In Search of Adventure and Moments of Bliss
SAILING THE SOUTH PACIFIC

Lois Joy Hofmann

First published 2012 by
PIP Productions
San Diego, CA 92109

Copyright © 2012 by Lois Joy Hofmann

All rights reserved. No part of this publication may be reproduced, stored in a retrieval system or transmitted in any form or by any means, electronic, mechanical, photocopying, recording, or otherwise, without the prior permission in writing of PIP Productions, Lois J. Hofmann.

Library of Congress Cataloging-in-Publication Data
0-9840913-4-3

Hofmann, Lois.
In Search of Adventure and Moments of Bliss: Sailing the South Pacific / Lois Hofmann.

ISBN-13:978-0-9840913-4-8

1. Hofmann, Lois —Travel. 2. Education 3. Sailing. 4. Geography   I. Title.

First reader and copy editing: Rebecca Brist
Development: Mel Weiser and Joni Browne-Walders
Book Design: Alfred Williams, Multimediaarts.net
Printer: Brittan Burns, LightSource Printing & Graphics
Cover design: Priya Garcia, LightSource Printing & Graphics
Photography: Lois Joy Hofmann, unless of Lois or otherwise noted
Book Production and Publicity: Melanie Kellogg, Media Melanie
Messing with Boats column and Technical Support: Günter Hofmann

Maps and Illustrations: Alfred Williams, Multimediaarts.net

AUTHOR'S NOTES
The coordinates of favorite anchorages listed in this book are shared with you only for planning purposes to show approximate locations and must not be used for navigation.

All sea miles mentioned are in nautical miles. One nautical mile equals 1.852 kilometers. All dollars mentioned are United States dollars, unless otherwise stated.

Information provided in the *Did You Know* columns are taken from Wikipedia, U.S. State Department Fact Sheets and other sources.

Printed in the United States of America

ACKNOWLEDGMENTS

Thanks to the many followers of my sailing website, www.pacificbliss.com, who kept asking me—not whether, but when—my online stories and photos would be incorporated into a book (or books).

Thanks to each of you—my family and friends—who followed our voyages and cheered us on throughout the eight years of our circumnavigation.

Thanks to Bob Bitchin, publisher, and Sue Morgan, editor, of *Latitudes & Attitudes* magazine for publishing the stories and articles that I sent to them while underway. Thanks to educational publishers who have purchased my cultural photos. This all gave me a start.

Thanks to those who helped me shape the final product: First reader and copy editor Rebecca Brist; editors Joni Browne-Walders and Mel Weiser, whose keen eyes, positive feedback, and energetic discussions took the manuscript to another level; web and graphic designer Alfred Williams, who kept his cool throughout the creative process; and to Melanie Kellogg, my publicist and production assistant.

Thanks to those who crewed on *Pacific Bliss* during her voyages throughout the South Pacific and on to Australia:

From San Diego to the Marquesas Islands: Doug
From San Diego to Tahiti: Armin
Around Tahiti: Paul, Janice, and Luke; Jeanne and Sarah; Phyllis and Richard
Around Fiji: Lydia and Helmut
From Bora Bora, Tahiti to Tonga and from Vanuatu to Australia: Richard

Thanks to family and friends who supported and encouraged us in our dream of sailing around the world.

And finally, a special thanks to Günter, my husband, partner, and Captain of *Pacific Bliss*. Without him, the voyages and this book would not have been possible.

The First Book in the Nautical Trilogy:
MAIDEN VOYAGE

What the critics are saying about *Maiden Voyage:*

A review by Mark Sutton, Marine Product Reviews
AN OUTSTANDING SAILING, TRAVEL, AND PERSONAL ADVENTURE BOOK THAT REALLY DELIVERS! 5 STARS!
Lois Joy Hofmann's In search of Adventure and Moments of Bliss: Maiden Voyage is a wonderfully written book about an adventure that just about anyone who has spent time on the water has dreamed of. Maiden Voyage is an outstanding sailing, travel, and personal adventure book that really delivers with its sailing stories, perspectives, cultures, and places, and incredible photography...

Mark Sutton
Marine Product Reviews
www.marineproductsreview.com

A review by Marie Chapian
A BEAUTIFUL BOOK!
Here is one of the most beautiful books you'll see this year. Packed with exquisite photos, the author has journaled a 34,000-mile sailing adventure on their 43-foot Catana catamaran, "Pacific Bliss," that will set your heart a-sailing. Hofmann and her husband, Günter, both in their sixties, decided to do what most of us only dream of at any age—they up and left their busy, and successful corporate lives and sailed around the world...

And! If you are simply a lover of beautifully and affordably produced books to enliven any coffee table or library, you won't want to miss this adventure book of the year...

P. S. Did I say exciting?
Marie Chapian
www.mariechapian.com

A review by Larry Jacobson
MORE THAN A COFFEE TABLE BOOK
Because this book has a beautiful cover, varnished to protect against spills, and is oversized, with 150 full-color photographs and maps, some might use MAIDEN VOYAGE as a coffee table book, and my guess is that's just fine with the author. If you're technically inclined, read all the blue sidebars, called MESSING WITH BOATS. And if you love history and geography, gravitate to the DID YOU KNOW sidebars with information about each country--trivia you won't find in the relevant State Dept website! But the best way to read this book is all the way through, beginning to end so that you understand the story: why and how Gunter and Lois decided to build the boat and sail around the world in the first place, how they felt, and how they changed. The adventures tell the physical story, their passages from country to country, but it is also the emotional journey, the psychological "inner journey," that you won't want to miss.
As a fellow author and circumnavigator, I respect Lois for her work and applaud this book's unique style.

Larry Jacobson
Author of *The Boy Behind the Gate*
www.larryjacobson.com

In Search of Adventure and Moments of Bliss

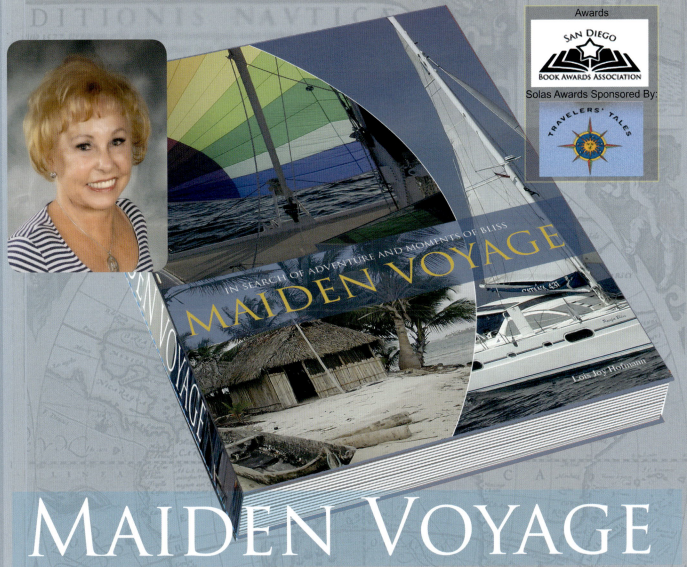

Maiden Voyage

Lois Joy Hofmann is the author of *Maiden Voyage*, the first in a trilogy called *In Search of Adventure and Moments of Bliss*. The book won first place in the travel category of the 2011 San Diego Book Awards. Hofmann also won gold in the Solas Awards, cruise story category, for *Force10!*, excerpted from chapter 7 of *Maiden Voyage*.

Her stories have appeared in magazines such as *Latitudes and Attitudes*, *Cruising World*, and *Living Aboard*. She has been a contributor to online magazines and blogs such as: *Multihull Magazine, Yacht Blogs*, *Multihull* newsletter, *Top Dekk* and *The Log*. Hofmann has been a keynote speaker for various organizations including yacht clubs, optimist clubs, book stores and libraries. She is currently working on the third book in her trilogy, to be called *The Long Way Back*. When she's not writing, Hofmann enjoys travel with her husband Günter to those countries they did not visit during their 8-year, 62-country sailing circumnavigation.

To learn more about Lois, please visit her author website at: http://www.loisjoyhofmann.com

Maiden Voyage was the recipient of the 2011 San Diego Book Award for Published Books, Nonfiction, in the Travel Category

Lois won gold in the Solas Awards, cruise story category, for her story *Force10!*

Dedication

TO SIGRID GLASSEL, MY MOTHER:
MAY YOU CONTINUE TO BE MY CHEERING SECTION IN HEAVEN.
MAY YOU SAIL ALONG WITH US,
TAKING IT ALL IN WITH YOUR CURIOUS EYES WIDE OPEN,
SEEING EACH PORT, TOWN, AND COUNTRY WE EXPLORE.
I WANT TO SAIL THROUGH THE REST OF MY LIFE WITH JOY.
YOU HAD A PURPOSE FOR GIVING ME MY MIDDLE NAME.
I WILL NOW EMBRACE THIS NAME
AND INCLUDE IT IN MY WRITING, ALWAYS.
I VOW TO EXPERIENCE JOY, LIKE YOU,
OVER THE SIMPLE THINGS IN LIFE—THE GLORIOUS SUNRISES
AND SUNSETS, THE CHEERFUL CHIRPING OF THE BIRDS,
AND THE THRILL OF NEW HORIZONS.

"TWENTY YEARS FROM NOW YOU WILL BE MORE DISAPPOINTED BY
THE THINGS YOU DIDN'T DO THAN BY THE ONES YOU DID DO.
SO THROW OFF THE BOWLINES. SAIL AWAY FROM THE SAFE HARBOR.
CATCH THE TRADE WINDS IN YOUR SAILS.
EXPLORE. DREAM. DISCOVER."

MARK TWAIN

TABLE OF CONTENTS

IN SEARCH OF ADVENTURE AND MOMENTS OF BLISS

SAILING THE SOUTH PACIFIC

PROLOGUE: San Diego: Decisions and Bon Voyage	10
CHAPTER ONE: Passage to the Marquesas Islands	16
CHAPTER TWO: Exploring the Magnificent Marquesas	34
CHAPTER THREE: The Elusive Tuomotos and On to Tahiti	62
CHAPTER FOUR: Navel of Nowhere: The Mystery of Easter Island	78
CHAPTER FIVE: Voyaging through Paradise: The Tahitian Islands	90
CHAPTER SIX: The Fabulous Cooks and On to Niue	110
CHAPTER SEVEN: The Proud Kingdom of Tonga	134
CHAPTER EIGHT: *Bula! Bula!* A Taste of Fiji	166
CHAPTER NINE: New Zealand Adventure	188
CHAPTER TEN: Fiji: One Country, Two Cultures	214
CHAPTER ELEVEN: Vanuatu's Remote Northern Bank Islands	254
CHAPTER TWELVE: Australia: The Land of Oz	288
EPILOGUE	296
APPENDICES	298

PACIFIC BLISS
CIRCUMNAVIGATION OF THE GLOBE
2000-2008

- 34,000 MILES
- 62 COUNTRIES
- 8 YEARS

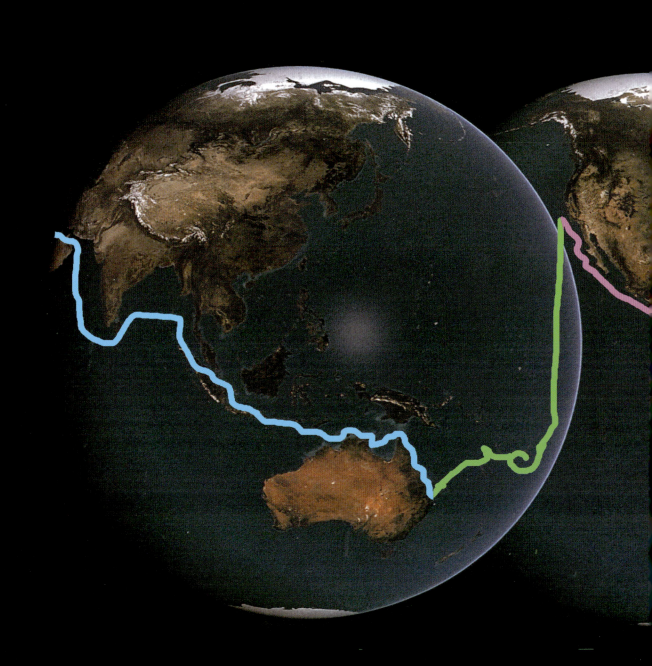

WE INVITE YOU TO JOIN US AS WE SHARE
OUR STORIES OF ADVENTURE AND MOMENTS OF BLISS,
SAILING AROUND THE WORLD ON OUR CATAMARAN,
PACIFIC BLISS.

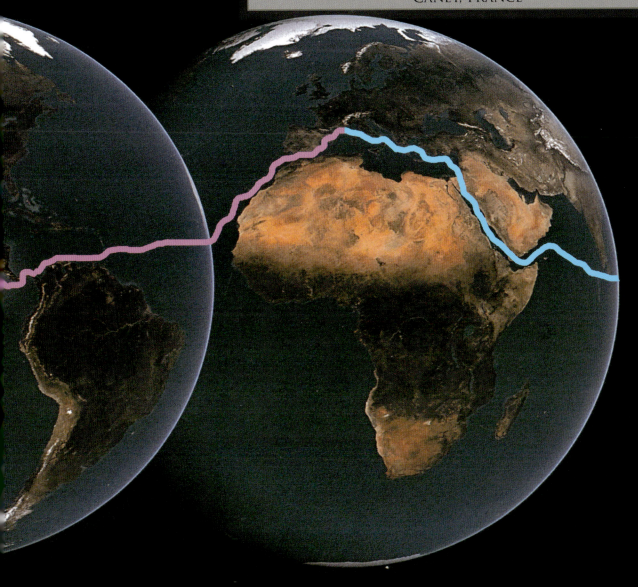

Prologue: Decisions and Bon Voyage

Lessons about Control
San Diego, California
September 18, 2001

Günter and I can't seem to tear each other away from the news. Neither can we tear ourselves away from each other. We have been nesting in the family room, mesmerized by the TV, for days. When we cannot bear the images of planes crashing into the World Trade Center and people mourning any longer, we take refuge on *Pacific Bliss*. She is now back on the dock on Shelter Island, looking prim and polished as the warranty repairs come to an end.

Some are saying that the hardest thing Americans are facing is the frightening loss of control over our lives. No one wants to admit loss of control, or accept it.

Günter and I had already learned that lesson, the hard way, during our Maiden Voyage. Caution is wise. Fear is debilitating. There are no guarantees in life. We all face dangers—whether terrorists, pirates, or simply the raging seas.

From Pain to Joy
September 20

I wake up hot and flushed, my heart pounding, my soul disturbed. The pain is more than I can bear. It is emotional, not physical. It's a repeat of the stabbing and jabbing I experienced those nights after Günter and I were thrust out of our company, and again while crossing the Atlantic. After months of sailing on *Pacific Bliss,* that pain had disappeared—forever, I had hoped. Evidently it has remained simmering beneath the surface, waiting to bubble up and burn.

This last week has seemed like a dark drama unfolding in slow motion. Images of planes exploding and toppling the towers, repeated ad nauseam, plowed furrows into my mind and drove stakes into my heart. I mourn for those who have lost loved ones. At first, my soul was raw and grieving; now it is deadened and sad.

For both Günter and me, the horrendous collapse of those towers has somehow revived our grief over the grim fall of our own biotech company to its very foundations. Obviously, we dare not compare our loss to those who lost their very lives or the lives of their loved ones. Yet new traumas have a way of re-awakening old grief, and we find we have not completely processed the loss of our company. Günter had devoted sixteen years of his life to the company; I had devoted eight. Most depressing was realizing that the wonderful technology Günter invented might never get to those cancer patients who need it so desperately. We now learn that the decline of the company since we were forced out has been worse than our most pessimistic imaginings.

In our condo, Günter and I sip our morning coffee in our favorite chairs, overlooking the sea below, sharing each other's pain. As has happened many times when we needed an answer from God, I open a book right to the page we need. This time, a phrase in a devotional called *Streams in the Desert* jumps out: "Joy sometimes needs pain to give it birth."

The text asks why human life is drenched in so much blood and soaked with so many tears. The answer: Trouble achieves for us something precious. There is a reward for every sorrow, and sometimes sorrow itself produces reward. The writer describes a shop in Brussels where special rooms are devoted to spinning the world's finest laces. The rooms are completely dark, except for the light that falls directly on the developing pattern from one small window. Lace is always more beautifully and delicately woven when the weaver is in the dark, with only his work in the light.

What web of lace is being woven in the aftermath of 9-11? How will the families of the victims find peace and comfort? Will the good we hoped to achieve through our former company be yet realized? Today all is darkness and debris, but what will be the result when these precious patterns—which only God knows—come to the light?

On with the Quest
February 25, 2002

After many discussions pro and con, Günter and I have made the decision to continue on with our circumnavigation—at least through the South Pacific and on to Australia. Beyond these voyages, we know that we will face more difficult decisions. Indonesia and Malaysia are Muslim countries. The people in the countries lining the Red Sea are Muslim and Arab. Only God knows whether those areas will be safe for yachts flying the American flag.

It is less than one month until D-Day, our departure for the Marquesas and ports beyond. Our days brim with anticipation and checking off endless To Do lists at a frenetic pace; our nights overflow with dreams of new adventures and Moments of Bliss in the South Pacific. Soon the day will come when we will bid adieu to family and friends and cast off on Voyage Two.

Although I had been concerned about my father dying while we were at sea during our Maiden Voyage, my mother actually went first, in December. I received a call to come to Texas quick; Sigrid was breathing only with the help of a ventilator. She held on until the last sibling, my youngest sister, arrived. She passed away that evening. The afternoon of her funeral, I visited my father back in the nursing home. "She was an angel," he said. "I don't want to live without her." I knew that he would be following her soon. He passed away last month.

After losing both parents during my sojourn on land, I find that I need time to delve into my own soul. As D. H. Lawrence put it: "That is the place to get to—nowhere. One wants to wander away from the world's somewheres, into our own nowhere." Through the soul searching and pain of these past few months, I realize that our Maiden Voyage was about losing ourselves. Voyage Two just may be the beginning of a quest to find ourselves.

Years later I would read Phil Cousineau's book, *The Art of the Pilgrimage: The Seeker's Guide to Making Travel Sacred*, and be astounded at how well the author captured the process Günter and I went through as we prepared for Voyage Two. We indeed are hearing an ancient call that many before us have heard:

> Yet the Lord pleads with you still:
> Ask where the good road is,
> the godly paths you used to walk in, in the days of long ago.
> Travel there, and you will find rest for your souls. (Jeremiah 6:16)

Goal: Build a boat. Mission: Sail around the world. How are these business terms different from a quest? I think back to my English Lit courses in college. Squire Trelawney and Dr. Livesey look at the parchment map the young Jim Hawkins has found in a dead man's chest. They sail off in search of it the fabulous pirate treasure. After the sack of Troy, Odysseus embarks with his men to return home to his far-off island kingdom of Ithaca and his beloved faithful wife Penelope. Jason goes after the Golden Fleece. King Arthur's knights leave to find the Holy Grail.

From Sunday School, I know of the quests in the Bible. Abraham leaves Ur to seek God in the desert. Generations later, Moses sees a terrifying vision of God in the burning bush, telling him that the Jews must flee Egypt. He leads the children of Israel for 40 years through the wilderness toward the Promised Land flowing with milk and honey. Paul, in the New Testament, takes off on his series of missionary journeys to Caesarea, Ephesus, Corinth, Athens, Philippi, and more.

Cousineau writes of the quests in other religions. In the fourth and fifth centuries, the Crusaders take off from their villages to retrace the footsteps of Jesus. By the eighth century, travelers are making the hajj to Medina and Mecca to visit sites consecrated by the prophet Mohammed. The holy texts of Buddhism and Hinduism tell their followers to travel to the tombs of the prophets, the places where miracles occurred, or the paths they walked in search of enlightenment.

Are we about to embark on a Quest as well? Certainly, we are treating the motions of leaving as a necessary ritual.

"Success is what comes when preparation meets opportunity" —a favorite motto in my business life—also works for cruising…and for a Quest. We've learned that preparation does not spoil spontaneity or lessen synchronicity. This time, we make better plans for the handling of our financial affairs. We put more comprehensive communications in place—including an Iridium phone—for keeping in touch. We take the time to make out our wills in case the Pacific swallows us whole.

We didn't want a welcome home party when we arrived in San Diego. We sneaked into port, tired and worn out, ill-prepared for the shock of re-entry. Now we know better. We realize that transition rituals like hellos and goodbyes are important. We are planning a Bon Voyage Party with over 50 guests. We will decorate with an island theme: bars and tables surrounded by grass skirts and tiki statues, serving tables full of catered "island" cuisine, and lots of music and dancing. Treasure chests will overflow with arrival gifts for us to take to the islanders—T-shirts, clothing, food items, drawing materials for the children, and cash donations to buy items along the way that we can give to the right people at the right time.

Our idea of building a boat and sailing around the world was a protective escape mechanism. We simply had to get away. Continuing on with our circumnavigation, though, is going to be something quite different. As Cousineau writes, "To people the world over, pilgrimage…is a journey of risk and renewal. For a journey without challenge has no meaning, one without purpose has no soul."

We are attaching a bigger meaning to our circumnavigation now, making it a Quest. I'm looking for what the pilgrim-poet Basho called a "glimpse of the underglimmer" (according to Cousineau). I sense that we will experience a deeper look into other people and places that we were not prepared for before.

Voyage Two will be a voyage of risk—of that I am sure—but it will also be one of renewal and reward.

There is so much more "out there" for us to explore and appreciate. There is so much more for us to learn. What new lessons does God have in store for us this time?

DID YOU KNOW?

CALIFORNIA

California is the most populous state in the United States and the third largest by area, after Alaska and Texas. It is the first U.S. state to have a non-white majority.

California is the most geographically diverse state in the nation and contains the highest (Mount Whitney) and lowest (Death Valley) points in the contiguous United States. Almost 40 percent of California is forested, a high amount for a relatively arid state.

California's gross state product (GSP) is the largest in the United States at about 13 percent. If California were a country, its GDP would be the eighth largest in the world.

As of 2005, 58 percent of California residents age five and older spoke English as a first language at home, while 28.21% spoke Spanish. In addition to English and Spanish, other languages spoken in California are Filipino, Chinese, Vietnamese, and Korean.

When I moved to California from Minnesota, I was told that the state was one big granola bar—a land of fruits, nuts, and flakes. It does have four seasons: floods, fires, famine (drought), and earthquakes!

California has always been as much a state of mind as a state of the union. Other states have

sunshine. Other states have beaches. Other states may even have decent organic produce and yogurt. But California promises something more: transformation. This state is a repository of America's frontier spirit, the notion that a better life is possible for anyone who wants it, regardless of birth. This is the California dream. A new Californian can leave his or her past at the border and reinvent himself, whether as a high-tech entrepreneur, a film director, a yoga instructor, or simply as a person who deserves a second chance. The state's motto is "Eureka," from the Greek, "I found it." The beauty of "it" is that "it" is whatever one wants "it" to be.

Wildflowers, Fiesta Island, San Diego

Three thousand victims from more than ninety countries lost their lives on that infamous morning when jetliners were turned into missiles and a new age of terrorism was born. Each anniversary of 9-11 brings back haunting memories of broken lives and shattered dreams.

"...THAT WE HERE HIGHLY RESOLVE THAT THESE DEAD SHALL NOT HAVE DIED IN VAIN—THAT THIS NATION, UNDER GOD, SHALL HAVE A NEW BIRTH OF FREEDOM—AND THAT THE GOVERNMENT OF THE PEOPLE, BY THE PEOPLE, AND FOR THE PEOPLE, SHALL NOT PERISH FROM THE EARTH."
ABRAHAM LINCOLN

MESSING WITH BOATS

A Woman's Perspective: Günter Gets a Mistress
February 15, 2002
by Lois

A strange addiction takes over men when they give up business life to become cruisers: It's called messing with boats.

I'm not complaining. This obsession taking hold can be a good thing, because not messing with boats could signal the end of a couple's cruising life. Men need to mess with boats because boats break—a lot. And if men don't learn to fix them and to enjoy the process, they will be frustrated in Paradise—thwarted from sailing from one exotic port to another—just to fix their boats. In remote areas, there is no one to come to their rescue.

I remember arriving in Nuevo Vallarta after a hair-raising night beating against the wind and the waves rounding Cabo Corriente. We arrived on a Wednesday, the night of the Weekly Cruisers' Potluck held on the docks at Paradise Village. During the party, it became apparent that the guys were deep into messing with boats and the women were heavy into shopping.

After a couple of days, I tried to entice Günter to the land life to get a much-needed haircut, but he was too busy messing with boats and negotiating for new treasures. A key part of the Vallarta Cruiser's Net was called "Treasures of the Bilge." His latest find was a pair of dinghy wheels. The day after Günter's lucky find, I hitched a ride in the Cruiser Car to buy the lumber that he needed. I returned to the dock, lugging boards of assorted lengths, to find my man seated on an overturned soup pot, grinning like the cat that swallowed the canary. He was shaded by one-half of a small wooden dinghy turned upright. I watched the sailor curls I loved drop slowly off the dock and waft into the water. Judy of *Quest* was clipping them off. I stifled a smart retort, forced to admire his ingenuity. He'd sleuthed out a way to get a haircut without ever leaving the dock!

Günter's addiction to messing with boats paid off during the Baja Bash. We were rounding the windy cape of Cabo Falso, where the Sea of Cortez collides with the Pacific. Angry seas hit hard against the rocks, at our lee, in ink-black darkness. At the Perfect Storm moment, just as the wind reached fury peak, the dinghy line broke. *Petit Bliss* hung helpless, motor and all, at a 90-degree angle to the sea. The other line could break, the dinghy could escape, and *Pacific Bliss* could race toward the dangerous rocks. Fortunately, though, during one of his messing with boats sessions, Günter had installed a backup line, and that line held the dinghy in place all the way to Mag Bay on the Baja California coast.

Here in San Diego, messing with boats took on yet a new connotation. It was at the repair dock that I first accused Günter of having a mistress. Evidently, not content with relaxing in our home on Sail Bay, he visited *Pacific Bliss* almost every day. I suspected he was in love, and this was confirmed at one of our dinner parties.

"Why is a boat always a *she*?" one of our landlubber guests asked.

"It shouldn't be," his wife added. "A boat is a neutral object, neither a *he* nor a *she*."

Her husband warmed to the subject. "I agree. A boat is a big hunk of fiberglass, with gleaming teak and high tech electronics. Such an object can be beautifully designed, but it is definitely an *it*."

A cruiser disagreed: "A boat is beautiful indeed. It has nice lines and curves and warmth. That makes it a *she*."

And the cruiser's wife added: "Each boat has her own personality, her own feeling. She puts up with a lot, and takes care of people. A boat is a *she*."

Then, Günter, sitting at the head of the table made his feelings known:

"A boat is definitely a *she*. The two bows of *Pacific Bliss* are like breasts. Her sides are smooth and sleek, yet rounded. And she's simply beautiful."

At that moment, I understood that Günter's messing with boats was more than merely an addiction or avocation. At that moment, I knew he was in love. And from then on, I began to call our boat *Miss Bliss, Günter's Mistress*.

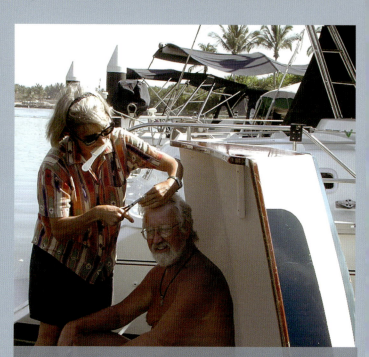

Judy cuts Günter's hair on the Nuevo Vallarta marina dock.

MESSING WITH BOATS

A Man's Perspective: Soothing the Soul
by Günter

Of course, everything starts with a list. Before we left France we had one; during our passage across the Atlantic, the list grew even longer; by the time we reached San Diego, our list had grown to 58 items to be taken care of under warranty. We had great cooperation from Catana, *Pacific Bliss*'s builders, and there was no disagreement about a single item.

However, one replacement produced an entertaining episode. Within our mountain of mail we found a letter from Catana. Why this letter was sent to our home when the factory knew we were in the middle of the ocean is a mystery, especially since it was a recall of the trampoline. It warned us that sun damage could cause the trampoline's fibers to break—Yes, the same trampoline that we had used to "network" crossing the Atlantic, the trampoline that Gottfried had used for exercise, bouncing wildly on it while underway!

Ironically, it was David, our yacht broker, who proved Catana's warning to be accurate. One day, I met him walking down the dock. His head was down; he was mumbling to himself and his clothes were sopping wet. When he saw me, he looked up. "No worries. Yours will be fixed before you sail off in March."

"What happened?" I asked him.

"I fell through the trampoline."

The new "net," as we call it, has just been installed and restrung, quite a labor-intensive task. It was the last item on my list.

Some of the other repairs and replacements:
- Change mast foot; replace stretched electrical cables in the mast
- Change anchor rollers
- Install new VHF antenna atop the mast
- Repair bubbles on hull
- Replace corroded port sail drive
- Repair anchor windlass
- Repair bimini shades and zippers
- Improve dinghy hoisting
- Apply new anti-fouling paint
- Correct plastic chafe guards
- Install safety steps on cabin roof next to mast (These steps would have prevented my accident in Malaga, Spain.)
- Replace holding tank valves
- Replace one bilge pump switch
- Make cosmetic improvements or small adjustments, e.g., on doors

But the Warranty List was only the beginning. As the sun-drenched days of summer turned into the coolest winter I've ever spent in San Diego, I wrestled with another type of list, the list of our own necessities, wishes, and dreams. This we called our Optional List.

We debated many items. One that we rejected was a generator to provide power for air conditioning, a luxury that we do not have. "We already have two engines on board, and I refuse to take responsibility for a third one," I argued. "We know how to sweat it out. We survived the stifling days in the Banana Bay Marina in Golfito, Costa Rica. Between noon and 1500 hours we just got naked, closed all the shades on the windows, moistened or sprayed our bodies, and rested in our master cabin, reading or napping." That argument shot down the air conditioning. Mine is a good low-tech solution, the kind I like.

But Lois won the washing machine debate. We had space for it and had the plumbing installed at the factory in Canet, but we waited to buy it in San Diego because the marine model we wanted is manufactured in Italy and would have cost much more in France than in the U.S., including shipping. Go figure! My low-tech solution of dragging the laundry behind the boat in netting was rejected. I also tried to make a point that not much laundering is needed on a cruise. One applies the method of relative cleanliness: Once you think something is dirty, put it into a bag; when you are out of clothes, go to the bag and start wearing it again because now it's relatively clean. Also, turning underwear inside out extends its clean life by a factor of two. Anyway, because we have a clothing-optional boat when just the two of us are on board, we also will need more suntan lotion than clothes. All this persuasion was in vain. What won out in the end was the specter of $50 laundry bills in Papeete, money which we would rather spend on French wine.

Other fixes were no-brainers: We had to add a third anchor and beef up our first anchor. During a stormy night, in a crowded anchorage, dragging toward a rocky shore is a cruiser's worst nightmare. Like a woman's never being too thin or too rich (or at least too rich), you never can have enough anchors out—with a long rode preferably made from heavy chain. That makes for a good night's rest. I will never forget our situation in the San Blas island of Mamitupu. That night the wind freshened up to Force 6, about 25 knots. *Pacific Bliss* danced wildly on the whitecaps. With four on board, each of us had come up during the night to check the holding, fearing we would drag and end up on the rocks behind us. We managed the night, but the next day I found the shackle on the bridle that attaches to the anchor chain was quite bent, but still holding. There had been a tremendous force on that anchor chain! A catamaran has more surfaces exposed to the wind and will exert more strain on the anchor gear than a monohull. That is one of the trade-offs for the comfort of a multihull.

Since we plan to stay in the South Pacific for a long time, we will need ample spare parts on board: fuses, batteries, light bulbs, hoses, screws, filters of all kind, engine oil, engine parts, auto helm parts, and more tools. All this requires diligent study of the inventory and sub-lists of lists. I enjoy going down to *Pacific Bliss*—secured at the yacht brokerage dock in the boatyard—to mull over all the big and little things the boat might need, just in case. Hopefully, many things will never be used, but an inventory of spare parts is like a car insurance policy: You are not unhappy that you paid for it and never had an accident.

Lois is the official navigator. She needs a complete new set of charts and guidebooks. With those, we can select nice anchorages. A pleasant way to dream your time away between voyages. Also, I installed an electronic chart system on the navigation laptop. I did this because I cannot get charts for the South Pacific for my built-in B&G electronic chart plotter. The new chart system also works with either of my two hand-held GPS units.

I had a second alternator installed on the starboard engine, which will double the charging current from 50 amps to 100 amps. With both engines, I can have 150 amps of charging current. We added a propane-powered barbecue, a night vision monocular, and a good second pair of binoculars with built-in compass and range finder. Because factory-supplied tools were of poor quality (a large screwdriver broke after the first use!), I upgraded our tool box substantially. I also added several power tools.

A nice addition to the galley is a breadmaker. (I tried it out and found that the drain on the battery bank was acceptable.) The smell of fresh bread on long passages will be wonderful. And if the crew does not use the breadmaker often enough, I threatened to use it as a fourth, emergency anchor. It weighs enough!

Completing little things on the boat is necessary to soothe the soul. *Messing with boats* gives me a sense of achievement. It also puts some control back into my little corner of the world.

15

Pacific Bliss is underway to the Marquesas Islands, a 3,000-mile passage.

Chapter 1
Passage to the Marquesas Islands: Twenty-One Days at Sea

Getting Our Sea Legs
At sea, 26°N, 118°55′W
March 27, 2002

Pacific Bliss glides through the starry night, a silent spaceship traveling to other worlds. On watch at the helm, I am lost in another dimension. Only the swish-swish of the water beneath the hulls and the occasional groan of sails against the rigging remind me that we are still at sea.

What a remarkable contrast to my first two nights on watch when *Pacific Bliss* tossed on steep and turbulent seas, on a beam reach, at 10 knots boat speed, in 20-25 knot winds! Feeling uneasy and a little queasy, I struggled to pull on long underwear, warm socks, a fleece pullover, and corduroy jeans, topping it all with a fleece-lined sailing jacket and gloves. I pulled my red fleece-lined cap snug over my ears and secured it with Velcro underneath my chin.

Whatever possessed me to leave a pleasant spring in San Diego to encounter these frigid northeast winds?

Strange, after sailing almost 10,000 miles during our Maiden Voyage, I considered myself a seasoned sailor. But after nine months as a landlubber, I had to learn the "cat-walk" all over again, crouching from one hand-hold to another with bent legs and a low center of gravity. And waves, exploding like "bombs" underneath the salon as they swept from one hull to the next, startled me again.

This third night at sea, I am more comfortable—resigned to this 3000-mile passage. My cap is off, my gloves are on the settee, my jacket is unzipped a little at the neck.

Oh, the freedom of unbundling! I yearn for the tropics and the shedding of more clothes. As the layers come off, I am gradually shedding the layers of care and worry and "stuff" that I brought with me from civilization.

Since we left our well-wishers behind, cheerily waving from the dock, I am amazed how little I've thought of home. Our home is now here, self-contained, in this 24'x 43'catamaran. As the seas have calmed, so has my spirit. Moving along, I can envision days and days of this, no hustle, no bustle, no cares (except for the safety of *Pacific Bliss* and her crew), and no deadlines—just chasing the wind.

I leave the helm to make a logbook entry at the navigation station. We are now west of Cedros Island off Baja. Memories of our long slog up the coast of Mexico toward the end of our Maiden Voyage flood my mind.

How tired of sailing we were back then. We debated whether to go on. And later that year, how eager we became to leave land life far behind!

Our Pacific crossing crew, Doug and Armin, is still sacked out in the crew hull. But Günter is awake and in the galley. I can tell he has his sea legs because the first words out of his mouth concern food: "What's on the menu today?"

For the first two days, no one felt like cooking, so it was good that our daughter-in-law and our friends had given us plenty of food. "Well, we finished off that wonderful goulash, the *Pichelsteiner* that Sabine had cooked for us…and her cookies…and her apple cake. We also scarfed up the sushi Doug brought on board."

"So?" Günter opens the big chest fridge, which is packed with three weeks' supplies. "So today, Captain,"

We enjoy a fun bon voyage party in San Diego before sailing off on Voyage Two.

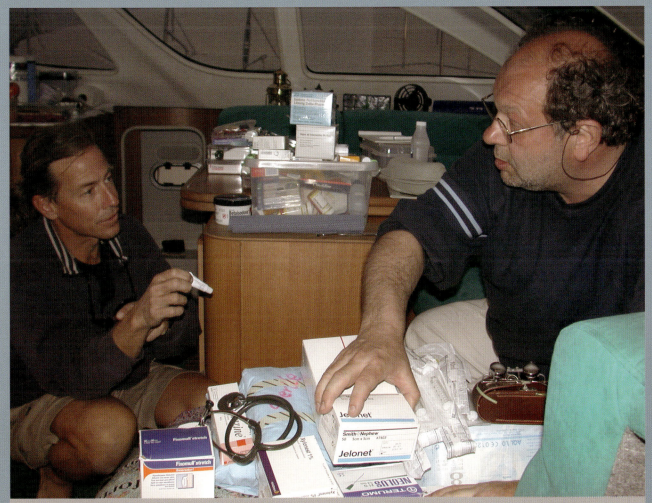
Our crew, Doug and Armin, both doctors, organize the medical supplies they brought on board.

I tell him, "will be our first day to actually plan a menu and cook on board. Get to it!"

He takes out a package labeled "Use First." Sausages! "Life's looking up." Günter turns on the SSB (single-side-band radio) and dials the numbers to the familiar Amigo Net.

But he leaves the cooking to me.

By afternoon *Pacific Bliss* ghosts through navy-blue seas, two-thirds of the way down Baja. Günter sits in the salon, reading a novel. Doug and Armin relax in their berths. I sit at the nav station, reading Melville's *Typee: A Peep at Polynesian Life*. We are moseying along at 3.5 to 4 knots in 8 knots of wind. Only the sloshing of the sea against the hulls and the tugging of the preventer on the main interrupt the silence.

There's no guilt on board: We have each completed our one obligatory task for the day. Günter searched for and found a spare light bulb in the clearly labeled spare parts box to replace Doug's reading light. I finally unpacked and stowed the last of the bags I had brought on board. Next, I unpacked the computer and began updating the 20-page provisioning list. "Save it," Günter orders. "Tomorrow is another day. We need to stretch out these tasks for the long passage ahead."

What a stark contrast from one week ago! Then we were still in San Diego, busily making boat improvements and conducting sea trials with Armin and Doug by day, packing and provisioning by night. We would collapse into bed complaining of aching muscles and mental exhaustion. Despite months of planning, there was never enough time. My lists were many pages long. I itemized even the simplest of tasks, e.g., making sure that the Egg Lady at the Farmers' Market brought the four dozen "fresh this morning" eggs I had ordered. There wouldn't be room in the fridge. They would be stored in a special compartment we had made underneath the floorboards in the hull—the coldest spot we could find.

I had been tempted to cancel the Bon Voyage Party because I was running out of time. But then I remembered what I had so recently learned: Rituals *are* important! We needed to have our friends and family with us in spirit, understanding (if not approving) of our quest. It was an opportunity for our new crew to meet and mix with those we hold dear. And what a party it was! Everyone was decked out as sailors or islanders. Grass skirts swayed to the hula (perhaps not the music for the Marquesas, but who cares about such details when contemplating the vast Pacific?). Bamboo vases

A large contingent of well-wishers sees us off to face the vast Pacific.

overflowed with orchids from Hawaii. At the grass-skirted Captain's Bar, Richard served the rum punch creations he had perfected on board in the Caribbean during our Maiden Voyage. We all partied like we might never see each other again. At the end of the evening we were left with the pirate's treasure chests filled with donations our friends brought for us to give to the islanders we would soon meet. Our goodbye ritual would flow into many hellos in the near future.

The Slow Boat to the Marquesas
24°42.7′N, 119°32.2′W
March 29

0400: You've heard the phrase, "Hurry up and wait." Sailing can take this concept to ridiculous extremes. *Pacific Bliss* is crawling now, inching along, under a full moon and a star-studded sky at a mere 1.8 knots in a 2-knot wind. Occasionally the wind increases to 7 knots, and she "speeds" along at 4 knots. Big deal!

In this passage to the Marquesas, we *must* use our sails because there is a danger of running out of fuel. I had expected to have windless days and nights in the doldrums (those "horse latitudes" near the equator where mariners threw horses off their ships in desperation to lighten the load). But here, only 560 miles into our passage? The chart shows our southwest course barely even with the tip of Baja!

I sit here on night watch and worry.

The moon is so bright it dims the stars. It creates a shimmering path of molten lead from the western sky straight to the starboard helm seat. I look around. No lights. No ships. I am in a void.

I continue to dream about Melville's description of *Typee* in Nuku Hiva: the land rising from the water, swelling to lofty and majestic heights, the shoreline heightened by deep and romantic glens, the clear streams forming slender cascades and eventually, noisy waterfalls.

I am impatient to get to the Marquesas. They say that one should enjoy the path. But the destination… For me, ahhh, that is the dream!

The moon sets as the sun rises directly opposite. When one is on land, this is barely noticeable. But at sea, the effect is dramatic. The liquid moonbeam flows to the starboard helm while the sun rises east of the port helm. The sky turns orange-gold. A yellow orb peeks above the eastern horizon at the same time the western sky lightens to blue-mauve. As another day begins, *Pacific Bliss* is alone in her own world. Cocooned by sea and sky, we glide through the water—imperceptible and ignored, except by God.

Easter Surprise
The guys hoist our "Spinnaker-of-Many-Colors"

while I prepare an Easter Sunday breakfast: buckwheat/banana pancakes with maple syrup. The Easter bunny arrived miraculously during the night, leaving white, hard-boiled eggs and gaily-wrapped truffle eggs in our basket. Our crew sits around the salon table ready for a feast. Handel's *Messiah* is booming from the surround-sound speakers and, despite the lack of sun, the weather is pleasant. During my early morning watch, I prepared a banana cream pie; it sits in the fridge, waiting to be devoured.

All day, the spinnaker balloons—a miracle of nylon and nature—pulling us gently along at 8 knots in a northeast breeze of 10-12 knots apparent wind. Armin stands on the deck snapping photos. Günter and I continue reading our books. It is an idyllic scene, just as I had dreamed it would be. After dinner we discuss rules for flying our multi-colored spinnaker. Günter's orders are to take her down at 15 knots apparent (Force 5).

"The conservative approach," he says, "would be not to fly it at all at night. There is no moonlight again tonight…"

Doug interrupts, "But we already flew it one night with no problems, and now we have practice taking it down."

"Yes, you guys did have it all together nicely." Günter's resolve is breaking.

"We seem to have it down pat," Armin joins in.

"The ride has been so nice all day," I add. "And with the main down, we wouldn't have that banging all night."

Günter stands up, persuaded. "True, and we might even gain on *Makoko*."

The decision has been made—the spinnaker will remain up.

Makoko is our buddy boat. Günter and Jean-Claude, her captain, had agreed that we would meet *Makoko* in the Pacific and sail together from then on. But *Makoko* found good winds while *Pacific Bliss* had floundered. And now *Makoko* is well into the NE trades and putting more distance between the two boats every day. An Amel-designed 53-foot Super Maramu ketch, she is not accustomed to being beaten.

But neither is *Pacific Bliss*!

"Okay, here's what we will do," Günter wraps up our discussion. "When the apparent wind is sustained at 15 knots, we'll call for all hands on deck to take the spinnaker down. Armin, you're the heavy. We'll need you for the chute. Work along with Doug, up front at the net, to hold it down. Lois, you're at the helm. I'll work the winches."

Günter and I retire at the end of early evening watch, but we cannot sleep. We are tuned to every gust. Instead of the steady downwind sail we had experienced during the day, the wind becomes fickle, veering from NE to N to ENE. Twice Günter leaves our bunk to go on deck. He adjusts the lines and changes the spinnaker angle, then comes back to bed.

By 2300, the wind is gusting steadily 13-15 knots apparent. It's still within our guidelines, but shifting to the east. Our downwind sail has changed to a reach. Armin is on watch. Doug is sleeping in preparation for what we call a "dogwatch" (12-3 a.m.).

"All hands on deck!" comes the cry.

We all rush topsides.

I take the helm as planned. I try to keep *Pacific Bliss* on a downwind course, but I can't hold it.

Günter starts the engines and then races forward. I'm reluctant to motor too fast with the three men upfront on the net. With no moon, they are in the dark. I can't see them. I turn the spreader lights on.

"Turn off the lights! We're blinded!" Günter yells. "We can't see the colors of the spinnaker lines!"

I turn them off. Suddenly everything happens at warp speed. The spinnaker balloons way up and out to sea, out of control.

"Don't let it catch and rip on the spreaders up there!" Doug yells.

Armin and Doug grab cords to pull the spinnaker in. Instead, the wind catches it and they go flying high above the net.

Oh my God! Please help.

Time slows. Now everything seems to happen in slow motion. I continue to steer downwind.

Keep her steady. Stay calm.

The main beside me flaps like a crazed bantam rooster. My mouth is as dry as sandpaper. Forget the spinnaker! I fear for our crew.

Doug is still flying. Armin, the heavier, drops first. He tackles the entire spinnaker bundle head-on, like an NFL linebacker, and wrestles it down to the net. The blue spinnaker line is tangled around the furled jib. It is impossible to untangle it in the inky night.

Adieu, Spinnaker-of-Many-Colors. The seams between the colors are ripped out; her collar is broken and one panel has a substantial gash. She will have to undergo extensive repairs at some facility in Papeete. Until then, we will have slower, less comfortable passages.

As fast as it began, it is over.

It doesn't matter. My men are safe.

Halfway
April 3

"Yuck!" I come up on watch at 0600. Just as I am about to sit at the helm, a flying fish lands right on my seat. "This one is going to get fried!"

Günter is coming off watch. He laughs as he and I search every nook and cranny for more creatures of the sea. We collect four flying fish and one squid. They're a gift from heaven, and we'll cook them later.

The water temperature has risen to 28.5º C. What a difference! Only two days ago it was 26º C and a few days before that it was 24º C. Now I wear shorts and a polo in the morning; by mid-day, I am barefoot in a *pareu*. We're moving south beautifully. Our destination, Atuona, Hiva Oa, is exactly 1500 miles away. We have passed the halfway point of our 3000-mile passage.

After my watch I bake an apple cake to celebrate our achievement. Armin cleans all the fish. Then I dip them in an egg/milk batter, coat them with seasoned bread crumbs, fry, and arrange them on a platter with sliced tomatoes. Soon they are history.

Contented, we take the opportunity to reflect and to decide what we want to accomplish during the last half of our voyage. Our minds and bodies have adapted to the long haul ahead, and we have settled into a comfortable routine. Everyone knows where things are and who does what; we have adjusted well to the three-hour watch schedule with a five-day rotation. We have become an interdependent, self-sufficient community—confident of each other's abilities, familiar with each other's likes, dislikes, and personalities.

We have even adopted nicknames. Armin became "Ironman" after he tackled the Spinnaker. He sits at the helm for hours during his watch, stone-faced and stoic. We call Doug *Big Smile Doug*. He is quick to smile and always eager to help. Günter becomes our *Capitania*, for obvious reasons. And I am known as *Island Queen*, in anticipation of my reign over this boat as we travel through the islands.

Life on board has its own order as things begin to fall into predictable patterns. Take my routine, for example: I take my coffee at the helm seat every day while watching the sun rise. Then I check the veggies and fruit stored in various cockpit lockers, taking into the galley those that should be used before they spoil. And I assemble the ingredients for any special foods to be prepared that day. Also, every morning at 0830, I monitor the Puddle Jump Net on the SSB.

The Big Pond, the Big Ditch, and now the Puddle Jump. Leave it to cruisers to find a way to make a long passage seem short!

This is no puddle. We are talking about the Pacific Ocean. In reality, it is a vast sea into which all the land masses of the world can fit. Fifteen times the size of the United States, the Pacific covers 28 percent of the globe's surface. Like a huge, inverted mountain, the bottom of this awesome ocean reaches a depth of 35,827 feet, deeper than the height of the Himalayas.

The Two That Got Away

The possibility of excitement exists for cruisers every day of a voyage.

Pacific Bliss glides along smoothly at 8 to 9 knots,

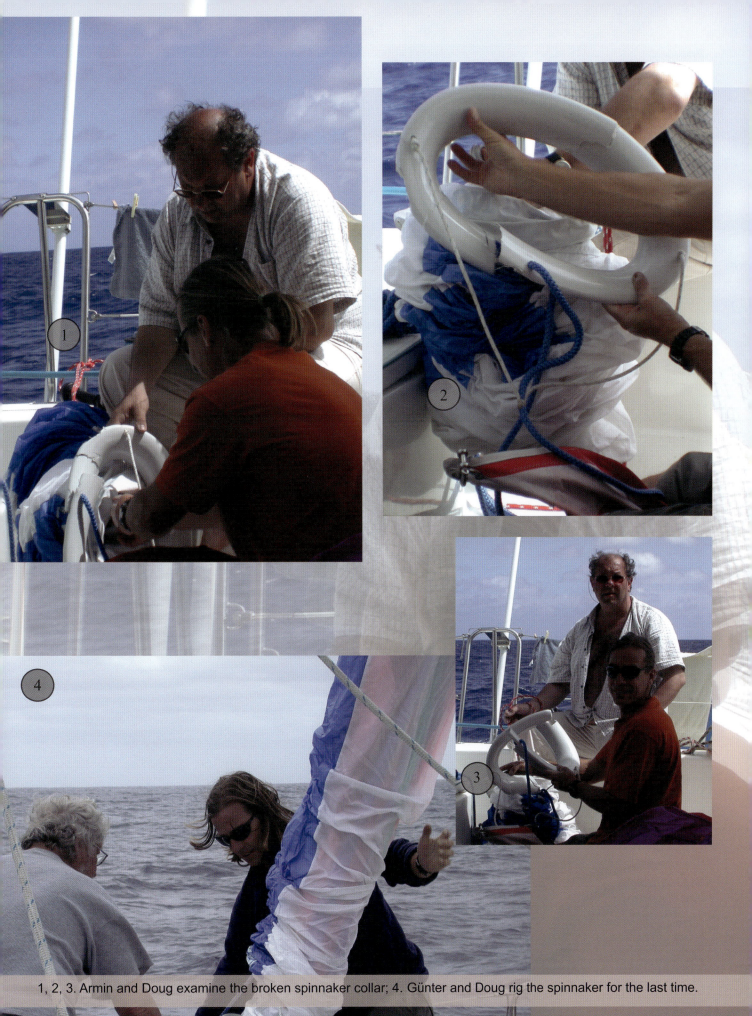

1, 2, 3. Armin and Doug examine the broken spinnaker collar; 4. Günter and Doug rig the spinnaker for the last time.

1. The men are deep into the sail locker; 2. Doug is hoisted up in the bosun's chair to fix the lines to the lazy jack; 3. Lois and Günter underway; 4. Doug relaxes at the helm; 5. Armin takes a bucket shower.

one reef in the main and one in the jib, gently rolling on the NE swells. Sparkles of sun dance upon small whitecaps. Puffs of sheep's wool crown the top of the swaying mast. Salt crystals, splashed on the trampoline, twinkle like a million diamonds.

We spot life out here today. Pairs of blue-and-yellow bonito weave alongside the hulls, pursuing schools of flying fish, which dash frantically from the crest of one wave to another. The four of us stand on deck for a long time and marvel at this wonderful show of marine life.

Suddenly the whir of the reel announces a fish on our line. Doug rushes to the rod mounted on the rail behind the port helm. The rod bows with the strain; the force is too heavy for him to lift it from the rod holder. By the time he cries, "Slow down the boat!" the line breaks, and the fish swims free.

"Could have been a tuna...had to have been over 40 pounds," he says. "That monster pulled harder than anything I've ever felt in my life."

Now with a new line and lure, we hope for another strike. It doesn't happen immediately.

Two days later I hear a commotion and race topsides.

"Lots of birds and dolphins," Doug informs me, "and where there are dolphins, there are fi-i-sh." All at once, the reel whirs and he rushes to the holder. He grabs the rod and begins to play the catch. "Slow her down!" he yells.

"How? We're sailing." Günter heads for the controls at the starboard helm.

"Turn into the wind, quick!" Doug can barely hold onto the rod.

"I'll backwind the main and go into irons! Lois, start the starboard engine!"

I start the engine.

Doug holds on as the fish swims out the line. He's forced to walk 40 feet to the port bow, with the rod bending over the lifelines.

"We need more control," Günter yells. "Help me pull in the jib."

I rush to help.

"Start the port engine," Günter orders.

I start the port. We push directly into the wind and rolling swells.

"She's down to 2 knots now," Günter shouts.

"Good." Doug grits his teeth. He walks the fish back to the port helm so he can brace against the seat. Armin has unpacked the West Marine belt from the center cockpit locker. Now he fastens it around Doug's midriff, giving him leverage to play the fish.

I turn off the port engine again to protect the prop.

Doug lowers the rod, reels furiously, then raises it again and again, pulling with all his might, keeping his stance wide as waves slosh against the hull. His forearms are tense and taut. His biceps bulge. His face is a grim mask.

"I know it's over 40 pounds, could be double that!" he grunts. "It's the largest one *I've* ever played." The monster pulls the line underneath the shade of the dinghy.

"Don't let him go under the boat!" Günter yells. He is still seated at the engine controls.

"I'm trying to prevent that," Doug shouts back.

Twenty long minutes pass. Doug is becoming exhausted. He hands the rod to Armin. "Here, take it awhile."

The fish plays out the line again, now directly in back of the swim ladder. "Keep the line tight or he'll take the opportunity to run," Doug instructs.

Armin gets the hang of it.

Lower the rod. Reel in like mad. Lift the rod. Pull back. He's all concentration—determined, focused. "He's re-ee-ally big," Armin growls. "And he's smart, too."

"You gotta respect him," Doug says. He takes the gear back. "But I'm gonna outsmart him." The fish is still fighting hard; there's no time for a Doug-smile. Instead, his every muscle is rigid.

"I see him," Günter says. "He's behind the dinghy now."

The fish flashes.

"A giant yellow fin," Doug answers.

Armin unhooks the stanchion to the swim platform.

Doug steps down for the kill.

"Don't let him pull you into the drink!" I shout. I'm afraid the monster will take our crew member with him in his struggle to escape.

Doug reels the giant toward the platform.

Suddenly this ogre of a fish gathers all his strength and makes one final leap.

Doug is almost pulled into the waves.

And then, in one second, the rod goes slack. The lure has broken, and the devil swims free.

Dejected, Doug climbs back into the cockpit.

Günter tries to put a happy face to the loss. "At least we're learning how to do it," he says as we trim the sails. "I didn't know anything about stopping a boat and going into the wind and all that, just for a fish."

Doug answers, "Well, now you know. It's a big deal, catching a fish from a sailboat."

"Wouldn't it be easier to drag him behind the boat on a cleat till he gives up?"

"We could do that," Doug agrees. "But it just doesn't seem fair. Sometimes the fish just has to win."

Ray Goes Blind.
3°29′N, 131° 20′W
April 7

It happens again. For the second time on this passage, Ray has fallen ill; but this time it appears to be serious. The three doctors on board fail to make a diagnosis.

"Ray's going crazy," Günter announces.

The four of us gather around the Nav Station in the salon, trying to make sense of Ray's erratic behavior. The COG (course over ground) in the PILOT menu of the Raytheon multiplex (Ray for short) wanders from our set course. We go from 202° to 156°, then over to 192° and back to 202°. Ray holds there for a short while, then goes bonkers again.

"Armin, steer manually to a course of 202°," Captain Günter commands.

"Okay." Concern clouds Armin's usual deadpan face.

"Ray can't die," I gulp. "He's our fifth crew."

"Maybe he hasn't had enough nourishment," says Doug, the retired baby-doctor.

"What do you mean? We give him all the juice he wants," Günter replies. "I even turned the freezer into a second fridge to save amps for Ray. I'll shut off all the instruments and reset the trip log; we can't give him more juice than that." Günter turns off the instruments while Armin steers. "Now, lay off and I'll punch AUTO again…."

My stomach clenches. Despite the crew's effort to maintain the humorous personification of Ray, I know that we all feel the same inside.

"He's in!" I shout. My stomach relaxes.

"But he's not holding," Armin calls from the helm.

Wild and erratic readings are coming from Ray.

"He's delirious," Doug says in a low, bedside-doctor voice. "We have to be prepared for Ray to go."

My stomach tightens again. I sense we're going to have a long "daymare" called "handsteering."

Grueling, two-hour watches instead of three…Can we even handle that, with a wind speed of 20 knots on the quarter? Maybe we'll be rotating every hour, rising from our bunks like robots, stumbling toward the helm, muscles aching, brains numb. For close to 1000 miles, we will have to continue on like this. Forget the saying on my cruising T-shirt: "Attitude is the difference between ordeal and adventure." It's not attitude. It's Ray.

Günter stares at the erratic readings. "I think it's his brain. But, just in case, we should pull out the Raytheon backup kit we bought in San Diego and put in a new computer."

Günter heaves the settee cushions aside and retrieves the kit stored underneath. He and Doug lay out the spare body parts for bionic Ray as if the salon table were part of a surgical suite.

"This is the new, improved version of the Raytheon computer." Günter points out the parts, as if he's giving a lecture, the way he used to do at the Max Planck Institute in Munich.

Thank God Günter had the foresight to purchase spare parts for Ray.

Doug carefully lifts the computer with both hands. "As the first step to potential installation, let's see if the new one even fits."

Günter and I unpack the crammed storage area beneath the nav station while *Pacific Bliss* rolls in the swells. Finally a path to Ray's brain, mounted way in the back, is cleared.

"Hand me the box," says Günter, still on his hands and knees.

Doug hands the computer to me, and I crawl in far enough to hand it to Günter.

A faint voice drifts back into the salon. "Bad luck. It won't fit. It's not even the same size." Soaking with sweat, Günter comes up for air.

"Do we even know that the computer is the problem?" I hand him a glass of water.

"No. In fact, it appears that the erratic input is coming into Ray from someplace else."

"He's blind," Doug says. "Maybe it's the compass and he can't see."

"This kit *does* have a compass," Günter answers. "Perhaps that *is* the problem, Doug."

I have an idea. "Before we go any further, let's call David and ask him if Catana has had problems with the compass before."

Günter picks up the satellite phone to call our broker. Fortunately, he connects immediately.

"That happened once on the Catana 471," David responds. "It was out for six hours, then came back on its own. Try leaving it off longer, like 20 minutes or so…Then reset it with the circle approach outlined in the manual."

Armin hand-steers for 20 minutes, then punches Ray's AUTO button. Nothing happens. We douse the sails and motor and circle over and over. Still no luck. We continue working on the problem through lunchtime; no one has an appetite anyway.

Günter calls David again. "Install the new compass by fastening it temporarily to a table or any convenient surface," he suggests. "Then disconnect the installed compass."

Our present compass is "conveniently" located on the wall down in the owner's hull, underneath the mattress and slats of the bed. The boat is still rolling. By the time they locate and disconnect the compass, the "doctors" have lost their bedside manners. **G-r-r-#*+@^##!!!! G-r-r-#*+@^##!!!! G-r-r-#*+@^##!!!!**

They make a temporary installation of the new

compass with a cable to the cockpit table, being careful to keep it away from anything magnetic. Doug and Günter relieve Armin at the wheel. They drive *Pacific Bliss* through the circle route again. This time, the compass takes the settings!

All this registers accurately onto Ray's brain. He springs back to life and steers *Pacific Bliss* again like the champ we all know he is. Collectively we breathe a sigh of relief.

Ray is back. Yay, Ray!

Stars of Wonder
0°47′ N, 133°09.8′ W

When I first come on the midnight-to-3 a.m. dogwatch, I forget that the purpose of being in the cockpit is to watch for ships in the night. I am star struck for the first ten minutes.

Pacific Bliss glides gently forward, skimming the ocean waves. I know she's moving because I hear the slosh-slosh of her hulls against the waves and the occasional creak-creak of her mainsail swaying as it tries to touch the stars. I feel like I'm encased in a giant dome, surrounded by stars crowded together so tightly they resemble a thousand Milky Ways. I am mesmerized. I find many sections of the sky so dense with stars that I cannot separate the individual star from the primordial soup. I am seeing distant constellations that I've never seen nor heard of before, lights that have taken millions of light years to come to me.

I feel unimportant, insignificant. That's how it is at sea, a mystical experience almost impossible to duplicate on land.

"A wonderful, starry night," I write in my logbook at the end of my watch, "the stuff of dreams."

Tomorrow, we will cross the line. And of course, we will do all the crazy things sailors do: perform saltwater initiation rites, dress up in costumes, and offer champagne to the mythological gods of the sea.

But tonight, before I turn into my bunk, I cannot help but turn my thoughts to the real God, the Creator of all of this. How could I possibly begin to think that an insignificant speck in a little vessel, way down here, could make any difference, could even get the attention of this God, who masterminded the creation of the universe? I think about it tonight, and it seems impossible.

Yet I feel that my prayers are being answered. Perhaps He assigns a guardian angel to His children down here. I cannot begin to understand it more than I can understand the reasons why God designed this whole universe. Did He design it for the race of man He would eventually create? Has He designed universes for other races of men, and did they also foul things up so badly that He needed to make a redemption plan for them?

Everything speaks for super-intelligent design, yet did all that design work go into creating a habitat for the imperfect beings who live here? God created the perfect universe: "God saw all that He had made, and it was very good" (Genesis 1:31).

NASA astronomer John O'Keefe said that, to the astronomer, the Earth is a very sheltered and protected place. A marvelous picture from Apollo 8 shows the blue and cloud-wrapped earth, seen just at the horizon of the black-cratered, torn, and smashed lunar landscape. The contrast would not be lost on any creature. The thought, "God loves those people," cannot be resisted. Yet the moon is a friendly place compared to Venus, where, from skies 40 km high, a rain of concentrated sulfuric acid falls toward a surface that is as hot as boiling lead. Then O'Keefe goes on to say that Venus is friendly compared to the cold and lonely vacuum that separates the stars, which is friendly compared to the crushing pressure of the white dwarfs or the unspeakable horrors of the black holes or neutron stars. He writes:

> We are by astronomical standards, a pampered, cosseted, cherished group of creatures…If the Universe had not been made with the most exacting precision we could never have come into existence. It is my view that these circumstances were created for man to live in…Someone made a lot of special arrangements and took a lot of time so that each of us could be alive and experiencing this just-right world.

When I read the passages in *Show Me God* (by Fred Heeren, Revised Edition, 2000) during the day, I did not know that it would be in preparation for this wondrous night.

During this long passage, I have been gazing at the stars that are the building blocks of the entire universe. They provide the heat, light, and materials necessary for life.

How fortunate I am to be here, in the vast Pacific, at this point in time!

Crossing the Line

I wake up to the strains of Beethoven and the welcoming aroma of Starbucks® French Roast coffee. The 0830 Puddle Jump SSB Net is just beginning. Some of the cruisers who crossed the equator earlier tell us they are experiencing SE trades; others say they are still in the doldrums, lolling about with no wind. They beg those who have yet to cross the line to "beseech Neptune for some wind when we cross" by giving him "a little extra champagne on our behalf."

"We're at 0.8° North Latitude. Come quickly," our Captain announces.

I hurry to see why we are being summoned.

We gather around the nav station as Ray calls out the latitude on the multiplex, and the B&G displays

Apollo 8 Earthrise. *Photo courtesy of Sky Lab Images, NASA.*

our location data. 0.4N, 0.3N, 0.2N…get your cameras ready…0.1… 0.0…Yes! We have crossed the equator!

High fives all around. Grins. Congratulations. What a feeling of accomplishment we share!

Since leaving San Diego, we have sailed 2,534 nautical miles.

Now an important ceremony must be performed.

But we decide not to perform it during the afternoon heat. Günter stretches the awning from the hard-top bimini to the lifelines, and we settle in. With the breeze on the stern quarter, this is a perfect siesta location. We relax and snooze.

Later, though, when the heat of the day has lessened, we welcome the required initiation rites. Captain Günter has transformed himself into Neptune, god of the seas. He wears a flowing, deep-blue robe (looking suspiciously like a bed sheet) and a staff (looking suspiciously like a boat hook) adorned with a fishnet. He does not explain the bright, yellow sou'wester he's wearing, but we suspect it has something to do with entering Neptune's southern domain. He calls us all to the trampoline. There, he dumps a bucket of seawater over Doug's head and pronounces, "I hereby christen you 'Old Salt Doug.'"

Next, he heaves a bucket of seawater at Armin. "As a dutiful crew member of *Pacific Bliss,*" he says, "and since this is your first crossing of the equator, I hereby give you your official sea name: 'Ironman.'"

It's my turn. I beg Neptune to give me a nice name. "It is predetermined," he says. "No special requests allowed." He heaves the bucket full of seawater over me and proclaims, "Lois will have three names: The first is 'Digital Lois' for her attachment to a digital camera. The second is 'Out of Memory.' (I believe this one had something to do with the fact that I'd requested a delay of the rites while I rushed to load another compact memory card into the camera.) And the third is… 'Island Queen,' because she is, indeed, our queen."

I am delighted.

Finally, Günter gets his. Doug fills the bucket to the brim with seawater. "I wouldn't want to shortchange our dear Captain," he says with a grin. Dumping the entire bucket of water over Günter's head, he adds, "You are now officially to be known as 'Capitania!'"

Laughing, we all head back to the swim platform for a freshwater rinse. The water temperature is a delightful 82° F.

The entire ritual has been great fun and something we'll all remember.

Now the sun sets. We busy ourselves with party preparations. I catch the crew searching the innards of *Pacific Bliss* for last-minute additions to their costumes. Meanwhile, I set out hors d'oeuvres, each with a special meaning: foie gras and crackers (it's a French boat, after all), smoked oysters (representing fruits of the sea), and dates, rolled in coconut (to represent the South Sea Islands). Then out of the depths of the fridge comes a magnificently chilled bottle of champagne. Ordinarily, we do not drink while underway. But crossing the line is a special occasion. The first sip will be something to die for. But wait! Before that first sip, Günter must appease Neptune. Dutifully he pours a few drops into the sea for the success of our voyage. Then, remembering the request of our fellow cruisers stuck in the doldrums, he stops.…With a twinkle in his eye, he makes an outrageous statement: "Why don't we drink the champagne ourselves, refill the bottle with saltwater and give it *all* to Neptune?" In one voice we all shout, "No! That would be bad luck!"

"Just kidding," Günter laughs and pours a few drops into the sea for the cruisers.

Then we all raise our glasses in a toast to Father Neptune and his sidekick, Poseidon. (We wouldn't want to leave *him* out.) After this comes a lengthy series of toasts: to each other, to *Pacific Bliss* and, finally, to Ray for bringing us this far safely.

But toasting is just the beginning. The grand finale is steak, grilled by Armin, and smothered with a creamy pepper sauce from Madagascar. He serves dinner just as the sun turns golden and rims the clouds on the horizon with shades of amber. The perfection of our festivities makes me wish I could cross the equator every day.

A Stressful Home Stretch

We have a cold breakfast of crackers, peanut butter, and juice. The seas are too rough to even turn on the propane for cooking. I watch a band of clouds rolls in and a sun that peeks out only intermittently. The Puddle Jump Net reports rain in Hiva Oa, our landfall. As the Brits would say, "It's a little lumpy out here."

Pacific Bliss gallops like a Derby racer; she smells land now and has become difficult to control. At the speed we are sailing, we may need to slow down in order to arrive at morning's light. She gave me a wild ride last night. I had to sit at the helm most of the night, with the wind from 20 to 25 knots and her speed always over 8 knots, sometimes even reaching 11. When Günter came topsides for his watch, he said, "We can rein her in a bit." We did.

Today the weather pattern continues: Coal-black clouds approach like a freight train; they dump their contents on us and then chug on.

"Lois, it's getting darker!" Armin shouts from the port helm. The sky is sullen and sodden—shades of gray and black.

I close the window to our cabin to prevent rain from blowing in. The rain hits hard and simultaneously with a terrific wind. This is different: usually the wind comes first.

"My God, it's Force 7," Günter says as he passes

Crossing the LINE

1. Lois, Island Queen; 2. Günter pours champagne for Neptune; 3. Latitude zero; 4. Günter as Neptune; 5. Crossing the line craziness; 6. Armin pops the champagne; 7. Doug christens Captain Günter.

the nav station.

I glance at the multimeter. "Now it's Force 8."

"Wake Doug."

I batten down the hatches, wake Doug, and then rush to the cockpit to support Armin. The wind drives the rain sideways so hard it stings like sleet. Waves curl angrily behind the dinghy, *Petit Bliss*, which is wildly bouncing on the davits at the stern.

Doug comes up.

"Take the starboard helm," Günter orders.

"Downwind?"

"Yes. We can't do anything about the main, but let's take in the jib some more." They furl the jib to a triangular handkerchief—just enough for stability.

The wind screams from the east at 40 knots true while the sea at our stern churns and froths. Going downwind, wind speed is reduced to 25 apparent. *Pacific Bliss* doesn't seem to mind the ride at all. She's taking it all in stride; she has been built for sterner stuff than this.

After hand-steering for a while, Doug punches in Ray, who continues to hold things together.

I examine the radar image. This weather system extends for two miles, with another following it. After that we will be home free…I hope. I slide open the door from the salon to the cockpit to give the guys the news. They are drenched. Water runs and drips from every surface, including their noses. Doug and Armin are wearing only their swim trunks; Günter, his yellow foul weather jacket. After 15 minutes, the wind eases to Force 7. But then the next squall hits like a steam engine, and the wind jumps up to Force 8.

I chide myself for not having watched more carefully for this storm. I had become complacent and had stopped monitoring the radar.

Günter is not feeling well; incredible stress always takes its toll. So I offer to stay on watch.

We're flying. With one reef in the main and one in the jib, we are doing 7-9 knots. The wind comes in from the east, varying from 15-20 knots. And, yes, it is raining—for the fourth time in the last 24 hours. Landfall is now only 165 nautical miles away. We have been at sea for 20 days.

Come, Neptune, take pity on us poor sailors! We don't want to arrive in port exhausted. I yearn to be in a beautiful anchorage, free of stress, leisurely sipping a cold white wine.

Land-Ho!
Atuona, Hiva Oa, Marquesas
Sunday, April 14

0330: I relieve Günter from his watch. He looks and acts exhausted; his forehead is warm to the touch; he is very short with me, but I am not offended. I can imagine how he feels. He cannot rest well under the strain of being Captain. It's a heavy burden.

The wind continues incessantly. When I take over, it is 18-20 knots. We are on a beam reach, so the waves slam against the hulls, creating bombs underneath. It wears on everyone; we have not had relief from this for days.

0345: My timer goes off, telling me to take the customary scan of the sky and the horizon. There are big, ominous clouds to the east. I turn on the radar. The multimeter shows the wind increasing to 22, 24, 26, 29 knots. The radar shows yet another huge squall system, some squall lines behind us, and others to the side of us.

I wake Doug.

Then Ray quits. Once, twice, a third time. He must be tired, too. The wind decreases to 12 knots, but I have no steerage. Doug and I change course, let out some jib, and Ray and *Pacific Bliss* begin to work in unison again.

0500: It doesn't seem dangerous to him, so Doug goes back to bed. I'm alone with *Pacific Bliss*, sailing through the night, the ride smoother now that the squalls have dissipated. I chart our new position: 9°40′ South and 138°34′ West. By dawn we should be able to sight land. I want to stay awake for that, but I'm so exhausted I have to crash at the end of my watch.

0700: Günter gently tickles my feet and wakes me. "There's land," he says.

I rub my eyes. A rectangular hunk of blue-gray juts out from the sea at our starboard, barely discernible in the haze. "I'm glad," I say. "No, I'm relieved." I turn around and crash again.

0900: I wake up again. A bright light is shining into my window. Finally, the sun! I stare out my window. We are motoring along the shoreline of Hiva Oa. It is totally green—a wonderful, deep, lush green.

I dress quickly and dash topsides. Three islands are in view, the largest of them very close. We are eight miles from Atuona Harbor. The brilliant sun puts the mountains into stark relief, and trees appear dark brown now. The rugged profile is spectacular!

We proceed into the little bay that is past the breakwater and take a slow pass around the bay, already crowded with 14 yachts.

1145: We drop the hook. Before we can set a stern anchor, we drift too close to a boat called *Free Radical*. The owner is already in his dinghy, offering to help us set the stern anchor. "It's better for me to be proactive now than a screaming asshole later," he chuckles.

Together, we set both bow and stern anchors. Then we sit quietly in the cockpit to catch a breath of breeze, fatigued and flushed in the warmth of

We view one last sunset during the home stretch.

the sun. The thermometer registers 97° F. No one says a word. There are no cheers, no high fives, no champagne. There are no words of wit or wisdom from our captain. We just drink water and then more water.

This is not the arrival I dreamed about during those long 21 days at sea. The only feelings I have are relief and sheer exhaustion.

"I'm going below," says Günter. "I don't feel so well."

"I'll follow shortly." One more glass of water, and I leave the cockpit to join Günter. He is already fast asleep.

A few hours later, I hear a faint, "*Pacific Bliss,*" followed by a tap on the hull. *Am I dreaming?* No, a male voice is repeating, "*Pacific Bliss.*" I look out the window. I see the hull of *Free Radical*. And in between our boat and his, the captain waits in his inflatable dinghy. Our stern anchor has been dragging and our sleeping ship had been gradually drifting toward his boat again.

I come on deck. "We were all asleep," I explain.

"I know. Sorry to wake you."

Doug comes topsides. He wraps the anchor line around the cleats a few times to move *Pacific Bliss* over a bit. Now everyone is up. Using *Petit Bliss*, Doug resets the anchor one last time, then fashions an impressive bridle system with our black dock lines, securing *Pacific Bliss* in all directions.

Sufficiently awake to feel some hunger pangs, our crew consents to a cold meal of potato salad and canned oysters with crackers. I take out a well-chilled bottle of Sheridan Sauvignon Blanc from California.

Oh, the marvelous taste of the first mouthful of dry white wine.

Ancient tikis at the archeological site near Baie Puamou, Hiva Oa.

Chapter 2
Exploring the Marquesas

Touring Hiva Oa
9°48.2′S, 139°02′W
April 16, 2002

It takes us a full day to recuperate from our long passage. Then, refreshed, we join our friends Jean-Claude and Claudie from our buddy boat, *Makoko*. Leading us all the way, they have arrived in Hiva Oa first. Jean-Claude is invaluable: He helps Günter to check in easily at the gendarmerie in Atuona; he leads us to the bank for an exchange of our dollars into CPFs (Central Pacific Francs); he even arranges an island tour for the following day.

At 0830, we are ready and waiting. A red Toyota pickup truck squeals to a stop on the gravel of the concrete jetty. Out jumps a friendly, thirty-something Marquesan. "Hi, I'm Sabine, your guide and also your driver for today," she announces in perfect English with a delightful French accent. "There is room for only three of you inside. The others can get in back."

Günter sits up front. Claudie and I take the next row, leaving Jean-Claude, Armin, and Doug to climb into the bed of the truck.

That arrangement works out fine; however, as we lumber past Atuona and up into the mountainous rain forests, a sheet of rain pounds the three in the open back until they look as if they've just come out of a steam bath. I check on them through the rear window. Armin, sits there stoically, a hint of smile cracking his face. I imagine he is relieved that this is a tropical rain, a far cry from the stinging sleet of his native Germany! I can tell by Doug's big grin that he is treating this as just another adventure. But Jean-Claude looks miserable. His knit polo is absorbing water and swelling like a puffer fish.

I inform Sabine. She stops at an orchard at the top of the mountain. Jean-Claude leaps out, heads to the back of the fruit storage shack, and returns soon. He has taken off his soaked shirt and tied Claudie's red scarf around his shoulders. He wrings out his polo, disgust clouding his usually cheerful face. No one dares say a word.

Underway again, we spot a souvenir stand selling flowery shirts. Claudie jumps out and returns almost immediately with a bright red shirt sporting huge white hibiscuses. Not Jean-Claude's style, but it will do. He struts around the truck, modeling it for us with a smug face, then climbs in the back again.

There is only one road to the tiki village, and we are told that road is constantly under construction. It begins with blacktop and soon turns into gravel. At one point, we even have to roll a large boulder out of our way.

But boulders are not the only obstacle to overcome. The fear factor is worse. I grip the roll-bars as the Toyota skids between ruts and veers around bends. Steep cliffs frame one side of the road, while the sea far, far below, frames the other. When I finally dare to look down, I view spectacular deep blue bays—serene, pristine, and empty.

"Why no sailing vessels down there?" I ask Sabine.

"It is not as calm as it looks. There are no coral reefs around these islands for protection. And the shores are rocky. Besides, the high surf, slamming against the cliffs, makes it all but impossible to get to shore."

A Land Rover, driven by Pepe, Sabine's husband,

The fruit of the Noni tree looks like a small, bumpy potato, green at first, turning to a yellowish white when ripe. "Canoe plants" were carried by Polynesian voyagers to other lands to meet their needs for food, fiber, building materials, and medicine. Noni fruit was known as the "queen" of all canoe plants for its medicinal qualities.

arrives at an overlook right after we have stopped. Pepe is guiding the captain and crew of *Raven*. From here on, the two tour groups travel together.

Pepe is a square, stocky Marquesan. He teaches us the Marquesan war chant posture: "You put your feet apart like this, with your knees bent slightly. Keep a low center of gravity."

"We know how to do this," Günter boasts. "It's the same stance as our cat-walk."

"So you know this. Now for the next part. You pull your arms down. Fierce. Then you chant, 'uh ooo, uh ooo.'"

We try it, and thereafter at every stop we all do the war chant. You can't possibly imagine a more comical sight!

At one stop we have tall, rocky spires at our backs and a bay below us. Pepe points to a high table-like formation. "This is the very rock where virgins were sacrificed, and the bay below is where they were thrown."

If sacrificing virgins isn't enough to shock us, cannibalism will.

"The last cannibalistic ritual in all of Polynesia was performed right on *this* island. In Atuona… in 1926." Pepe puffs with the pride of his fierce ancestors. "When the Marquesan girls go on to school in Papeete, they do not speak the Marquesan language. They speak only French. Why? They don't want to say where they are from." Pepe pauses for effect. "But the boys—they are proud of their warrior heritage! They call those Tahitians 'wussies.' You see, Marquesan heritage is different from Tahitian. Here, when two tribes used to fight, the head of the losing chief would be cooked and brought to the winner. Then, in front of the followers, he would first eat the chief's lips, to take his authority, then the eyes, to take his vision. Then he would open the skull and eat the brain, to take his mental strength. In this way, the loser's men would follow him willingly."

Back in the Toyota, Sabine tells us that her 12-year-old son can now repeat the stories his father tells. "But most modern Marquesans," Sabine adds, "are no longer interested in the island's gory history and legends."

"I read that there was a large population here at one time," Günter says.

"Yes. There were 50,000 to 80,000 during the pre-European era. Before they 'discovered' us. At the low point there were only 800."

"Wow! What happened?"

"Syphilis…leprosy…elephantiasis…all brought by the so-called civilized white man. But the French tackled the problem and reversed the trend."

With vivid images in our minds, we pile back into the vehicles. The road leads us now to the town of Iipona. We stop for drinks, which Sabine says we can take with us to our lunch. "This store is owned by the great-grandson of Gauguin," she adds.

Later, as both tour groups leave their vehicles, Pepe points to the only intersection of the dusty main street.

Jean-Claude uses a scarf for warmth after rain drenches his shirt.

"There he is…that's him! How lucky can you be?"

A huge gray horse clomps along carrying the local celebrity. Ponytail swaying, a red bandana wrapped around his forehead, the man could double as a Polynesian Willie Nelson.

The group then follows Pepe to the Iipona *me-ae* temple grounds. We pause before *Takaii*, the largest tiki in the world. It stands 2.43 meters (8 feet) high on a massive stone-ringed platform. The statue of his wife kneels submissively behind him and to his side. Pepe invites us to mimic the poses. "I like this," says Jean-Claude, striking a dominant pose next to *Takaii*. But Claudie refuses to kneel. Her reaction surprises Pepe. "Go ahead," he pleads.

Instead, Claudie reclines seductively on the stone slab—a French model's classic pose. Pepe doesn't think it's funny, but we laugh until our sides ache.

Though failing here, Pepe succeeds in engaging us in other role-playing activities. We walk past stone terraces, called *me-ae,* which were used for religious ceremonies. Here, human sacrifices were offered to the gods. One of these stone gods is an oversized turtle, the god of fertility. Pepe points to an area used for mating. "This is an unusually large center," he says. "At one time, it was used by seven tribes."

Seven tribes! A lot of mating must've gone on here.

Not one to waste an opportunity for drama, Pepe calls on members of our tour group. "I will now demonstrate the legends that happened here….Günter, you will pose as the chief."

The idea of being a chief pleases Günter. He sits on a stone "throne," legs tucked underneath, yoga-style.

Claudie and I watch warily.

Pepe climbs up on the *me-ae*. But he has left the mating theme behind him by now, and he begins another story: "After the year 1400, the population expanded so much that terraces and irrigation ditches had to be built to provide more food. Günter, as chief, you would have been in charge of digging those ditches. And you would have ordered huge public plazas for dancing and festivals."

Pepe's stories are endless and fascinating and make us wonder how many more we would hear if we were to remain at this *me-ae* site. However, we have to move on, so we trudge back to the vehicles. Sabine drives. Her voice drones on.

I drink the rest of my water from the bottle that I refilled from those water pitchers set on the table during lunch. Then I nod off to sleep.

I lose the entire next day to the Marquesan version of Montezuma's Revenge.

After the solitude of three weeks in the middle of the Pacific, I find all the hubbub in this bay disconcerting. Imagine waking to the rousing horns of a military band!

Sabine, our Marquesan tour guide.

I stumble up to the galley for some coffee and squint toward the French garrison stationed on the hill. Do I detect a distinct Polynesian accent to these patriotic chants and commands I seem to hear?

Doug is in the galley. "You missed the show yesterday, when you were down there, sick," he says. "The big event was the Marquesan war chant. The same one Pepe taught us." (From this point on, my men would perform it at almost every sundowner!)

Still weak, I am nevertheless determined to become part of the action. I climb down into the dinghy and join the three men for a trip into town. They pull *Petit Bliss* up on the sand. Sweating in the heat and humidity, we follow the path into town.

We are pleasantly surprised to discover all the modern conveniences of civilization in Atuona. Located 740 miles northeast of Tahiti, the town boasts a gendarmerie, small hospital, banks, weather station, Air Tahiti travel office, restaurants and snack bars, stores, and shops. In addition to all of this, we find electricity, telephones, a postal system, and even television.

One must admire the French for the infrastructure they have developed in this remote town.

At the post office, I e-mail my "puddle jump" story to my webmaster, after struggling with the French keyboard. Although the government building is air-conditioned, I can't help but notice the clerks, all men, wear khaki short-shorts as part of their uniforms.

Great legs! I won't repeat our crew's derisive comments. They're just jealous.

We hike to the Gauguin museum and learn it will be closed from 11:30 to 2:00. So we find the closest restaurant for lunch. In my condition, I make sure to order a bland chicken-with-rice dish. And only *bottled* water!

An hour later we head back to the museum, this time taking a different route. It leads us behind the village to a path to the Calvary Cemetery. The graves are simple here, but we find the resting places of Paul Gauguin and the Belgian singer Jacques Brel, who spent his last years here. On his marker I read, "In these islands of pure solitude, I have found a sort of peace."

I can relate to that sentiment.

We enter the museum to learn more about Paul Gauguin, whose search for an unspoiled island ended on Hiva Oa. We find that he painted his final masterpieces here: *Deux Femmes* and *Where Do We Come From? What Are We? Where Are We Going?* The museum display shows that his 18-month stay was not without controversy. Allegedly, he traded a sewing machine for a 13-year-old native girl. But it was in 1903 that he was fined and sentenced to three months in prison in a dispute with the church and government. At 54 years of age, he died of syphilis before he could even start that prison sentence.

How convenient!

Outside the museum, we're amazed to find an impressive re-creation. For the lazy, timid tourist who won't brave the Puamau Bay road that we dared to traverse the other day, the museum has provided a duplication of the ancient *me-ae* platform and its magnificent tiki god, *Takaii*. Though it's impressive, it pales beside the real thing.

Cruising Is Never Boring: The International Incident

"Lois, come up here quick. We have an international incident," Günter calls.

I scramble topside to see that a new yacht has entered the bay.

"You bloody British!" Jean-Claude is screaming at the boat.

The return salvo is quick: "Typical bloody Frenchman!"

The new yacht had plopped its anchor right in front of *Makoko*, then pulled back, hooking onto *Makoko's* bow anchor.

"*They* had the nerve to ask *me* to pull back because *they* were getting too close," Jean-Claude fumes. Claudie just happens to be taking her afternoon swim. She heads for their anchor and tries to untangle the mess, but she can't do it alone.

"Doug, Armin," Günter commands. "Launch the dinghy. Quick! They need a U.S. peacekeeping force out there."

In a flash, our crew reaches the offending anchor, followed by the Canadian contingent, Ed and Julie, of

Fueling in Atuona was a difficult set-up; there is no fuel dock. Armin hands the fuel hose from the pump on land to Doug in the dinghy, and from there he will bring it over to *Pacific Bliss*.

Free Radical. The four of them struggle to free the lines and, finally, the British boat slinks away to anchor somewhere else.

The conflict is resolved. The peacekeeping force returns to *Pacific Bliss,* and the afternoon is spent rehashing the incident and laughing about French-English hostilities that have been going on since the 17th century—all with more than one "cold one" in our hands.

Who says cruising is boring?

Nothing Is Ever Easy.
How I love my washing machine!

Doug helps me string additional lines between the mast and the jib halyard. I hang our sheets on the new ropes—and our passage-soiled clothes on the lifelines—as I watch other cruisers plunging their clothes into buckets and wringing them out by hand. The wind that whistled through the night and tugged at our anchor is welcome now. No fabric softener in the world could make my sheets this fresh! While I continue as the ship's laundress, the three men perform maintenance duties. They clean the boat's filters—all of them: the watermaker, galley sink, heads, and shower filters. After that, they head for the fuel dock to exchange our propane tank.

We experience first-hand the newest phrase bandied about by the cruisers in Polynesia: "Nothing is ever easy."

Our original propane tank was *blue*, installed in Canet, France. Its size, shape, and fittings are the same as the *green* tanks approved here. That should suggest an even exchange, right? Wrong. Even on this remote island, bureaucracy prevails. Here, French blue does not equal French *Polynesian* green. The exchange is refused. Frustrated, Günter enlists the help of Pepe, our guide. Whether Pepe used sweet-talk or threats, we'll never know. What matters, though, is that he manages to effect the exchange, and we now have cooking propane for the next three to four months.

Refueling the boat will not be easy, either. Ordinarily the refueling tank is located on a dock and we can bring *Pacific Bliss* right up to it. Here, in Atuona, the tank is located on a hillside 50 yards away from the dock. What makes it even more difficult is the fact that the dock is raised above the water to a height that makes it impossible for the dinghy to tie up. Consequently, we have to take the dinghy close to the rocks where one of the men must jump out and climb. After that, he must trudge to the tank on top of a hill and haul 50 yards of hose back to the dinghy. Then the dinghy must bring the hose out to *Pacific Bliss*. And the whole process has to be reversed once the boat's tanks are full. All of this takes most of the day.

By 1715, with only one hour to spare before dark, we make it back to our anchorage location. Then it takes another two hours to set and secure the anchors. To make matters even more difficult, the stern of

Paul Gauguin was buried near Atuona after spending the last two years of his life on Hiva Oa.

Pacific Bliss now faces the steep, rocky shore, and an unnerving wind begins to blow and continues all night long.

Günter is concerned, enough to mumble, "I'll be more comfortable back at sea," as we toss and turn and try to sleep.

Meditations and Reflections on Viatahu
9°54.5′S, 139°06′W
Baie Hanamoenoa, Tahuata

Our overnight passage here was uneventful. We are anchored now in one of the most beautiful bays in all of Polynesia, according to Eric Hiscock, a sailing legend. This Sunday, I awaken to the aroma of French Press coffee and *pancakes a la banana.*

Doug ladles on the maple syrup. Um, um, good! As we enjoy this tasty breakfast, we gaze at the village of Viatahu. It is so much quieter here than that crowded anchorage of Atuona. Except for *Makoko,* not a soul is in sight.

Later we see the children whooping and cavorting on the ferry dock. Four older Marquesan boys perch on the cliff overlooking the pier. Just their presence stirs us. It's time to explore!

With *Makoko's* Jean-Claude and Claudie, we head our dinghies toward the pier. The swell bounces *Petit Bliss* against the dock. This is dangerous. Jean-Claude grabs the painters and, instead of tying us to the pier, pulls us onto the beach. We are surrounded immediately by exuberant children.

The area seems to be a communal playground. Children follow us eagerly but drop off as we walk along the paved main street that takes us beyond the school. We stroll past a fleet of colorful fishing boats and a stand of palms, their trunks bent and bowed by the winds. We examine a gnarled tree, stretched and hunched over the pounding surf, and discover a bunch of hibiscus growing wild. The delicate yellow blossoms contrast with their knotted and knobby stems. A monument next to a colossal ship's anchor proclaims the true Marquesan name for the islands—*Fenua Enata,* the Land of Man. Here in 1842, the plaque says, the Marquesans turned over the islands to Admiral Dupetit-Thouars, who signed the treaty linking them to France.

We continue our walk along the seaside road. We're determined to find the charming church with the red spire that dominates the view of this village from the bay. When we reach it, we see it is positioned perfectly for an inspiring view of the sea and elevated on a high platform to catch the breeze that swirls through the town. As we watch, the sun ventures from behind the omnipresent clouds drifting over the mountaintop. It bathes the church in a holy light. We stand in awe.

A lush garden, overflowing with blossoming trees, surrounds the entrance. Gently, we push aside palm fronds hanging across the entryway. We find ourselves in a vacant sanctuary, facing a statue of Mary looking up at Jesus on the cross. A stained glass at the front captures sunlight and beckons us inside. A sweet fragrance from the dazzling array of potted plants near the altar——azalea, bougainvillea, frangipani—is overwhelming.

The church is named *Eglise Sainte Marie de L'Enfant Jesus.* It was built in commemoration of the 150th anniversary of the arrival of Catholic missionaries to the island. The structure combines local wood with discarded stones, which had been used as ballast for 19th century trading ships.

Günter and I sit on the bench in front and bow our heads: *Thank you God, for bringing us here safely, 3000 miles across the vast Pacific. Thank you for giving*

The Marquesas

Fatu Hiva

Hiva Oa

Ua Pou

Tahuata

"The first experience can never be repeated. The first love, the first sunrise, the first South Sea island are memories apart."
Robert Louis Stevenson, *In the South Seas*.

Nuku Hiva

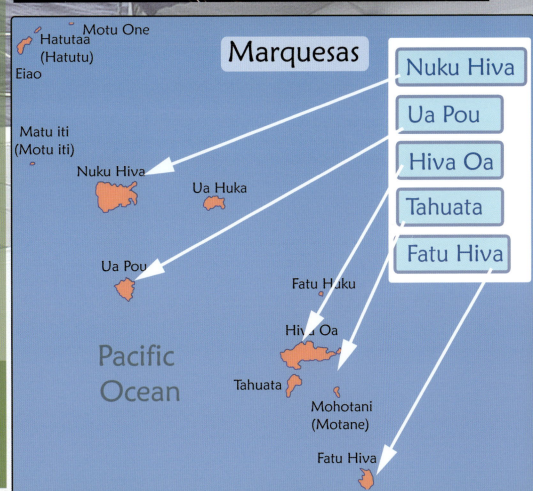

us the opportunity to see these marvelous Marquesas. And thank you for all of your creation. The moment is magical. We are filled with a sense of peace and contentment.

We rejoin Jean-Claude and Claudie. It's time to head back to our yachts for Sunday siesta and a wonderful dinner.

After a rejuvenating siesta, we enjoy urchin appetizers before dining on New Zealand steaks and some local fish we had purchased at the market in Atuona. During dinner, Doug regales us with information he learned from a young Marquesan man with whom he spent the afternoon catching sea urchins. He tells us about the typical family house here. He says it rises from a stone foundation, it has wooden walls which enclose the bedrooms, and the kitchen and living areas are always open. The structure will contain indoor plumbing and electricity, and, usually, display a TV dish on the roof.

"Most of the younger generation live like this now," Doug says. "They sit inside watching TV, while *we* are out here in *their* bay—without TV."

Truthfully, we don't miss the tube at all.

Later our men retire below. I sit at the helm seat, gazing at the moon. It lurks behind drifting clouds, as if playing hide-and-seek. I think of my mother, Sigrid, up there somewhere. Tomorrow will be her first birthday since struggling to take her final breaths via ventilator last December. Mom doesn't seem as close as she did in those grief-stricken days that followed.

Have I grown more used to the idea of her being gone? Is she done hanging around, finished with her initial earthly duties, finished comforting us all? Maybe it was time for her to move on to more heavenly pursuits and time for us to move on without her.

⚓

I'm baking up a storm this morning of April 23 in honor of Mom's birthday. She would have turned 83 today. Mom would be proud of me, baking up two loaves of banana bread—reducing the big bunch swaying in the bimini holder by six bananas. "It's good you're not letting them go to waste," she would have said. A child of the Great Depression, she wanted to save everything. I'm making these for her: "Mother's Banana Bread," a great recipe from Mike Greenwald's *Cruising Chef.*

After another day of exploring, we return to *Pacific Bliss,* who tells me that she has had enough of relaxing in this idyllic anchorage. She tugs on her anchor, her bow headed out toward the sea, as if to say, "Let's go. It's time." I pat her hull as I climb on board. "I know. Tomorrow we head for Fatu Hiva."

I wake up during the night, my sleep suddenly disturbed.

Just nervous the night before a passage. The usual.

Then I sit up straight in my bunk. The moon! I throw on a robe and head for the cockpit. It's 0300. The moon is larger now; it casts an ethereal glow onto the rugged mountains as it descends into the sea. I feel like I'm in another world, but that's not a sufficient explanation for the eerie feeling that descends upon me.

Of course, I am in another world! This is Haratefau Bay in the Marquesas, one of the most primitive and remote places on earth, smack in the middle of the Pacific, 4000 miles from either Australia or Panama, 1950 miles from Hawaii, and 850 miles from Tahiti.

But that's not it. There's something else. I can feel the hairs of my arms stand up on end. Yet there is no breeze.

Mom is here.

Her pale blue fish eyes are bulging out of her round face, trying to take it all in. Curious, as always.

"I'm happy to see you here after your long passage, and I know you're just exploring now. You did good…"

The gentle voice is hers. She's here, but she's not here. I know no one else could hear her—even if anyone else were here in the cockpit.

"Lois, I know you like to explore, and there is so much left for you to see in *your* world, but if only you could see me now…"

The voice fades and I am transported back to her funeral with the chorus of one of her favorite songs, performed by Truth:

> If you could see me now,
> I'm walking streets of gold.
> If you could see me now,
> I'm standing tall and whole.
> If you could see me now,
> You'd know I've seen His face.
> If you could see me now;
> You'd know the pain's erased.
> You wouldn't want me
> To ever leave this perfect place
> If you could only see me now.

"You cannot imagine the beauty of this next world. You'll have so much more to explore…"

The voice is back.

"I *do* try to keep an eye on all of you down there. I'm sorry if you miss me. But oh, there is so much to do, so much to see up here. You would not believe…"

The voice fades. Sigrid is gone again.

I sit at the helm seat for a long time. The stars brighten with the moon gone. I focus on the Southern Cross and gaze beyond it into the galaxies, far into the

Church on Baie Hanamoenodi on the island of Tahuata.

Eglise Sainte Marie, the church where we gave thanks for a safe passage to the Marquesas.

world beyond.

I feel a sense of relief, of affirmation, that taking this voyage around the world is the right thing to do.

I want more. I try. But I cannot bring her back.

Passage to Fatu Hiva

We escape Haratefau Bay in the dark. *Pacific Bliss* rounds the island of Tahuata as the sun climbs the mountaintops. The receding island is in stark silhouette. Jagged outlines resemble a landscape from some fictional planet.

A pod of over 20 spinner dolphins swims over to check us out. They pirouette, leaping into 180° and then 360º spins, totally free of the water. Flying fish scream from crest to crest, evading predators. High above our mast, snow-white tropicbirds, their red plumes behind them, carry the bounty of the sea in their crops. They streak toward the head of the valley, where they are rearing their young.

It is a grand day to be alive!

The rollers are long and low as we leave the lee of the island. The wind picks up to Force 3 from the east, 10 knots apparent. Our crew raises the main and unfurls the jib. We are sailing again! *Pacific Bliss* is in her element. With the sails full and the wind increasing, she gains slowly on *Makoko*, who left the anchorage first.

I turn to Günter to make her case. "I think *Bliss* wants to surge ahead."

"I don't want to race. I'm just enjoying this super day. I don't feel competitive."

"It's not what *you* want. I don't think you'll be able to hold her back. She has racing in her sails today."

Günter agrees to humor *Pacific Bliss* by adjusting her sails: 8 knots, 9 knots. Yes, our Mistress *Bliss* is in fine form, and all is well with the world. We had set the alarm for 0530, allowing for an 8-hour sail. That is a 50-mile passage, at a little over 6 knots average speed. Plenty of time to anchor in Fatu Hiva.

"*Pacific Bliss, Pacific Bliss,*" crackles the VHF.

Günter picks it up and we all eavesdrop. "*Makoko* concedes the race," Jean-Claude announces. "You'll be preceding us into the anchorage."

"Wow!" Doug jokes. "I wonder if they'll still lend us ice cubes."

A gust of wind smacks her tail, and *Pacific Bliss* gallops ahead. She doesn't care that the race has already been won. But she's going a little too fast for Günter.

We douse the main and furl in the jib, slowing her to a trot, and soon we glide into the anchorage.

High spires of rock greet our arrival. They have been carved by nature into colossal monoliths and minarets that soar to the heavens. They are like enormous stalagmites, jutting to heights of five and six stories. In shadows, they suggest ominous figures—a demented King, fierce knights, demons from hell. They form a battlement of towers. Slowly we motor toward them. We drop the hook into the weirdest world I have seen in my entire life.

Our Anchorage in Fatu Hiva
10°28′S, 138°40′W
Baie Hanavave, Bay of Virgins, Fatu Hiva

It is our first full day in this bay, and we are unable to leave *Pacific Bliss*. Blasts of rain, thunder, lightning, and wind funnel through the mountaintops down onto the bay. I watch the anemometer swing from a steady 4-8 knots all the way to 30-plus. My nerves are grated raw. *Pacific Bliss* swings wildly on her anchor, clocking all directions.

Charlie's Charts had warned us about this place. But glowing reports about the waterfall hike have trumped caution. We had difficulty anchoring, as did others, but our anchor is holding securely now.

Once anchored, no cruiser moves in this weather. Not if it can be helped.

Three boats were here when we arrived; now we are seven. We spot two Japanese yachts, the first we have encountered during our circumnavigation: *C'est la Vie* (skippered by a solo Japanese cruiser) and *Flying*, with a family on board. *Flying* sways dangerously close to us. Quickly, the guys lower our dinghy to help its skipper set a second bow anchor closer to the shoreline. Much better. I feel safer.

The view is awesome, constantly changing. Periodically the sun peeks out. Its light plays on the brooding water, reflecting threatening clouds overhead. For a fleeting moment, the sun beams onto a little village below. Sadly, by the time I grab my camera, it has disappeared again. But the vision remains vivid, and our determination to leave *Pacific Bliss* intensifies.

The Waterfall Walk

"A one-hour's walk behind the village," says *Charlie's*, "is a spectacular 61m (200′) waterfall." After a long walk through the paved village and along the soaked and muddy dirt road, then another hour's hike through the tropical rain forest, stumbling under and over logs, climbing rocks, shoving branches out of our way, and detouring around yet more boulders and thick brush, we finally cross a stream to view the elusive falls. We crawl down to the base to see the water from below. It drops like a silken veil.

This is truly spectacular!

Günter and I are not alone, of course. The crews of *Pacific Bliss* and *Makoko* are accompanied by Sarah, who is crewing on the Canadian yacht *Nootka Rose*, and by the family on board the Japanese yacht *Flying*— Captain Tess, his wife, and their two very well-behaved children. Like one body, all of us leap into the cool pool

DID YOU KNOW?

THE MARQUESAN ISLANDS

According to legend, Polynesians sailed their ships into the darkness of the unknown to emerge where the sun shone on a group of volcanic islands they hailed as a world of light. These islands were grouped together under the name of Hiva, but centuries later they were renamed the Marquesas by the Spanish. This wrinkled land, whose virginal beauty is mostly untouched to this day, tells a long and captivating story.

Legends refer to the first comers as the Take, meaning the cause, or root. They were the life that spread from the center of Polynesia to take root in the deep isolated valleys of the rugged isles of Hiva—so long ago that the legends have left the names of the discoverers and their ships far behind.

The first settlement in the land of light was thought to be on Hiva Oa, most likely in the 10th to 12th century. Some settlers migrated to nearby islands and founded new tribes. The island of Nuku Hiva became a second cultural center. Then the others—Tahuata, Fatu Hiva, Ua Huka, and Ua Pou— followed. It is probable that some of the voyages north to Hawaii passed through the Marquesas. The Marquesas may have become a center for the development and dissemination of culture in the entire eastern Pacific.

In 1595, Spaniards Alvaro de Mendana and Pedro Quiros—commanding fast, small caravels—discovered the Marquesas, the first islands in Polynesia touched by Europeans. Surprisingly, the Incas of Peru were the ones who gave the Spaniards precise navigational instructions: Sail 4,000 miles due west. The Spaniards found the islands of great beauty and the people peaceful, but they could not control their crews, who killed 200 Marquesans without provocation. Mendana named the islands Las Marquesas de Mendoza, for the wife of his patron.

The next outsider, Captain James Cook, arrived in 1774. He estimated that 100,000 Marquesans inhabited the isolated valleys and reported that clans often fought wars across the intervening mountains. After a handful of men died, he added, these wars would be called off and feasting would begin—often with the flesh of the enemy.

The islands' reputation for human sacrifice and cannibalism spread. When the whale ship *Essex* was rammed and sunk by a whale in 1820, the captain opted to sail 3000 miles upwind to Chile rather than 1400 miles downwind to the Marquesas. (Ironically, many of the survivors of the shipwreck resorted to cannibalism in order to survive.)

The American navigator Captain Joseph Ingraham first visited the northern Marquesas while commanding the brig *Hope* in 1791, giving them the name Washington Islands. In 1813, Commodore David Porter claimed Nuku Hiva for the United States, but the US Congress never ratified that claim. In 1842, France took possession of the whole group, establishing a settlement (later abandoned) on Nuku Hiva. In 1870, France re-established control over the group, which was later incorporated into the territory of French Polynesia.

These islands, far from shipping lanes and unprotected by barrier reefs, remain remote to this day. Tourism has not tainted them, and there are no major hotels.

of spring water. It is frigid and shocking.

"Swim with me out to that tree," Günter says. "Then we can go *behind* the sheet of water."

"Just give me a minute to catch my breath."

"Come now," he goads.

"Okay." I swim out into the chilling water underneath the falls. Günter, always the intrepid scout, is already there.

"Hold onto the tree."

I grab it and hold on for dear life, pulled by the pounding water.

"Now, look up."

I'm holding on for dear life, and he tells me to look up!

I do—and see one long 200-foot drop of water rushing over a sheer cliff. The spray around us is deliciously fresh as it fans like a lawn sprinkler in a breeze.

What a sensual, delightful Moment of Bliss!

I turn my face up. I taste the exquisite liquid and thrill to the emotional rush the water produces.

Günter and I rejoin the group. We sit on boulders, talking and drying off. After an hour's respite, we pack up reluctantly and head back. We follow the creek all the way back to the town, where we use stones from the riverbed to clean our muddy shoes. On the village main street, we are amused to see an upside-down sign, in broken English, warning visitors to leave their "shit up the street to the right."

How should we understand this? Do they mean "shit" as "garbage" or "trash?" Or are the villagers just plain tired of tourist excrement?

The crews return to their own yachts. Back on *Pacific Bliss* we all take fresh showers and, after dinner, collapse into our bunks.

But we can't sleep; we're still wondering about that sign!

Nothing This Good Lasts Forever: Passage to Ua Pou

Our plan for the 100-mile passage to Ua Pou is simple: Depart before sunset, sail under a full moon, arrive in the morning. We all know we *should* sleep, but no one does. We're too energized with anticipation.

At 1700, we pull anchor, slip out to sea, and look back on the shrinking Bay of Virgins. The sun sheds its final rays on forlorn peaks, dimming centuries of primitive secrets. We navigate through an area of swooping frigate birds, boobies, and flying fish.

Dusk transitions into a magnificent world of semi-darkness. Even under the glare of a full moon, the Southern Cross sparkles. *Pacific Bliss* is also enjoying––no, relishing—the night ride as she rushes ahead on a beam reach that brings us 8 knots, 9 knots, 10 knots. The four of us sprawl in the cockpit, savoring this evening of enchantment.

But by 2200, everything has changed. *Pacific Bliss* is wallowing now. The wind is down to 8 knots, and she bumps along at 4, sometimes even less. Joy has turned into misery. The boom preventer, rigged on the port side, bangs against the lines holding it in place. The sound is magnified inside the hull as if it comes from giant amplifiers. There is no rest for anyone—even in our bunks.

It is time for my watch. I hear Günter talking with Jean-Claude. *Makoko* is wallowing also. I join Günter for awhile. Eventually, the wind *does* pick up from the east, and on my watch I experience a nice one-hour sail, with *Miss Bliss* gliding along at 7-8 knots.

But nothing this good lasts forever….

My peace is interrupted by our autopilot alarm. The reading on the multimeter says "LST CSE SE6." This is serious. Ray has lost his course: He is no longer steering. The compass is out-of-whack again. I hurry to the nav station. Same message. Soon *Pacific Bliss* is drifting out of control. I race back to the helm to hand steer. Ray says 260º. Our compass course should be 306º. "Gü-ü-ünter!" I call through the screened window above our berth. "*H—e—l—p!*"

He is beside me in a flash, taking over. Soon Armin rushes on deck, followed by Doug.

"It's a new compass!" I ask, "How can it be broken?"

Günter considers my question but doesn't immediately respond. Finally he turns to Ironman. "I can't figure this out. My brain is scrambled. Take the helm and hand steer."

The waves are higher now, with a long fetch, rolling toward the beam. No one has had much sleep tonight, but Günter has slept far less than any of us. Groggy from deprivation, he says, "Armin, take it for one hour, then Doug will take it for an hour, then give it to Lois. I *must* get some sleep!" He stumbles to our cabin and collapses on the bed.

I am surprised that our captain has failed to troubleshoot the situation.

Doug is silent, lost in thought. Then suddenly he exclaims, "The *cable*! We changed the compass, but we didn't change the cable!"

With Ironman steady at the helm, Doug decides to replace the entire cable with our back-up. He struggles in the stifling, claustrophobia-inducing area beneath the nav station.

Pacific Bliss reels with the waves.

Finally, Doug straightens up, sweat dripping from his body. He has brought Ray back to life! He was right. It *was* the cable.

The next thing I see is Doug heaving his guts out over the leeward side.

By 0600, a new day is born. I am on watch at the starboard helm. The moon is bright white against the navy sky to our west. 180 degrees across our domed world, a faint glimmer of sunlight surfaces over the horizon. Soon Ua Pou beckons on my port.

Pacific Bliss sails merrily over the waves, toward

We hike to this spectacular waterfall, one hour's walk from Baie Hanavave, Fatu Hiva.

Günter can relate to this Polynesian voyaging canoe belonging to the Canoe Club in Ua Pou.

our waypoint at the northeast end of the island, and all is right in our world.

What a luxury to have Ray back again, with the autopilot, compass, and computer all working together, in sync!

The Benefit Feast in Ua Pou
9°22′S, 140°03′W

At 0945, we anchor in Baie D' Hakahetau. The town of Hakahetau, according to *Charlie's*, welcomes cruisers and has made every effort to provide services. Because of this, there are 14 boats in this bay. *Makoko* anchors behind the breakwater.

The VHF crackles an announcement: "A benefit lunch will be held ashore to raise money for the town's rowing team."

Shoving fatigue aside, we're off. The hefty swell makes getting there an acrobatic feat: We must board our dinghy *Petit Bliss* and motor her ashore, attach her to the sea wall, then climb the wall's wet and slippery surface while waves bounce us in every direction.

But a Polynesian feast—that's an occasion worth the effort!

We arrive to find what may be the only sand beach in the Marquesas. It is packed with families on a Sunday afternoon. The children frolic in the water while the adults set out their coolers and spread towels on the sand.

The party is in full swing in the canoe clubhouse. It is a huge, shed-like structure with high rafters, wide metal roll-up doors, and cement floors. Long portable tables covered with banana leaves groan under a bounty we haven't seen since our Bon Voyage Party in San Diego: *poisson cru,* made with coconut, lime, and shark meat; curried goat; octopus; and the traditional *poi* and rice—all topped dramatically by a suckling pig, which has been roasting in a pit for the past 24 hours. The donation is 2000 francs each (about $16). We are happy to contribute. The band plays while a soloist belts out all sorts of tunes, including some in English.

We experience another of the wonderful, unexpected surprises of cruising that can happen anywhere. Here we are, on a remote Marquesan island, and we discover that Clark and Suzy of *Final Straw* live only a few miles away from us in San Diego! We had met them over the Puddle Jump and Coconut SSB Nets, but never in person. Now we greet each other warmly and spend time exchanging cruiser stories.

When the benefit ends, we head back to the wide beach. There we strike up a conversation with two charming teenage Marquesan girls. Günter wants to practice his French on them, but they want to practice their English on *us*! Next we engage a couple of sun-wrinkled Marquesan men. They are amazing! They entertain us with remarkable stories about Polynesian sailing, and they boast that Ua Pou is the center of the ancient Polynesian voyaging culture.

This is fascinating. Without realizing it, we have been sailing our yachts on the same routes used by the ancient Polynesian voyagers, who over 2,000 years ago embarked on a series of epic migrations that would

Doctors Doug and Armin treat Claudie's infected leg.

result in the discovery and settlement of the entire Polynesian world!

From beginning to end, our experience at the Ua Pou benefit party has been an absolute joy.

The Boat Docs

Injury and sickness are often unavoidable. When they happen, one wishes for a crew member with a medical background. God must be smiling on us: We have two.

Claudie is experiencing a flare-up of the shin injury she suffered while provisioning *Makoko* in La Paz, Mexico. After swimming here in the Marquesas, her wound became infected. This is a dangerous condition because tropical heat and dampness can cause bacteria to go wild. Fortunately, Doug and Armin have been like resident Doctors without Borders. They have made numerous house/boat calls. With Claudie, they disinfect and wrap the wound, order "boat-rest," and provide antibiotics.

In addition, they have been checking and redressing the wound twice daily. Consequently, it is healing nicely. Claudie is relieved. Now she'll be able to make the next leg of the journey (no pun intended!) without the help of additional "boat doctor" calls.

I am relieved, too. *Makoko* and *Pacific Bliss* were meant to buddy throughout our circumnavigation. Now with Claudie's recovery progressing, she and I spend hours talking boats, politics, and every other subject we can think of while the men shop for supplies to take us to the Tuomotus.

Günter plans to leave Ua Pou in a few days. Our next stop will be Nuku Hiva.

A Bloody Market in Paradise
8°55′S, 140°06′W
Baie de Taiohae, Nuku Hiva, Marquesas

We arrive at Taiohae on a 20-knot wind. Two rocky islets, called Les Sentinelles, guard the entrance to the horseshoe-shaped bay, which is shallow, lush, and pristine. We settle in among 25 other yachts and, as quickly as we can, head into town.

Taiohae is the largest town in the Marquesas. It is also the Marquesas' administrative capital. Though it lies in an open volcanic crater, it is quite civilized. Red roofs line the hillsides. A helicopter pad sits on a high hill. The town sports a radio station, a hospital, an air-conditioned post office, satellite telephones, three markets, a gendarmerie, and administrative offices. There's even a yacht services shop on the wharf, which

Even this remote village on Fatu Hiva has electricity and a paved main street.

contains one computer with internet access. While I send out my e-mails, Doug purchases a ticket to fly home to tend to personal business.

The next day, he makes a connection to Tahiti and from there he heads back to the states. We miss him. But we still have Armin. Meanwhile, Günter heads for the gendarmerie for our exit papers and visa and to report Doug off our crew list.

We had hoped to leave early today or tomorrow but, on reaching the post office, we learn it is closed and won't be open until Monday. One thing a cruiser must learn is to be flexible and to expect the unexpected. So instead of leaving, we go to the hairdresser-souvenir shop. Everyone gets a haircut. While we're there, we are persuaded to buy $30 tickets to a benefit dance for the Taiohae sports team. Another buffet — *and* a band from Rangiroa! I look forward to the excitement, but the last buffet brought me down with diarrhea, and I dread the possibility of that happening again.

Lots of rice, don't eat the fat, and don't drink the water.

The dance is great fun, the food is delicious, and, this time, I escape the Marquesas Revenge.

On Saturday, the alarm jangles at 0430. Twenty minutes later and half asleep, Günter, Armin, and I climb into the dinghy. Günter's miner's flashlight, worn on a band around his head, throws a beam on the dark, rippling bay. We motor around tangles of anchor and dinghy lines; we bump into unlit fishing boats. At the wharf, Armin jumps out and pushes aside the four or five dinghies already tied there.

"Where were you?" Jean-Claude asks, his dinghy already secured.

"We were at *Makoko* at five minutes 'til, as planned," says Günter. "You were already gone."

"Well, you need to come early for *this* market. Come on, the fish are already laid out."

It is bedlam here. Madly chopping heads off fish, the fishermen crouch over makeshift tables and stand in pools of blood and water.

"Good size fish," Armin observes, "but only half the size of the one that got away from us."

We order four kilos (2.2 lb) of tuna. The fisherman hacks a big hunk from one huge fish. The kilo of redfish I want is pulled from a picnic-style cooler. Then I head straight for the lobsters. I buy four of them. The fisherman shoves them into a plastic bag that is much too small. I throw all of it into to my large canvas bag, which is already soggy and smelly.

I move quickly to the veggies. Rarely available throughout the islands, vegetables have to be bought quickly before they disappear entirely. The metal folding tables are surrounded by cruisers and islanders, all frantically groping for the few vegetables there. In the faint light of dawn, I can begin to see without my flashlight. I fight my way up to the table and grab two packs of green onions, two Chinese celery, two bags of green peppers, and two bunches of carrots. Tomatoes…tomatoes…where are the tomatoes? There are none.

I hurry to the bakery table. I shoulder the crowd to grab three sweetbreads, two quiche, three little pies, and a bag of croissants. I'd like baguettes, but they will be found only in stores later, I'm told.

By six o'clock, the big rush is over. The tables are bare. The vendors begin to pack. Fishermen are cleaning their mess of eyes and heads and guts by hosing it all into the sea. The filthy water gushes down the wharf steps, picking up other fish parts along the way, and flooding everything into the dinghies tied below.

I slide down the oozing steps, the soles of my

Tevas® sloshing in the bloody water. I settle into the gory dinghy and prop my shopping bags into place next to Armin. Then Günter, glumly handling the outboard, steers us across the bay and back to *Pacific Bliss*. No one says a word. Everything—our clothes, our shoes, our bags—is saturated with mud, blood, and saltwater. I feel I'll never be clean again. Back at *Bliss*, Armin secures the painter. I disembark first. He hands me the filthy bags, one by one. I set them on the starboard swim steps; I can't have them messing up the interior. Günter splashes seawater all over the dinghy, rinsing it as best he can. I strip off my Tevas®, clean my feet in the bay, and then pad inside.

Armin sets up a fish-cleaning operation on the steps of the port hull. He spreads out our old oilcloth, then cleans and guts the fish, and finally washes them with the freshwater hose. As he cuts the tuna into steaks, he passes each of them to me, and I slip them into plastic sealer bags. We get a smooth assembly line going: Armin cuts, I pack, Günter seals, and I put each one-meal package into the freezer.

That done, I unpack and wash the vegetables. Those that cannot be peeled must be treated in a bleach solution. Then they are spread on the trampoline to dry. Later I will put them into green Ever-Fresh® bags and into the fridge.

The process has been hectic and exhausting. We flop on our berths to rest, but not for long. Market day hasn't ended for us yet. Today is Saturday. We want to leave on Monday right after we get our visas stamped at the post office. Also, on Sunday all stores will be closed. Who knows how long they will be open today? Is their frozen meat still available? After a one-hour respite, we drag ourselves back into the dinghy, back to those dreaded concrete steps on the wharf, back to the dusty road into the town's markets.

We have to accept it...there is a price to pay for Paradise.

Sunday Mass on Mother's Day

On Sunday, May 5, Günter and I accompany Jean-Claude and Claudie, who are Catholic, to the local Catholic Church for 8:00 a.m. mass. Two tall pines frame the twin-towered building. A brick pathway leads to wonderfully carved wooden sanctuary doors.

Inside the church, sixteen wooden sculptures of Biblical events flank three sections of pews.

It is the first Sunday of the month, Communion Sunday, so the service is especially long. After the first few minutes, we are using the printed handout of service and songs to fan ourselves. I love the Marquesan songs. Their strong, separate parts for men and women move me deeply. The men resonate profundo from deep barrel chests; the women sing soprano like angels. It is all sung without musical accompaniment—purely a cappella—and is thoroughly enjoyable.

At the close of the service, something happens that moves me even more than the music. At least a dozen teenagers circulate through the sanctuary asking all the women if they are mothers. To each woman who answers yes, one of the teenagers gives a simple, colorful bouquet of local flowers—with a loving smile. I accept mine, and my heart fills with affection and appreciation. I am touched that these wonderful youngsters gave up their Saturday night to assemble these lovely bouquets to honor the mothers of Nuku Hiva. I will remember this Mother's Day always.

Our Men Become Hunters and Gatherers.
8°49′S, 140°03′W
Bay D'Anaho, Nuku Hiva

A nine-foot, southwest swell from a New Zealand gale is reported in Tahiti, and it's heading straight for the Tuomotus. Aware that these swells can affect the currents going in and out of the passes, we decide to stay in the area until the forecast is clear. Here in Anaho Bay, we can swim right off the boat. Both *Charlie's* and *Sailing Directions—Pacific Islands* warn cruisers about the coral reefs and bombies (coral heads) here, rare in the Marquesas, but both fail to mention what a fine bay it is for snorkeling.

The bay is a veritable aquarium! Electric-blue neon fish dart through soft, pastel-colored formations and hard brain coral. Blue-and-gold striped angelfish and orange fairy basslets swim past pale-blue goatfish with thick, yellow stripes. There are delicate butterfly fish, and blue-green parrot fish, and who knows how many other magnificently colored species. All that riotous color is accompanied by groups of ink-black spiny diadema (sea urchin), moving more slowly than turtles, feeding on the algae of the sandy bottom.

Armin and Jean-Claude stare at a green moray eel slithering out of its cave, its menacing mouth open wide, its sharp teeth flaring. It's all exciting, but after a few days, the guys want more action! They take *Petit Bliss* to the shore, where Jean-Claude spear-fishes, darting like a fish himself all over the bay, while Armin and Günter shuffle along in knee-deep water, both looking...

"What are they looking for?" Claudie asks.

"I don't know," I answer as I watch them through my binoculars. "They're searching for *some*thing."

Soon they are joined by a Marquesan boy. The lad takes Günter's spear and brings up an octopus at the end of it. All eight legs are curling and twisting as it squirms frantically to get away. The boy dashes the octopus back and forth on the rocks, then drops it into Armin's pail. Success! From there, the process is repeated four times, and with the pail full, the guys return happily to *Pacific Bliss*.

The men have become hunters and fishermen.

While waiting for a weather window to sail to the Tuomotus, the men become hunters and gatherers.

I wait for them to return, and as they climb on board, I ask, "How did you find them so easily?"

"The boy showed me," Günter puffs proudly. "I looked for a pile of small rocks in front of a small opening, like a little cave. Then I pushed the rocks aside. After that, I jabbed my spear into the hole. Either the octopus would come out, or it would shoot a jet of ink. After the ink cleared, I could locate the octopus. Then I speared him and smashed him against the rocks. That stuns him. Then I turned him inside out. That kills him. It's simple."

At the swim steps, Armin pounds each octopus with a rubber mallet to soften the flesh. And Günter throws the lot into our stock pot. We boil them for 45 minutes and prepare them in three batches for our voyage to the Tuomotus: one batch in a Fijian curry; another in a lime/ginger/soy sauce marinade; and the third without anything, to be frozen as is.

It may sound gross to some, but octopus can be delicious.

Our Women Become Nesters.

A woman may have been a professional or a high-powered executive before she became a cruiser. No matter. Prior to a passage, she takes on the traditional housewife role.

The day before our passage to the Tuomotus, Claudie and I morph into "galley slaves." Since we know the weather forecast is good, frenetic activity ensues. We bake cookies and bread. We boil our remaining potatoes and most of our eggs. I make potato salad; Claudie makes salad niçoise. We check the status of all the fruits and vegetables, prioritizing the ones to be eaten first, and make sure that sufficient toilet tissue and paper towels are available and easily accessible.

I strip the galley of breakables, store the blender and breadmaker below, depress all the latches, vacuum the floors, and shake out the rugs. A little bit overboard? Perhaps, but all female cruisers do it. Some will say, "It's best to be prepared for anything, especially for foul weather." But I believe that all this frenetic activity is the cruiser's version of Every Mother's Warning: "Always wear clean underpants in case you're caught in an accident!"

One never knows what to expect on a passage. However, the truth of the matter is this: Before passages, while he keeps the boat sound, she always feathers the nest.

DID YOU KNOW?

POLYANDRY IN THE MARQUESAS ISLANDS

Polyandry is a notorious practice common in Eastern Polynesia that was noted by Western visitors and writers in the 1800s. It is a situation where a woman had a primary husband and one or more secondary husbands, who were to some extent, domestic servants. This was different than the fraternal system that still exists in the parts of the Himalayas in which brothers share the same wife. Edward Robarts, a beachcomber who lived in the Marquesas from 1798 to 1806, was quite candid about his male European views: "In this liberty, these people differ from any other class of people that I ever met with. One man may have several women, but for a woman to have several men I think is a pill hard to digest." Linton, a field researcher, made some conclusions in 1939, based on his field work done fifteen years earlier, which proved overly simplistic but do provide one of the best descriptions of domestic arrangements:

"The Marquesan household was polyandrous, there being usually two or three men to one woman, while in the household of the chief, there might be eleven or twelve men to three or four women, one head wife and subsidiary wives... All members had sexual rights to each other, the arrangement constituting a sort of group marriage. A chief or head of a rich family would sometimes arrange a marriage with a young woman because she had three or four lovers he wished to attach. The men would follow the woman; in this way a man could build up the "man power" of his household. Only the poorest households at the lower social levels were monogamous, and there was much envy of the rich households by the poor ones.

"Household, rather than family, is the proper term for the basic social unit of Marquesan society...the more active adult males the household had, the more work it could do, and the more wealth it could accumulate."

Linton claimed that the ratio of 2.5 males to each female was the basic cause of polyandry, and despite the Marquesans' denials, suggested that they practiced selective infanticide.

In the households of that time, all children were considered as the sons or daughters of the principal husband, even if he could not have been the father. In other cases, men who had been the woman's partners during adolescence remained with her when she married an older or wealthier man. According to Melville, sometimes two men jointly offered themselves to a woman, who chose one as the principal and the other as pekio (secondary husband). The more substantial households consisted of a principal husband and wife, several pekio, and also a number of female and male servants who were not pekio. A man could remain a pekio after the sexual relationship ceased.

The signature peak that distinguishes Ua Pou rises like the prow of the boat that serves as the altar in the nearby church.

Plants with exotic red stamens bloom in profusion near the waterfall.

Dancing trees typical of the windy Marquesas shoreline.

In the Wake of ANCIENT EXPLORERS

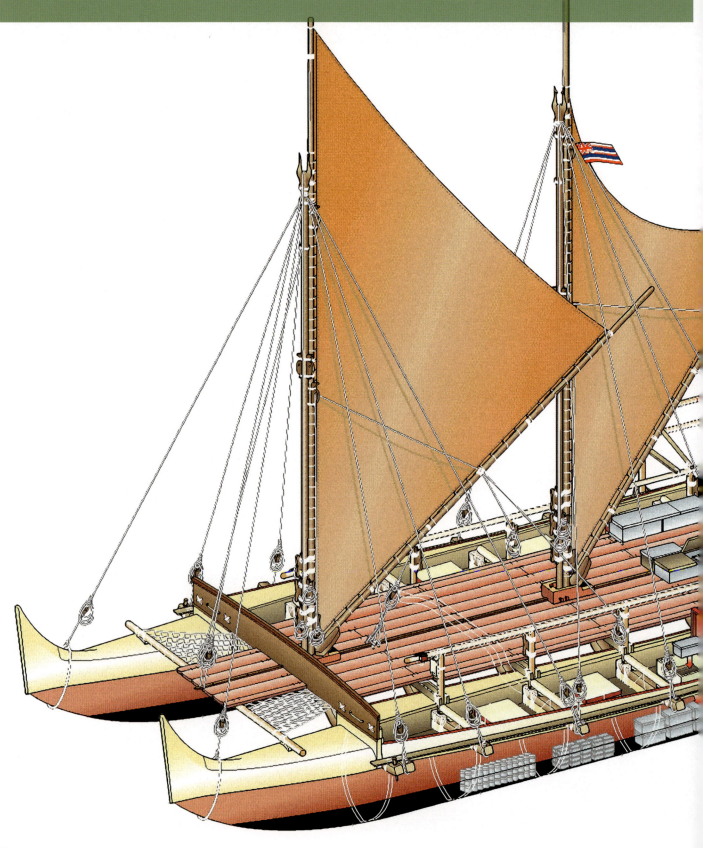

Polynesian Voyaging Canoes

For hundreds of years, the rugged islands of the Marquesas gave rise to the voyaging culture. These very islands served as the springboard for reaching every corner of the vast Polynesian triangle that extends from Hawaii on the north to Easter Island on the east and New Zealand in the south. Double-hulled voyaging canoes from the Marquesas, held together with flexible sennit lashings and propelled by sails made of woven pandanus, slid onto the Big Island of Hawaii around the 4th or 5th century A.D. A few hundred years later, Marquesan explorers reportedly settled Easter Island and centuries later, New Zealand.

Based on pottery fragments, most historians believe that the first inhabitants of the Marquesas came from Samoa, more than 2000 miles away. Unlikely though that may seem, their route was against the prevailing winds and currents. Sailing their great wooden canoes carved from tree trunks with Stone Age tools, they crossed the world's largest ocean over 2000 years ago, at a time when legions of Roman soldiers were marching through Europe. Marquesan legends refer to their ancestors as coming from "below" and "up" the wind, meaning that they had sailed from the west. When the westerlies blew, they could have sailed their canoes due east; when the prevailing southeast trades resumed, they would have to tack against the wind. This course would have taken them not only east, but a little north as well. It was inevitable that the high islands of the Marquesas, rather than the Society Islands, became their final destination. These nine islands would have stretched in a 200-mile chain at right angles to their path.

The 1985-1987 Voyage of Rediscovery took *Hokule'a*, a double canoe replica without navigation instruments, on a 16,000 mile journey along the ancient migratory routes of the Polynesian Triangle—from Hawaii to the Society Islands, the Cook Islands, New Zealand, Tonga, Samoa, and back home via Aitutaki, Tahiti, and Rangiroa in the Tuamotu Archipelago. This voyage showed that it was possible for Polynesian canoes to sail from west to east in the Pacific when the prevailing easterly trade winds were replaced by seasonal westerlies. The Polynesian Voyaging Society has revived the ancient art of guiding canoes by celestial bodies and ocean swells.

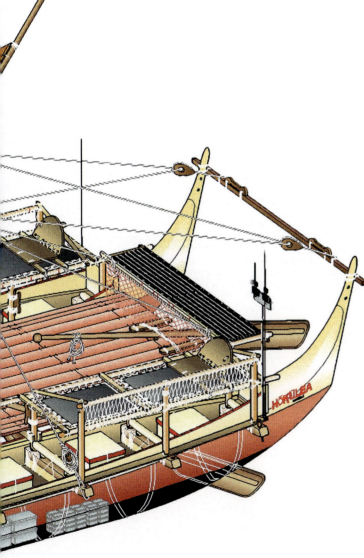

Sources: Polynesian Voyaging Society: *Hokule'a*: *The Way to Tahiti* by Ben R. Finney and others (see bibliography).

Chapter 3
The Elusive Tuamotus and On to the Societies

The Dangerous Archipelago
8°47'S, 140°W
May 13, 2002

I leave my charts and sailing references below. "Captain, your navigator reporting on deck." I make a playful show of saluting. "This will be a difficult and dangerous entrance. It says here in the pilot manual that we must plan our approach to the Ahe atoll between 10 a.m. and 2 p.m. on a sunny day with the sun directly overhead. Right now, the atoll is over 500 miles away. Besides watching out for reefs, we must time our approach with the tides. We will need to enter the pass at slack tide or the start of an ebb."

Günter pulls me tight into a big bear hug. "Good plotting job, Navigator. Okay, here we go, off in search of another adventure."

Not so long ago, most sailors wanted only to sight and successfully pass the Tuamotus. For centuries, these low-lying atolls, called the Dangerous Archipelago, have been littered with the carcasses of sunken ships. We'll probably see numerous wrecks stranded on those reefs, some of them ancient, and others, recent. Even though we modern sailors are blessed with GPS, accurate depth meters, and better on-board weather forecasting equipment, exploring the Tuamotu Islands is still no walk in the park.

Seventy-eight in number, the Tuamotus sprawl right across our path to Tahiti. All but two of the islands are made of coral. This means their low-lying character makes them almost invisible at a distance of only a few miles.

I turn toward Günter. "Let me read to you this warning in *Charlie's Charts of Polynesia*: 'Typically, the motus (islets) on the reefs are clustered to a greater degree on the northern and western sides while the southern sides are often bare, awash in coral reefs. This is very dangerous, since even in daylight the reef cannot be seen until close-to and the sound of the wind and sea often masks the sound of the breakers.'"

"But you wanted to go there," Günter teases me.

"Of course. I especially want to see the island of Tikehau. It's part of your past, before *me*."

Günter had lived with the locals on Tikehau in the '70s, with nothing but his windsurfer and a backpack. He had lived on rice and fish until he came down with the area's dreaded *ciguatera* (fish poisoning). After days of sickness, he survived. But for the remainder of his stay, he lived only on rice.

I am willing to risk the reefs of Tikehau to see the island that had threatened my husband's life.

Pacific Bliss is sailing along nicely at an easy 7 knots, her main sail full under fair winds and a following sea—every sailor's dream. The sun climbs above wisps of striated clouds. Flying fish leap across crests, leaving luminous streaks of silver in the sun-specked sea.

"The next land you'll spot will have tall palm trees and white sandy beaches stretching for miles on end…a different kind of paradise," Günter says.

"I'm dreaming about it already," I reply, "but it was in Anaho Bay that I learned the art of the 'slow snorkel,' just lying on the water, alongside schools of fish, letting my body wash back and forth with the incoming tide. It was in Anaho that I gathered arms full of hibiscus growing wildly beneath the trees just beyond the beach. It was in Anaho that you and Armin learned how to spear fish, to gather coconuts, and to hunt for octopuses.

We leave the brooding, mysterious peaks of the Marquesas behind and set sail for the Tuamotus.

Anaho Bay was the perfect refuge, and Tuamotu will have to be something very special to top it." I interrupt my reverie. "What happens if a strong wind develops while we're inside the lagoon?"

"Well, if we get a forecast for strong winds, we'd better not be on the wrong side," Günter says. "I remember *flying* across the lagoon on my windsurfer. I know it can get nasty real fast. Three-foot waves. Once bad weather hits, moving the boat will be out of the question."

As we sail on through this perfect day, I dream of what is to come.

When Friendship Counts

"Something is wrong with *Makoko*. I can tell by her sails she's hove to." I set down the binoculars on the cockpit bench where I have been keeping Günter company. "We've been steady, never more than two or three miles ahead of them. But now she's dropping back."

Both vessels have been motor sailing all day. "Jean-Claude radioed earlier about having some problems with his engine," Günter explains. "Let's just turn this bucket around and go see. Armin! We're going to douse the mainsail. Lois! Steer into the wind."

Günter performs his slick, turn-on-a-dime maneuver and stops near the bobbing *Makoko*. He keeps both engines idling. The waves slap against the hulls while the captains talk back and forth. Then, Günter rushes below decks for Nigel Calder's "Bible," a reference book that covers everything about electricity on boats. Over the VHF, he reads the section on Hurth transmissions… "What the heck, I'll bring it over to you," he tells Jean-Claude.

"Don't jeopardize your safety," Jean-Claude warns.

"Don't worry."

We motor *Pacific Bliss* as close to *Makoko* as we dare. The swells are high. Armin stretches precariously over our dinghy, *Petit Bliss*, and unties the safety lines. Plunk! She drops into the ocean swells. When Günter is seated, I hand him the thick volume, wrapped in a plastic garbage bag for protection.

He yanks the cord on the outboard. Silence. He pulls it again. No go.

Günter is drifting away from us—fast.

On the third try, the welcome *brm-m-m!* is music to my ears.

Makoko rolls miserably from side to side like a drunken sailor. Günter powers toward her.

Armin and I take turns watching the action through our binoculars. We see Günter cut the engine. He rides the swells. The rubber dinghy bumps the hull of *Makoko*. Armin frowns and glances at his watch. He's worried. "Less than one hour till sunset. Is he going to board? I

DID YOU KNOW?

THE TUAMOTUS

The Tuamotu Archipelago, a chain of atolls in French Polynesia, encompasses 78 coral atolls and islands, the largest chain of atolls in the world. All of the islands of the Tuamotus are coral "low islands": essentially high sand bars built upon coral reefs. They span an area of the Pacific Ocean roughly the size of Western Europe.

At the 2002 census, the Tuamotus (including the Gambier Islands) had a population of 15,862 inhabitants. 769 inhabitants live in a 215-nautical-mile (400 km; 250 mi) radius around Morurua and Fanguataufa, the sites of the French nuclear tests. The language spoken in the Tuamotus is Tuamotuan, a collection of Polynesian dialects, except for in Puka-Puka and the Gambier Islands, where Puka-Pukan and Mangarevan are spoken, respectively.

The tourism-related income of the Tuamotus is meager, especially by comparison to the booming tourism industry of the neighboring Society Islands, although Rangiroa and Manihi are favorite scuba diving and snorkeling destinations. The most important sources of income are black pearls and copra. Agriculture in the islands is predominantly subsistence in nature.

Archaeologists say that the western Tuamotus were settled from the Society Islands by 700 A.D. Flat ceremonial platforms made of coral blocks (called marae) similar to those on Tahiti have been found on the islands of Rangiroa, Manhihi, and Mataiva. Tupac Inca Yupanqui may have stopped in the Tuamotus during his 10-month voyage of exploration of the Pacific around 1480.

The first European to discover the Tuamotus was Ferdinand Magellan in 1521, during his circumnavigation. His visit was followed by Portuguese sailor Pedro Fernandes de Queiros in 1606; Dutch mariners Willem Schouten and Jacob Le Maire in 1616; Jakob Roggeveen, who also first sighted Easter Island, in 1772; John Byron in 1765; Louis Antoined de Bouganville in 1768; James Cook, during his first voyage in 1769; and German navigator Otto von Kotzebue, sailing in the service of the Russian tsars, in 1815.

At the beginning of the 18th century the first Christian missionaries arrived. During the late 1800s, the islands' pearls became a coveted possession of Europeans.

In 1880, following the forced abdication of King Pomare V of Tahiti, who controlled the Tuamotus, the islands were annexed as an overseas territory of France.

The Tuamotus made headlines around the world in 1947, when archaeologist Thor Heyerdahl sailed from South America to Raroia on his raft, *Kon-Tiki*. Heyerdahl wanted to prove that the ancient settlers sailed the trade winds from South America instead of originating from the East, as archeologists maintained.

1. Günter hands over the manual to Claudie and Jean-Claude so they can troubleshoot *Makoko's* transmission;
2. *Pacific Bliss* stops to help the ailing *Makoko*.

At 0535, the wind picks up to 10 knots. *Makoko* is abreast of us now. Jean-Claude and Claudie are busy, trimming their sails to catch every precious breath of this elusive wind. Perhaps today the breeze will allow them to shut down their cantankerous engine!

Thank you, God, that Pacific Bliss *has two engines. And please see that* Makoko *enjoys a better day!*

By 0545, the clouds begin to glow. They fringe the entire horizon like fluffy ballerina skirts. Imagine a Super Bowl half-time performance, with the star performer waiting eagerly in the wings. At this hour, the sun is that performer. And right at 0600, as if on cue, it leaps onto the stage of the sky! Mesmerized, I warm in its glow. Another day has begun.

But a day that began with such a glorious show degenerates into dreary duskiness as the night curtain falls. I see flashes of sickly yellow lightning. Radar tells us a line of squalls is approaching. My stomach is churning.

I hate electrical storms!

During his watch, Günter calls on Armin for help. They douse all sails before the first squall hits. After the second, Günter sits inside, at the dry nav station, like a steamer pilot. Whenever the wind direction changes, he sets Ray to whatever direction would give *Pacific Bliss* a 45° apparent wind angle against the main. It works—we're sailing by the wind. Nevertheless, with one squall after another hitting us, watches become very hard work. Tension caused by the flaky winds, the driving rain, and this complex method of sailing has me close to tears.

Then, at 1030, I witness a most terrible sight: *Makoko's* largest sail flaps uncontrollably as part of it falls into the sea. Their Genoa has ripped, and I know they do not have a replacement. Not only are they without a working transmission, now they have torn their largest sail!

The VHF crackles. It's Jean-Claude. "You on *Pacific Bliss* are unfortunate enough to be paired with the most unlucky boat in the Marquesas and Tuamotus—no, the most unlucky boat in all of the South Pacific. We feel so sorry for you."

"Don't," I reply. "We're sticking with you. How's the sail repair going?"

"Slow. We have about 70 centimeters to stitch by hand. And the tear is not uniform along the seam. We need to take our time and make it strong."

By the afternoon, we're underway again. Jean-Claude and Claudie have completed the repair, and they fly their genoa in a gentle 10-knot wind. By 1815, though, the wind increases to 17 knots. *Pacific Bliss* is in her element, scooting along at 9-10 knots. Before long, we have to take a second reef in the main so *Makoko* can stay with us. But during my early evening watch, the wind increases to 25 knots. I become concerned about *Makoko's* sail; however, she manages to stay even with us.

Later, at the helm for my 0300 watch, I note that the wind is still going strong. After one hour, it turns ugly. When I see "Force 7" on the multimeter, I remember the Force 10 of our maiden voyage, and it sets off a Pavlovian response. My heart pounds; my tongue feels like sandpaper.

I check the radar. It shows a big squall line. I wake Günter to keep me company. By 0445, it hits us hard. But, thank goodness, it's only rain.

On *Makoko*, Claudie is on watch. She has Jean-Claude right by her side. The rain lasts only 25 minutes, and by the time it ends, the wind has decreased to 12 knots, a mere Force 3. More squalls appear and the wind increases to Force 6. Now *Makoko* is three miles behind us. I feel sorry for them; with only two on board to share the watches, ship problems are always multiplied.

By the afternoon, we on *Pacific Bliss* have recovered from the two miserable nights. Jean-Claude calls. "I'm so ashamed of my boat," he begins. "Usually this is the perfect wind for *Makoko*, but now she is chugging along at only 6 knots. Propeller drag, I guess, since the blades will not fold now."

"We'll reef some more," I reply and hang up the receiver.

At sea, 14°10.7′S, 148°02.5′W, May 17: Our latitude keeps changing ever farther south. *Pacific Bliss* continues to shepherd *Makoko*. We have decided to skip the Tuamotu Archipelago and, instead, are now headed for the Society Islands. But we can't go to Tahiti yet, because only Raiatea has the repair facilities we will need. *Makoko* has lost all of her forward power. Jean-Claude has ordered a new gearbox that will be ready for installation in the shipyard. *Pacific Bliss* may have to tow her through the pass and into her berth there. The good news is that, thanks to Jean-Claude's farsightedness, both yachts have dock space reserved. That means electricity, all the water we want, and a respite in civilization!

I predict some raucous partying in our future!

Preparing for the Worst

But before the gain comes the pain. Günter and Jean-Claude discuss towing procedure. They try to determine how to rig a towing bridle out of our spare 250-foot anchor line. Then he and Armin bring out all the extra dock lines we have in preparation for the eventuality. Nevertheless, we concoct back-up plans and hope they won't be necessary. Concern about towing *Makoko* through the pass keeps everyone on edge. The wind continues at over 20 knots. No one can sleep. We keep *Pacific Bliss* to 3 knots average speed for a landfall at dawn. It's not easy; a strong wind can push our catamaran at 3-5 knots with no sails—just the rigging!

By the end of my watch, I can barely see our buddy boat, she has fallen so far behind. Günter puts both engines into reverse and reduces our speed to 1.5 knots.

Finally, we reach the entrance to Raiatea's lagoon, and the wind decreases to 12 knots on the beam. "Good news! I think we can sail through," Jean-Claude radios. "We'll lead, but be prepared to tow us into our berth, if need be."

We are set to power through the rough-water pass. But, just as both yachts reach the channel, the inter-island ferry appears from around the bend.

"What do we do now? We're under sail and cannot stop," Jean-Claude worries.

"Call *pan-pan* immediately," Günter answers. "Then explain the situation in French."

The call is successful; the ferry stands by and lets us pass.

"*Pacific Bliss*," we're instructed by the port operator, "pick up the mooring labeled 'Private' between the red and the white boats. *Makoko* will be escorted to the shipyard."

However, as we close in to pick up the mooring, a sailor in the vessel on the adjacent mooring calls out, "No! Private."

Günter shouts back, "We have permission."

"The owners will be back to this mooring today!"

We head toward the mooring anyway. Suddenly an 18-knot wind arises from nowhere. It throws us about, but Armin and I manage to grab the buoy on the third try and run the line through the ring.

Finally, moored safely, we have a quick lunch and fall into our bunks, "dead on arrival." An easy three-overnight trip had morphed into seven long days and nights at sea.

Nine hundred fifty miles. Half the distance of our Atlantic Crossing and a third of the Pacific Crossing. More stressful than both because this long crossing was not in my plan.

Just as we're settling in, two men in a dinghy marked Raiatea Marine appears at our stern. "You have to move," we're told. "You can anchor out by those reefs. It is shallower there."

Günter's face tightens; he is ready to explode.

"This mooring is promised to another Catana."

I take a wild guess. "Is it *Adelaide II?*"

"You know them? They are your friends?"

"Yes. I'm sure it will be all right with them." We had met Francoise and Bernard in Cartagena, Colombia.

The dinghy turns back to the shipyard. Finally, we can relax and let go.

Just as we are about to retire, *Adelaide II* swings by the mooring. My heart sinks.

But Bernard thoroughly understands. "Stay," he says.

Once again, we receive proof of the strong bond that unites cruisers. We seem to be a band of brothers, willing to help, confident we can count on each other in difficult situations.

Günter tells them, "You're both invited for sundowners tomorrow. We want to thank you properly, and we want to introduce you to our other French friends on *Makoko*. They'll be coming to our party, too."

During the night, I sense *Pacific Bliss* pulling and jerking the mooring. I climb topsides. Way off, in the sky above the reefs, bolts of lightning illuminate the red-and-white hull of *Adelaide II*. An ear-splitting crash of thunder follows. Then I remember that it could have been *us*, anchored out by those reefs, sleepless, worrying about our anchor dragging.

I feel sorry for Bernard and Francoise. I hope they don't regret their generous offer.

Decompression and Celebration

Claudie and Jean-Claude arrive as the western sky softens from its bright gold; the clouds have become gentle and limp. Claudie hands me a tray of appetizers and a bottle of champagne. "First of all, we want to express our thanks."

"It was nothing…"

"We can't relax until we express our gratitude. *Pacific Bliss* was always there for us. That was so good for our morale."

"But as it turned out, you didn't need to be towed after all." Günter joins the conversation. "You could have made it on your own."

"Yes," adds Jean-Claude. "But it would not have been the same. I was ready to sell bloody *Makoko* when I came into port."

"And now?" Günter asks.

"Of course not."

"Was this the worst passage you ever had?"

"No. But it came close. In the Balearics in the Med, with our previous boat, I was at the helm for thirty-three hours nonstop."

"While the two children and I were inside, throwing up in the sink," Claudie adds.

"But you kept on sailing," Günter says.

"Well, you know how it goes: Two or three days on shore and you forget how it is," answers Jean-Claude.

"Like childbirth, you forget the pain." Claudie turns to me and smiles like a co-conspirator. "But you men wouldn't know about that."

Francoise and Bernard arrive, bearing more food

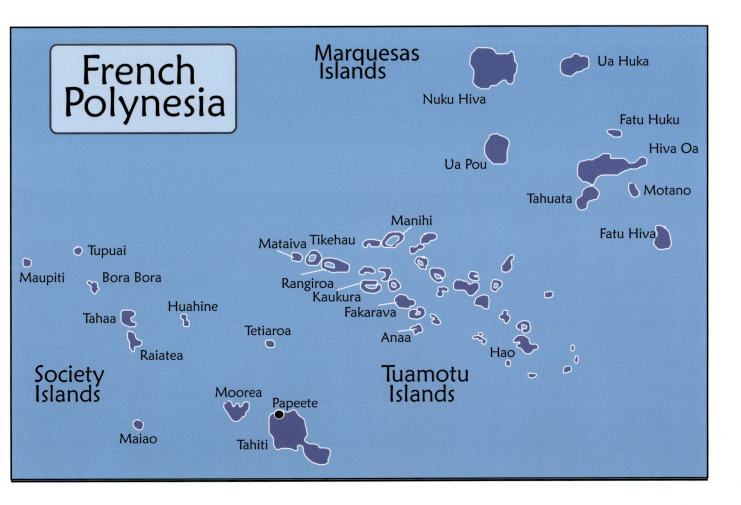

and looking sharp, tanned, and as cheerful as always. They don't even mention the electrical storm.

Armin comes up from below, freshly showered.

Claudie hands him another bottle of champagne, decorated with multi-colored streamers. "Thank you, Dr. Armin, for your excellent attention to my wound. It's healed nicely now."

"Happy to help." Armin grins and pops the cork.

Along with the food and drink, story-telling goes round and round. In Cruiser Talk, this is called "Decompression." Günter repeats the details of our Force 10 storm off Colombia and ends with a sequel describing how we had met *Adelaide II* during another "decompression." Francoise tells the story of their French friends who had worse luck than we did there, actually losing their boat on the reefs near Cartagena. Jean-Claude expands on the horror stories of the Med, which he and Claudie had sailed off-and-on for ten years.

Why cruisers insist on recounting their worst misadventures when they come into port, I swear I'll never understand. I guess it's like soldiers exchanging war stories to other buddies who have "been there, done that."

French Polynesia has the reddest sunsets I've seen anywhere in the world. As we party, the sky turns to a brilliant red-orange, changing to claret, and then gradually to a deep maroon. We take photos of each other against the seascape.

We examine the visa situation. We Yankees want to stay in French Polynesia more than the 90 days allowed. Our French friends come up with a solution: Günter and I are the problem, not *Pacific Bliss*. Before our visas expire, we can fly out of the French territories, then fly back in and get a new visa stamp on our passports, good for another 90 days.

Easter Island—that's the answer!

Jean-Claude and Claudie are eager to come with us. "It will be fun," Claudie laughs. We proceed to work it all out: *Makoko* must stay in Raiatea for repairs, but *Pacific Bliss*, needing only her spinnaker mended, can leave for Papeete, Tahiti. Jean-Claude and Claudie will sail with us. Then, we four will fly out to Easter Island, while Armin stays on board *Pacific Bliss* in the harbor. It will be another great adventure with two of the closest friends we've made in the wonderful cruising community.

Easter Island, here we come!

The two boats motor toward the Raiatea Marine shipyard.

MESSING WITH BOATS

A Cat Out of Water
by Günter

Zinc electrodes prevent electrolytic corrosion of a boat's metal parts. Periodically, it is necessary to replace them. Unfortunately, one set of zincs is located on the Catana propeller under the boat—a bad design—and can only be replaced with the boat out of the water. That is because the entire propeller must first be removed.

Hauling one's boat out of the water is always tricky. And scary, too, unless a professional marina repair service is available. Fortunately for us, the haul-out facility at Marina Apooiti in Raiatea was well equipped for this procedure.

Pacific Bliss had to be hauled up on the marina's rail system, which was set into the shallow blacktop landing. So I drove the boat up the rails, and a tractor gradually pulled *Pacific Bliss* out of the water. I must say, the marina mechanics were fast and efficient. Once underneath the boat, they managed to change the zincs and have her back into the water within one hour.

Next, the mechanics had to repair the cantankerous outboard motor for *Petit Bliss*. Here's how that problem occurred: We had returned from a walk to a village from Anaho Bay in the Marquesas to find our dinghy deflated and half submerged, not by accident is my guess. Before it was hauled back onto the beach, it had probably flooded the engine with saltwater. We cleaned as much saltwater from the engine as we easily could, and we got the engine to start, though in a sputtering mode. Fixing the outboard was easy for these mechanics.

Finally, our Spinnaker-of-Many-Colors was sewn onto a new collar and the seams were re-stitched. Good as new!

Back in the water, the marina gave us a berth outside the walls, but with a line to electricity and water hook-up on shore. The set-up was complex, but once in place, it worked fine. We placed our dinghy between the stern and the shore and pulled ourselves along a dock line to get on and off the boat. Compared to the bedlam inside the marina (which did not have space for a Cat), we enjoyed a peaceful existence and wonderful sunset views over the neighboring islands of Tahaa and Bora Bora.

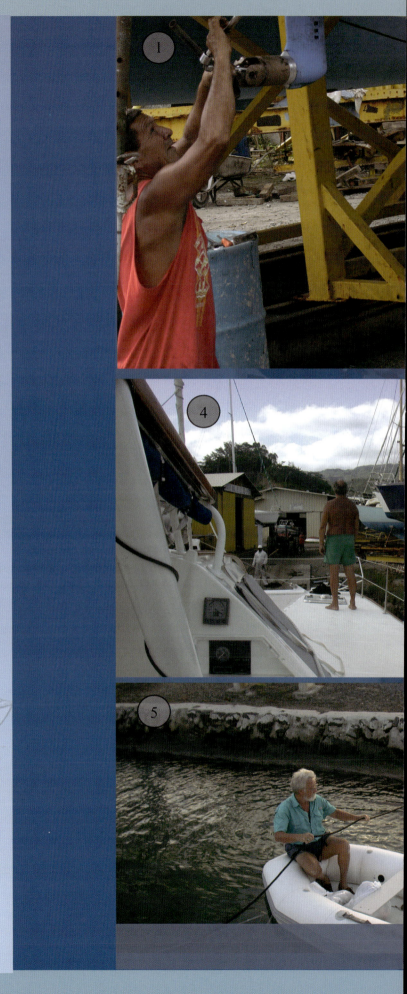

1. Replacing the zincs; 2-3. A tractor is used to pull *Pacific Bliss* onto the hard; 4. This is the scary part; 5. Günter uses the dinghy to pull ourselves along a dock line to get on and off the boat.

Decompression and Celebration in *Raiatea*

"EASTER ISLAND HAS THE DUBIOUS DISTINCTION OF BEING ONE OF THE MOST MISINTERPRETED AND MISUNDERSTOOD AREAS OF ITS SIZE IN THE WORLD."
PATRICK MCCOY

Chapter 4
The Navel of Nowhere: Easter Island

An Island Shrouded in Mystery
27°9′ S, 109°26′ W
June 2, 2002

The LAN Chile jet drones through the night. It leaves the lush, tropical air of Tahiti behind, crosses four time zones, and begins its descent as the sun rises in the eastern sky. With us on the 727 are Jean-Claude and Claudie and the couple's friend Gerard, whose Super Maramu ketch is also under repair in Carrenage Raiatea. The jet dives through a layer of thick clouds and glides along the extra-long runway, upgraded by NASA to serve as an emergency landing for the space shuttle program.

As we disembark, I zip my *Pacific Bliss* sailing jacket all the way to the neck, a comforting protection against the blasts of rain and wind that assault us. This has to be the most godforsaken place on the planet! Torrential rains continue to pour down from a gloomy, vengeful sky as fierce winds whip across a barren landscape.

While I wait for our lone duffel to arrive at the outdoor carousel, I stare at the weathered wooden sign at the entrance to the terminal: EASTERN ISLAND. (The Spanish translation, *Isla de Pascua*, is engraved below.)

They have added an "n" to "Easter." Incredible! Is this a sign of carelessness, or do the islanders not know their own name given to this place by a Dutch explorer?

In 1722, Jacob Roggeveen sighted the island on Easter Sunday and named it Easter Island.

Today's Polynesian name for the island is *Rapa Nui*, dating from the 19th century. The Tahitian sailors who had first discovered it likened it to the island of Rapa 2400 miles to the west—but added the name *Nui*, meaning larger.

Immigration is straightforward; soon Günter and I have the *Isla de Pascua* stamp in our passports. One objective for the trip has been met. Now we can proceed with a more important objective: learning and understanding the island's perplexing history, legends, and culture.

Martin Hereveri, our host, arrives as scheduled and drives us to our guesthouse, one of ten motel-like rooms that he and Anita maintain. We find the couple very helpful and friendly. They laugh with us as Günter and I adjust to communicating in Spanish, rather than French—easier for us. The couple speaks both, along with limited English.

Günter sets down our duffel as we look around the room. Rather basic: a double bed and two nightstands, one with a lamp; a bare light bulb, hanging from a cord centered in the A-framed ceiling; a standing fan in the corner. No other furniture—not even a chair. Neither a painting nor a photo breaks the expanse of green wallpaper. But there *is* a bank of built-in shelves at the far end of the room, with a hanging area for clothes, as well as a small private bathroom with a tub. Drapes, with filmy white curtains underneath, cover a picture window that faces a pathway overhung with shade trees.

After unpacking, we walk through the courtyard to the dining area and ask for *agua* to take back to our rooms. We receive two glasses instead of a bottle, but eventually Anita understands and brings us a bottle.

I turn toward Günter. "I think *la pension* could be

79

charming on a sunny day. Look at those orange-gold Canna lilies. They're an unusual color. And I like the rose bushes next to the white iron furniture."

"It's not charming today," he says grimly.

Later, the five of us trudge through the rain. We pass through a neighborhood filled with simple, unpretentious houses, past a stucco church and souvenir shop, and then down to the town's center. We search for a restaurant and find one, Restaurante Cuerito Regalon. After seating us, the waitress informs us that this is the only restaurant in town that is always open. "And Hanga Roa is the *only* town on the island," she adds.

We learn that most of Easter Island's 2000 inhabitants reside here.

Fortified with a hearty lunch of steak, fries, and red wine, we are warm enough to brave the cold wind and driving rain. We amble downhill toward the sea, gesturing and laughing all the way.

At the bottom, I stop cold.

I stand there at attention, incredulous, silenced. Slowly, my gaze travels upward.

Towering over me is a 30-foot gray stone figure with no arms or legs—a lone giant that stares back at me with vacant, black, obsidian eyes. He faces the village as if he is guarding it, his back to the sea.

I'm dumbfounded, rooted to the spot. I am intrigued. I am hooked.

The Mysteries of Rano Raraku

The rain pounds the roof and whips through the garden outside. The wind whines all night. Günter and I snuggle to keep each other warm. In the morning, I see the rain relentlessly driving against the window pane, and I pull the covers back over my head. I don't want to leave our cozy bed to face the elements. But we must—adventure beckons!

The five of us breakfast in the little dining area of the *pension*. Methodically, I spread butter on a couple of tiny baking powder biscuits, add a few squares of cheese, and sip a second cup of instant coffee.

Basic, like our room. But it will hold us for a morning of exploration.

We all joke with the couple at the next table, the only other guests. They are blonde, thirty-something backpackers from Holland. One by one, we look toward the rain outside the lace-curtained windows and repeat a common travel refrain: "What is, is."

After breakfast, layered with most of the clothes we brought for a three-day stay, Günter and I climb into the driver/guide's truck with everyone else. We're heading for Rano Raraku. The road is bumpy all the way, and once there, the group must trudge along a murky path, dodging oozing black puddles everywhere. Red-clay mud clings to the tread of my ill-suited sports shoes. Each step produces a giant sucking sound, followed by a loud "splat!" Eventually the muddy path turns into a grassy slope, and we follow our guide up the slope to a volcanic crater. No wonder this crater is described as an "open-air museum!" It is one of the most intriguing archeological sites I've ever encountered.

The main quarry for the Easter Island statues, this crater is virtually a moai graveyard. Here we find the stone-faced giants lying in various states of production. Some are half-carved, some are broken, and some appear to have been abandoned in mid-transport. Rushing eagerly around the base of the quarry while our guide lingers behind, we discover moai half-buried in the grassy slope—hidden by centuries of erosion.

The site sends chills up my spine. I am witnessing a snapshot of history, frozen in time.

Something awful happened here. Whatever it was, it stopped moai production dead in its tracks.

The abrupt stoppage is ideal for archeologists because they can look closely at exactly how the moai were carved from the available rock. Also, it is on this staging area—the quarry and the adjacent transport road—that speculators base their theories of how the moai were transported to various ceremonial sites on the island.

I remember learning about it from our books on board *Pacific Bliss*. Experts say that fewer than one-third of the carved moai made it to a final site. This raises intriguing questions: Was the problem due to the difficulties in transporting them? Were these remaining moai deemed culturally unworthy of transport? Were they meant to remain here? Did the islanders run out of the resources necessary to complete the herculean task of carving and moving them? What are some of the "expert" conclusions?

Well, in 1989, archeologist Jo Anne Van Tilburg did a survey that reported 887 monolithic statues on the island. Of those, 397 are here in the Rano Raraku central production center. Another 288 were successfully transported to various *ahu* (ceremonial platform) locations, and 92 were recorded "in transport." The remaining 110 were lying throughout the island.

On average, moai stand 13 feet tall and weigh 14 tons, all human heads on torsos, carved in the male form from rough, hardened volcanic ash.

"Look! A giant one!" Günter cries. He is already way ahead of us, halfway up the hill.

Lying on his back, this moai is, indeed, a Giant. He is called *El Gigante*, and he is 71.93 feet long (21.60 meters) and weighs about 145-165 tons. (The largest standing moai is called *Paro;* he is about 32 feet tall and weighs a mere 82 tons.)

A favorite pastime of the guides and tourists here is to imagine how these statues were moved to stand in place on their *ahus*. The explorer Thor Heyerdahl was told by the village elders that the statues walked from the

Jean-Claude, Claudie, Gerard, Lois, and Günter explore Easter Island's mysteries during unfriendly wind and rain.

quarry to the *ahu*. That may have meant that the statues were merely moved in an upright position, as a Dutch drawing from 1728 seems to show. In this illustration, the statue is on a base and workers are doing something underneath while others pull. Several experiments have been carried out to prove that the statues could have been moved by "rocking and rolling" their bases similar to the way we would move a refrigerator or a large piece of furniture. But this would have caused too much damage to the base and perhaps was used only for the final positioning atop the *ahu*.

American geologist Charles Love successfully moved a replica moai by placing it on two logs cut to fit the bottom of the statue. When raised onto a track of wooden rollers, his 10-ton moai could be moved 145 feet in just a few minutes, using 25 men and two ropes.

Van Tilburg of UCLA used computer models that took everything into account: manpower, available materials, type of rock, most efficient route for transport, and even how much food the workers would need. In her view, each statue was laid on two logs. Under these were positioned smaller logs upon which the larger logs were rolled. Her calculations showed that a standard sized moai could be moved from this quarry to Ahu Akivi (10 km) by 70 men in 4.7 days. Hers is the explanation given by our guide.

Now that we have exhausted the "how" possibilities of transportation, the bigger question "why?" remains. *Why* did the population turn to statue construction, and on such a large scale, in the first place? And *why* did the islanders continue the practice to their own detriment and eventual demise? Ultimately, the islanders deforested more and more of their land and conscripted more and more of the population into their grand scheme until no one was left to produce the food. Why didn't they see their end coming? And an equally intriguing question would be: Who felled the last tree?

Of course, although speculations have existed for hundreds of years, neither our guide nor anyone else has offered incontestable answers.

We walk back from the quarry silently, each of us lost in his or her own thoughts. The conundrums haunt my soul.

This is clearly statue building run amok. There may be a lesson here: Is this the inescapable punishment for extreme obsessive/compulsive behavior?

We leave the quarry and climb back into the truck to view the ceremonial sites along the coast. Most are along the southeast shore. Here the moai are more standardized, erected between 1400 and 1600 A.D. They stand in a row atop the *ahu*. These, too, have their backs to the sea. Our guide proposes that these moai

1. Moai stand watch, their backs to the Pacific; 2. Fifteen restored moai stand watch at Ahu Tongariki, the largest of Easter Island's ceremonial platforms.

may have held a sacred role in the life of the Rapa Nui; however, what it could have been, no one can say with certainty.

At Ahu Akiva, we visit an *ahu* with seven standing moai. The sky clears just long enough for me to take a wide-angle photo of the entire row. I approach the *ahu* for a close-up shot. A local woman with a short, stocky build and jet-black hair waves me away frantically. "Not too close to *ahu*," she admonishes me, stern-faced. "Sacred."

Even though most islanders are friendly, clearly she is not.

"She is out here protecting their local customs," explains our guide.

There are no written records and few oral histories to tell the story of this remote land. Conjectures fill over 4000 books and articles.

I am fascinated and determined to find out more. But that will have to wait until tomorrow.

Right now, dripping wet, we stop at the restaurant in Hangaroa for an early dinner. Günter persuades me to try a frothy Pisco Sour (in memory of a "Before-Lois" trip to Peru). I cannot identify the liquor, but the lemon and sugar pep me up. Following cocktails, the five of us share a bottle of *Vinotiuto*, a cabernet from Chile, and hot *sopa verdums,* vegetable soup.

Gerard finally quits shivering; he has layered his three shirts and a light jacket, but he has packed only shorts for this brief trip. A stocky man, his body temperature usually runs hot. Now, though, he yearns for long pants!

The special tonight is *pollo grille con rizo exotica* (grilled chicken with exotic rice). We attack it *con mucho gusto,* while we relive the day's experiences and engage in the usual retiree dinner conversation: why our children don't discipline our grandchildren like *we* disciplined *them*, how the world is *not* becoming a better place—what with wars and ethnic hatred—and how we can continue to cruise, have fun, and avoid it all without feeling guilty!

At ten o'clock, our taxi is waiting for us in the unrelenting downpour. We dash into the vehicle and then out again at our *pension*, trying to avoid the rain.

Silly. With layers of clothes already drenched, what difference could a few more drops make?

In our room, Günter and I strip and heave all our clothes over the fan standing in the corner. Then Günter turns it on, full force. Not a bad solution.

More drastic measures are needed, however, for our soaked socks.

By pushing the hair dryer into each sock and then turning it on, I manage to get Günter's socks relatively dry. But when the effort turns to *my* socks, we blow out the fuse protection. The *pension* has no spares. My socks will have to dry—or not dry—*au naturale*.

The good news: Günter has remembered to bring his "universal" bath stopper so the small tub will stay full. We run hot water almost to the top, and then soak together in a tub with barely room for one until we're warm and cozy again. Günter finagles a thick, warm plaid blanket from the manager. While the wind wails and howls, we cuddle and stay toasty all night.

The Mysteries of Orongo: Caves, Craters, and the Strange Bird Cult

We awaken to a fierce wind, whipping through the garden of callas and roses. We don't want to face the elements. Really. But we have lined up another tour for our last full day here.

We five jam ourselves into the four-passenger four-wheel-drive vehicle, with the bald tires. We head straight for Orongo, where we stop first at the Visitor Center.

"Sorry, we have no map or guide," says the Polynesian clerk, as she takes our money. "But there *is* a little one-room museum back in Hanga Roa. They might have one."

A lot of good that does us.

We follow our driver/guide to the rim of a volcano called Rano Kau. Tall rusty reeds line the bottom of the crater. Delicate yellow flowers line the ridge. The sun peeks through briefly, revealing patches of green moss clinging to the opposite side.

Along the way our guide describes what happened after all the statues had been built. "The first westerners to discover this island wondered how anyone could have survived in such a desolate, treeless place. For centuries, it had remained a mystery."

"Was it ever solved?" I ask.

"Possibly. Core samples taken from these craters show that the island had been heavily forested... with giant palms. These are now extinct, of course. But the original Polynesians were greeted with a lush, tropical paradise. They must have thought that the island's resources were inexhaustible. So, they cut trees for housing. They cut wood for fires. And, eventually, they cut trees to make the thousands of rollers and levers necessary to move and erect the moai."

We reach the top of the crater and look across.

"The moai building competition turned into an obsession...with bigger and taller moai."

"Like the 70-foot monster we saw in the quarry?" I ask. "The one that could no longer be moved?"

"Right. And still the trees came down. The land began to erode, with the topsoil vanishing into the sea. Crops failed, and clans turned on each other to battle over the scarce resources. The moai were once the symbols of power, but now they were toppled. Eyes were smashed out of them. Some were decapitated."

We climb partway down into the crater, where our

Günter gazes at the statues.

guide leads us into a spooky cave.

"There was even evidence of cannibalism. The victors in the many battles would eat their enemies to gain strength. In fact, one of the caves I will show you is called *Ana Kai Tangata*. This means cave-where-men-are-eaten."

He takes us to a cave where, he claims, even children were eaten. "We found bones here. That's how we know."

Outside the cave again, he explains that such cannibalism may have been a case of hunger rather than ceremony. Just when we think this story of Easter Island's gruesome past cannot get any worse, our guide says, "But there's more." We hike past the ridge to an overlook. "The islanders were cut off from the world as never before," he continues. "Any dreams of escaping had disappeared, for they no longer had wood. The only boats they could build were made of the *tortoro* reeds that grew in the crater lake you just saw. Even fishing became difficult.

"All this led to the next weird custom, called the Birdman Cult. This cult became the dominant religion of the island and was practiced until 1866 or so. High on this rim we are now walking was the ceremonial village of Orongo. It was built to worship the god of fertility, Makemake.

"You see those three little islands way down there?" Our guide points toward the sea. Whitecaps roil the surface.

"Each year, the people of this island picked a new leader in a very strange competition. Strong young men had to scale down these sheer cliffs, swim out to one of those three small islands…these waters have sharks, by the way…and bring back the egg of the nesting sooty tern—unbroken. They had to swim with the egg held high. The man who did this successfully was named Birdman of the Year, and he enjoyed special honors."

"But the winner was a young man. How did he know how to rule?" asks Jean-Claude.

"He didn't. He didn't really *rule* the people. He just sat alone in the forest by himself, like a guru."

It sounds crazy. But after being here for two days, I'll believe almost anything!

Next, we enter small, damp caves that contain petroglyphs of birds, carved into solid basalt. Over 480 Birdman petroglyphs have been found, mostly near Orongo.

It's difficult to imagine what might have happened next. "But as if things were not bad enough," our guide continues, "by 1862, a succession of slave traders landed on the island, taking away all the strong and healthy to work the guano fields of Peru. At first, the islanders greeted the ships with open arms. Later, they wised up and hid in their caves until the ships departed."

The entrances to the caves are hidden and small. Only locals can find them. Bent over like animals, the five of us, one by one and in single file, enter the caves.

What a miserable way they had to live!

We are reaching the end of our tour. Our guide leads us to a round black stone about four feet in diameter. "This is called The Navel of the World. This is the translation of the ancient name: *Te Pito o Te Henua.*"

It figures. Whoever they were, those very first

Lois pretends to move the stone called The Navel of the World (*Te Pito o Te Henua*).

discoverers of this remote island thousands of miles from nowhere, they must have conceived of this place as the spiritual epicenter around which their entire universe revolved!

The downpour had stopped briefly but renews now with a vengeance, as if the sky gods are furious. Our guide wants each of us to come forward to touch the surface of the smooth lava stone.

"To the Navel of Nowhere," I pronounce. Then I return to our circle standing around the stone. Streams of water run from my umbrella. My rain jacket drips like an old faucet. "It's time we get *outta* here," I mumble to no one in particular.

After we cram ourselves into the car, we discuss just how remote this island is. We *are* Nowhere. Easter Island is isolated from the rest of the world geographically and culturally. It sits in the South Pacific Ocean, 2300 miles west of South America, 2500 miles southeast of Tahiti, and 4300 miles south of Hawaii. The closest inhabited island is Pitcairn, the tiny island where the mutineers of the *H.M.S. Bounty* settled in 1790. But even *that* is 1260 miles away.

Back in Hanga Roa, we stop for souvenirs (I *must* have one of those gray statues with the rust-red top hat for our collection of primitive art). Then we step into the one-room museum where we learn about the *rongorongo* script, the only evidence of Polynesian script found to date. The island's chief, heirs, and rulers were the only ones who could read and write the script, and they had been captured by the Peruvian slave traders. To this day, no one can decipher the script.

The lady who is running the museum tells us the story of the Long Ears and the Short Ears.

As if statue-building-run-amok were not enough!

Later, this story dominates our final dinner conversation at the now-familiar Cuerito Regalon.

"I have Thor Heyerdahl's book *Aku-Aku* with me," I begin. "I brought it to read on the plane. I looked up the Long Ears. Heyerdahl says that legends talk of an earlier time of greatness, when another people, the Long Ears, lived in peace with their ancestors, the Short Ears. But then the Long Ears demanded too much labor of the Short Ears, and, in the end, there was a war. It's only legend, but it's believed that all of the Long Ears were burned in a ditch. From that day on, no more statues were made, and many of the existing ones were pulled down with ropes."

"So what's with the two peoples?" asks Günter. "Were they from two separate races?"

"That's the Heyerdahl take on it. He says that Father Sebastian, a missionary he met when he first came here, was convinced that two separate races, with two separate cultures, came here."

"Who were they?"

"One race, he says, was white, with blue eyes and red hair. He says that Roggeveen and the first European discoverers claimed that they saw people like this, too."

85

Migration Patterns of the South Pacific

Some 25,000 islands are scattered across the Pacific, encompassing Micronesia, Melanesia, and Polynesia. Geographically, the three corners of the Polynesian Triangle—Hawaii to the north, New Zealand to the southwest, and Easter Island to the southeast—are almost the same distance away. The Society Islands are at the very heart of the triangle.

"And the other?"

"Ordinary Pacific natives, he called them."

"So how did the Long Ears end up in the ditch?" asks Jean-Claude. "And why were their ears long?"

"Oh, I know the legend of the ears," says Claudie. "The lady in the museum explained that. They all pierced their ears and then put heavy weights in the lobes to pull them down—almost all the way to their shoulders."

"The Long Ears were supposedly very energetic." I jump back into the conversation. "The straw that broke the camel's back was that they wanted to rid the island of all the stones, so that the island could be cultivated. The Short Ears were supposed to take all the stones and fling them into the sea, beginning with the Poike Plateau, which is now grassy and free of stones, by the way."

"But the Short Ears thought they were taking the project too far?" asks Jean-Claude.

"Yep. So they decided on war, instead. Supposedly, they dug this great trench 2 miles long—which, by the way, scientists say is natural, and not built—to separate the Poike Peninsula. Supposedly, they filled it with branches and tree trunks, ready to be set on fire if the Long Ears tried to storm the slope."

"Which, obviously, they did," adds Günter.

"Yep. But one of the Long Ears had a short-eared wife who was a traitor, and she warned the Short Ears of the attack. Heyerdahl had the locals dig up sections of the ditch. Surprisingly, they found signs of a great fire."

We sip our wine and dive into the new Special of the Day. Research can wait for another time.

We leave this desolate place with more questions than answers. But my fascination continues. The only other site in my travels that has filled me with such awe was the Israeli archeological site of Megiddo (Armageddon).

But that's another story.

⚓

The next morning, on the plane back to Tahiti, I think back—and forward. We'd had no desire to brave a *sail* to this remote island, but we always wanted to *visit* here, first, because of the intriguing statues and other mysteries, and second, because it will add to our understanding of all Polynesia. Easter Island is one of the three key islands that form the vast Polynesian triangle. Northwest of here is Hawaii and southwest is New Zealand. Our plan was to fly to all three "anchors" of Polynesia, and to sail through much of the middle.

I can't wait to see how that plan unfolds !

DID YOU KNOW?

EASTER ISLAND

Easter Island, called Rapa Nui by the Polynesians, is a small, hilly, and treeless island located in the southeastern Pacific Ocean approximately 2200 miles (3600 kilometers) off the coast of Chile, which considers it a special territory, annexed in 1888.

During the 1900s, it was a sheep farm managed by the Chilean Navy. In 1966, the entire island was pened to the public and the remaining Rapa Nui people became citizens of Chile.

As of 2009, Easter Island had a population of 4,781. The official languages of the island are Spanish and Rapa Nui; the main ethnic groups are Rapa Nui, European, and Amerindian.

The island became a UNESCO World Heritage Site in 1995. The entire island is only 63 square miles. Much of the island's land belongs to the Rapa Nui National Park. Formed geologically by three extinct volcanoes, Easter Island also has no permanent source of fresh water.

Easter Island is one of the most famous, yet least visited, archaeological sites in the world. Exploring it is like visiting a vast open air museum: Each corner of the triangular island has an ancient site. The amount of world attention this small, remote island—only fourteen by seven miles—has garnered is extraordinary! Anyone who has delved into the volumes written about the island becomes enthralled with its mysteries.

We all recognize the photos of the giant stone images. They fire the imagination: Who built them and why? Where did the great stone architects come from, and why did they leave?

The mysterious *rongorongo* tablets raise more questions: Who were the master scribes that understood what they mean? What valuable information has been lost?

Next follows the mystery of how such a remote island was discovered and populated: Did they come by raft from the Americas, or did they arrive by Polynesian voyaging catamarans? Was there one wave of immigration or more?

And as if that isn't enough intrigue, there are the legends: the legend of Hiva, the homeland of the gods, supposedly destroyed by a flood; the legend of the strange Birdman cult; and the legend of the red-haired kings from the east. Each enigmatic archaeological discovery fuels the world's fascination, yet fails to solve the island's many mysteries.

Chapter 5
Voyaging through Paradise: The Society Islands

Anchoring Bedlam
Papeete, Tahiti
June 7, 2002

Even in Paradise, the cruising life is not perfect. Heavy vehicle traffic along the quay drops a layer of soot on the white hulls of *Pacific Bliss* every morning. Except on Sundays, the crane across the street winds up each morning and drones on until eight o'clock at night. (The workmen are building the foundation of a new *Supermarche*, a French supermarket.) And, even though we have an extra dock line system in place to pull the dinghy the short distance from the quay to *Pacific Bliss*, Günter manages to fall into the filthy harbor water. "I give up," he growls, as muddy water oozes from his shorts. "But thank God we have that fourth anchor...I mean the washing machine...on board."

This washing machine is proving its worth!

I load Günter's T-shirt and shorts into the washer while he loads himself into the shower.

Later, after Günter changes to fresh clothes, he and Armin take off for the parts store. They plan to purchase two new batteries for *Pacific Bliss*. Boat batteries are large and heavy, and Günter is determined to take advantage of Armin's strength. Armin has taken good care of *Pacific Bliss* during our trip to Easter Island. But he will be leaving us soon; his flight back to Germany is only three days away.

With my men gone, I'm content to do my own chores uninterrupted, including three loads of laundry. However, the Ferocious Gust of Wind whips one of the sheets off the line, clothespins and all, and blows it into the lazy jack. This evil Ferocious Gust simultaneously causes *Pacific Bliss* to veer dangerously close to the quay. I rush to the sail locker, pull out a fender to protect the boat, and shove it between the cement and the swim ladder just in time, all the while hoping that the sheet does not sprout wings and fly into the harbor! Eventually I am able to retrieve the sheet from atop the solar panels on the cabin roof.

The guys return and struggle to heft the heavy batteries from the quay to the dinghy and into the boat. Focused as they are on installations and repairs, they do not seem too interested in my story, or the fact that one of the two anchors we had set during our perfect Med-mooring process could possibly be dragging.

Forget it! They don't listen to me anyway.

The next morning, Ferocious Gust reappears at the worst possible time, as if beckoned by the devil himself. The guys are into their chores again: filling the dinghy gas tank, changing all the filters, and then changing the oil in both engines. I have a garlic-filled lamb roast in the oven and couscous boiling on the top of the stove. I set the table for a special lunch—including a bottle of Merlot from Napa Valley, which has traveled with us all the way from California. We planned this lunch as a reward for completing our To Do lists, and afterward we will have a long, well-deserved siesta. However, "the best laid plans..."

This time, Ferocious Gust causes *Pacific Bliss* to swerve so that the other stern hull is close to the quay. I dash for the fender and hold it between the boat and the quay.

"Stay there!" Günter yells.

Visions of burned roast and couscous dance in my head, but, of course, the boat always comes first, and I

The Papeete boardwalk.

The fish market in Papeete.

do as I am told by The Captain.

The guys struggle to winch in the anchor line, to distance *Pacific Bliss* from the quay.

"Use your engine," calls the captain of motor yacht *Wild Wind IV*, in the line of danger on our port side.

Why didn't we think of that?

Günter now realizes that our main anchor is dragging, while our secondary bow anchor line remains taut. He and Armin continue to winch the line to the secondary anchor while I rev the engine. It works! With our boat out of danger, the men finish their chores, and I hurry to the galley to save what I can of our "rewards luncheon."

But work is not over yet—we spend the rest of the afternoon (or so it seems) attempting to reset the primary anchor. We'd never done this before. Med-mooring is a space-saving technique used in European countries and territories. It is not a skill that most American yachties have learned to do well. Three dinghies are now gathered in the harbor out by our anchor: ours and one from our neighbors on either side of us, who, *because* they are our neighbors, have a stake in our learning experience.

To make a long, agonizing story very short, the anchor that once dragged manages to catch on the bottom again. But to what, we don't know. And at this moment, we don't particularly care. When we finally leave here, we'll learn the rest of the story.

Maybe the solution will involve hiring a diver. Who knows?

Clearly, though cruising has its wonders, all is not heaven in Paradise.

The Papeete Market

I awaken to the blood-red glow of the rising sun outside my starboard window. It's the most colorful sunrise I've seen here in Papeete! I grab a one-piece island dress and pull it over my head. I pick up my camera, station myself on deck, and begin shooting away. Later, Günter and I sip coffee as we watch the sky change to orange-gold, casting a glow over the entire harbor. Then, since we're wide awake before 7:00, with Armin gone, Günter and I decide to preview the "Sunday market," which reportedly runs from 5:30 to 7:30.

We find the market bustling with activity: Vendors refill their produce stands from trucks as the market spills over from the inside, onto the sidewalks, and then onto the street. We purchase onions, papayas, limes, carrots, and white radishes.

The produce has been carefully packaged in plastic. I am amazed. I turn to Günter: "What a change from the 'Bloody Market' in Nuku Hiva, Marquesas! What an abundance of veggies!"

"Here in Papeete, life is easy…and very civilized… yet, exotic. I love it."

We stroll around. We purchase a chocolate croissant and hot chocolate. Then, casually, we buy additional fruit and proceed to the meat section. There we see freshly caught fish from the Tuamotus, still alive, in long, wooden trays filled with ice. Here tuna steaks are neatly sliced exactly to our liking. Fresh pork, veal, and lamb can also be cut to order, and I envision filling our freezer here before we depart for the outer islands.

"Life is good here!" Günter is in his element.

Sometimes it takes difficulties to make one appreciate what is good.

My Most Embarrassing Moment

The heat of the Papeete harbor is excruciating. Unfortunately, I had selected this day to bake cookies for an afternoon coffee klatch with fellow cruisers. As I open the oven to put in the second batch of cookies, steam pours out. Rivers of sweat run from my hair and drip into my eyes, smearing my mascara. But most irritating is the sweat that I can feel accumulating around my breasts. "What the H—!" I fling off my one-piece sundress. I'm in a state of temporary amnesia. I forget that the galley of *Pacific Bliss* opens into a wide cockpit that can be seen from passersby walking along the quay. We are not at sea!

"Hi, Lois," a man's voice calls out. "Haven't seen *Pacific Bliss* since the Marquesas!" My brain is on autopilot. I step out into the cockpit to answer him, stark naked.

Oh my God!

The man is Keith, a retired judge from Sacramento, the capital of our home state of California. He and his wife, Susan, are standing on the quay, looking in. I can feel the flush rise from my throat to my cheeks. Recovering my composure seems impossible, but I try. "Oh, Keith…just a minute till I throw on some clothes."

I can hear them snickering as I turn. I dash back to the galley, slip the sundress over my head, and step outside, trying to act as if nothing had happened.

"Forgot you were not at sea?" Keith asks. "We also go naked on *C'est la Vie,* when we're sailing out there."

This story will spread around Papeete harbor as fast as a cockroach has babies! By the time I attend the coffee klatch, everyone will know.

Strangely, the story never comes up in the afternoon conversations. The cruisers have more important subjects to discuss. Some are planning their cruises around the Tahitian Islands. Others, like us, are making plans to pick up and drop off guests. The rest of them, having completed their provisioning, are already saying goodbye and leaving for The Cooks.

My embarrassment remains my secret.

It Could Always Be Worse.

"Worse" is what happens to *Adelaide II* at the Maeva anchorage in Papeete, a short distance from us.

Our new crew, Paul, his wife Janice, and their son Luke, have joined us. They arrived at the Papeete airport and came straight to *Pacific Bliss*. Paul is an oncologist who consulted for our company's clinical trials program. We had developed an electroporation product for delivering drugs to cancerous tumors. It was in Phase III clinical trials when we retired. He and his wife Janice have become our good personal friends. Previously, Günter and I were used to seeing Paul in a business suit or hospital whites; now he sits in the cockpit of our catamaran, wearing shorts and an island shirt. It seems strange!

But we are ready to shove off. *Pacific Bliss* backs from our complex Med-mooring setup. (Fortunately, we were able, after all, to free both anchors without hiring a diver.)

Francoise and Bernard pass by in their dinghy, see us leaving, and stop at our stern.

"You would not believe what happened to our Catana…" Francoise begins.

"We were hit by lightning…just last night," Bernard continues.

"Did it hit your mast?" Günter asks.

"No, just the water," says Bernard. "At least that's what we thought."

"But most of our electronics went out," Francoise says, "including one engine and one alternator, radar, VHF, GPS, and—well, you name it."

"Wow! I feel so sorry for you!" I cannot believe their calm demeanor. "You appear to be taking it quite well."

Bernard shrugs. "What can we say? It happened."

"What will you do?" I ask.

"Our guests are due here in Papeete in two weeks. We will have them bring all the parts, and then we will see."

"What if the cables are also affected?" Günter asks, frowning.

"We will find out," Bernard shrugs again.

We say goodbye, wish them well, and leave for Raiatea.

After navigating the pass, I turn to Günter. "They took it so calmly."

"They're still in shock, I'm sure," says Günter. "This will take them two months to fix, and their guests will be disappointed."

"We have to count our blessings while we cruise," I say. "Things can always be worse."

Full Moon in Tahaa

We motor through the channel to Moorea and anchor there overnight. In the aftermath of the storm, the sea is lumpy and confused all the way back to Raiatea. What a way for our guests to experience their first overnight on *Pacific Bliss*! Queasy, they stay in the cockpit all night long. "Look out at the horizon; it will be better," they keep advising each other.

With such an inauspicious beginning to their vacation, how can it go anywhere but up?

A couple of days later, we are anchored deep in Tapuamu Bay. At 71 feet, *Pacific Bliss* gently tugs on 150 feet of chain, swaying to the beat of the drums coming from the shore. A steady rhythm emanates from the well-lit shed

we see there—the one with the corrugated tin roof.

All of French Polynesia is practicing now for the *Heiva,* the July festivals and competitions that celebrate the Maohi culture. The festivals are carryovers from the French Bastille Day celebrations.

But why would the Polynesians celebrate the independence of France?

Clearly, French Polynesians have turned what was Independence Day into a dramatic month-long cultural extravaganza. Throughout the anchorages of the Marquesas, we saw canoe teams rowing and lance teams throwing. In Papeete, we heard dancing and drumming almost every night. And here in Tahaa, it becomes apparent that the rehearsals and performances will continue.

The fast Tahitian beat from shore lends an exotic background to the twang of Luke's guitar as he sits at the pulpit seat at the bow, his profile silhouetted by the full moon. Luke's parents have given him this sailing trip as a graduation gift. He will leave for college in a few months. Günter and I know Luke from the summer when he worked as an intern for our biotech company. He is a nice lad, blonde, fit, and poised for a wonderful life.

The caressing breeze and mellow music soothe our souls.

The Coral Garden

After breakfast, *Pacific Bliss* and *Makoko,* which has rejoined us, motor two miles west from the east side of Tahaa to an islet called Tautau. We anchor easily, and everyone dons swimsuits.

The two dinghies, *Petit Bliss* and *Mokoquette,* loaded with snorkeling gear, carry our two crews to the shallow water between the small islet and an even smaller motu.

Snorkeling in the channel is like floating above an intricately planned aquarium, an exquisite coral garden. The pathway is carpeted with the usual muted brown, gold, and orange coral, occasionally interrupted by bright yellow and lavender formations. While wending my way through schools of fish, I am startled by a skull-size, bright orange-fuchsia object. What could it be? I dive down to check it out. Soon I realize that the "skull" is a brain coral with a waving, wiggling mop of hair! Darting in and out of the swaying mop are tiny orange-gold fish with white stripes that ring their heads.

Janice, snorkeling alongside me, points to a geometrically designed fish, quartered into red and blue panels in the front, and yellow and white panels with a blue stripe in the back. She stands in the shallow water. "Look at that Picasso Fish!" she says.

"I've never seen one like that before!"

I remove my mask and snorkel. The Picasso Fish darts out every so often, leaving behind hundreds of

black spiny sea urchins and gray sea cucumbers. The sun fractures the clear green water into prisms, intensifying the kaleidoscopic effect of the fish and coral. Because the lagoon is only five to ten feet deep, the sun's rays bounce off the sandy bottom, providing a surrealistic glow of enchantment. The channel is like a fairy tale—a veritable Wonderland.

Back on *Pacific Bliss*, I can't wait to identify the unusual "Picasso Fish." I select *The Snorkeler's Guide to the Coral Reef* by Paddy Ryan from our Ship's Library. What we called the "Picasso Fish" turns out to be a species of goatfish dubbed the "half-and-half goatfish," or *parupeneus barberinoides*. The sensitive barbells (feelers) tucked under the chin and lower portion of the gill help it find prey under sand or rubble. Interestingly, the guide does contain a different fish dubbed a Picasso Fish. The common name is *humuhumunukunukuapuaa*.

Seriously!

One can be spoiled very easily in Paradise. The next morning, Giuliano, the croissant man, delivers our morning croissants right to the boat! We banter with him, as usual. He has been asking us to visit his restaurant on Motu Atara. Today, we decide to accept his offer.

Loaded to the brim with five passengers, snorkeling gear, and extra clothes, *Petite Bliss* groans and crawls through the waves to the motu. Snorkeling is marginal there, and we have to wade through a long, shallow, stony area to get to the reef.

But the tiny island itself is idyllic and charming. And the restaurant and food are fabulous.

The proprietors are Swiss. Weary of all the rules and regulations in Switzerland, they yearned for a less structured life. They found it by leasing the operation on Atara. While Juliana and his wife serve lunch, their two little girls run, naked and free, throughout the restaurant and then, giggling and laughing, splash directly into the sea.

What a marvelous way to grow up!

Heiva in Huahine
16°42.8′S, 151°02.4′W

Pacific Bliss is anchored near the village of Fare, in Huahine, another one of the Society Islands. The sun rising over the mountains turns the fluffy cumulus clouds to amber, trimmed with edges of silver gray. The smaller fluff balls over the sea to the west have turned white, fringed with blue.

By now our friends Paul, Janice, and their son Luke have left for home. Other friends, Jeanne and Sarah, who had visited for a few days, are also gone. And Jean-Claude and Claudie have flown home to France. For this part of our Voyage through Paradise, our friends Phyllis and Richard have joined us; they had sailed the Caribbean with us during our Maiden Voyage and are familiar with *Pacific Bliss*.

Fare is a delightful little settlement; although it is

Luke goes up the mast of *Pacific Bliss*.

Giuliano, the croissant man, delivers right to our boat.

the big town on the island, it is still a village by most standards. Most of Huahine's 5,400 citizens live here and along the west coast.

We were fortunate to anchor the evening before Bastille Day, the most important of the month-long celebrations. Close to the village, the bay was very deep, but close to the Bali Hai, we could anchor in 20 feet with 110 feet of chain, in bright blue water so clear that we can still see the bottom.

By now, I've researched the *Heiva*. In Tahitian, the word *hei* means to assemble and the word *va* means community places. In ancient times, music, dancing, singing, and sporting events held an important place in Polynesian community life. They were essential components of religious ceremonies. Dance was one of the most sophisticated and ritualized art forms. During the 19th century, missionaries condemned these demonstrations as an erotic form of debauchery. In 1819, King Pomare II outlawed them. After France annexed a large part of Polynesia, July 14 became symbolic for Polynesians because on this one day France allowed sports and dancing. In 1977, French Polynesia gained greater political autonomy from France, and by 1985, the country organized *Heiva I Tahiti* and named it *Tiurai*, meaning "July, the month of festivities." The dances are unique creations for which the dancers train six months or more. The music, choreography, and costumes are based on historical or legendary themes. Orchestras are made up of five to fifty musicians playing traditional instruments such as a nasal flute called *vivo*, made from bamboo, or *pu*, made from shells, and more recently, the *ukulele*, a Hawaiian guitar.

The four of us take *Petit Bliss* to shore at 8:10 a.m., thinking we will have plenty of time. (Most events begin on Polynesian Time.) Surprise! The parade has already started. The Queen's float passes by. *Miss Huahine,* with her dark hair curled in tight locks, sits primly at the center, wearing a long sarong-style white dress, draped with a wide ribbon of red, white, and blue, the French colors. Behind her is the Polynesian flag, red on each side and white in the middle, with artwork depicting a boat. One float is saturated with thousands of flowers; it pulls another containing an outrigger canoe, overflowing with flowers. The floats remind me of California's Rose Bowl Parade on New Year's Day. Every organization on the island, it seems, has entered a float in this parade. Marching between the floats are the Boy Scouts, the Girl Scouts, the Mamas' dance troupe, the Children's dance group, the Huahine equivalent of the FAA, and all of the island's canoe teams. The town's residents and visitors line both sides of the streets. The VIPs sit under a tent set up especially for them. It is a memorable spectacle!

After the parade, we witness the flag-raising ceremony in a square near the mayor's building with the *Heiva* Royalty seated upfront. Then the entire group descends on refreshment stands prepared for them in the artisans' square. Visitors check out the crafts displayed there while parade participants enjoy the free food and drinks set out for them.

Fortunately, the queen and her attendants are posing for official photographs there. I stand by and take my own photos. A group of Huahine teenage boys gawks at the beauty queens.

We leave the crowd to walk across a bridge, which crosses a stream that empties into the bay. We stroll past charming houses, much more elaborate than those in Raiatea. All have the typical display of flowers throughout the yard. Most of the homes have older planted hedges of hibiscus and bougainvillea.

The sound of war chants draws us to an event outside a church where more than a hundred children, in matching T-shirts, watch a performance of chants and dances by a visiting group of older teenage boys. Because the chants are familiar to us, we surmise correctly that the performers come from the Marquesas.

Satisfied and happy, we return to *Pacific Bliss* for lunch and siestas. Afterward, I doze to the joyous sounds of children swimming and shouting and to the laughter of kayakers, who row out to *Pacific Bliss* and right under her belly, between the hulls.

The wonders of the day are far from over. Rested, we go ashore again for the official Huahine *Heiva*. This event is held in a massive wooden structure, with sand covering the floor, and with Christmas lights and branches of banana leaves strung from the rafters. A spotlight shines on the stage. It's a lively, inviting setting.

The *Heiva* will begin at seven o'clock, and the auditorium is filling up fast. Ladies arrive in dresses of starched white or a variety of colorful prints. A fat-bellied grandpa sits next to me and keeps watch over his rambunctious two-year-old grandson. A masculine-looking teenage boy in girls' clothing (common in the islands) sits in a chair diagonal to mine and daintily crosses his legs.

The speeches begin. And go on. And on. And on. This process takes about an hour, while various dignitaries and officials are introduced and praised.

Finally, the dance begins. This *Heiva* is different than those we had attended in Raiatea: The *Heiva* here is more like a summer festival than a serious competition. It's not exclusive, as it was in Papeete. Here almost anyone who wants to can take the stage. One precocious girl, about ten years old, is definitely destined for greater things. In her grass skirt, yellow-and-brown print bandeau top, with greens and garlands woven through her long black hair, she dances the hula to raving cheers. Then, after the entire group of girls, ranging in age from five to eighteen, has completed an overly long routine, she returns to the stage for an encore. A gifted performer who loves to show off in front of an appreciative audience, the girl revels in the rousing cheers as she takes one deep curtsy after another.

DID YOU KNOW?

THE SOCIETY ISLANDS

These islands, called "Paradise on Earth" by savvy travelers, were explored by Captains Cook and Bligh, but they were made truly famous by the paintings of the artist, Paul Gauguin, and by the words of author, James A. Michener.

Captain James Cook named them in 1769, after England's Royal Society. And Royal Islands they certainly are, with the high prices to match!

The Society Islands are an island group within French Polynesia, divided into the Windward Islands (Iles du Vent) and the Leeward Islands (Iles Sous le Vent), originally claimed in 1843 as an overseas territory of France. Tahiti is the largest island and the administrative center of French Polynesia.

The locals called their island "Tahiti"—or, as Bougainville first wrote it in 1768, "Taiti," and Cook in 1769, "Otaheite." Europeans applied the name to all of the indigenes there. If the Tahitians had a name specifically identifying themselves, it is not known. What is known is that all of those living in the Society Archipelago, including Tahiti, referred to themselves as "Maohi."

The love of Tahiti gave rise to the mutiny on the *HMS Bounty*, and more than any other, this island has represented the notion of escape to a Polynesian paradise. The society was not as freewheeling, however, as the popular culture suggests. Tahitians disapproved of marriage between close kin, but how close was never made clear. We do know that marriage was not permitted between those of differing social classes; therefore, children resulting from a sexual relationship between partners of differing classes were killed upon birth. In the 18th century, young couples had to obtain the permission of their parents before marriage, and among the chiefly class early betrothal was the norm. Marriage ceremonies consisted of prayers at a marae, an open air place of worship. Divorce was by common consent.

Men and women ate separately, and there were a variety of restrictions regarding who might prepare another's meal. Fear of divine retribution was a major control; others were human sacrifice and a variety of corporal punishments for antisocial behavior. A district chief determined justice, and the accused could appeal to one's paramount chief.

We leave the venue, agreeing that we'd rather watch a homespun Huahine *Heiva* any time, rather than the professional Papeete performance. Here the announcers made off-hand remarks; the audience tittered during the performances of small children; they even laughed wholeheartedly at their local teenage boys attempting the war chant and dance. We left feeling that we had participated in a very special, yet casual, "family affair."

⚓

The next day, we go ashore again to witness various contests. We begin by watching the canoe (*vaa*) races, the most traditional of Polynesian sports. After the racers disappear far out to sea, we watch a group of boys compete in spear fishing. They throw wooden spears at fish that only they can see while standing knee deep in the splashing surf on the reef.

The most intense contests of the day pay tribute to the coconut tree, called the "tree of life." Using javelins, athletes stand 22 meters away from a 7.5 meter pole and attempt to spear a coconut. The athletes have seven minutes to throw ten javelins each. The one whose javelin is stuck at the highest point of the coconut wins the prize. It takes great dexterity to win this contest.

However, the copra preparation contest combines dexterity with *danger*. In this contest, each team is composed of three candidates, who have to split, open, extract, and put into bags the almonds of about two hundred coconuts in three minutes, using only an axe, a curved blade, and hemp bags. I'm amazed that no one loses hands or fingers!

In a third contest, coed teams compete to prepare coconut milk by husking the coconut, cutting it open, extracting the juice, and then squeezing the meat through their fingers and into a measuring cup, while their enthusiastic families cheer them on.

But of all the contests, I find the fruit carrier races to be by far the most aesthetically exciting. Bronzed and muscular Polynesians, simply dressed in *pareus*, run a two-kilometer race with bamboo rods across their shoulders. Hanging from the rods are huge bundles of luscious and colorful fruits, each one more artistically arranged than the other.

Our stay in Fare could not have ended better.

Hunkering Down in Huahine
Haapu Bay
16°47′S, 151°W

We leave Fare enveloped in a mysterious mist, her mountains like a Japanese painting in shades of charcoal and green. Two hours of motoring to the southwestern side of Huahine brings more misty bays. One bay has a motu in the middle of its entrance. The entire bay is cobalt blue, reminding me of a deep northern Minnesota lake. Cute red-roofed houses surround the bay. The muted rain clouds to the west blend like watercolors into purples, lilacs, and grays. A luminous brushstroke outlines the surf at the fringing reef.

As we turn at our waypoint to enter this picturesque lagoon, the clouds burst. We slow to a crawl. We can't see a thing. We try to anchor, letting down 120 feet of chain, only to drag, with our stern too close to the coral. Our second attempt—plopping about 60 feet of chain straight down in quick-release—is successful. When the rain stops, we look around, surprised: *Pacific Bliss* is all alone right in the middle of the anchorage.

A series of clouds blankets the mountains in mist, but the sun comes out to grace our lunch. We enjoy a tasty French baguette filled deliciously with turkey and ham (purchased in Fare), cherry tomatoes, cucumbers, and lettuce, and because wine and beer accompany this, we succumb to siestas shortly thereafter.

This delightful, quiet bay has a charming little village on one side and coral reefs on the other three sides. It's too lovely to ignore. Richard and Günter snorkel directly from the boat. They return to describe new fish that they had never before seen.

"And then," Günter adds, "we saw white-and-pastel corals that spread throughout the bottom like an Easter bouquet."

Poetic words, coming from the analytical scientist!

The rest of our stay becomes quite focused. Here in this bay we enter the new age of sophisticated navigation: We install the multiple discs of a *Max Sea* software navigation program that includes charts of the entire world! The installation takes most of the day. The GPS inputs directly into the laptop and the system. The planning component will allow us to chart our course and set our waypoints. Then we'll have only to activate our course once we're underway, and the software will control the navigation. What a marvelous program!

This morning, July 17, we anchor in Baie de Avea, 16°48.7′S, 150°59.5′W, a delightful bay to the south of the island. We see only one monohull and one catamaran as neighbors. On shore, the bay contains two restaurants and a few bungalows. I look up and see a variety of clouds. They glut the sky on three levels. Intrigued, I run for my cloud booklet. The highest level contains streaks of purple cirrus; just below it are circles of purple-and-gold cirrostratus, and at the lowest level I see gray-and-white fluff balls of cumulus.

The soft and steady rolling of the surf against the reef is almost hypnotic. A tree-covered ridge lines the entire shore, leading to a sandy beach.

By 11:30 we're ravenous, and we decide to eat

lunch on shore. Once there we look for a snack shop, but the one bearing a sign that says SNACK is part of an exotic bungalow complex. And, though it is nicely decorated with woven peaked roofs, tiki statues all over, and a round rattan table facing the sea, the food and service are the worst we've found in all of French Polynesia! We order "The Killer" and *poisson cru* from the sandwich board. The food: tasteless. The price: sky high. And the fish has soaked through the rubbery bread, which is enclosed in plastic wrap.

Pacific Bliss is a welcome retreat after this disappointment. She sits there pretty as a picture, nicely framed by the sea, with the distant charcoal mountains of Raiatea in the background.

After our siesta, it rains, clears, and then rains again. There will be no snorkeling today! Some serious rain settles in after dinner. We group in the salon and discuss kids, grandkids, the state of the world, and whether human beings are innately good or evil. Conclusions? None, but the talk is amiable and satisfying.

This first day of rain is only the beginning. We will be hunkered down here in this bay for three more days. We cook on board, troubleshoot, learn how to use the new navigation program, defragment the hard drives of our computers, eliminate software programs that we no longer need, and download photos. In addition, I spend some time researching and writing.

By mid-afternoon of day three, our crew is bored out of their skulls. We succumb to hot chocolate laced with Kahlua while staring at new waterfalls that scream down the mountain bluffs. The once-clear water beneath our boat even turns muddy.

By late afternoon, there's a break in the weather. We find the dinghy one-third full of water. It's a blessing. "Shower time!" Günter calls.

Eagerly we climb down the swim ladder and directly to the dinghy, shampoo and conditioner in hand. Günter fills the plastic "Bailer Bucket" and dumps the freshwater over my head. After days of being cramped in the salon, doors shut during torrential downpours, we laugh in this sudden freedom and, soon, we all feel clean and refreshed again

By evening, the weather has cleared enough to grill some steaks and to celebrate!

⚓

Sailing is surely a study in contrasts. A night of continuous squalls changes to a morning of clear and calm weather. I'm up in the cockpit at 0600. A baby blue sky breaks through the puffy gray clouds. The mountains tower in dark green silhouettes, reflected in the waters below. As the sky lightens, I can barely make out the exotic umbrella-topped trees lining the mountain ridges, while the palms and ferns stand out sharply at the water's edge. A few white terns fly near *Pacific Bliss*. I reach for a hunk of old baguette and break it into pieces; the bits dimple the clear water as they fall. Strangely, no birds fly down to catch the bait; no fish swim toward the boat to grab the leftovers. Neither fish nor fowl is inclined to interrupt this calm morning.

But not for long! The ubiquitous island roosters never miss an opportunity to crow. The rude sound interrupts my reverie. I hear stirring in the cabins below.

With the crew topsides, we decide it is time to blow this pop stand. I program our new navigation system to route us back to Raiatea. Despite the weather, Huahine has become one of our favorite islands in French Polynesia.

Marina Apooiti, Raiatea (Again)

It has been too rainy and chilly to swim, an activity that had been good therapy for my ongoing sciatica pain. And the humid weather here is causing rust and mildew, big time. Our pillows are musty; our books are beginning to rot; even on the toilet seat, light gray spots are spreading. Mildew on plastic—is that even possible? Today I must spray and clean the bathroom, back pain or not.

Ugh! This is the unpleasant part of cruising that our friends back home never understand!

Surprisingly, the sun comes out for most of the next day. I work on the bathroom; we hang out all the rugs; I air out the lockers. Still, everyone is grouchy.

Right now, I'd rather be a landlubber, squirreled away in a house, all by myself, for a long, long time.

But after one whole week of rain and humidity, the weather is finally perfect again, and we'll soon be off to beautiful Bora Bora.

The Sun Rises over Bora Bora

Like an old photograph,
Time can make a feeling fade,
But the memory of a first love
Never fades away.
—Tim McGraw

Bora Bora. The island that novelist James Michener proclaimed "the most beautiful island in the world." My first impression of Bora Bora is the one I want to keep forever. That's why I always hesitate to visit, for the second time, a place that I have loved. But here we are, motoring toward those famous distinctive peaks, Mount Pahia and Mount Otemanu, the remnants of an extinct volcano. One peak rises ahead of us like a perpendicular sheet of polished rock, ascending straight to heaven. The peak levels off in some places and protrudes in other places in small, jagged points. At its base are rolling hills, lesser peaks, and dense vegetation.

Heiva festivities in Huahine include a parade, a beauty contest, and various competitions such as coconut husking.

Tourist catamaran in Raiatea.

An orange glow begins to appear behind the peaks, and as the sun rises, the navy blue sea turns into sapphire blue, which contrasts dramatically with the emerald green of the shallow lagoon. The barrier reef surrounding this island is as close to perfect as nature can provide: a circular ring of glittering sand and motus topped with high waving palms. No wonder many travel brochures describe Bora Bora from the air as "a tiny emerald, in a setting of turquoise, encircled by a sheltering necklace of glowing pearls."

I'm reminded that these same brochures say the original name for Bora Bora was Pora Pora, because no "b" sound exists in the Polynesian language. When he arrived in Bora Bora in 1769, Captain James Cook named it "Pora Pora." Since that means "first born," he had assumed that the Polynesian Taaroa god would have created it immediately after Raiatea.

There is only one entrance, named Te Ava Nui, through the coral reefs, and all cruise ships, cargo ships, yachts, and sailboats must proceed through it. As if this isn't enough congestion, the brochures call this pass the "White Valley" because it teems with gray sharks and barracudas. Amazed tourists watch local divers feed four-to-five-foot reef sharks by hand.

I watch a huge iridescent green cloud descend over the lagoon and wonder if it is a reflection of the aquamarine below.

After we drop the hook near Motu Topuua, I perform my "cats-and-dogs" stretches on the cockpit bench to relax my back. Every time I sit up, I face the ever-changing view of spectacular **Mount Otemanu, 728 meters above the sea.** It is the same gorgeous scene I remember from sailing to Bora Bora only three years ago. This new view sharpens my memory even more.

Some things, though, have changed—and badly: Richard swims to shore from *Pacific Bliss* and returns to tell us his disappointing news. At the reef he found only dead colorless coral, murky waters, and few reef fish. Later we learn that the reef was damaged during the cyclone of 1998.

After breakfast, we tune into the Coconut Net. Then we motor to the dock at Viatape, the main town. We tie up behind another Cat. The town square appears as we remember it from 1999, but then we had watched a lively game of boules in the main square. Today, cars crowd the concrete wharf.

Phyllis will fly home from here. But Richard will stay on as crew, leaving us in Tonga. Our farewell lunch for Phyllis consists of cheeseburgers and French fries (*pommes frites*) at the SNACK Bora Bora. Prices are sky-high here, too, despite a 50 percent fall-off in tourism since 9/11. The French newspaper we purchase tells us that the Dow Jones Average continues to plunge: 7800! The paper also reports that two cruising yachts

were wrecked on the reefs around Papeete harbor. Both disasters occurred within a space of 48 hours. And, foolishly, both vessels had attempted to navigate the reef-lined pass to Papeete at night.

I resolve never to take such a chance during the remainder of *our* circumnavigation.

We walk along the main street for a while, snapping photos. Phyllis will take a ferry to the Bora Bora airport, then fly to Papeete and on to Los Angeles later tonight.

The airport, created by U.S. forces in 1942, is built on the palm-fringed motu about 20 minutes by boat from Vaitape. This was the main airfield for all of French Polynesia for many years. In fact, Americans built much of the transportation on the island from 1942 to 1946. The U.S. set up a refueling/regrouping base in 1942 and arranged eight huge naval guns to defend the base from a surprise Japanese attack. The attack never came, but some of the guns remain. In addition, the Americans built a road around the island, still in use. Until the Tahiti airport was built, all visitors to French Polynesia flew into Bora Bora and then took seaplanes to other islands.

We escort Phyllis to the ferry depot and say our goodbyes.

Richard, Günter, and I return to *Pacific Bliss* and prepare for our departure to The Cooks. But, just as we are ready to leave the Viatape dock, the wind comes up. It stays at 8-9 knots, and gusts to 18 knots, pressing *Pacific Bliss* against the dock, as if to say, "Don't leave quite yet." We put off our departure for another day and motor over to Bloody Mary's instead.

Bloody Mary's is a well-known celebrity restaurant; the names of the world's rich and famous who were here are carved into the sign outside. We have fond memories of how we partied and laughed as a gay waiter told jokes and entertained us here on our last visit. We want to see if it's as wonderful as we remember.

With Günter at the helm, Richard attempts to pick up one of the restaurant's mooring balls. The wind makes it difficult. One try…two tries… this mooring process is clearly not working. Then Günter remembers a technique another Cat owner had mentioned: Go to the back swim steps and pick up the ball from the rear, where one does not have to contend with the boat's high freeboard. We try that, and the mooring line wraps around the prop. So much for this technique! We free the line and motor to another mooring ball, only to see the first mooring ball drifting off by itself. We then repeat the from-the-bow mooring method one last time, despite wind gusts. Success! Elated, we dinghy to shore—only to find that the restaurant is closed on Mondays. A repeat experience is not to be. But we'll forever remember that we are the ones who cut the mooring line at Bloody Mary's!

We feel really ready to leave Paradise now. Our impression of the Society Islands, especially Bora Bora,

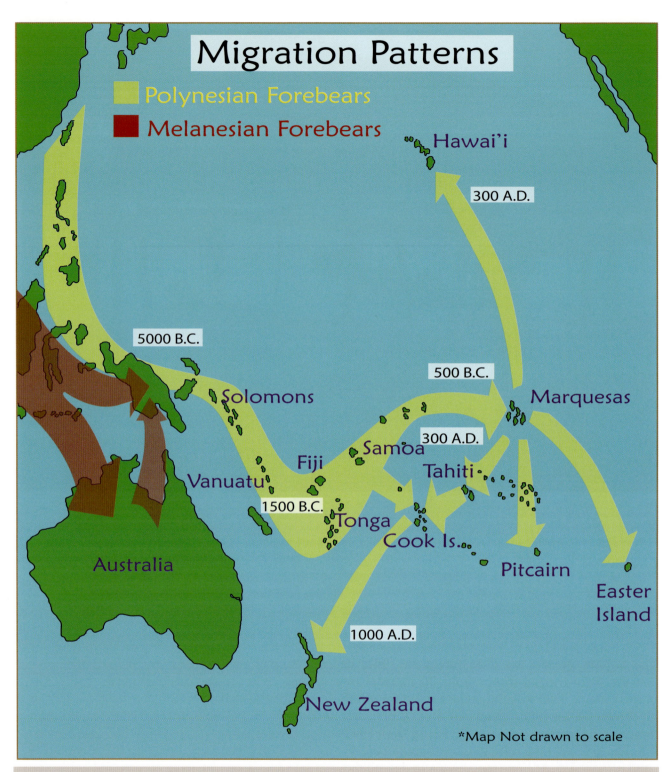

The Society Islands are located at the heart of the South Pacific. Their Polynesian forebears came from the Marquesas Islands as well as Samoa. All of the Pacific Islands can be grouped into three regions defined by their ethnicity. Melanesia (black islands) embraces the islands from New Guinea to Fiji, where people are predominantly dark-skinned, having ancestors in Africa; Micronesia describes the archipelagos of the Caroline Islands and other "micro" islands, inhabited by people of Mongoloid size and appearance from Southeast Asia; Polynesia (many islands) encompasses a widespread, seafaring people who share similar linguistic, cultural, and physical characteristics. When picturing the story of the Polynesians, imagine a spearhead laid out across the Pacific, with its tip pointing east and its shaft reaching back toward Southeast Asia. Polynesians sailed east toward the sunrise—a symbol of life, hope, and new lands. For them, the sunset represented death, their spirit ancestors, and the lands from which they came.

Günter with friends Sarah and Jeanne, who join us in Raiatea.

had been formed during that first trip. Nothing will ever change that. It's like your first date—or your first kiss.

We loved the *Heiva* performances this time around. We hated the rain. And now, we are looking forward to new horizons: The Cooks, which are named after my seafaring hero, Captain James Cook.

Who knows what we'll find there?

"If there are places left where a man can grow old contentedly, it is on some such drowsy atoll, where today is forever and tomorrow never comes; where men live and die, feast and sorrow, while the wind and the waves play over the wet sands and gleaming reefs."
Julian Hillas, "South Seas Paradise"

Chapter 6
The Fabulous Cooks and On to Niue

Passages: What's Not To Hate?
At sea near Aitutaki, The Cook Islands
August 2002

Frequently, there are glorious days at sea; sometimes, a passage is simply terrible. Our passage from Bora Bora to Aitutaki is one of those terrible times.

We are a crew of three miserable, smelly, salt-encrusted sea-rats, trying to keep a stiff upper lip while grumbling, "I hate passages!" Since we pulled anchor over two days ago, I have not been able to brush my teeth for fear of ramming the toothbrush through my cheeks. I sleep spread-eagle on my tummy, bouncing up and down like a bungee cord. Richard has turned ashen under his new tan—terribly seasick, yet stoic, he continues to stand his watches. Günter catwalks about with wide stance, absently stroking his beard and moustache and continually checking all the systems on board.

The timer rings. Time for my watch. Ocean weary, I slide the salon door open. My bare feet search for a foothold on the slippery cockpit floor. I grab salty handholds and edge toward the bench seat behind the wheel. There I squint through the mist toward the bow. No lights on the horizon. An angry sea froths and sloshes from crest to crest, and wind moans through the rigging. *Pacific Bliss* sways and jerks from side to side like a four-wheeler barreling through a desert wash. Humongous waves crash into her port hull. Trapped in the space between the hulls, they explode like bombs under the salon floor. The entire vessel quivers with the aftershock. As the waves escape from the starboard hull, our precious boat creaks and groans like an old lady as her joints twist. Lines flap and supplies roll back and forth as she straightens herself for the next onslaught.

Friends back home in San Diego probably think I'm out here in my bikini, sipping a piña colada, while the sun bronzes my bod. Isn't that the way the South Seas are supposed to be? *Where is that bliss of the South Pacific for which we've named our boat?*

Why do cruisers beat themselves up like this? Is it the challenge of living on the edge, the adventure, the adrenalin rush? Is it to prove we are still alive? Or is cruising just better than the alternative? Günter always says, "It's better than sitting in a rocking chair, complaining about our aches and pains."

Perhaps we are simply deluded, crazy, stubborn, independent, freedom-loving fools just willing, for no good reason, to brave monstrous swells like these that we're experiencing now.

Safe in the Bosom of Aitutaki
Inside the lagoon at Aitutaki, The Cook Islands
August 7

Aitutaki has taken us in. The arms of her shallow lagoon embrace and cuddle *Pacific Bliss*. Her emerald seas lap gently at the hulls while her cheerful sun beams through clear blue skies. On shore her palm trees sway in sugar-white sands. With a brotherly friendliness, cruisers on boats already anchored here—*CheckMate, Alii Kai, Infinien, Da Capo,* and *Red*—had helped us anchor and settle in.

We had sailed 480 terrible, demanding miles from Bora Bora and spotted Aitutaki gratefully at dawn's first light, a hazy gray-green smudge to our port. And it was a very welcome sight, indeed, to this utterly

Richard and Günter focus on fishing during passages to the Cook Islands.

Günter was able now to rev the engines full throttle forward. We met the outflowing current at the mouth of the pass head-on.

Richard and I stood at each bow and directed Günter toward the changing center of the ever-winding channel. The pass, lined with coral heads on either side, is reportedly less than 40 feet wide. *Pacific Bliss* is 24 feet wide. There was no room for error.

My heart pounded. My mouth was as dry as cotton.

The yachts in the basin had pulled in their stern anchors so we could wind our way through the channel to the front of the group––to the innermost part of the basin. They were all busy putting out fenders. *Pacific Bliss* passed by them, one by one, with only a foot to spare.

Can we make it through this gauntlet?

We passed three yachts. Two to go. *Scra-a-a-pe*. It was sand, not rock. Thank God! I glanced at the depth meter. It read 1.9 feet.

exhausted crew. We had slowed to a crawl and headed toward the entrance believing all would go smoothly. But it didn't.

Suddenly Günter yelled, "Lois, come up here, quick! We're heading toward the reefs!"

I scrambled topsides.

Günter and Richard were pointing at the reef in front of the bow. Günter slammed the engine into neutral and then into reverse.

Pacific Bliss swerved horizontal to the reef.

Squinting through the haze, Günter and Richard looked for the entrance. The reef appeared completely solid.

"Call the Port Captain," Günter ordered.

I called. There was no answer. But a couple of cruisers in the basin answered immediately.

"It's pretty laid back here," one said. "Don't expect an answer."

Another said, "The pass is very tricky. And when you get inside, it's worse yet. Lots of rocks and coral heads. Only three to six feet deep in most places. But come on in. We'll help."

Instructions from the yachts kept coming. We slipped slowly forward through dangerous areas. Finally Rick, of the yacht *Infinien*, came out with his dinghy to guide us all the way. He led us into the narrow pass.

We pushed on, our fenders bumping theirs. It was a concentrated community effort. Finally, after what seemed like a month, we dropped anchor inside the lagoon, in six feet of water. We set a stern anchor to keep us from swinging into coral heads if the wind should change. Our work done, we collapsed in the cockpit.

Now, sitting in the cockpit having a cold beer, we look at the beauty that surrounds us. My gaze falls on the five anchored boats behind us. Wow, this was *really* a tight pass! I can feel my tense and tired muscles relax. It's time to make lunch before I lose whatever energy I have left.

Together we cook our first hot meal in two-and-a-half days. Then we turn in to our bunks for the well-deserved deep sleep that only arrival in port can bring.

By evening we have spruced up *Pacific Bliss* enough to have the crew of *Infinien*—Rick, Patti, and six-year-old Jessica—over for a "thank you" sundowner. Jessica immediately falls in love with our ship's mascot, a stuffed dolphin. Her cruising parents join us in the cockpit. They seem so young. We have children their age! Rick is athletic and analytical; Patti is pert and fun-loving. And little, blonde, blue-eyed Jessica is simply adorable.

The sun sets, and the evening becomes surprisingly

We attend the Cook Islands Christian Church in Aitutaki.

cold. Near 19 degrees South, we are still in the tropics, but barely. This is the middle of the Cook Islands winter!

We sit and talk for a long time while Jessica sleeps on the settee, cuddling the dolphin. Of course, our conversation turns to the difficulty of the entrance to the lagoon.

Rick raises a question: "Do you realize that the charts for this area are the ones first plotted by Captain Cook?"

"Aha!" Günter replies. "That explains it. Modern GPS navigation systems tell us exactly where we are, not where the old charts expect us to be."

"No wonder we were a quarter of a mile off in our calculations!" I add.

At that moment, little Jessica groans and turns in her sleep. Her parents realize that it's long past her bedtime and time to take her home.

"We'd better be going," Patti says. They lift her gently and leave.

The next morning, on the SSB Coconut Net, cruisers in Rarotonga ask me about Aitutaki. They report high winds coming into Rarotonga and wonder if we'd had a good passage sailing here. I assure them that we did not.

"A group of us are thinking about joining you there in Aitutaki," one of them says. "But it may be too shallow for monohulls. What's the depth under your keel?"

"We're a catamaran; we don't have a keel, but let me take a look…." I switch the instruments to the depth meter. I report, " It says 1.2 feet under our hull."

"That settles that," he replies. "We'll stay put. See you in Tonga."

Now the local VHF is abuzz. "Glad you discouraged them," Rick laughs. "We don't need any more yachts clogging the channel. They would have to anchor outside of the reef, and that would be a miserable roll."

Another advantage to owning a catamaran.

Günter and Richard launch *Petit Bliss*, and we head ashore to see what Aitutaki has to offer. First we must check in with immigration and customs. Everything goes smoothly. So we have lunch at a restaurant near the wharf, after which Günter asks around and locates a hairdresser who works out of her home. He needs a haircut again. As she trims his beard, I ask where we can find an internet connection. I want to upload my latest blog.

"It's not far—just to the outskirts of town, turn onto the dirt road, then up the long driveway to your right."

Not far. Where have we heard those words before?

We walk for what seems forever. Finally we arrive

DID YOU KNOW?

THE COOK ISLANDS

To comprehend the Cook Islands, picture 93 square miles of land sprinkled across 750,000 square miles of ocean. Fifteen specks dot the map between Tahiti to the east and Samoa and Tonga to the west—the largest a mere 26 square miles and the smallest, a miniscule 100 acres.

The first Polynesians from Tahiti may have arrived about 500 A.D. About 1300 A.D., other Tahitians sailed via The Cooks to New Zealand and back—which explains the Cook's Polynesian-Maori culture.

Modern history begins about 1595 when the Spanish explorer Alvaro de Mandana de Neyra saw the first of the 15 islands called Pukapuka (Danger) Island. His countryman Quiros noted Rakahanga in 1606.

The islands were named after Captain Cook, who first sighted them in 1770. Cook, who never sighted the main island of Rarotonga, called these remote specks "detached parts of the earth." Bligh from the *Bounty* sighted Aitutaki in 1789. Legend has it that the mutineers brought the first oranges and pumpkin seeds to Rarotonga.

The Reverend John Williams of the London Missionary Society first called on Rarotonga in 1823. The European and Polynesian missionaries he brought there soon converted the native population to Christianity; subsequently, the church gained the dominant role in Cook Island affairs.

The islands became a British protectorate in 1888. By 1900, administrative control was transferred to New Zealand; in 1965, residents chose self-government in free association with New Zealand. Cook Islanders are New Zealand citizens.

The estimated population of these islands is 18,200; about 12,000 live on the main island of Rarotonga. About 1000 Maoris per year migrate to New Zealand; there are now more Cook Islanders in Auckland than in Rarotonga.

The first language is a Cook Island Maori (except for Palmerston); but almost everyone speaks English. The culture is conservative; the dress is Polynesian, and the lifestyle holds to traditional practices. The church still maintains a strong influence. About 75 percent of the islanders belong to the Cook Islands Christian Church (formerly the London Missionary Society). But that doesn't rule out dancing; in fact, the islanders dance the same energetic dances as do the Tahitians.

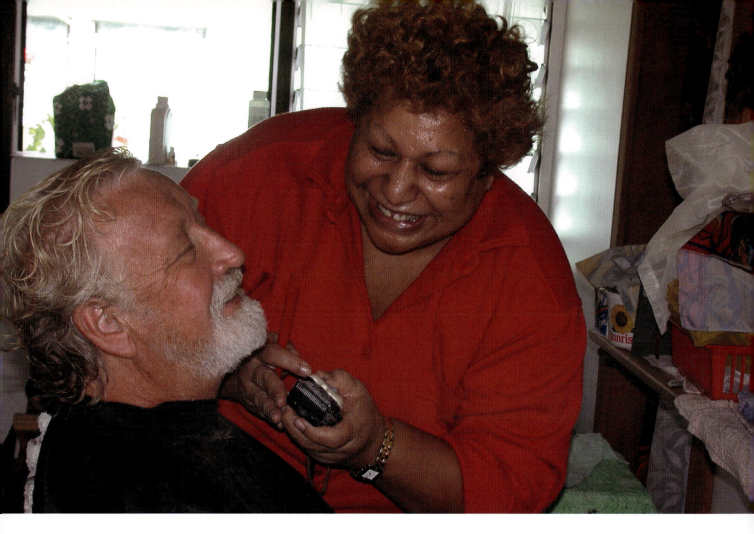

at the house.

"Internet? Yes, you can access it from the computer we have in the entry. I must warn you though, it's expensive. They tell me that the signal goes to Rarotonga first, and then on to Auckland, New Zealand. And then, for you, back to America."

One hour costs me $100 U.S.! It is the most I have ever spent anywhere for internet access. At that price, my website followers had better appreciate my posts!

Richard, Günter, and I walk through the manicured grounds of Aitutaki Resort and Spa, the only hotel on the island's famous blue lagoon. Luxuriant spreading coconut palms adorn the beach's white sand, which is swept clean every day and is always immaculate. We pause to swing lazily on the hammocks and to gaze at the idyllic scene. The morning sun casts palm frond shadows onto the sand; the colors of the shallow lagoon change from a light green near the crystal beach, to an aquamarine, and then to turquoise, and farther out to a shimmering cobalt blue. We relish this special Moment of Bliss, the perfect "Wish You Were Here" postcard.

At lunchtime we find a restaurant with tables facing the lagoon. The specialty, Island Burgers and Fries, is like none we've ever tasted: huge hamburgers topped with onions and a thick slice of pineapple and a slice of beet. Excellent! We savor the food slowly. Later, as we walk along the beach, we come upon a crew filming a movie. A wooden Polynesian catamaran, the kind used for trading, is part of the set, along with barrels of produce and casks of rum. We venture closer; surprisingly, no one waves us off the set.

"Are we allowed to take photos?" I ask someone who acts important.

"Yes, when we have our break, which will be soon."

We wait, and during their break, I walk around taking photos of everyone and everything while Günter and Richard talk to the cast. "They say they're not sure of the eventual title," Richard says, "but they think it'll be called *Island Trader*. We'll have to watch for its release date."

I agree, of course. This has been a fascinating experience—another of those totally unexpected but perfectly enchanting adventures that only cruising can offer!

Later, after a siesta back on the boat, we decide to enjoy the local main Saturday event, which is called "Island Night." For the first time, all cruisers come together in one place. The islanders offer a marvelous feast, a lavish buffet with all the usual Polynesian dishes. And they put on a floor show, too—a family affair with vigorous, non-professional dancers of all ages, performing with grace and agility. We stand and clap after each event and laugh along with the parents

Yachties discuss the weather and make plans for their passages to the next island.

as a group of small children show what they can do. Afterward, we are all invited to dance. And we do. It helps to burn off the heavy dinner!

Nothing is as rich and unique as a Cook Islands Sunday church service! Islanders sing songs called "thunder hymns" in rounds, and the renditions, in native tongue, are passionate and powerful.

The Cook Islands Christian Church was constructed in 1828 by the London Missionary Society. It was the first church built on the Cook Islands, only 50 years after Bligh landed here. Fashioned of coral and stone, the church is well preserved, although the white limestone façade has faded and blackened in places. The interior looks colorful and vibrant in shades of green, yellow, and red. Lovely stained glass windows grace the sides and front. The highlight, however, is the colorful mural over the altar, depicting angels proclaiming "Holy, Holy, Holy."

Günter and I follow a group of ample-bosomed ladies in lacy white dresses and broad-brimmed hats up the steps and into the building. The pastor and deacons greet us and the other cruisers warmly, with wide smiles, and motion us toward the front pews.

For the first time since we left home, we hear a sermon in English. Because I can finally understand the words, I enjoy it immensely. During the service, we recognize one pony-tailed worshipper as an exotic male dancer from the night before. He was my favorite! Now he is dressed in his Sunday best, singing loudly from the hymnal. After the service we do not dare turn down the invitation to stay for the Sunday afternoon buffet, even though Richard is not with us. We will not lose weight here! Dishes brought by the ladies line the entire length of the four folding tables set up end to end on the lawn behind the church. After a short prayer, we are asked to form a line. We notice that the entire line is composed of visitors and sailors. Following the island custom, the locals hang back until their "guests" have their fill. They sing while we eat.

What heartfelt hospitality! These islanders have made me feel so special.

We pick up Richard and take a Sunday afternoon stroll. All is quiet in the town of Arutanga. Gigantic banyan trees dominate the scenery. Manicured yards surround cyclone-proof cinderblock homes where children smile and wave as we pass by. Families walk together, still dressed in their Sunday best. Life is wonderfully relaxed; there is no rush, no bustle. It is obvious that Cook Islanders march to the tempo of a different drummer. Out here there are no big box stores,

nor fast food chains, nor even a single traffic light.

We walk along the beach where fanning palms line the shore. Through the trees, we see six yachts bobbing gently on the sea, waiting to cruise again. Total serenity.

I may never want to return to civilization again.

Passage to Palmerston
17°52′S, 162°43′W
At sea, 192 miles from Aitutaki

Palmerston, an even more remote Cook Island, will be our next stop.

I turn over my watch to Günter at 2100. "Beautiful watch. You'll like it out here."

Soon I hear: "Lois, dress and come back up here!" It is only 2330, almost midnight, and Günter is calling me topsides again. *Pacific Bliss* is racing over some mighty waves. The main and jib sails are full. We discuss reefing.

"If we're even talking about it, it's time," Günter decides.

I wake Richard. Force 6, 20 knots already. While we prepare to reef, "Force 7" appears on the multimeter. Günter mans the electric winch at the stern; Richard and I pull in the sheets. We can reef in our sleep by now; in fact, we are half asleep! But that is the end of my off-watch rest.

Sometimes, life out here just doesn't seem fair. We are only interlopers out here, where the sea holds sway.

Whatever happened to the forecast that we so carefully analyzed before we left port? The swells are always higher, the winds faster, than they say.

We're getting slammed and, frankly, I'm tired of it.

All day and into the night, winds continue a steady Force 6, sometimes up to 30 knots, but *always* above 25. To think that during the first day out of port, we had actually barbecued while underway! Tonight, dinner is grilled cheese sandwiches on paper plates. Nothing to bounce around and no dishes to wash. Back to the basics. We'll cook again in Palmerston.

I still hate passages!

Our biggest problem remains how to slow down *Pacific Bliss* so that we can arrive in the daylight. She rebels against being held back in strong winds! Right now she is moving along at 5 knots, with no main and no jib. That's right: She is just being pushed by the wind and the following seas.

As the passage drones on, we change our waypoint to go farther north of Palmerston, before we jibe (technically, doesn't one need sails up to jibe?). Anyway, our new course works to our advantage; it lengthens the time to get there, and now we'll be arriving in the morning.

This promises to be another difficult, shallow

Günter and Richard with the Marsters brothers of Palmerston Island.

passage through a reef. We have heard that the passage has been dredged to two meters. But rumors are rampant in the South Pacific; we'll know when we get there.

Until then, it is a challenge for this Captain and crew not to let fear reign. There's a very real fear of a tricky and windy landfall, and then there is just this plain free-floating anxiety whenever we hear wind chasing us like a freight train…which is what I'm hearing and feeling now.

"But I am determined to stay strong," I write in my journal. "I am determined not to give in to the sea."

The Marsters of Palmerston Island
18°02.8′S, 163°11.5′W

When we reach our waypoint, 5.7 miles from the island, we change course to head directly to the atoll. I check in with the Coconut Net via SSB; then I pick up the VHF to contact Palmerston Island. A man identifying himself simply as Marsters answers immediately with a strange, almost-Shakespearean, accent.

"Just pick up a mooring outside the reef," he advises.

What a relief!

During our visit here on Mahine Tiara in 1998, Captain John Neal had decided to stay with the yacht because of the unsafe "anchorage." If we hadn't been here before, we would never have attempted this landfall. I turn to Günter. "They have moorings now." I was dreading another tricky entrance or the alternative: anchoring near the reef.

By 0930 we are motoring slowly toward breaking surf that is lashing the reef. Scary. Richard, at the bow, spots the mooring ball and we inch toward it. We put a double line through for safety. Our depth is 34 feet, but we are only 30 yards or so from the reef.

"*Pacific Bliss. Pacific Bliss.* Welcome to Palmerston!" says the Shakespearean voice over the VHF. "We will pick you up for lunch after you are settled in. Is two o'clock okay?"

"Fine, thank you very much," I answer, relieved that we do not have to launch our own dinghy. I can see sticks in the water marking a zigzag course through the narrow canoe passage to the atoll.

Right on time (unexpected in Polynesia), Edward Marsters comes with his fishing boat to transport us to the island. At his home his wife, Shirley, greets us with their two sons, David, six, and little John, three, at her side. Shirley serves a lunch of parrot fish and chips to us and their two male cousins, also named Marsters. It is simple but delicious. After lunch Edward invites us to a tour of the atoll.

No planes can land here and very few yachts stop by. Edward tells us that even the Cook Islands supply boat often fails to stop at Palmerston on its way back to Aitutaki. He points to the omnipresent coconut palms that greet us along the dirt footpath. "These are our

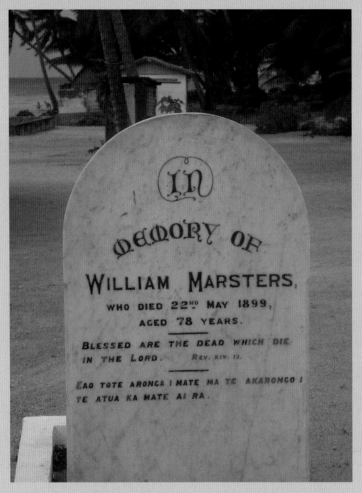

lifeblood, our major cash crop; we use them for cooking, for weaving, for their shells, and even for safety."

He shows us a sand hill—all of six to eight meters high—surrounded by a taro patch. "We call this our mountain," he laughs. "But during hurricanes in the past, it was called Refuge Hill. This taro patch forms sort of a drain around the hill to keep the waves off. During the hurricane of 1936, William Marsters II ordered everyone on the island, about a hundred or so, to make their way to this hill with all their belongings. Each family was tied to a rope that was strung to a big building so none would be lost to the sea. I remember being in another hurricane as a child…climbing this coconut tree here…and hanging on for dear life."

What a lesson in true grit and perseverance!

Our tour continues to the island cemetery, a graveyard full of whitewashed tombstones. Curiously, each name is Marsters. The story Edward tells us is amazing:

William Marsters was the man who made it all happen. He was quite the South Seas character. After a fight with his family, William left Leicestershire, England, and ran away to sea. He served on whaling ships, finding his way to the gold fields of California and finally sailing to Hawaii. Once in the South Seas, he jumped ship at Penrhyn, a remote atoll in the northern Cooks, in 1856. Despite having a daughter with a Penrhyn local, Arehata, he married the Penrhyn chief's daughter Akakaingaro, whom he called by the name Sarah because it was easier to pronounce.

Marsters worked on trading vessels around The Cooks and other island groups, sailing as far as Australia. He often took his wife, Sarah, and their two young daughters with him. But during one of these voyages, tragedy struck: His older daughter, Ann, drowned. The family returned to Penrhyn from where they sailed around the South Pacific. In Manihiki, Marsters recruited laborers for Suwarrow; then he sailed to Manuae, where his second daughter, Elizabeth, died of unknown causes. After some time the family found its way to Aitutaki and then to Palmerston. Accompanying the family was Sarah's cousin, Tepou, who had been brought to the island to help Sarah. A friend and fellow trader, Jean Fernandez, also came along with his wife Matavia.

Life was not easy, but William was a remarkable leader. He was a competent shipwright and house carpenter. He built homes for the family and his workers, houses strong enough to withstand the violent storms that lashed the island. He planted coconuts, which provided his growing family with food and drink and also gave them an income from copra. All slackers were expelled from the island. The women became skilled weavers of hats and mats, and the excellence of their work made them famous.

Marsters created a little village in which the inhabitants, mainly his own family, were firmly established.

After several years, on May 12, 1888, he established legitimate ownership of the island by applying for and receiving a license from the government of the United Kingdom.

According to our host, the stories about the three "wives" of William Marsters became more interesting and conflicting over the years. Apparently, Sarah, the Penrhyn chief's daughter, was not happy about sharing her husband's affection with her cousin and, later, with the wife of his friend. Jean Fernandez had left his wife Matavia in Marsters' safekeeping while he worked the local whaling ships. Fernandez was a dark-complexioned Portuguese. Matania was bearing fair skinned children. Reportedly the extramarital affair did not affect the friends' relationship as drinking buddies. But one time, when Fernandez returned home to find his wife pregnant yet again, he was furious. He had a terrific row with Marsters, abandoned his wife, went to Aitu, married again, and ultimately drowned drunk in Avatiu Harbor, Rarotonga.

Marsters died in May 1899, survived by the 3 wives and 23 children, who in turn produced 54 grandchildren. By the fifth generation, his descendants had surpassed 1000 souls.

During his lifetime, William established rules and regulations that enabled the three families to live as harmoniously as could be expected. Each had a designated plot of land on the main island and on the sandy islets around the lagoon. The property lines were identified by double rows of coconut palms or *puka* trees. Each Marsters clan has its own leader—a family structure that holds true even today. Eventual population growth created difficulties for sustainability, and some descendants left for New Zealand and Australia. For many of those who have left, a claim of relationship to the Marsters family will always connect them to the island and especially to their common patriarch, William Marsters.

From the beginning William would not allow his children to speak any language other than English, with the result that today the entire family speaks with a distinctive old English (Gloucester) accent. Now the children learn Cook Island Maori as a second language, enabling them to fit in if they should choose to emigrate to other Cook Islands.

My curiosity gets the better of me. "How did William handle intermarriage?"

"He never allowed the marriage of a full brother and a full sister," our host answers. "But in the beginning, marriage between half-brothers and half-sisters was allowed. Today, of course, our children have easier matrimonial access to other Cook Islanders—and to the rest of the world."

It's an amazing story, one where truth is better than fiction. And it makes us eager to learn more about the island. In the cemetery the sun casts shadows from the yellow-blossomed Frangipani tree over the faded white tombstones. The grandest headstone of all is that of William Marsters, a rounded white limestone structure that reads: IN MEMORY OF WILLIAM MARSTERS, WHO DIED 22ND MAY 1899, AGED 78 YEARS.

As he shows us around, young William relishes being our host. We walk past cinderblock houses, and he introduces us to this Marsters and that Marsters. We can no longer keep track of all the brothers, uncles, and cousins with the same last name.

Our island tour includes a sturdy church built from timbers of old shipwrecks. We also view canoe storage huts and an impressive array of solar panels for radio and satellite communication. Masts from shipwrecks are used as antennas. Shortly after the first Marsters arrived on Palmerston, a three-masted schooner carrying 16′ x 16′ Douglas fir beams from Seattle to Australia was shipwrecked on the tiny island. This provided lumber for the original great house, which still stands. The next year, another schooner sank here, and Marsters salvaged more timber, with which he constructed even more buildings. An enterprising man, he sold the remaining lumber to passing ships.

Next William takes us to a schoolhouse where delightful pictures drawn by the children hang below a thatched roof. I find it enchanting, but William is more enthusiastic about the new schoolhouse being built nearby. "It won't be as cool as the old one here, but it's larger and we're even advertising for a teacher now," he says proudly.

I feel for them. Is there any teacher out there who would want to come to this remote place? Good luck.

We finish our walk around the main part of the island. (The entire island is only four miles wide and six miles long.) Small, but the tour has been fascinating, intense, and exhausting. Günter thanks William and explains that we are really tired after our passage.

"Will you come back tomorrow?" he asks hopefully.

"Of course," Günter answers.

Behind the reef, the sky darkens and the wind howls. One hundred percent cloud cover, 25-30 knots, Force 6. We are relieved that we are no longer "out there" at sea! My only concern is that the mooring, drilled into coral and secured by two independent ropes, will not hold and send us crashing into the reef.

"No worries," Richard says. "If it does break, the wind's direction will simply drift us out to sea."

123

The shallow channel to Palmerston Island is navigable only with small boats.

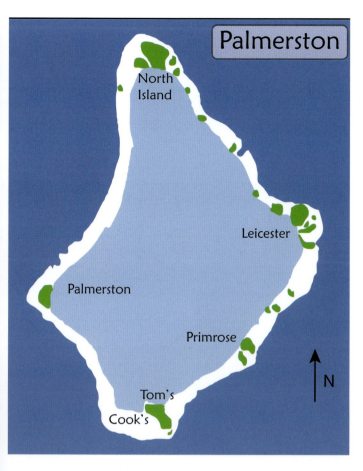

I don't know if that would be any better, but somehow it's a comforting thought, and I sleep easier this night.

William arrives in his aluminum fishing boat to pick us up for lunch again. We have packed a bag of canned food and gifts for the Marsters. They are very grateful. This time, they serve us coconut land crabs, a Palmerston specialty.

Afterward the men relax on the patio while Shirley and I talk. She shows me a purse that she has made from half a coconut shell. I compliment her, and the next thing I know, it's mine! There is no way to graciously refuse a Polynesian gift.

Shirley shows me her refrigerator. "Not all of the homes have this," she says. "But they all have freezers."

Parrot fish, coconuts, and crabs are the island's exports. The freezers provide storage until the trading boats arrive.

Cousins stop by. "We're going fishing on the reef. Want to come with us?" William asks.

Richard jumps at the chance, but Günter elects to stay with me. From the bow of *Pacific Bliss*, we watch Richard "reef fishing" through our binoculars.

"They don't use lines or hooks," I say. "Just nets. They just reach down and scoop them up."

"Amazing!" says Günter, taking a look.

Richard returns, grinning proudly.

"How's fishing?" Günter asks.

"Incredible! I've never had such fun fishing before." He holds up two strings of parrot fish. "They're going to take these and give us frozen fish in exchange."

"Already frozen…that's great," Günter says. "Saves electricity."

Günter, always the amp man.

Just then, a Marsters' aluminum motorboat screams to a stop. Cousin Edward cleats the line to our stern.

"Just wanted to say goodbye," he says. "We want to give you this…from the women." He hands up a bag of fish-head cakes, still warm, and a starchy coconut dessert. "Just a little something extra. Take it."

"You are too kind."

With what they've already given us, we certainly will not go hungry through our passage to Niue.

Niue—Here We Come—Again

It's time to go. A rainbow hangs in the western sky. Could this be a lucky sign? I believe this until we run into a snag…a big snag.

Günter is performing his maintenance check before we sail off to Niue. White-faced, he comes up from the starboard engine compartment underneath the swim steps. "The engine is smoking! We can't leave now." He slumps onto the cockpit bench while Richard and I gather around.

"What's the problem?" asks Richard.

"Don't know. Come with me down into the engine room to take another look."

Soon the men surface, glum and discouraged.

"What's smoking is the diode going into the house battery bank." Günter shakes his head. "The lead is also corroded and burnt. I have no idea how we can fix it here. But we must sort it out before we sail on to Niue."

I have an idea. "How about using our Iridium® to call David at Yachtfinders?"

"Small chance he's in, but let's give it a shot."

Günter cradles the hefty satellite phone with one hand and punches the keyboard with the other. He smiles and signals with a hands-up. David is in!

David is more than a yacht broker; he is a technical man and a troubleshooter par excellence. Together, he and Günter devise a temporary solution. Then the guys go down into the engine room once more; they move the house bank lead to an empty diode post and disconnect the additional alternator, limiting the charging current to 50 amps.

"Whew," Günter announces. "We are back in business. As long as we motor part way, we'll charge up the batteries, and we'll be okay. I'll order a new part

125

The wonderful caves of Niue.

from San Diego and have it shipped to Tonga."

Now we're ready. We loosen the mooring fastened to the coral. Niue, here we come!

"Thar she blows!" Richard yells.

"You're kidding," Günter says.

"No, I'm not. Out there! I see two of them now. Humpbacks. Heading from the reef out to sea. Starboard bow."

Two whales. Breaching in unison. What a good omen for our passage!

And so it is. When my logbook says "uneventful" for two days, that's good. We experience a brisk sail, averaging 6.5 knots for the full 456 miles.

I pass the time reading up on Niue. I'm curious. Why did Captain Cook call Niue "Savage Island?"

Stories circulate about how Cook thought that there were cannibals on the island because as he tried to land, he saw warriors with blackened legs and chests and blood dripping from their lips. Revolted, he left and named Niue "Savage Island."

In fact, cannibalism was unknown in Niue. The locals had always expressed a horror of this practice. They never liked this name for their island and felt that Captain Cook gave them an unnecessarily bad reputation.

Sailors' lore claims that what Cook thought was blood was in reality the red juice of betel nuts. That's not true, either.

Niueans claim that they never injured any of Cook's crew but merely made a demonstration to prevent his landing because they feared that he would introduce disease among them. That had happened before, during a visit by seamen from Tonga. This version of the story was confirmed by the *Encyclopedia Britannica* in 1911.

What did Cook himself say in his journals? As *Pacific Bliss* sails in the wake of Captain Cook's second voyage in June of 1774, I imagine myself in his boots. He has recently named Palmerston Island after one of the Lords of the Admiralty. Now he sights land again. He sails down Niue's west coast and launches two boats to go ashore. They land on a small creek and take a position on a high bank, display the colors, and begin to collect plants to show peaceful intent. The coast is so overrun with vegetation that they cannot see 40 yards in front of them. The men enter a chasm that opens into a woods, and suddenly menacing men throw stones at them and then disappear into the bush. The bush is too tangled for them to follow.

The landing party leaves. It lands again about seven miles farther down the coast. There they find the country "nothing but coral rocks, all over-run with bushes; so that it was hardly possible to penetrate." This time, a group of warriors threw spears at them. Cook records,

DID YOU KNOW?

NIUE

Niue is commonly known as the "Rock of Polynesia," but the inhabitants call their island simply "the Rock." Although it is one of the world's largest coral islands, any news and tourist reports claiming that Niue is the world's largest coral atoll aren't even close. Most of the world's coral islands can be found in the Pacific.

The country has steep limestone cliffs along its coast and a central plateau. The highest is about 220 feet (68 meters). The country has no harbor and few beaches.

Niue is located northeast of New Zealand with Tonga to the southwest, the Samoas to the northwest, and the Cook Islands to the southeast. The nearest land is Vavau, Tonga, 240 miles west. The country covers only 100 square miles (260 square kilometers).

The population of Niue, less than 2,500 and decreasing yearly, is predominantly Polynesian. Because of emigration to New Zealand, the island is suffering a serious loss of population. Though self-governing, Niue is in free association with New Zealand. All Niueans are New Zealand citizens, and Queen Elizabeth II is Niue's head of state in her capacity as Queen of New Zealand. Most diplomatic relations are conducted by New Zealand on Niue's behalf. Up to 95 percent of Niuean people live in New Zealand, along with about 70 percent of the speakers of the Niuean language. Niue uses New Zealand currency.

Niue had no national government or national leader until the beginning of the 18th century. Around 1700, the concept of kingship was introduced. From then on, a succession of *putu-iki* (kings) ruled the island. Tui-toga, who reigned from 1875 to 1887, was the first Christian king of Niue. Christian missionaries then converted most of the population. Finally in 1900, in response to renewed requests, the island became a British protectorate, and the following year it was annexed by New Zealand.

Like other Pacific islands, Niue's economy suffers from geographic isolation, few resources, and a small population. Government expenditures regularly exceed revenues, and to cover the shortfall, critically needed grants from New Zealand pay the wages for public employees.

The island's natural resources are fish and arable land, which comprises almost a fifth of the country. Forests and woodlands comprise another fifth. Although some cash crops are grown for export, the agricultural sector consists mainly of subsistence gardening. Industry consists primarily of small factories that process passion fruit, lime oil, honey, and coconut cream.

This out-of-the-way country has found clever ways to capitalize on its uniqueness. In 2003, Niue became the world's first "WiFi nation." Free wireless Internet access is provided throughout the country by The Internet Users Society—Niue.

The coral cliffs surrounding the island have been deeply eroded by waves, creating the chasms and caves which are Niue's greatest tourist attractions. The relaxing lifestyle of Niue offers the few tourists who visit there a way to get off the beaten track. Air New Zealand has a weekly flight from Niue to Auckland.

"Seeing no good was to be got with these people, or at the isle, as having no port, we returned on board, and having hoisted in the boats, made sail to W.S.W.... The conduct and aspect of these islanders occasioned my naming it Savage Island."

Now that I understand the reason for the misnomer, "Savage Island," I wonder why Niueans now call their island "The Rock of Polynesia." I learn that this name has a double meaning: It describes the rough terrain throughout the center of the island and its jagged coral reef, but it also refers to the tough survivor spirit of the Niueans. Niue is a harsh land in which to scrape out a living, quite different from most Pacific islands. One has to be "a rock" to live here.

Niue is a raised coral island, quite inhospitable to sailors. Geologists speculate that the island was once an atoll with a shallow lagoon, like the present-day Tuomotus, because the center of the island contains the brown-red earth of decomposed coral. The island's topography is like an inverted soup plate: The rounded edge represents the lower terrace; the rim, the old margin of the lagoon; and the bottom, the surface of the old lagoon. The island is about 40 miles around, with the average height of the raised interior about 220 feet above sea level. Its fringing reef is quite close to the shore—about 60-80 yards.

The southeast trade winds blow for eight out of twelve months onto the eastern reef, making landing impossible. Narrow, deep chasms intersect the reef on the western, leeward side. The island's only port is the town of Alofi, on the western side. We must round the top of the island and then sail along its western shore.

⚓

At 0500 on August 18, our radar tells us Niue is only 12 miles away and under black skies. I adjust our waypoint so that, again, we can make landfall in daylight.

Finally I spot a break in the clouds: three thin horizontal streaks where the orange of the morning sun peeks through. A shadowy strip of land is barely visibly in the gray. It is an airstrip! Then I see the white froth of the incoming surf pounding the reef surrounding the coral atoll.

Günter sneaks up behind me at the Nav Station and plants a kiss. "Niue, Lois' favorite coral island."

"Yes, we've been here before—with Captain John Neal on the *Mahine Tiare*. I wonder how it has changed." I turn to give him a long kiss. Then I go back to staring at the radar. *Pacific Bliss* motors along at 6.5 knots; both engines hum as she glides over southwesterly swells. The wind is benign—only 8 knots.

As the sky lightens, the long, low-lying coral atoll of Niue begins to take shape. A ridge of trees, like stray hairs out of place, lines the flat top. A whale spouts and then we see a second whale breach.

Another good omen? We have enjoyed a marvelous passage... for a change.

Pacific Bliss alters course: We round the island, motoring on calm seas, to head toward Alofi. Once there, we grab a mooring in water so clear that we see a water snake lurking below.

I study the island: I see a flat table top with cliffs on all sides and a dense verdant center. No threat of tidal waves will cause these people to run for the tops of coconut palms! The island rises straight from the sea for 40 meters (120 feet) or so. Its circumference is studded with glistening rock pools, like natural amphitheaters, filled with sparkling emerald water.

After settling in, Richard, Günter and I launch *Petit Bliss* to go ashore. On an island made of coral, there is no shallow dinghy landing. Although this is a "roadstead anchorage," protected from winds except from the west, going ashore is quite the feat. The guys fashion a bridle setup that allows a crane to lift our dinghy from the deep water onto a high shipping wharf. We climb up handholds to the top of the wharf while *Petite Bliss* is lifted, set down, and wheeled to a storage area.

After checking in with immigration and customs, we rent a car in Alofi. Günter automatically takes out his driver's license and shows it to the clerk. "What would I need this for?" she asks.

"For documentation?" Günter is confused.

"No need. Where could you go? There's only one road around the island. We call it the 'ring road.' We'll know where you are." She hands his license back.

We drive to the Niue Yacht Club to pay for our mooring. *This must be the strangest yacht club in the world!* It is a club in name only; it has no clubhouse or docks because Niue has no harbor. What it does have, however, is wonderful friendliness.

"Welcome to the Rock of the Pacific!" The buxom manager smiles and sets her granddaughter back in her playpen. "Would you like to join our club? You'll get a membership card and this club burgee." She shows us a green and white pennant.

How can we resist?

"It will be interesting to show *this* at the entry gate of the San Diego Yacht Club, where they share reciprocal memberships," Günter laughs, reading my mind. He even buys a Niue Yacht Club T-shirt.

Niue is an island virtually untouched by tourism. We "yachties" (as we are known in this part of the world) and a few divers comprise the majority of tourists. And it's this paucity of tourists that adds to the island's charm.

We want to give Richard an overview. It shouldn't take long. Niue is bigger than all the Cook Islands

and soft drink can crusher is a gift from New Zealand!

Rounding Niue—Again

Despite a continuous rain, the next day we go ashore again. "We had some sun two weeks ago," says the manager of Matauai Resort. We sit at one of two tables set for lunch. The hotel has a massive double-level deck, with a 180-degree view of the west Pacific, perfect for viewing spinner dolphins, turtles, and humpback whales. There are bars inside and outside, two swimming pools, inside dining and relaxation areas, tennis courts, a fashion boutique, and a tour desk. But it serves only 14 guests.

"So business is good!" Günter jokes with the manager, who happens to be from New Zealand.

"Well, yes, at least it is this week," she smiles. "This hotel is 57 percent owned by the New Zealand government and 43 percent by private investors. It has never made a profit since it was built in the early 1990s."

The front desk phone rings, and she runs to answer it. "I'll be back," she says. "I also handle reception."

When she returns to our table to take our order of sweet and sour meatballs (one of the three lunch selections), she explains that her receptionist is off for the remainder of the week. She is handling it all. "I'm on a two-year contract," she adds.

I wonder what happens then. This slow-paced hotel is probably part of a government training program for bigger and better things.

As we leave, Günter inquires about the carvings displayed in the unlit, un-manned souvenir shop.

"Oh that's Charlie; he lives in Hakupu, three villages back."

"We just passed that—I remember the sign," Gunter says as we return to our rental car. "Let's go back."

The carvings are of ebony, native to the island. "I only think of ebony in relation to Africa," Gunter says. He fingers the little wooden figures and the highly polished necklaces. He chooses a whimsical seahorse on a cord.

We are almost at the end of the second rounding of the island and the rain is coming down in sheets. This stop ends our second Niue tour. Richard is disappointed, of course. We've built up the Niue experience.

Back on *Pacific Bliss*, I explain to him why I continue to get a kick out of this island. "It's terribly tiny to be its own country, yet it's full of kinky characters.

combined, but that's not saying much. Rush hour here, they tell us, is four cars on the entire 42-mile ring road. The entire population, numbering about 1800, is spread out in 14 widely dispersed villages. And so many of the houses are empty that some villages are almost ghost towns.

Even the local jail has closed down! The key has been hanging in the station closet since 1991. A couple of cells are kept clean, but for whom? Maybe somebody who has guzzled a few too many Fosters?

No prison, no prisoners. What a glorious thing to say about a country.

Our tour of the entire island has taken only four hours.

A wharf worker operates the crane to lower *Petit Bliss* back into the surf. Once on *Pacific Bliss*, I wonder: How does this sparse population, clearly in decline, manage to stay in business at all? Who pays for the maintenance of underground power lines and telephone cables and for the one remaining primary school? I grab a book from our ship's library and read up on Niue. New Zealand, I learn, is the island's rich uncle. The island uses Kiwi currency and receives Kiwi aid. (Much of the population lives off the earnings of thousands of people who left Niue for greener pastures.) Even the local beer

The residents come up with all kinds of schemes to keep the people here—and employed."

"In fact, last time we were here," Günter adds, "they had set up banks, yes…banks and shell corporations…for tax evaders. It became a problem for the 'corporate officers' to come here, though, when the local island-hopping airline closed down and Air New Zealand became the sole airline serving Niue."

"And now they've come up with an internet scheme," I interject. "This year they'll be the world's first and only Wifi Nation. Instead of .com, it will be .nu."

I convince Richard that there are many outdoor things to do and see, but only if weather permits.

The Razor's Edge and the Stairway to Heaven

All is not lost; the downpour becomes intermittent.

Between the rains, we go ashore and take some tours by car, stopping off to hike whenever we can. First, we head for Togo, past the Village of Hakupu, on the southeast side of the island. Günter stays with our rental car while Richard and I take off on foot for Togo Chasm. As we leave a dense forest, a sweeping vista opens to a sea of coral, sculpted by the elements and ending with the real sea far, far below. The view looks as if an ancient giant had deliberately arranged a million sharp coral razor blades pointing toward the sky. Photos cannot do justice to this view: Each of these huge needles rises from 5 to 8 meters (15 to 24 feet). And among them, coral spikes fill the spaces between these pinnacles like a bed of 18-inch sharp nails. An amazing sight! If not for the Niue government's pouring a narrow pathway of concrete through this coral jungle, access to the beach would be impossible.

Farther on a rock stairway, with a necessary safety rope, is the way we descend. It is treacherous, slow going. Negotiating the track around the coral pinnacles takes us another 30 minutes, but the panoramic view all the way down is worth the effort. The track dead-ends at a long 32-step wooden ladder that leads even farther down to a small sandy beach. I affirm my inner Indiana Jones and take that first tentative step. The ladder is steep but sturdy. Soon Richard and I are standing on the beach surrounded by huge coconut palm trees. (They shouldn't grow in such a difficult environment. Yet they seem to thrive here.) Interestingly, the beach itself has no water; but it does have an intriguing cave with a unique sea arch through which we're able to view breaking waves.

We relax and enjoy the view for a while.
But now for the dreaded long hike back!

Avaiki Cave and Our Reef Tour

Günter drives us to Avaiki Cave. This time he joins us. Avaiki Cave, named after the legendary Polynesian homeland, is where Niue's first settlers landed. The cave used to be an exclusive place for Niue's ancient kings. Actually the site has two caves in the same complex. One, at the entrance, is full of huge stalactites, stalagmites, and colorful pillars. The second is accessed by following a narrow gorge and then walking across a reef flat and into a cavern that opens to a heavenly rock pool. It is very difficult to say which cave is more beautiful. But the pool is gorgeous and inviting, full of coral formations and colorful reef fish.

Richard dons his mask and snorkels to explore the pool while I take photos. He comes back to the coral ledge, takes off his equipment, and nods his head. He is beaming along with the sun. Now he understands our love for Niue.

Niue has some of the best caves in the South Pacific. In fact, these caves are so large and numerous that until the 19th century the majority of the residents on the island actually lived in them. We know that we cannot possibly find most of them on our own.

The best guide on the island, we were told, is Tali, who works in the tourism office in Alofi. We arrange a cave tour and reef walk with him.

The next day at low tide, Tali leads us to the reef. We follow him in ankle-deep water while he points out various examples of reef life and explains how the locals fish for oysters and octopuses. We squeeze through several caves filled with stalactites and stalagmites to get to crystal-clear freshwater pools. Saturated with these awesome sights, we head for Vaikona Chasm, the best cavern of them all. We descend through a sloping cave to the chasm floor to find a small freshwater pool, fringed by lush green ferns. An oval sapphire of sky peeks through from above. Niue's caves are the most magical I've ever seen! Everywhere, I stop to take photos of magnificent sea arches and listen to blowholes whooshing as the tide returns.

We check out of Niue, return the car, and walk back to the wharf for the last time. Günter and Richard operate the crane to lower *Petit Bliss* back into the sea. We prepare to leave on yet another South Pacific passage.

Goodbye, Savage Island. I am very happy that we came here again. I hope that Tonga—called the Friendly Isles by Captain Cook—will be as friendly to us as you have been.

BOAT DAY AT PALMERSTON ISLAND

In Aitutaki, we stumbled upon a set for a movie with the tentative title *Island Trader*. That experience piqued my interest in how traders contribute to the welfare of these remote islands, mere specks on the vast Pacific. The arrival of a trading vessel at an island like Palmerston represents a huge event in the lives of the residents. The activity is carefully planned, although it may appear feverish, confused, and uncoordinated. Frenzy builds until arrival time. Then systematically the islanders transport their produce from storage sheds to the boat landing. The men have to be ready for work, and the smaller boats must be ready to leave as soon as the vessel arrives. On Palmerston the primary product for sale is copra, the dried flesh of coconut; the second most important product is frozen reef fish. The residents prepare accommodations for the people who intend to stay and assign hosts to entertain the visitors who will be there only a few hours.

A journal entry by W.H. Percival from 1956, reprinted below from the book *Sisters in the Sun*, provides a lively account of "boat day." In 2002, "boat day" here is much the same as it was then.

The Pacific sun sent fierce heat down upon the *Charlotte Donald's* deck, as she swung at anchor a short distance from Palmerston Island's reef. Beyond the reef the large lagoon scintillated in the sunlight, the dark blue where it met the reef three miles away merging into subtle tones of turquoise and emerald in the nearby shallows. Palmerston, the largest of the motu threaded like green beads upon the connecting string of the reef, lay half a mile away, its narrow strip of white coral sand blazing beneath the drooping plumes of the coconut palms and the green tangle of pandanus and *ngangie* bushes. Six canoe sheds of brown palm thatch stood out boldly against the coral sand and a boat was drawn up on the beach.

Across an unwrinkled ocean of technicolour blue I watched three boatloads of islanders coming out to meet us. The leading boat had six people on board and it flew the New Zealand flag from its stern. In the sternsheets sat a grey-bearded man wearing a blue shirt, long trousers and a peaked, flat cloth cap. He was Ned Marsters, grandson of William, the founder of the Marsters clan, and the recognized chief of the three families living on Palmerston.

Ned Marsters climbed on board and went straight to the wheelhouse where he shook hands with Captain Andy Thomson and other old friends. Then, as soon as preliminaries were over, he pulled papers from his shirt pockets and began to talk business.

After spending several hours ashore, I was able to make friends with the islanders…

Back on the ship, I saw the last of the outward-bound passengers curving toward us through the reef passage. The whaleboat was borne swiftly on the outgoing current—and it had a green-painted outrigger in tow. The oarsmen slowed their progress, easing the heavily-laden craft carefully through the shallow channel. The tide was on the ebb and there were only inches of water beneath their keel. Then they were safely over the lip of the reef and rising and falling on the ocean's smooth swell.

Minutes later the whaleboat rubbed and bumped along the *Charlotte Donald's* side. Lines were heaved and secured. Then the business of boarding began.

Shouts and good natured laughter floated across the water as brown-skinned islanders of both sexes and all ages scrambled up the ship's side. Infants were handed up to the people who crowded the bulwarks, then came rolls of sleeping mats, crates of dried fish, bunches of coconuts, and baskets of plaited coconut fronds filled with reef fish and taro.

The black-bearded helmsman of the whaleboat, Bob Marsters, who is also one of Palmerston's policemen, bartered with Captain Andy during this apparent confusion. Bob offered live chickens and freshly caught reef fish, which were finally accepted after the usual haggling…

The engines shuddered into life, bells clanged, and we began to go ahead. Polynesian seamen moved about the well deck and fitted hatch covers into place over holds, partly filled with Palmerston copra. Tarpaulins were then rigged, tent fashion, over the derrick's boom, forming a shelter for the deck passengers, who then moved into their temporary home. They spread sleeping mats over the hatch covers, sorted out their various belongings and arranged themselves into family groups. The remainder of the deck was cluttered with the ship's work boats, crates of chickens and tethered pigs. The odours of dried fish and copra hung everywhere, and as the *Charlotte Donald* began to roll in the swells the first signs of seasickness appeared among the new arrivals.

This catamaran was built for a movie being filmed on the island of Aitutaki.

Chapter 7
The Proud Kingdom of Tonga

Tongan Time
At sea, 18°32′S, 173°54′W
August 28, 2002

0500: During this night, on Günter's watch, we crossed the international dateline and entered the Kingdom of Tonga, the only Polynesian monarchy. Now I'm on morning watch, and I note in my logbook that we have skipped a day. Although I understand the reasoning behind losing an entire day when crossing the dateline, the reality seems strange. Crossing an invisible line, made by man, gives me a weird sense of disorientation, and it seems as if my internal calendar has gone crazy.

Despite the early hour, the almost full moon lets me see the first island rising, a ghostly apparition to our port. During our first night out on this passage from Niue, the three of us marveled at this moon as it rose from the eastern sea, like a squashed orange pumpkin. Now he is a dented white soccer ball suspended in the sky at the top of our mast.

My senses are on full alert, anticipating landfall. The radar is on. Our automatic tracking system makes navigation easy. *Pacific Bliss* glides gently over the swells, filling her double-reefed main with the 16 – 20 knot northeast wind.

Perhaps there will be other vessels headed slowly for Neiafu, waiting for the first light. I hope so. I feel lonely out here.

The Kingdom of Tonga. The name evokes mystery, a sense of the exotic, perhaps because I have never been here before. Or perhaps because it is one of the few remaining absolute monarchies in the world. Tonga has a fierce reputation: It is the only island in the Pacific that was never colonized.

This Polynesian country of over 170 islands has intrigued me ever since I viewed a TV broadcast of Tongans on the beach greeting the New Millennium on January 1, 2000, with exotic, feverish dancing. Later that year, I was intrigued again by the news that 444-pound King Taufa'ahau Tupou IV had gone on a diet-fitness program and had lost over 100 pounds!

I've been longing to see the "real thing" for two years!

The legends of the islands tell two stories of their origin: In the first, the mighty Polynesian god Tangaloa went fishing and snagged his tortoise-shell and whalebone fish hook on an opening in the island of Nuapapu, located in the Vavau Group to which we are heading. The islands emerged as one continuous land mass, but the fishing hook broke, allowing bits of land to sink back into the sea. In the second legend, the demi-god Maui was fishing, using a hook borrowed from an old man named Tonga. Maui yanked up the islands one by one and named the entire island group after the man who had made this strong and dependable hook.

The origins of Tongan royalty also have their place in the legends. The first Tui Tonga (Tongan ruler) was formed from the union of the sun god Tangaloa and a beautiful young earthling named Ilaheva. When the god discovered her shell-fishing on a small island near Tongatapu—the southernmost island group—he became irresistibly amorous; nine months later, she gave birth to Aho'eitu, who became the first king in a long line of Tuis. Tongans even date this legendary event to A.D. 950!

Tonga's first known European explorers arrived in

A dancer who performed at the dedication of a new school in Tonga.

1616. A Dutchman named Jacob Lemaire encountered a Tongan sailing canoe. He killed at least one Tongan and took others captive. He never actually landed in Tonga. The next visitor was another Dutchman, Abel Janzoon Tasman, whose two ships traded with the Tongans in the southern islands in 1643. Then, in 1767, English Captain Samuel Wallis explored Tonga. Seven years later, Captain Cook visited Tonga during his second Pacific expedition. Today, Tonga's Vavau Group is one of the world's great sailing destinations. Both The Moorings and Sunsail charter companies have operations here in Neiafu, and it is a mecca for cruisers.

I can't wait to swap sea stories in the many bars and restaurants that line the Tongan port.

0700: Günter and Richard are up. We relish the longest, most beautiful sunrise that we have enjoyed for a long time. The colors gradually change from pastels to vibrant oranges and reds that merge at the northeast point of Vavau Island. Eventually the colors flow on to join the wispy mare's tails covering half the sky.

I'll never tire of such beauty!

This two-day passage has been what South Pacific cruising should be about (and hasn't been, so far, this season). For the most part we have experienced following winds in the 10-20 knot range and moderate swells with clear skies overhead.

To add to the perfect passage, last night we were treated to a double green flash. A green flash is a green rainbow. It occurs when the sun disappears into a totally clear horizon and only the green of its spectrum remains for a moment. Günter had never seen one. And when I had reported seeing one, he had the audacity to question its reality. But when the sun sank below the horizon, we experienced green flash #1. Then waves came up on the horizon, and the sun dipped a second time, resulting in green flash #2. "Like an emerald in the sky," Günter exulted like an excited child.

What an omen! The three of us could barely contain our enthusiasm as we looked forward to the adventure ahead.

1000: We douse the sails and motor through Faihava Pass on the western side of the island. Then I navigate us through the long fjord-like entrance to the Port of Refuge. We tie up to a mooring ball owned by Beluga Diving. We spot more yachts in this harbor than we ever expected: charter boats, adventure and diving boats, cruising boats with flags from all over the world, and live-aboards that look like they haven't moved in years. Tonga is a sailor's haven. I breathe a huge sigh of relief and contentment.

We will be happy here. I can feel it.

I had temporarily forgotten that well-known South Pacific cruiser adage: "Nothing this good lasts forever."

Cruising Talk and Hunkering Down
Port of Refuge, Neiafu, Vavau Island Group, Tonga

Days after our arrival, Günter, Richard, and I are sitting here in the rain, "hunkered down" again on *Pacific Bliss*. We are still moored in port; it has been too rainy to go out to the snorkeling anchorages. *Miss Bliss* is cozy and dry; we have no leaking, so far.

The big issue is our collective dour mood. Our complaints about the weather in Paradise have been building. "We've had about 50 percent cloudy or rainy weather since mid-July," Günter reminds us. "Many times we haven't had a drying spell for days on end!"

Richard sits here with a glum look. He has only a few days before he flies back. He had so looked forward to more than this in Tonga!

However, we can be thankful that the pervasive dampness has not invaded our electronics: The two computers, digital camera, and remotes are all in working order. (I backed up my laptop this morning, just in case.) But keeping mildew under control on such things as pillows, life preservers, and foul weather gear, and even on fiberglass surfaces in the heads, has become a daily challenge.

The locals blame the weather pattern on El Niño. All we know is that this is not the South Seas cruising weather that the guide books rave about! Everyone is talking—and complaining—about the weather. And when the weather turns really ugly, sailors return to port. No wonder Neiafu is named the Port of Refuge.

When the weather is miserable, the bars and cafés here do a bang-up business. The Mermaid offers arriving yachties their first drink free in the hope they will choose it as their primary hangout. Günter, Richard and I decide to join the crowd at the Mermaid for Richard's last event before he returns to his home in California. The dinghy dock is bursting; dinghies are tied up three deep. Everyone who can fit is squeezed along the bar, an old ship's bow with a carved wooden mermaid at the bowsprit. Those who can't fit crowd around three tables in the bar area. We pull up chairs to one of the tables and order bottles of the local beer, called *Mata Maka*.

Cruising Talk among new arrivals turns first to the recent passages: what the seas were really like "out there," what broke down, and finally, as tongues are loosened, to a frank assessment: *Why are we doing this, anyway?*

"I think cruising would be great if it weren't for sailing and anchoring," says Ed of *Free Radical*. The table erupts with laughter.

I tell everyone that we managed our own rough passages—from Bora Bora to Aitutaki and then on to Palmerston—by being stoic. We just went through the motions of passage-making like zombies, without saying much. But I wonder how it works for families with children on board. Do they discuss their fear? Or do they hide it for the benefit of the children? On *CheckMate*, the UK grandparents of seven-year-old Oliver and three-year-old Gillian say they just keep on sailing, acting as if nothing bad ever happens. Is that true? It's hard to say because negativity rarely passes through those stiff, British upper lips. But Americans? We're very different. American families let it all hang out.

"After we come in from a bad passage—and they have *all* been bad lately!—my parents, my brother Jesse, and I sit down on the deck and have coke and a debriefing," says Sarah, 14, from *Windarra*.

"What did you discuss this last time?" I ask.

"We all agreed we'd *never* go out there again," she says, screwing her face into a cute frown.

This family has sailed *Windarra* all the way from their home in Seattle. Difficulties had beset them even before the start of their passage. Elaine shares this with us: When their vessel was new to them and unproven, and they were taking it home from Long Beach, crucial systems broke down at the worst possible place and time. They were fighting, head-on, against the wind and waves of California's Point Concepcion.

"So what was the consensus after that experience?" I ask Sarah.

"Like I said—we all agreed we would *never* go out there again...." She pauses, and then we all laugh along with her.

Full of stories and beer, we dinghy back from the bar to *Pacific Bliss*, dripping like drowned sea otters. The rain is pounding the salon roof; it is beyond raining "cats and dogs." I'd call it a torrential downpour.

Aventura and *Mobisle*, two yachts familiar to us from the Puddle Jump Net, made it into the anchorage last night in the rain and early evening gloom. Now more yachts from that group are straggling in. They hail us via the VHF. Their captains and crews are dog-tired and thankful for a non-rolly anchorage after facing up to 40-knot winds at sea. I listen to the familiar names calling each other: *Final Straw*, *North Road*, *Silent Runner*, *Hallelujah*, and *Little Gem*. One thing is certain: After this new group recovers, there will be a lot more Cruising Talk tomorrow night!

It's like childbirth, says Leslie of *North Road*, reminding me of my earlier conversation with Claudie. As we eavesdrop on the "party line," Leslie continues, "One forgets what it was like after a while, and then, foolishly, one goes out and does it all over again."

These yachties *will* go out and "do it all over again," I am certain. I do not see any "For Sale" signs around.

When wind and sea touch the soul, one can never be totally free of them again.

An island scene in Tonga.

Out in the Anchorages
Port Maurelle, Anchorage #7

I sleep through sunrise. Even though I hear Günter making his regular Sunday morning satellite call to his mother in Munich, I doze off again, pulling our comforter tight around my neck.

"You slept through, for a change," Günter says, as I join him later in the cockpit. "The sunrise was cloudy, but pink. You would have loved it."

Now, the sun bursts through clouds of silver onto a powder blue sky. We have come into a mostly-sunny weather pattern. I notice that *Blue Yonders* is no longer next to us. It must have been their windlass chain that was clanking through my morning dreams. I must be getting really relaxed out here—all alone with Günter now that Richard has departed for home.

"You are keeping royal hours befitting a Queen," Günter teases. Always the scout, he is already reading the Fiji guide, dreaming about new adventures while I'm still "taking in" Tonga. I count 11 yachts in the bay. Some are charterers, who, in their haste to fit it all in, only stay one night in each anchorage. They are a stark contrast to us cruisers, who stay until we become bored.

Coffee in hand and still in my PJs, I journal about the outstanding Island Feast we attended on Barnacle Beach last night. There we met New Zealanders John and Val, who own a powerboat named *Tutakako*. They told us we will need two months to see their country, rather than the three weeks we have planned; they invited us to visit them there. They also filled us in on Vuda Point, Fiji, where we plan to "winter" *Pacific Bliss* during the tempestuous southern hemisphere summer.

I tell my journal how Tali, the hostess, greeted us underneath a long, green canopy positioned over a long table, which was being laid with banana leaves and an array of salads. Nearby, her husband Naita and two sons were barbequing two small pigs. The thick, crisp skins crackled over the fire as Günter and I watched, salivating. Another son was slowly turning four scrawny chickens that were skewered on a spit. He looked up and gave me a wide smile. Since it appeared that the preparations would go on for some time, we took a walk with John and Val into the village. The narrow trail into town wound around two dozen homes, most of them fenced to keep out wild pigs, then up a small hill, past dozens of trees uprooted by a cyclone, and past a plain but clean church. Beyond the church, we enjoyed a wide-angle view all the way down to the sea where the path ended at a concrete jetty and a few small fishing boats. Off the jetty, posing against the setting sun, a few cruising yachts bobbed peacefully. It was all so beautiful and enchanting!

But the feast awaited us, and we hurried in the twilight back to Barnacle Beach. By the time we returned, more guests had arrived. We were 22 in all, seated on long, wooden benches under the canopy. The villagers brought basket after basket of food, including pan fish, taro with corned beef, and octopus with coconut sauce. Before long the flower arrangements on the table gave way to huge platters of pork and chicken.

The host family explained how to eat it all—on banana leaves, with our hands. They placed small bowls of water on the tables for finger dipping. "Let's bring home a lesson from this," said Val. "Everyone, plant a banana tree in your backyard. No more dishes!" Everyone laughed.

The dessert was sweet papaya and watermelon, and the wine flowed endlessly.

What a feast it was! No wonder I slept in this morning!

Church in Falevai
Island of Kapa, Tonga

This Sunday morning, Günter dons his slacks and short-sleeved shirt and I pull on my trusty "church dress," an ankle-length cotton sheath with a blue sails print. We will attend yet another island church. We had asked the pastor, who had given the long prayer of blessing at the Island Feast, whether we could come. He is such a nice, friendly man!

Günter guns the dinghy motor to make a run up the beach. I hike up my skirt and he his trousers, and this time, we manage to stay dry. We don't see our host family at the beach, so we presume they have already gone to church.

We walk tentatively toward the front door of their home. The father, Naita, has gone on, but Tali has stayed behind to wait. "I'm waiting for one other group," she tells us. "They are also from the feast. My son Sione will take you."

Sione (John, in English) is a bright ten-year-old who leads us down a few paths, over a fence, and up a hill. I try not to step in any animal droppings with my "dress Tevas®." Sione approaches a white stucco building. He leads us to the doorway, where he takes off his sandals. We follow suit. We enter. Mats cover the floor of the room. A cotton curtain partitions the room, and four men sit cross-legged around a large carved *kava* bowl.

A kava ceremony before church?

I am confused. Naita is there. We shake hands with the men and introduce ourselves. "Sit down," Naita says. The men are well dressed; two even wear ties. They refill their bowls with the muddy-looking brew.

"*Kava?*" asks our host.

I sit awkwardly with my legs crossed underneath

DID YOU KNOW?

THE KINGDOM OF TONGA

Tongans are a proud people who inhabit the only island nation in the region that escaped formal colonization. The country is a hereditary, constitutional monarchy;  the government is largely controlled by the king, his nominees, and a small group of hereditary nobles. The king in 2002 was Tupou IV. His son, George Tupou V, came to the throne in 2006.

Polynesians have lived on Tonga for at least 3,000 years. The Dutch were the first to explore the islands. British explorer James Cook landed on the islands in 1773 and 1777 and dubbed them the Friendly Islands. The current royal dynasty of Tonga was founded in 1831 by Taufaahau Tupou, who took the name George I. In 1900, his great-grandson, George II, signed a treaty of friendship with Britain, and the country became a British protectorate. The treaty was revised in 1959. But Tonga gained its full independence on June 4, 1970.

Tonga consists of some 150 islands; only 36 are inhabited. Most of the islands contain active volcanic craters; some are coral atolls. The Kingdom stretches over a distance of about 500 miles, but the land area is only 277 square miles (717 square kilometers). The population in 2002 was 106,137. The Tongans attend Wesleyan Methodist, Anglican, Roman Catholic, Seventh-Day Adventist, and Mormon churches, but everyday life is heavily influenced by Polynesian traditions and, especially, by the Christian faith; for example, all commerce and entertainment activities cease from midnight Saturday until midnight Sunday. The constitution declares the Sabbath to be sacred, forever.

Tongans speak Tongan and English. The literacy rate is 98.5 percent. The monetary unit is the pa'anga, worth about 50 cents to the U.S. dollar in 2002.

Tonga has the first of the world's time zones, or the last, depending on how one looks at it. The country holds the world's only time zone of GMT +13, a bulge that extends the eastern hemisphere into the west, stealing one hour from yesterday to make it today.

The land rules are strange and confusing: All the land in the kingdom technically belongs to the crown. Much of it consists of hereditary estates that were bestowed upon various chiefs, who lease the lands to farmers at a nominal annual rent.

All important occasions—weddings, funerals, and church-related functions—are marked by drinking *kava*. When a new king takes his throne or a new chief is established in his title, he must participate in the *pongipongi*, ancient *kava* ceremonies, to make his rule official. *Kava* is drunk nightly at *kava* clubs, kalapu, where only men are allowed to imbibe the drink. The server is usually an unmarried, young woman called the toua.

my long skirt.

Thank God it has slits so I don't have to hike it up! But kava *right before church? With no water afterward to wash down the taste? What if I choke?*

Günter keeps his head. "No, thank you," he says with a smile. "It's too early in the day for us."

Our host smiles back and puts the bowl to his lips, not putting it down until the bowl is empty.

The host offers Sione a drink. He accepts, proud to be included among the men. He handles it well. I can tell it's not his first time!

"You don't clap your hands afterward, as they do in Fiji," Günter observes.

"Sometimes we clap," Naita replies.

This must be an informal pre-church ceremony. Perhaps clapping is the custom only when the chief is present.

Naita, Sione, and Tali, the family who takes us to church on the island of Kapa, Tonga

Günter seems to be reading my mind. "Where is your town's mayor?" he asks.

"Oh, you mean our chief. He is in Nukualofa right now. He is a member of our country's Parliament," Naita responds with pride as he sits up straighter.

"How many people are in your village?" Günter asks.

"Five hundred. About 200 are children," says the large man in the black suit. His buttons are straining across his mid-section so hard, I wonder when one will pop. I look at my watch. Although it is 10:55, these men seem in no hurry to leave.

"Are we going to the church?" Günter asks, reading my mind again.

"Soon," says the black-suited man. He scoops up yet another bowl of *kava*. The other men do the same, even little Sione.

"The pastor is also in Nukualofa right now," Naita explains, "so this man will give the sermon." He points to the black-suited man.

I'm amused. What kind of sermon will this be?

At exactly 11 o'clock, they all stand. We do the same. We follow them up the hill and into a white stucco building with red-painted window frames.

Men in suits and ladies dressed in their finest fill the little church. The sermon is in Tongan, so we have no idea whether the stand-in pastor is doing well. The impassive faces of the parishioners tell me nothing. When the sermons and songs are over, a bag is passed around for the offering. Then the stand-in gives a prayer of dismissal and walks to the door of the church, where he shakes the hand of every person individually. They are all smiles and appear to be congratulating him for a job well done.

After lunch and a siesta, Günter and I take the dinghy to explore the many coves indenting the island of Kapa. A flock of white terns gracefully heads for the palm trees lining the coves. Along the reefs and shores, schools of fish jump frantically; there must be some mighty chasing going on.

We search for Swallows Cave, a local attraction that one can visit only with a small boat. We find it quickly because we see a motorboat filled with children, dressed in their Sunday best, exiting the cave. Shouting and waving, they point to the cave's entrance as we slowly motor forward. Before we enter, the water becomes such an intense blue that it rivals Italy's Blue Grotto. The depth is 250 feet. No wonder anchoring here is impossible!

Our guidebook has informed us that the best time to visit is about 1500, when the sun from the west lights the multicolor stalactites. Our timing is perfect. The sinking sun shines a path across navy water to magnificent coral formations. Inside, the walls of the cave are covered with a mixture of recent graffiti and ancient art that dates back to whaling days. Overhead we see, ironically, the mud-built nests of starlings, not the swallows that give the cave its name. As we leave, Günter remembers to pick up a dinghy oar and hit the pulpit-like rock rising from the left side. As the locals had promised us, we hear a deep, resounding bell tone.

At the turn of the 20th century, entire feasts were lowered down into Swallows Cave. With this breathtaking beauty, it's no wonder this cave was used to entertain important visitors! Back on *Pacific Bliss*, we find that we can snorkel directly from the swim ladder. Here, we see fish with yellow on top and blue neon underneath; some with turquoise and neon blue

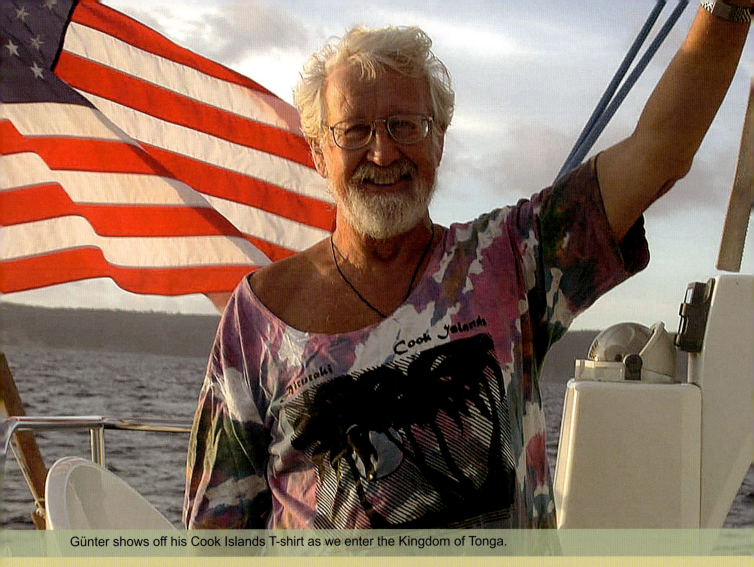
Günter shows off his Cook Islands T-shirt as we enter the Kingdom of Tonga.

coloring; others with a brown-and-amber geometric pattern. I swim among yellow-and-black angel fish, my favorite. And my eyes discern a bright blue starfish enjoying itself, just floating to and fro within the motion of the waves.

The brochures we had found in Neiafu claim that the remote and unspoiled waters around Vavau are crystal clear with visibility exceeding 100 feet. They are not exaggerating! The brochures also claim over 100 species of colorful tropical fish, giant clams, manta rays, sea turtles, and spinner dolphins. And from July through October, the humpback whales reign here. Vavau is a water wonderland not to be missed by any South Pacific cruiser.

The Birthday Boy
18°42.83´S, 174°08.25´W
Blue Lagoon, Vavau Island Group

On the morning of Günter's birthday, September 9, we depart Anchorage #7 and zigzag for eight miles through a string of islets, some with sheered-off sides and others with sun-drenched beaches. The smooth sea glistens like sapphires and surrounds each island with a ring of emeralds.

"This is a day of bliss." A contented smile fills Günter's face. "I like birthdays."

"And you don't even have to help with the lunch or dishes." I sway my hips in what I hope will be an enticing stroll to the helm seat. There, I kiss the Captain. He responds so nicely that I kiss him again.

"We'll be dining out tonight, Birthday Boy. And afterward, I just may have a surprise in store for you."

We enter the Blue Lagoon from the east, passing through the 3-fathom (18-foot) channel shown on our chart. I note that the lagoon lies within the southern fringing reefs of Hunga Island. I head for the bow to look out.

Günter motors around two marked coral heads. The sun is behind us; I can easily distinguish the brown reefs through emerald waters inside the lagoon. A perfect passage, with exquisite timing! I walk back to the helm where we congratulate ourselves with our usual high fives. Then I return to my lookout, and we wind carefully around the rest of the reefs. Soon I spot the blue tarp of the Blue Lagoon Restaurant on the hill, far above the long sandy shoreline. "Günter, drop anchor," I call out. "We're in the protected southeast corner in about 15 feet of water." Günter motors a little farther. "It looks very shallow now," he says, "and I see another green-brown reef in the middle." He puts the

A classic Tongan church.

engine into neutral; we coast closer. "Look, there's a mooring here. Call them on VHF 16 and find out if it's okay to tie-up here."

I go to the salon to make the call. The response is muddled. All I can make out are the words, "anchoring ball."

I rejoin Günter in the cockpit. "He must mean for us to pick up the ball," Günter says. He motors forward, then slows, as I reach over the side to grab the mooring ball with the boat hook. No luck. We repeat the maneuver two more times.

Even using our extra-long bamboo boat hook, I cannot grab the line beneath the ball. And there doesn't seem to be a loop to put our mooring line through.

"Darn!" I yell.

"You take the wheel and I'll try." Günter is the patient one, this time. On his second try, he succeeds. Together, we find the loop and put two lines through it to secure *Pacific Bliss*.

We feel safe now, but are we? We scope out our new neighborhood. Reefs surround us, and the charming little island of Foe'ata will not protect us much from ESE winds. If the winds should shift, there will be even less protection.

"Let's keep our options open," Günter says. "We may have to leave."

"Right. I think we should forgo lunch and our usual siesta. Let's go ashore first. Friedel should know how safe this is here. Perhaps he'll make us a birthday *lunch* instead of *dinner*."

We first heard about the eccentric German, Friedel, from Rolf, who hails from Berlin. We were enjoying a candlelight dinner at his *Pua Tale Fusi* waterfront restaurant in Neiafu when he mentioned Friedel's name. After the meal, Rolf sat at our table for a while. "I can tell that you two appreciate good food. When you go out to the anchorages next week, you must go to the Blue Lagoon. A crazy German named Friedel runs the place; only cooks when he's in the mood. Or if he likes you. He's quite the character, but Günter, *you*, another German, will be able to talk him into cooking for you."

The following day, we researched the area in our guidebook, *The Lonely Planet: Tonga*. It told us:

> This lodge and restaurant has six large fales (beach cottages) beside a truly idyllic beach on Foe'ata. Constructed from local materials, each fale is unique and built around its immediate environment. Part eco-lodge, part eccentric dream resort (some of the bathrooms are particularly wacky), it offers reputedly the best food in Vava'u. It's already popular with yachties and boat trippers...offers glorious white beaches and good snorkeling in a secluded atmosphere. At low tide, it is a simple walk across a sand bar to Foelifuka.

That did it. We had to go there. We also looked up Blue Lagoon in our *Cruising Guide to the Kingdom of Tonga*, published by The Moorings. "It says that it's only a day anchorage," Günter cautioned. "Maybe it will have to be just a birthday lunch."

"But remember what the New Zealand couple at Barnacle Beach said the night of the Island Feast," I reminded him. "They said that it seemed plenty safe for an evening stay and thought that Moorings was only being extra cautious because they wanted to protect their own charter boats."

"Let's check it out, and then decide," said Günter. "After all, how could Friedel have the best food in Vavau Group if yachts couldn't stay there overnight?"

Discussion closed.

I throw on a *pareu* over my swimsuit, and we

dinghy to the shore. We hitch the dinghy to a post dug into the sand. Children frolicking on the pearly white beach pay no attention to us as we pass by.

We step into the pan of water on the wooden plank steps outside the building to clean the sand off our feet. Barefoot, we tackle the three flights of wooden stairs up to the restaurant. A tall, stately mermaid, exquisitely carved from wood, greets us at the top. The room, large and wide, offers a magnificent 180 degree view of the beach and the sea. The high, circular, coconut-thatched roof is supported by one huge log standing in the center; live trees, complete with leaves, protrude through parts of the roof. In the whimsical dining area, large chairs made of crooked tree limbs and painted white or bright green, surround round varnished tables, which are decorated with shells and flowers. A long lacquered bar dominates the far side of the room, but customers can still watch the chef as he works diligently in the kitchen. We venture further.

The entire room is dark, empty, and still.

"Friedel!" Günter shouts.

A tall, heavyset, balding man with an uncontrolled beard and mustache slowly saunters into the big room. He wears a dirty T-shirt and cut-offs; his glare tells us he does not welcome this rude interruption to his lazy afternoon.

Günter greets him in German and explains that he was born in München. Friedel's surly demeanor improves immediately. The men chat for a while, and then Günter introduces me as his American wife. The conversation changes quickly to English.

"My radio doesn't work so well," Friedel says. "I was trying to tell you *not* to pick up that mooring. It is for fishing boats only. It's held only by a chain. I do not think it will support your catamaran."

I envision a chain just lying there on the bottom of the sea and our Cat dragging it and the mooring ball all the way across the bay, ending up on the reefs.

"Is anchoring good here?" I ask.

"Very good. It'll hold in sand. That's what all the yachts do."

"Okay. We'll anchor, then. Do you think we'll be safe overnight?"

"Very safe. Six boats were in here a few weeks ago."

"So, we can have dinner here, then dinghy back to our boat with no problem?"

"No problem at all. It just gets a little choppy at high tide."

It is still morning, but we make arrangements now for an early dinner. I discuss the menu with Friedel and settle on salad, grilled snapper, and an apple cake for Günter's birthday. I select an Australian Riesling from the display of empty bottles on the bar. Friedel says he will chill one for us in advance.

We hightail it for *Pacific Bliss* and undertake anchoring maneuvers. We have to anchor twice before we are satisfied, making certain that we have sufficient swinging room should the wind direction change.

Günter snorkels in his "birthday suit" to check the anchor. It is sufficiently buried in sand. Now we can have lunch on board *Pacific Bliss* and, after that, our usual siesta!

To pass the time until dinner is ready, we dinghy back to the beach, tie up to the post, and strap on our Tevas®. Then we walk across the reef, which is now exposed at low tide. This is the one that connects the Blue Lagoon's island of Foe'ata with the neighboring Foelifuka. Toward the middle of the reef, we introduce ourselves to two sure-footed Tongan women who are collecting rock oysters. We watch, fascinated as they use mallets to pound the oysters free from the slippery reef and then pile them into woven banana-leaf baskets. We continue to walk the reef. Farther on another woman, grinning proudly, shows us a handful of live shellfish she has found. I count five blue starfish hugging the rocks.

Turning to Günter, I remind him, "Just like the ones we saw earlier, while we were snorkeling in Anchorage #7! Should we take one back?"

"Nein! It would just fade to that white, bleached kind that you can buy at the pier in San Diego."

As the tide turns, we head back to *Pacific Bliss*. We sit there, contented, in the late afternoon sun. The sea slowly covers the connecting reefs again. "This is not only a Moment of Bliss," Günter says. "It is a Day of Bliss." As if on cue, a huge turtle lazily swims past the hull, spotlighted in the golden glow.

At dinnertime, Friedel greets us like long-lost friends. He introduces us to his wife, Ma'ata, a long-haired, buxom brunette who is obviously Tongan. She wears a full-length pink-and-red sheath. With a sweet voice, she greets us warmly.

Seated at a private table in an alcove directly overlooking the beach, we visit with Friedel, sipping chilled wine from antique crystal goblets. A burgundy cloth covers the square table, and a white starched linen cloth lies diagonally across it. In the center of the table sits a colorful hurricane candle, while a bouquet of bright fuchsia bougainvillea graces the table's edge. All very picturesque.

Behind my chair stands an dusty old wooden hutch filled with books in German and English. I cannot resist. I turn and select a well-worn, hardcover book, *Queen Sālote of Tonga*.

"Do you know about her?" Friedel asks.

"All I know is that she made the Tongan royalty famous on the day she rode in a torrential downpour to Queen Elizabeth's coronation in London. It is

1. The birthday boy shows off his buns; 2. The beach at the Blue Lagoon, Tonga; 3. Friedel poses with the wooden mermaid at his restaurant.

said that she refused to let them raise the top of her carriage out of respect for the Queen."

"Yes. The Tongans may criticize the King, but they never had anything but good to say about Queen Sālote. You may read the book. Just make sure to return it."

I promise to get Friedel's book back to him. Günter promises to bring some German books from our ship's library.

Conversation roams from Tongan to German politics, then to how 9-11-2001 and the hurricane of 1-1-2002 have hurt Tongan tourism. Günter queries Friedel about his background. "How did you happen to end up here, with Ma'ata, your charming Tongan wife, and four children?"

"I just got tired of Germany," he says.

"So did I," Günter replies.

Friedel tells us that he went to chef school in Germany, then worked for two famous Munich restaurants before coming to Tonga. He was en route to Hong Kong when he ran into an old chef school friend from New Zealand who said that Tonga Resort, on Tongatapu Island, needed a chef. After a few years of working for others, he started the Blue Lagoon from scratch. That was three years ago. He had leased the island for 50 years. He has steadily built up this remarkable, funky-but-special resort. "And I do what I want here," he adds. "If I don't feel like cooking some days, I don't."

By the time we begin our second glass of wine, we have switched to Cruiser Talk. "I can't believe how cheap some cruisers are," Friedel complains. "Once we had twelve boats in the lagoon for ten days, and all they bought were two orange juices. Two! But those who only stop on the island to throw their trash on the shore are the worst."

I feel ashamed. That kind of behavior reflects badly on all cruisers. Günter talks about the Seven Seas Association to which we belong and explains its motto: "Leave only a clean wake."

Friedel isn't mollified. "And some of them come on to the island and just start fanning out, looking at the *fales*. They even entered one of the bungalows, where a couple—my guests—were there in bed!"

"Can't you just tell them to leave, that this is private property?" I ask.

"I do. One of them told me: 'The beaches belong to everybody.'"

"How about a sign marked PRIVATE?"

"No, I couldn't do that," Friedel says. "It would remind me too much of Germany, where *everything* is VERBOTEN."

"Well, I have to cook for you now." Friedel lights the candle on our table. The sun beyond the beach slowly drops into the sea.

And what a cooking this is! We start with a cream of mushroom soup like none we have ever had before.

"This is great!" Günter says with relish. "I have not tasted such good food since French Polynesia." He dives into the pasta that accompanies the main course, trying to restrain himself, but to no avail.

I revel in the moist red snapper slathered with a delicate sauce. The accompanying salad, papaya with lettuce and vegetables, is topped with yet another delicate sauce.

"I'm in heaven here. I love birthdays," Günter pronounces.

But I'm no longer paying attention to the food. I'm looking out at the beach. "I hate to destroy your mood, but the sea seems to be slapping our dinghy around."

Günter rises abruptly and heads for the railing. "Uh, oh. It's not even hooked to the post any longer."

I follow him to the railing. "I think it's taking water over the transom!"

"I'll go down and check. You stay here and finish your meal."

But Ma'ata and I follow him.

Günter has raced down three flights of stairs and along the beach. He has reached the dinghy when we catch up with him. We see him struggling with *Petite Bliss*, which is half-filled with water by now. He is standing knee deep in the water. He motions for me to join him.

Ma'ata and I jump into the water and hurry to him. Günter is bailing furiously. We grab other containers and begin to bail as well. Soon the dinghy is manageable and the three of us tug and pull it back and higher onto the beach. The wet sand sucks at my bare feet. I'm soaked with saltwater to my waist.

"I thought we'd pulled it well up…we even secured it," Günter mumbles.

Ma'ata shrugs it off. "It happens sometimes at high tide with a new moon. Slips right off the post."

Back in the restaurant, we ask Friedel about the tides. He tells us that, at this time of the month, they can change by as much as two meters. Sometimes the sea spills over the fringing reefs from three sides. Günter slumps in his chair and sighs. "Looks like we can never relax. Even on my birthday."

"That's cruising." It's my turn to shrug.

Well into our second year of this cruising life, I'm used to it. I know by now to always expect the unexpected.

I pick at the rest of my meal. After a few minutes, the restaurant lights flicker and die. But we have a candle on our table. Soon the electricity is on again. Günter's apple cake arrives; it is square, with one large white candle in the center. He blows out the candle with one puff, but he doesn't share his wish. All I know is that he has regained his birthday spirit.

"My treat, birthday boy." I settle our bill and we

rise to leave.

We hug goodbyes with Ma'ata and Friedel, promising to return someday.

"I will *never* forget *this* birthday." Günter shakes his head. Then he breaks into a wide grin.

Boarding the dinghy at high tide is quite an exercise. The confused waves have run over the fringing reefs from three directions, racing toward the sandy beach. We can see the night light of *Pacific Bliss* bobbing frantically as if to say, *come rescue me*. I hike my *pareu* around my waist. We pull the dinghy into the water.

"The Queen enters first. I'll hold it," Günter says. But there is no way to keep dry, with waves slapping at my behind. By the time I make it over the slippery side, I am soaked for the second time!

Now, it is Günter's turn. He makes it almost over the top, but then slides back into the drink. With one huge lunge, he pulls himself over the side again. He is totally drenched.

Our next hurdle is the outboard motor. Will it start? Fortunately, we had bailed out the dinghy before the motor could get soaked. But this will be the moment of truth. Hrrrruuummn! *Petite Bliss* purrs. We're in business, and we reach the boat over choppy waves.

We strip naked before we enter the salon. Then we pile our saltwater-drenched clothes into the galley sink, lay dry towels over the salon seats, and collapse with loud groans. We stare at each other across the table and, suddenly, burst into uncontrollable laughter.

"I'll never forget *this* birthday!" Günter gasps.

"You mean it was all worth it after all?" I giggle.

"Worth it? Absolutely! It's the best birthday I've ever had in my life!"

"It's not over yet, birthday boy. I still have that surprise for you.…"

Heavy Weather in Anchorage #16
18°43.4′S, 174°06′W, the lee shore of Vaka'eitu

"The sky is crying," Günter says as he snuggles next to me at the salon table. "It's pouring cats and dogs again."

"So we hunker down… I don't mind. There's so much to do in our little world. And with just you and me, I'm cozy and content."

Last night, we watched the first two installments of the TV series *Horatio Hornblower*. Hornblower joins the British Royal Navy at the outset of the Napoleonic Wars and rises quickly from raw recruit to seasoned sailor. We were cuddled close, just as we are now, with the laptop in front of us. The family on board *Windarra*, anchored next to us, loaned us this DVD series, part of their 125-DVD collection. They planned ahead for entertaining their two children on board. We look forward to viewing more of this series tonight. There were 15-knot winds outside, but our anchor didn't drag, so I am confident we're secure against any weather that might kick up tonight. This is a lee shore; however, it is sandy, should we drag anchor. It's a cozy little neighborhood out here today in Anchorage #16. *Gitano* has just anchored between us and the shore. A long navy-colored monohull, *Bucephelous*, is on one side. *Harmony*, *Final Straw*, *Windarra*, and a charter boat take up the other.

After clearing breakfast, we transmit our e-mails and my website update via SailMail. It is an unusually fast connection today. Günter plays a Jimmy Buffet CD. Then he sits back at the salon table to begin a book by a German author, Richard von Weizsäcker. "Some food for the mind," he says, "after a diet of junk detective novels." I'm deep into the biography of Queen Sālote, the book I borrowed from Friedel. All is calm on board. But not for long.

At 1050, the rain changes into sheets of wind that blow sideways. *Pacific Bliss* swings 180° so that our bow is facing the sea, with the stern towards the shore. We worry about *Pacific Bliss* slamming into *Gitano*. By 1055, the wind increases to 32 knots. With gusts to Force 7, a near gale, Günter starts both engines. He guns the boat forward a little to release the load on the anchor. Then he takes the engines back to neutral but keeps them running. The anchor, even with the 180° twist, appears to be deeply buried in the sand. We are relieved that we have put out 120 feet of chain; the longer the chain, the less chance of dragging.

I fix a hot tea, laced with lemon and rum to calm our nerves. Then Günter goes back into the storm to bail buckets of water out of the dinghy.

I set up the laptop again. We settle in to watch more of Horatio Hornblower, the ultimate high-seas hero, encountering roiling sea battles, mutiny, plague, and love, but always proving himself equal to the task. The storm rages outside our cozy salon as we cheer on Horatio in "The Duchess and the Devil." Our anchor is holding. I insert the next DVD: "The Wrong War." The storm continues as I insert "The Mutiny." Horatio's getting out of one scrape and into another, reminding us of our own adventures at sea. Finally, the storm eases as night descends peacefully on Anchorage #16.

Unlike Horatio Hornblower, we cruisers do not have to seek adventure; it comes to us!

The *WhaleSong* Tour

We have returned from "the anchorages" back to Neiafu harbor. We see the *WhaleSong* tour boat docked in front of the Mermaid restaurant every time we dinghy from the boat to the bar. Of course, we've known all along that we *will* take this "must do" tour out of Neiafu. We've just been waiting for the weather to clear. By now we realize that it will rain every afternoon, but we don't want to take the tour in an *all-day* rain. My goal is

Günter poses with our helpers in Hunga.

to not only *see* the famous mother humpback whale and her baby, but to *photograph* them. Today is the day.

The pilot steers the tour boat from one bay to another as the tour guide drones on. I presume that she knows where the whales are; she just wants to build up the suspense! We spot a few humpbacks, too far away for a good photo, but finally we come upon the key attraction. The guide spots the mother with her baby. The driver slowly motors toward them. Then he stops and the boat drifts. "Time to get on your equipment," she yells. Günter is ready to jump in. I'm ready with my camera. The guide leads the group of snorkelers. "Follow me, and do not leave the group!" she admonishes.

From here, I'll leave the story telling to Günter, as he wrote it for our website:

The Eye of the Whale: A Moment of Bliss
By Günter

Our guide spots a mother humpback whale with her calf; she orders the driver to approach them slowly. Then at the spot where we had last seen them, the four of us on this excursion, along with our guide, take to the water with our snorkeling gear. With my face down, I do not see anything right away. Suddenly, I see something right below me—big and white. Then I realize that what I am seeing is the mother on her back, letting the calf drink her milk. In the next moment, the calf begins to surface very close to me, just a few arm lengths away. It comes up and looks at me with a large black eye as large as a dinner plate. I am mesmerized. I cannot move.

I feel intimately connected to this animal in a very friendly way. I have a very strong urge to touch it. So I swim a few feet toward it and reach out with my arm. That is too close for the whale's comfort! The calf rolls on its back and paddles away from me with a few powerful strokes of its large flippers. In doing this, one of its flippers hits me on the right shoulder. It feels like being slapped with a big piece of wood. I'm not injured, but the spell is broken. I become concerned that the mother will surface and toss me into the air. However, she doesn't; she is a gracious creature who forgives my intrusion.

The Moment of Bliss in which I felt deeply connected to this fellow animal is gone. What is left is a scolding from the guide. I had violated the rules of engagement in the Whale Watcher's Guide. I feel like a little schoolboy being reprimanded by the principal. But she is right. It is a very dangerous thing that I did.

Back in the anchorages, we find a houseboat with a sign saying ARK GALLERY. We motor over with our dinghy. We tell Sheri, the artist/owner, about Günter's experience. "Then you will want a souvenir of that experience," she says. "Here's a set of plaques that I painted of those whales. One of the humpback surfacing. The other, as you can see, of the baby swimming above the mother."

I love them! There is no need to negotiate. I pay the price. I know exactly where they will hang in our home.

Shark Attack!

"Volunteers needed!" says a loud voice on the VHF6, the Tonga Cruisers Net in Neiafu. "We are asking for volunteers to give donations of A-positive blood to be stored for Felipe. He will be transported to the hospital in Nukualofa. We also need contributions. We just learned that the Army will not—I repeat, will *not*—pick up the cost of his flight."

It had first been reported that the accident had occurred near the *WhaleSong,* where the sharks were evidently attracted by the baby whale. Felipe had been leading a group of snorkeling whale watchers. But later another story came out: in a bag at his hip, fastened to his belt, Felipe had been swimming with a dead fish that he had recently speared. A lone tiger shark lunged for that bag, and in the process gouged a hole in the swimmer's thigh. All whale watching expeditions have been cancelled. The authorities are concerned that even snorkeling here might be dangerous.

At first it was reported that the boy would lose his leg. But Dr. Bob on *Harmony*, one of the cruising fleet, had managed to tie off the blood vessels and ligaments before he would be transported to the main hospital in Tonga's capital city.

By evening the cruisers and the islanders have put together a fundraiser at Ana's Waterfront Café. (The café is a remarkable success story in and of itself: It is fashioned around the hull of a sailing vessel swept into the café by Cyclone Waka. The owners just left it there and reconstructed their restaurant around it!) The fundraiser is successful: Over 4000 pa'anga (US $2000) have been raised to date. The army had reportedly asked for 2000 pa'anga for the transport. The remainder would be used for Felipe's rehabilitation.

Upon returning to *Pacific Bliss*, I research "shark attacks" in our three guides. The only other reported tiger shark attack was in 1992, off Tapana, when a Spanish man was attacked while spear fishing there.

Thankfully, Felipe recovers. We wonder when the *WhaleSong*—a key attraction here—will resume its tours.

Voyage of the *Victoria*

In the early morning mist, Günter and I sit in the cockpit, enjoying our morning coffee, when a ghost ship from the past pulls into Anchorage #8 and drops anchor. The big, brooding vessel, over 60 feet long, made of unpainted wood and iron, flies a Czech flag and has the letters V I C T O R I A chiseled into her squared-off wooden transom. A couple of unkempt young men wearing cut-offs and T-shirts let the chain down, hand over hand. It seems to clunk on forever. Clearly, quite a few young men and women are on board. We are intrigued. What is the story behind this ship? We intend to find out.

We befriend the sailors and are soon invited for a

tour. "The original *Victoria*," says Ivan, the captain, "was the only surviving ship of the five ships that Ferdinand Magellan started out with when he circumnavigated the globe. Only 18 sailors lived through that voyage. Most died of hunger and disease. And Magellan himself died during battles with the locals in the Philippines."

No wonder this *Victoria* looks like a ship from the past! She is a replica of a 16th century vessel, 1519 to be exact. That's when Magellan sailed from Seville, Spain, with 5 ships and 270 men to become the first to sail around the world.

"What made you want to build and sail this boat?" Günter asks.

"We wanted to repeat the circumnavigation of *Victoria*," Ivan says. "So we started by purchasing a forest in Czech, in the Orlické Mountains. Then we looked for the perfect tree for the mast. We began building the boat in 1995 and didn't complete her until 1998, when we launched her from Stetten, Poland."

"What are her statistics?" I ask.

"She is 23 by 5 meters long; she weighs 60 tons and draws 3 meters."

"How long have you been sailing the *Victoria*?" I ask.

"We had planned our official start of the circumnavigation in 1999 and thought we would be in Athens in time for the 2004 Summer Olympics. Unfortunately, we didn't make it. Now we have no long-term plan, no sponsors anymore. We just want to remain independent."

"Where have you been so far?" I am still curious.

"Of course, we took the route through the Strait of Magellan, as the original *Victoria* did in the 16th century. Basically, we've been following Magellan's route through the Sea of the South, which he named the Pacific Ocean."

"What about crew?" Günter asks.

"Martina and Mirek here joined *Victoria* in Chile six months ago. They will leave the ship in New Zealand. Martina and Henry always get seasick; they pass each other to and from the head. Michael here even had his father on board for a time. Rudolf is the most experienced. He made a voyage from 1990 to1993 around Antarctica in *Polaris*, a homemade boat. But we are all tired. I plan to put *Victoria* in dry dock in New Zealand. I plan only one year ahead now."

We walk and talk throughout the boat. The winch had been taken from an old railroad. The hull is made of spruce because it has the most epoxy. The chain locker contains 150 meters (450 feet) of chain, which the crew feeds out by hand.

In the galley, an old metal bread pan sits atop a decrepit stove with the metal rusted through in spots. "We made wood fires in the cold climates," Ivan says. "But here in the tropics, baking down below is Hell."

The sleeping quarters have bunks for 12, the maximum they have had on board. "Obviously, we lost some of our original crew." Ivan shakes his head. "This kind of life doesn't appeal to everyone."

I can't imagine getting any crew who is not conscripted agreeing to live in these conditions.

In return for the tour, we are asked for something cold. We dinghy back to *Pacific Bliss* and return shortly with a supply of beer. "To the Czech Navy," Günter toasts. Cold beer goes over very well with this disillusioned captain and his crew. As we leave, I wish them well. But secretly, I feel that Magellan's chances for success were far better than theirs.

Lucy's Hair Salon

Having one's hair colored in a foreign country is always an opportunity to get in on the local gossip. Lucy runs the Unisex Salon. Her salon is the best because it is the *only* one in town. Lucy is also the hairdresser to the Royal Family, she tells me. A mother of seven, she doesn't sit around, even though she had a stroke three weeks ago. "Just do what you love," the wise Tongan doctor told her. "You will gradually improve." Before opening her shop today at 11 o'clock, she had a doctor's appointment at 8:45. And before that, she had done the princess' hair at 5:30! Yesterday, beginning at 9:30, she had done the entire Royal Family's hairdos.

"For how many?" I ask.

"Seventeen."

I gasp. "And how long did that take you?"

"All night. I didn't sleep last night. I left the palace at 4:30."

Given the circumstances and her illness, I'm surprised she opened her shop today! I love this plucky woman. I can't stop talking with her. "What do you think of the Royal Family?"

"We love them. We love our princess. She is a princess of the people. She is beautiful, like Diana. She comes to all of our functions. She likes all of us."

So much for democracy in this kingdom. They love their royals!

I discover that Lucy had five children with her ex-husband, who is now in New Zealand. Her present husband is a doctor, and she has two boys by him. "I have a nice home," she volunteers. "It has hot water. Here, only cold water. Ladies love cold water. In my shower here, I sit on a plastic chair and just let cold water run for a long time."

"We can't do that on our yacht," I tell her. "We have to make our own water from the sea, so we use it sparingly."

"You can come in here and use my shower any time you want," Lucy offers. "All the water you want…I know you have to get that salt off."

"Thanks Lucy, but that's okay. We take short

showers."

"I mean it. Anytime. And you're welcome to bring your jugs to fill up here. I only pay three dollars a month for water."

After washing the dye, Lucy comments on my fine hair. "Europeans have thinner hair than us. That's because of our diet. We Tongans are a strong people and we have strong hair. I will put this product on to strengthen your roots. It's like a fertilizer, the kind that makes plants grow. It will make your hair thicker. This first application is free. You try it. Then come back in three days to show me."

"I can't do that, Lucy. We'll be back out at the anchorages."

"Okay. You come back before you leave Tonga, then."

"I will. Where does the product come from?"

"America." Lucy stands up straight and grins. "It's a new thing. My sister in Seattle sent it to me."

Dedications in Tonga

Dedications in Tonga are a big deal. The first one I experienced was shortly after we arrived in Tonga when I attended the dedication of an elementary school. I arrived at the stated time, but apparently these events run on island time. And island time means take your time. Being early, I had the privilege of watching the preparations. Teachers decorated the speaker's podium with Tongan mats, then they fastened them in the back with rolls of duct tape. The King was in attendance, but he was hidden from view from most of the audience by a pole holding up the canopy! His wife slept through part of the long speeches, even though one of them was given by the president of French Polynesia.

Today's dedication of the new Arts and Handicrafts Center is more elaborate—perhaps because this event is managed by artists instead of educators. A wide platform at the front spans the width of the long rectangular hall. Tapa cloth is positioned on the steps where the governor of Vavau and the princess will walk to their seats. Their chairs are also draped with mats. Huge, woven mats are hung at the same height on all of the walls. Tables piled with handicraft displays line the sides and back of the hall.

Surprise. The event actually starts on time! The princess takes her seat on the stage and with a desultory stare fans herself during the long dedication speech. After the speech comes a long-winded prayer. Halfway through the speeches, an intermission allows us to walk around the hall and study the handicrafts which are for sale. The governor and princess dutifully round the tables. I watch them walk up to each display and talk with the artist. At one booth, I see a humongous carved wooden whale hanging from the rafters. At other booths, I find beautifully woven bags, placemats, baskets, and bowls.

The ceremony continues. The princess speaks in Tongan and then English. "We have so many guests visiting us in Vavau. Welcome! May you enjoy your stay here." Her warmth is contagious. After the princess speaks, the dancing begins: First, small children perform, facing her. Then a group of boys dance in front of her, with their backs to the audience! Lastly a group of Tongan women, with one lone white woman, dance gracefully, and yet sensuously.

At the end of the performances, we all rise as the princess and royals step down from the dais and walk along the aisles toward the rear of the hall, shaking hands. I'm seated right on the aisle. The princess reaches out and grasps my hand with a firm, confident handshake. She looks me right in the eye. Her smile is genuine, warm, and inviting.

I like it here. I appreciate the Tongan community, its people and events. I enjoy the camaraderie of other cruisers, the enchantment of the outer islands and anchorages, and the warmth of shopkeepers and restaurateurs. Life is good here. I could settle in for a while.

Giving Is Receiving.

Hunga Lagoon, Ika Lahi Resort, Vavau, Tonga

Branches flailed against corrugated iron roofs. The wind rose like an approaching freight train, moaning through the shuttered windows and doors of the little village on the hill above Hunga Lagoon. Fierce gusts found their way deep into the homes of the huddled occupants, causing the flames of their kerosene lanterns to flicker and tremble. Entire groves of Frangipani trees toppled like lines of dominoes. The angry wind had already ripped away their leaves and flowers.

But that was only the beginning of Cyclone Waka's fury this past New Year's Eve.

What sadistic irony! Exactly two years after they appeared on television channels around the world—the first to celebrate the New Millennium—the joyous dancers of Tonga entered this New Year frightened and full of despair.

In Vavau, Tonga's most beautiful and treasured island group, the sea slammed against the shorelines, devouring everything in its path. Waka destroyed docks, overturned boats, and ground churches, schoolhouses, and hospitals to rubble. Even in the relatively protected harbor of Neiafu, a catamaran broke loose of its moorings and flew right into Ana's Waterfront Café, where for some weeks afterward the owners continued to carry on business around it.

Most of the waterfront docks and structures had to be rebuilt. The governments of other South Pacific countries such as French Polynesia contributed workers and materials to rebuild schools and hospitals.

Ika Lahi Resort in Hunga Lagoon.

Missions and charities rebuilt churches and handed out food necessary for survival. But for the inhabitants of Vavau, there was no such thing as government aid to rebuild. Nine months later, these poor people are still recovering.

In Hunga, the village near where *Pacific Bliss* is anchored, the villagers staggered drunkenly in the wind as their homes fell around them, the sand stinging their faces like icy sleet. They ran for cover to whatever dwelling was still standing, carrying a few meager possessions with them. Coconuts thudded on roofs and cisterns with the force of exploding cannonballs. Shade trees were uprooted and torn apart until none were left standing in the little village. Every gust of wind hurled more branches and debris against any structure left standing until the landscape was finally flat.

Then came the rains.

Water rushed and swirled until horrid, twisting ravines replaced pleasant, tree-lined paths. When it was all over, the villagers struggled to rebuild their simple homes out of the muddy mess.

But then came the sun.

The rays shone mercilessly down upon their barren and ugly world. They had no protecting shade. They labored under the sun's cruel glare for weeks on end.

Afa, the storm, was over in a few days. But the devastation it wrought would seemingly last forever. During this time of misery, the villagers found it hard to believe that beauty would ever again come to Vavau.

But it has! Lush vegetation *has* returned to Tonga's beloved Vavau. Nevertheless, there's no escaping the lasting effects of Cyclone Waka. Overturned boats and canoes still line the shores and reefs of the anchorages and lagoons. And the luxuriant new growth cannot hide Vavau's uprooted trees, sawed-off tree trunks, and stacks of old wood. For the 80 percent of the population who live off the land, recovery is particularly painful and slow. It can take ten years for a coconut tree to bear fruit. Replanting right after the storm meant using nuts the farmers could have used immediately for food. Newly-planted banana plants will not bear fruit until the following year. The most immediate crop is the *papalangi* (European) vegetables—such as tomatoes, cucumbers, lettuce, string beans, and cabbage—the produce that we have been enjoying here. These vegetables could be produced quickly and sold at the markets in Neiafu in return for nails and building materials. Fish from the sea, of course, was another source of income.

Nine months after the horrible effects of Cyclone Waka, Günter and I are enjoying all the bounty that Vavau has to offer. We have purchased fresh produce at the markets. We have feasted our eyes on the lush landscapes, pearly beaches, and multihued rock formations of the islands. We have frolicked and snorkeled in the emerald green waters of the lagoons. By the time we anchor off the Ika Lahi Gamefishing Lodge in Hunga Lagoon, Günter and I have decided that we want to give back.

I consider how to go about it. In the past we have had unfortunate experiences with giving to village chiefs and matriarchs. We would find out later that our

Loaf Island in Vavau, Tonga.

gifts were not distributed to the needy families and children. Many times our donations were resold for profit. So after breakfast at the Lodge, I seek the advice of the friendly New Zealand proprietress.

"I've had bad experiences with giving as well," she says, tossing her long red hair. "One of my vacationers, a doctor from New Zealand, gave a box of medical supplies to the clinic in the village up over the hill. Hundreds of dollars worth. That should have lasted the little village an entire year or more! Yet a few days later a villager came asking at the resort for a tube of antiseptic cream. He had a badly skinned knee. 'Have you been to your nurse?' I asked him. 'He should have some.' It turned out that the nurse at the clinic had sent the entire box to his family in Nukualofa, where they sold them all!"

"Would it be better if I walk house to house and distribute gifts where they're needed?" I ask.

"Hmm," she answers. "You could, if you had someone to point out the needy families. I know! I'll ask Moule to accompany you after her shift. She is done working at the Lodge by noon. She herself comes from a family of nine, and they could use some help."

I return to our table where Günter is picking up the tab. I tell him what I've discovered. Then I suggest that we start with our unopened box of 96 servings of Idaho potato flakes. "Moule's family would be perfect for that."

Before we leave the Lodge, the owner introduces me to Moule. She is a teenager with a wide but shy smile and an unusually slight frame for a Tongan. She agrees to lead us to her village at noon. When she calls on the VHF, we find that she has enlisted the help of two Tongan girlfriends who live in the village high on the hill.

The girls accompany us to *Pacific Bliss*. There we gather tins of food, clothing, shampoo, bars of soap, and cosmetics. Then, back on land, we trudge up a narrow footpath for what seems like forever, carrying everything in bags and backpacks. Finally we reach the crest of the hill. Cyclone Waka has destroyed everything! Not a tree stands. There is no longer a jungle, not even a path to lead to the village clearing. Such devastation is shocking. All I see is a pitiful assortment of run-down, hastily built bamboo huts. What misery and poverty! I feel like crying.

Moule leads us to the first hut, where her own family lives. I give the introductory speech I have prepared. Moule translates for her family. "We travel and live on a boat called *Pacific Bliss*. We are moored by the Lodge in your very beautiful Hunga Lagoon. You are blessed with such wonderful Nature here. Because your lagoon has given us so much pleasure, we want to give back to your village. We understand that your village suffered a horrible cyclone and that it will take a long time to recover. So we want to help by giving you some small gifts and food."

I explain how to use the Idaho mashed potatoes by heating water and then stirring it in. Then we let each of the family members choose a T-shirt from our bag. Afterward, I distribute cosmetics and soaps to the women.

The King of Tonga (left) and the President of French Polynesia (right) speak at the dedication of a new school in Vavau, attended by students, teachers, and cruisers.

One of the needy families in Hunga to whom we distributed gifts.

Günter holds up a petite princess-waist dress that we had purchased in a used-clothing store. "Who can fit into this?" he jokes.

"Not any of *us*!" Everyone laughs.

Moule appears to be the only lean one of the family, but the dress is too small even for her.

Our second stop is a bent-over widow with scraggly gray hair whose children had left Vavau for Tongatapu, the main island of Tonga. She seldom hears from them. She lives alone in a tiny dilapidated one-room shack. We leave her a supply of tinned food and a bag filled with soaps and shampoos.

"I'll begin to eat this today," she says haltingly, holding up a can of chicken breast.

Next we visit a man whose leg has been crushed in an accident. He sleeps on the floor, on a woven mat. There is no other furniture in the hut. We leave him cans of stew and trust that someone will come in to make it for him.

After this a wizened grandmother, who looks to be over a hundred years old, breaks into a wide, toothless grin as she sees the food we carry. We can't imagine her being able to chew! So Günter hands her a stack of canned soups.

We go from home to home on bare ground that is broken only by thin tufts of grass. No landscaping or flowers grace these homes.

This is the poorest, most downtrodden village I have ever seen in my life!

Later, Günter turns to Moule, "You chose the eight needy families well." He tries to lighten the mood. "But I'm still worried about finding a Tongan girl to fit into this small dress."

"I know a lady who has a small daughter," Moule laughs.

We head toward their house. The daughter is quite small. The dress will fit. After my standard speech about our enjoying the bounty of the lagoon, the mother says, "But I don't have anything to give *you* in return."

Moule assures her that it is okay; we expect nothing in return.

Our trip has been well-planned. Our bags are empty—except for some nail polish and costume jewelry. We give these to the girls who have helped us so cheerfully. They are amazed and flattered. As they walk us down the hill and back to our dinghy, we again emphasize how much we appreciate the beauty of Vavau and the wonderful friendliness of the Tongan people. I do not know whether they understand what I mean, but I do know that Günter and I will treasure this special day in our hearts for the rest of our lives.

A special thanks to each of you who contributed clothing and gifts at our Bon Voyage Party in San Diego.

The Puddle Jumpers' Party

No, these jumpers are not a kind of clothing; they are the Pacific Crossing Class of 2002.

The Coconut Milk Run begins with the Puddle Jump—the crossing of the Pacific. It ends in Tonga, where cruisers converge one last time before heading to New Zealand or to Fiji to "winter" their boats through the cyclone season.

And this is the big night out—with lots of food, music, and dancing. The liquid flows tonight!

Teri of *Tauranga* (meaning safe harbor) introduces herself and her husband as we enter the hotel. "Dennis and Tina of *Alii Kai* told us to be sure to meet you," she tells us. "They said you two are a lot of fun."

"We look forward to seeing them again in Fiji," Günter says. "We'll tell them hello for you."

Keith and Susan, from *C'est la Vie,* greet us with equal friendliness. They are managing the T-shirt sales of the event. We can choose a white, black, or blue shirt displaying a dancing dolphin and the words *Puddle Jump 2002*. We choose blue.

"I love you guys." Keith hugs both of us at once. "I want to go through the Red Sea and the Suez Canal with *Pacific Bliss*," he says.

"We don't want to go the Cape of Good Hope route," adds Susan.

"Okay." I reply. "I hope we can all form a flotilla and hire a gunboat, complete with AK47s, to lead the way through Pirate Alley."

"We'll be sailing the Med together, then," Susan says, her voice certain and sure.

As we walk farther into the long room, a group of New Zealanders takes the stage. They belt out some sort of Kiwi song, loud and off-key. They are feeling no pain.

The fiddlers from *Gitana* and *Irish Melody* perform an Irish jig; Leslie of *North Road* and Louise of *Little Gem* croon western tunes; cruisers from *Free Radical* and *Zephyr* hand out free CDs from their websites. And the hit of the program is a parody of "The Man Who Never Returns," written especially for Clark of *Final Straw*. Clark had been the master organizer of the Puddle Jumpers; his voice was a mainstay on the SSB and VHF. After the song Clark and his wife Suzy join us for a drink. We kid Clark about his reputation for being the most talkative of the Puddle Jumpers, and they kid us about our sitting so close, like lovers, on our yacht's double helm seat.

Later, little Sarah of *Windarra* tells us about how she handles cruising and home schooling. "Our official school-on-board lessons began yesterday," she says. "Our lessons are mailed to us from our school in Seattle. We pick them up in each port."

Her brother Jesse joins us to thank Günter for helping him with a science project.

Cruising boats anchored in Vavau's Harbor of Refuge.

The garden behind a restaurant on an island in Vavau.

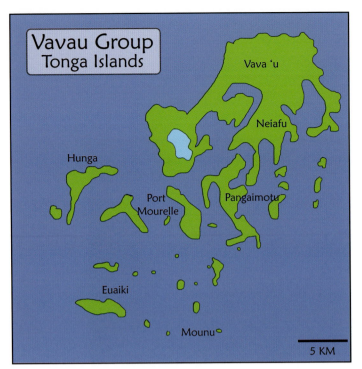

The room is packed with cruisers who fill the evening with wonderful stories, music, laughter, and dance.

As we return to the anchorage, we're thinking how lucky we are to be part of this cruiser culture. Back on *Pacific Bliss*, we can still hear Louise belting out country western songs.

The Long Goodbye

It is early morning and the deck is wet with dew. A dozen masts are reflected in the still waters of the harbor. The rising sun is still hidden behind the hills of Vavau. Wispy, mauve-pink clouds line the entire sky. The roosters of Neiafu have been crowing for over an hour now. It's a beautiful morning to say goodbye.

I know that Tonga will always hold a special place within my heart. I draft a speech for the morning VHF Cruisers Net. "Because *Pacific Bliss* is leaving your beautiful Vavau Group at dawn tomorrow for Vuda Point in Fiji, Günter and I want to say goodbye to all of you who have made our five-week stay here so special. We'll miss Vavau. It will go down as one of our favorite places in all of our circumnavigation."

After my announcement, we tune into the Fiji SSB Net. Dennis and Tina of *Alii Kai* are there now. They inform us that the strong wind advisory for Fiji has been lifted. Good news! Dennis shares the waypoints for the route they took, far south of the Lau Group, skipping Suva as a stopover. We plan to sail straight through and to stay overnight in the Lautoka anchorage, where we will check into Fiji and provision.

Once again, I become a nester, and Günter prepares *Pacific Bliss* for the passage.

Günter and I make one final stop at Fisheries Depot, where the inter-island supply boats dock. We purchase red wine and cheese, but are disappointed to learn they are out of chocolate bars, yogurt, and butter. "Till the ship comes in," the clerk says. We know that line by now. We devour a final pizza at the Ifo Ifo Bar. From there, we stop to say goodbye to Lucy.

"Just a little more fertilizer to thicken your hair before you leave," she implores. "Just sit here for a minute."

I can't say no to her.

"I had to take a nap yesterday afternoon," she gossips. "Too many *palangis* in here, after *you* spread the word."

"But are you happy to have the business from these foreigners?" I ask.

"Of course! Thank you. But I was tired."

After leaving Lucy's, we sign out on the Yachtie Board at the Mermaid, the final cruiser ritual prior to departing.

We motor out of port in the morning. I photograph the King's red-roofed palace, high on the hill and, next to it, the newly dedicated elementary school which glows in the sun. To our port is the island of Hunga and straight ahead, the open sea.

Luafata shines brilliantly in the sun, while surf slaps against the majestic shores of Matahunga. I say goodbye to Swallows Cave on Kapa, to Mariner's Cave on Nuapapu, and to the loaf-shaped islands of Oto and Ava. Finally, I say goodbye to Hunga, an island laced with precious memories.

I change to bareboat essentials: hat, sunglasses, and cotton panties to protect my buns from the hot vinyl seat. Then I slather on suntan lotion. I keep looking back at the Vavau Group until the islands fade from sight and only the blues of sky and water remain. Perhaps we *will* be back. Who knows? Now, almost halfway into our circumnavigation, I don't remember missing a place quite this much.

The sea swells are higher now, but with a full main and jib, on a broad reach, in a 12-knot wind, the sailing is nice and easy. This is our final passage of the season. In Fiji, we will prepare the boat for storage in Vuda Point's hurricane hole.

Goodbye, Friendly Isles. You are aptly named.

Cruisers celebrate the end of the season at the Puddle Jumpers' Party. Dancers at the dedication of a new cultural center in Neiafu

MESSING WITH BOATS

Lists and Lessons Learned
by Günter

We are now in the Kingdom of Tonga, at Neiafu in the Vavau group of islands. This is cruising heaven: scenic islands close together, nice bars and restaurants on the waterfront, and everything is reasonably priced. There are many boats here, waiting to continue their voyages either to New Zealand or to Fiji, just like us. This is a good time, because it has been raining for a few days, to reflect on our experience with *Pacific Bliss* from a hardware and performance point of view.

The following list appears long, but when we compare our experience with that of other cruisers we have met along the way, it is not excessive. And we never once regretted having bought a Catana 431. We are still very happy with, and proud of, *Pacific Bliss*.

1. Spinnaker

We had a rule not to fly our spinnaker at apparent winds above 15 knots. Well, one night on the way to the Marquesas, the wind gusted up to 20 knots. When we tried to get the spinnaker down, making some mistakes, it wrapped around the forestay. The sock did not come down anymore, and we had to lower the spinnaker by the halyard. The wind got very nasty and banged the collar against the forestay and broke it. It also ripped the spinnaker foot at several places. A big mess. We needed to get a new collar from San Diego and had the spinnaker repaired in Raiatea. Our mistake caused a $400 problem.

Lesson learned: Don't fly your spinnaker at night, and take it down early.

2. Alternators

Starboard: We had a second 50-amp alternator (a Volvo upgrade kit) installed on the starboard engine to boost the starboard charging current to a total of 100 amps. This worked very well and reduced the running time for charging batteries. This was necessary because we wanted to keep our freezer and fridge running. The auto helm in strong winds and heavy seas also draws heavy currents.

In Palmerston, just before we wanted to leave on our leg for Niue, I noticed that the SB charging circuit provided 70 amps, but only 40 amps were going into the house bank. Checking the isolator, I found the diode of the house bank lead extremely hot and smoking. The lead was also burned and corroded. After checking with David from Yachtfinders (we could contact him, thanks to our Iridium Satellite telephone), I moved the house bank lead to an empty diode post and disconnected the additional alternator so the charging current was limited to 50 amps.

This worked well for our passage, when we had to motor for about 10 hours.

Now that we are at a mooring in Neiafu, I reconnected the second alternator again, but I am charging only with a maximum current of 70 amps, which I get at 1200 rpm. This works fine.

I ordered another isolator (from San Diego, being shipped to Tonga) rated higher at 160 amps (the old one was 130 amps) and also ordered a much heavier cable. I think the problem started with a marginally-sized cable that corroded at the post and led to higher temperature on the diode, killing the diode. Otherwise, the upgrade is a blessing, because it drastically reduces the charging time.

Port: In Raiatea, I found that the port alternator did not charge anymore. The alternator turned out to be faulty and I had it replaced with a new one coming from Papeete. Since then it charges okay, but always less than the SB single alternator.

3. Windlass

For the second time, the chain stripper on the windlass bent and finally broke loose. I had it repaired in Raiatea. It turned out that the last repair in San Diego was marginal because the screws were stripped, and the mechanic, instead of tapping and putting in the next bigger size, just epoxied the old size back in. I had the whole windlass taken off, which turned out to be difficult, because the axle was not greased at the factory and had rusted to the bushing. We also found out that the contacts of the windlass were completely exposed, so if there is a spare anchor in the locker where the windlass motor is, there is a chance that the anchor will shorten the windlass motor contacts. Not a nice thought considering the hundreds of amps in the windlass circuit! I had a housing built around the contacts to protect them.

Lesson learned: At a minimum, put some tape around the contacts.

4. Watermaker

I have a Spectra® watermaker with two high-pressure feed pumps. One feed pump stopped working. This reduced the flow from about 12 gallons/hr to 6 gallons/hr. This is not a catastrophe; however, I ordered a new feed pump.

5. Sails

One lazy jack line broke twice, which required going up the mast to fix it. Also, most of the bands tying the sail bag to the boom ripped off and need to be replaced. I did a temporary fix with short lines. The lines holding the bag to the mast are also worn and need to be replaced.

6. Water pumps

The port-side house water pump (Johnson)

failed, and I replaced it with a spare one that I had on board. I have a seawater pump installed in the anchor locker to wash the decks. It failed for the second time. (It was replaced in San Diego.) I purchased a new, better one from Papeete that is waterproof and specified for heavy-duty use.

7. Fluxgate compass and cable

At the worst possible moment in the middle of the night with heavy wind and seas on the way to the Marquesas, with over 1000 miles to go, our Autopilot failed. I had an expensive spare kit on board, consisting of fluxgate compass, computer, and rudder position monitor. So we installed the new fluxgate compass on the paneling at the side of the 200-liter fridge (taping it to the fridge) and plugged the cable into the computer (easy, because all the wires are color coded and snap into the connector). After steering a slow 360 to recalibrate, all was okay again. In the next harbor, thinking the faulty part was the fluxgate compass, we replaced the old fluxgate compass (located under the bed in the master cabin) with the new one and connected it to the existing cable.

All worked fine for a while on the next passage; then the same problem occurred again: no Autopilot. Now we realized that the problem was not the fluxgate compass but the cable to the computer. We tried to pull out the old cable but were unsuccessful. It goes around so many inaccessible corners, it would not move.

Lesson learned: Install the fluxgate compass on the side of the steps down to the owner's hull and run the cable through the navigator seat, through the door to the computer. It will work very well that way.

8. Holding tank valves

The plastic valves switching the heads to the holding tanks are about the flimsiest design I know. On the way to San Diego, they froze on both sides and, in the effort to free them, the valve mechanism broke internally. Both were replaced. Large clumps of deposits are forming on these valves. They need to be operated frequently to keep them clear. We missed that chore for a few weeks, and now our SB valve broke again during an effort to free it. Because there is no need for holding tanks in the South Pacific, I thought, to hell with it, we don't need it. However, it is a good idea to regularly exercise all the valves on board.

9. Batteries

On the way to the Marquesas, I observed twice that the battery voltage after charging was not coming up beyond 13 volts and that there was a drain on the batteries, though the Link did not register any currents. We found twice that a battery was getting hot, indicating an internal leakage. We disconnected the faulty batteries and continued on with a reduced house battery size. In Papeete, we could not get any gel batteries at all—especially not the Sonnenschein brand we needed. We moved both engine batteries, which are the same size as the house batteries, into the house bank, replacing the faulty batteries.

For the engine batteries, we purchased regular sealed lead acid automotive batteries of about 80 amp-hour capacity each. This arrangement worked well, and the house batteries held up. That is the good news. The bad news is the following:

The warranty labels on the two engine batteries showed a date of October 2000, close to the date on which *Pacific Bliss* was completed at the Catana factory. The two faulty batteries showed a date of May 1998, more than two years before the boat was completed at the factory. Clearly, these were old batteries beyond their useful life and beyond warranty. The warranty on batteries is typically two years.

10. Solar panel/boom

When reefed, the boom needed to be lifted with the topping lift; otherwise it was not high enough and it hit the solar panels. On one stormy night, we had to put in a triple reef and did not lift the boom high enough. We were running downwind. The boom was resting on the outside SB solar panel and worked a groove into the aluminum frame. The solar panel glass itself shattered like a car windshield after a collision; however, the output did not change. It must still function.

Lesson learned: Keep the boom up when reefed!

Lesson to Catana: Make a bar across the solar panels, so that the boom never can touch the solar panels.

11. Dinghy

Our dinghy deflated on one side twice without any apparent reason. No leaks were observed in the rubber, and after re-inflation it held air well. The first time, in the Marquesas, it happened in the water, resulting in flipping and immersion of the outboard. It took half a day to get the outboard marginally going again. Only after complete disassembly of the carburetor in Raiatea, cleaning the salt out of it, did it run well again. The second time it happened, in Niue, the dinghy was hoisted onto the jetty. Again, no cause for deflation could be determined.

Lesson learned: Always carry a dinghy pump with you. It is a disheartening sight to face a limp dinghy when you are returning from a fun excursion on land.

12. Bilge pumps running

The port engine room bilge pump started to run one day and did not stop. I pulled the little circuit breaker to stop it. Later, in Raiatea, a smart electrical technician found that at the edge of the flat cable in the circuit breaker box in the engine room, a very fine hair-like copper wire bridged the contact of the bilge pump circuit and provided power to it.

Lesson Learned: Clip to solve the problem.

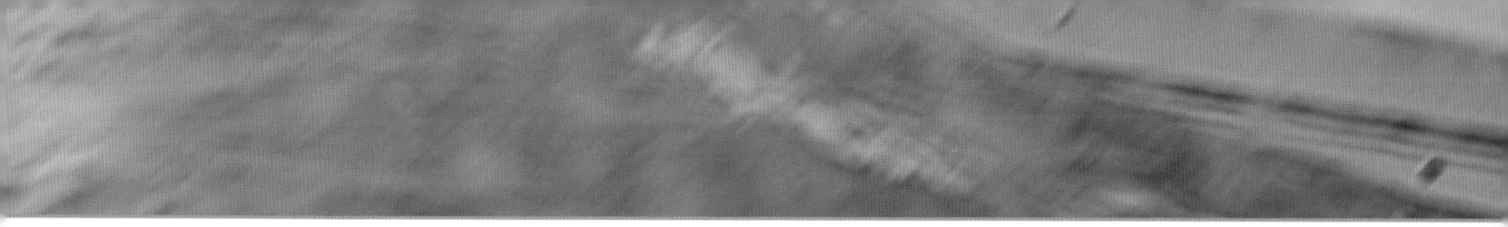

CHAPTER 8
BULA BULA! A TASTE OF FIJI

Passage to Fiji
At sea, 19°S, 176°E
October 4, 2002

We experience an ideal first day at sea: During the day the winds never increase beyond 18 knots, and we fly a full main and jib. Günter wears a wide, contented smile that I haven't seen for quite a while. And despite our three hours on, three hours off watch schedules, he says that my face looks calm and rested this morning.

Life on board is so much simpler without crew. Our scheduled crew—a couple with sailing experience—cancelled. Had they come, we would have been ultra-concerned about making a weather window that would fit their two-week holiday, one that would allow some time in Tonga and more time in Fiji before they'd rushed to catch a flight out. They would have arrived all stressed-out from work. And all that land stress would have come onto our *Pacific Bliss*. We vow to keep our yacht *blissful,* to live up to her christened name!

I've been immersed in Polynesian culture since we left San Diego. Now, nearing the end of Voyage Two, I'm studying the differences between two cultures: the Polynesian and the Melanesian. Historians agree that Melanesians came to the Pacific from Southeast Asia by way of the Indonesian archipelago. Some researchers claim that the first settlements date back 8,000 years. We do know that archeological finds prove that people lived on the Fiji Islands at least 3,000 years ago. According to Fijian legend, the great chief Lutunasobasoba led his people across the seas to the new island of Fiji. Later, voyagers from Polynesia mixed with the Melanesians to create a highly developed society long before the arrival of the Europeans.

As early as February 6, 1643, Abel Tasman sighted islands and reefs northeast of Taveuni. Captain Cook visited the islands in 1774. However, it was not until 1789 that these islands were recorded in detail by Captain Bligh himself when, having been cast adrift by the mutineers of the *HMS Bounty*, he sailed through the archipelago during his 4,000-mile epic voyage in his long boat. In fact, sea charts still refer to the passage between the two largest islands, Viti Levu and Vanua Levu, as Bligh Passage.

Bligh did not set foot on the islands, due to the reputation of "Feejee men" as cannibals. When almost out of the group, Bligh's craft was chased by two canoes carrying war lords from the Yasawas. "Even though his party was desperately short of supplies," reports Robert Kay in *Fiji Guide*, "Bligh was unwilling to find out whether the natives' interest was friendly or dietary."

I'd been to Fiji once before, as a part of a ten-day charter sponsored by *Cruising World* magazine. That trip included a visit to the Yasawa Island Group. I loved the island dancing, feasts, and church services and yearned to return someday.

As the nautical miles pass underneath our hulls, my love affair with Tonga is quickly forgotten.

Like a fickle lover, I fall in love with one country, only to dream about the next!

Dreamy Kandavu
Anchored near Cape Washington and Denham Island
19°1′S, 177°6′E
October 6

The wind continues blowing a steady 25-30 knots for the next 24 hours. Then on the third day, it lessens to

The tricky entrance to Vuda Point Marina's outer basin.

a steady 20-25 knots, with following seas. The passage from Tonga to this Cape Washington Anchorage, our first landfall in Fiji, is fast. Our average speed for the three-day, three-night passage is a respectable 6.8 knots, and that's with a double-reefed main at night. Nothing harrowing happens (thank goodness!), and all is pleasant and serene.

The island of Kandavu, Fiji's fourth largest, lies east-west (to our port) like a giant statue reclining on its back. Sometimes she rests in a foggy vapor as if from some other-worldly, perhaps mystical, fairy tale. Now, awakened by the sun, the island is beautiful to behold. I do hope we are able to visit it next season! Kandavu is about 50 miles south of any place on our itinerary, so sailing back here would take a special effort. Günter says that the diving and snorkeling should be excellent here, with clear waters and reef entrances every ten miles or so around the south of the island. On the top of the cliffs perches the charming village of Nabuketevuiva. Near the reefs to our port bow reside a few small houses tucked in below the cliffs.

What a lovely anchorage!

Silhouetted by the sun, I sit here in the starboard cockpit seat, jotting down my thoughts. The island of Denham, its tall pines bent by the southeast wind, flanks our starboard side. The wind stabilizes at 15-20 knots, gusting to 25. We anchored here at 39 feet in a sea of cobalt, so clear that we can see the sandy bottom. We are secure, swinging on 120 feet of chain. The tide sweeps in to cover the exposed reefs. I watch while a couple walking the reefs scurries toward the land. Then I spot a little resort on Denham, nestled beneath the pines. It contains half a dozen log cabins. Except for the couple on the reef, it is very still this Sunday morning.

I'm continuing to describe the scene because I want to etch this anchorage into my memory. A local power boat with three curly-haired Fijian men passes by. The boat disappears into a crevice that juts through the cliffs in the main island of Kandavu. It is a high island, about 30 miles long and 5 miles wide. My view from the cockpit is of its westernmost peak, called Nabukelevu, usually the first land sighted by yachties arriving to Fiji from Australia or New Zealand. When we arrived this morning, the great peak was brooding in the clouds. Now, in the sun, it has taken on a completely different character: rugged, rough, and proud. The lighthouse on Cape Washington rises from the mountain's northwest bluff. The land extends into the sea like an arm embracing a long curved beach of sugar-white sand.

As the wind swings *Pacific Bliss* around on the anchor in a pivoting arc, I face the open sea to the stern, the sea that will soon take us to the island of Viti Levu, Fiji's largest island. Viti Levu (pronounced Vee-tee Lay-vu) is home to 70 percent of the population (about 600,000) and is the hub of the entire Fijian archipelago.

At the nav station, Günter and I plot the rest of the trip: We will enter the island's reef at Navula Passage

The tight turning space in the inner basin.

on the island's west side, pass Vuda Point and then meander 22 miles inside the reefs to check in at Lautoka, a point of entry. Returning to the cockpit, we lower our Tonga flag and hoist the Fiji courtesy flag on the bow spreaders. Now is the time to catch some zzz's before making the overnight passage. That way, we can enter through the reefs in the daylight.

But we're too excited to sleep!

An Eerie Passage
October 7

We depart Kandavu at 1810 in a gentle 16-knot wind with following seas. By midnight the small island of Vatulele will be to our starboard. The evening is stark dark. No stars. No moon. After my watch, I fall asleep easily in the soothing motion of the ocean.

"Help! Lois! Come up here!" Günter's cry jolts me awake. It is 2330, almost midnight. I rush to the cockpit. The weather is damp and drizzling. I can understand why Günter probably spent most of his watch inside. But it doesn't take me long to understand the bigger problem. White lights are coming at us straight for our starboard bow! Also, I see one red light to the port bow. When a sailor sees lights coming right at him, it's time to get out of the way. Fast! But *which* way?

"Günter, how did you get yourself into this predicament? Didn't you see those lights long ago? You should have figured out what the situation was by now."

"I didn't. Why do you think I called you up here?"

Günter has already jibed to avoid whatever it is coming at us. Now *Pacific Bliss* is back-winded and dead in the water. Günter starts both engines. They idle in neutral. He pushes both levers forward. No response. This is weird: The GPS does not respond; the knot meter does not work either!

An electrical problem? Or could we have been caught in a fishing net and immobilized?

I call the vessel on the VHF. No response. My heart pounds as I attempt to think through the problem. Could those two white lights be at the front and back of a long freighter?

"Oh…the white hull of a *sailboat*! There!" I shout.

"Only the red light on its mast is showing," Günter says. "No other lights. Well, that solves the red light problem. But, whatever that is up ahead, it's going in the same direction we're going."

I've taken over the helm while Günter adjusts the main. "Why are we going *against* the wind and waves, instead of *with* the wind? We must have turned around!"

"Just give the engine more gas."

"She's not moving."

Günter comes to the stern. "Uh-oh," he says sheepishly. "The engines aren't engaged!"

He turns them on. Then I steer back on course. It seems to take ages, but the radar finally warms up. It shows two boats running parallel with each other. Now that we've turned around, they are *ahead* of us. We take two 10-degree turns to our port. Each time, it appears that the boats are imitating us! Finally we can make out what is going on: Two fishing boats ahead of us are crossing our intended path diagonally. Because they are not heading directly at us, we are in no danger.

Later Günter describes the incident in our logbook's Navigation section merely as "captain lost control." What he does not enter is that he didn't wake up in the salon when the timer went off. He slept through! No wonder he was disoriented.

New rules are needed when there are only two of us. We would never allow a crew to set the timer and sleep during a watch. Why should Günter be allowed to trust himself to wake up? Never again!

A few hours later, we are entering the reef system of Momi Bay. We see some anchored yachts ahead. Identifying the white light that marks the port reef is easy; but the starboard channel identification turns out to be only a simple black marker on another reef much farther ahead. However, with both engines on just in case, our catamaran takes the pass easily. We sail through the traffic lane marked on our chart and past Vuda Point.

By 1430 we have successfully anchored in mud near the sewer outflow northeast of Queen Anne's Wharf in Lautoka. We receive no answer from the Port (supposedly on 24-hour duty). Another yachtie anchored nearby informs us that today is a Fijian holiday, called Family Day.

Günter hoists our quarantine flag. We won't be checking in today, and we may not leave the ship until port opens tomorrow and approves our arrival. But that's all right. We stay on *Pacific Bliss* and enjoy a well-deserved siesta. In the evening, we are treated to another South Seas sunset that seems to last forever. A freighter is silhouetted in the setting sun: I never knew a sight like this could be so stunning! A cruise ship leaves the dock and the freighter pulls in, unloading piles of pipe and containers. There's plenty of activity here to watch. We don't mind being quarantined on "island time."

A Clumsy Arrival
Vuda Point Marina, Viti Levu, Fiji
17°41′S, 177°23′E
October 10

I race around the deck of *Pacific Bliss*, struggling to fasten dock lines to cleats. We have two on each side of the boat, and I'm rushing from port to starboard and back again as Günter moves toward our designated slip at the marina.

"Slow down!" I shout. "I'm not ready with the lines and fenders! They told us to stop at the big buoy in the center of the harbor!"

"But the guy in the dinghy is motioning us to follow him in!" Günter yells back.

"That's doesn't mean you have to go right away!"

Günter goes in anyway.

Surprisingly, I spot our friend Rolf at the quay, to our stern. We're backing in. I heave the line toward him with all my might and feel my body following it. I land in the cesspool of the hurricane hole that is Vuda's inner basin. Luckily, I catch the ladder and somehow manage to swing myself back on board before my head goes under.

Meanwhile, Günter throws the other stern line to Rolf, who quickly fastens it to a cleat on shore. Günter shuts off the engine, and both men run to the bows to attach the Med-mooring set-up strung to the center buoy.

"Rolf, I'm *so* glad to see you again." I stand there grinning while my shorts drip filthy water onto the deck.

"Tell that husband of yours that he has only one crew on board, and she needs time to set up before he roars on in."

"I have. He forgets. Rolf, I haven't seen you since Huahine, when you helped us install navigation software! It's still working, thanks to you. Where are you headed?"

"New Zealand. But not until I get my bucket in working condition."

Rolf, an adventurous sailor who was born in a land-locked European country, also owns a Catana 431. But his is faster than *Pacific Bliss* and cutter-rigged. He has chosen yellow and white for the décor and *Yelo* for her name. We've always compared notes. And I know we'll be sharing sailing yarns tonight!

I change clothes and come back into the cockpit to see our friends Tina and Dennis standing there; they are a couple who hails from the American Northwest. We have shared many tall tales on their small monohull, *Alii Kai*, and even befriended their huge amber-colored cat. Tina's laughter is infectious. And Dennis' ample girth adds dimension to their "jolly couple" reputation. Dennis and Tina explain that they have rented a condo on the hill for the cyclone season. "You'll find the heat in this hole oppressive. You'll not want to live on your boat for long," Tina warns us.

After Günter explains that we are going back home for the season, the couple offers to watch our yacht for us. "We're already taking care of three others," Dennis adds, "so we'll be down here in the marina every day making our rounds."

Even though we've arranged for the marina's "hurricane service plan," we are relieved to have Dennis and Tina watching over *Pacific Bliss* as well.

Imitating Men's Messing with Boats

When Dennis and Tina come on board for sundowners, we get to hear one of their great stories:

One day, while living on board, Dennis returns to *Alii Kai* to hear an awful commotion, a metallic pounding and ringing sound like he'd never heard before, interspersed with groans and cusses. He rushes down the hatch of the small monohull and into the galley.

"What's happening?" he manages to shout through a mouth dry with fear.

He finds Tina, his wife and trusted sailing partner, gone crazy. She has a butcher knife in one hand and a large serving spoon in the other. She is pounding on the bottom of a pan and occasionally banging on the counter!

"Honey, stop! Look at me!"

Tina stands barefoot in a red T-shirt and raggedy capris. Sweat drips onto her brow and nose from her thick dark brown hair. She quits pounding and turns calmly to face her spouse.

His short, stocky frame is rigid. Concern clouds his face.

"I'm just practicing for when I might have to fix something on this boat myself," she says with a frown. Then she bursts out laughing. At first, Dennis is shocked speechless; then he joins her laughter.

No wonder Dennis and Tina are one of our favorite cruising couples. When we are in the same port, there is never a dull moment. Even the most ugly, gruesome stories become humorous when they're around.

As we cruise from port to port in the South Pacific and the beer and wine start to flow, many are the captains' mates who will tell similar stories about horrendous noises and cussing coming from their otherwise in-control partners. Invectives begin as soon as an unexpected problem arises and finally end with a cold beer when the problem is solved.

Celebrating Our One-Half Circumnavigation!
October 12

Halfway! We crossed the line at 180° West during our passage from Tonga to Fiji. Now we are heading back toward decreasing east longitudes. We began our circumnavigation on November 3, 2000, in Canet, France; now we're 16,337 nautical miles away, according to our ship's log. The circumference of the earth at the equator is 24,901.55 miles (40,075.16 kilometers). Including all side trips, we estimate that completion of the circle for us will take us about 34,000 miles.

Quite the adventure. Quite the accomplishment. This is definitely cause for another celebration!

We mark the route we've taken so far on our

DID YOU KNOW?

A TASTE OF FIJI IN FOUR, FOUR-LETTER WORDS

Bula. Nowhere else in the world will one hear a more heartfelt greeting than in the Fiji Islands. The renowned Fijian greeting *Bula!* welcomes the visitor with affection and sincerity. Fijians say this word with enthusiasm, as if they are welcoming a long lost friend. The word is universally used to say hello, or welcome, and is even exclaimed if one sneezes! It's a way of wishing good health and fortune to the recipient. The formal phrase is "*ni sa bula vinaka.*"

Kava. The word *bula* is used in all *kava* ceremonies. *Kava* (also called yaqona, or grog) is a drink made from the root of a pepper plant, used for its sedative and anesthetic properties. Its active ingredients are called kavalactones. The drink is non-alcoholic and non-narcotic, and it's a part of daily Fijian life. No wonder Fijians have a reputation of being the friendliest people on earth—smiling, generous, and relaxed! The *kava* drinking ceremony is a highlight of all important local happenings. The liquid tastes like watered-down mud and it makes one's lips and tongue tingle. Later, it brings on a relaxed, meditative state. It's rude to refuse the drink if it is offered by a village chief or if you have agreed to participate in a special event that includes a *kava* ceremony. When presented with a cup of *kava* (half a coconut), here's the protocol: Clap once with cupped hands (not flat palms); say *bula*; drink all the *kava* in the cup; clap three times with cupped hands; say *bula, bula.*

Sulu. A *sulu* is a colorful Fijian sarong. It has many uses and is worn by both men and women. Visitors find it ideal for covering their shorts when visiting a Fijian village or as a swimsuit cover-up or shawl for a cool evening. Of course, it makes a convenient beach blanket, a bench cover, and it's an easy-to-pack souvenir to take back home.

Meke. The *meke* is an indigenous dance that tells the story of ancient gods, historic battles, or just everyday life. Along with *kava* ceremonies, *mekes* often mark significant events. They are forums for entertaining VIPs and visiting dignitaries. Most Fijian hotels offer "cultural nights" so that tourists can participate in *mekes* as well.

inflatable globe and hang it from the bimini. We set out the champagne, and Günter pops open the first bottle. The cruisers in the marina begin to walk up the gangway.

"You think of more excuses to party," Rolf jokes. He's the first guest to appear.

"Well, this party is for you, too," I reply. "*Yelo* is also halfway from Europe." Other guests arrive quickly. We all toast to safe passages the rest of the way.

"Seriously, it's good to celebrate these milestones," Manfried says in English that's tinted with a German accent.

I explain our new emphasis on rituals: "We've posted stories on our website about many of our milestones."

"The last event was our equator crossing party, on the way to the Marquesas this spring," adds Günter. "So we're really due for another party."

"Here's to our Catana that got us here," he toasts.

We reminisce with our friends about building and launching our boats and about fighting the storms and nasty weather we've all encountered.

The best of times and the worst of times.

Günter and I first met Manfried after he'd stopped at the Marina restaurant here. He was still shaking. Now he recounts in detail what happened that night. He had been on his way to New Zealand from Musket Cove when damage caused by 40-knot winds in the channel forced him into this marina. He'd missed the entrance and gotten hung up on the reef outside the pass. With help from his bow thrusters and a dinghy driver sent by the marina, his *La Rossa* was finally freed, only to scrape its long beautiful hull against the fuel dock as darkness descended. "My bow thruster then gave up the ghost," he frowns. "But all is fixed now, and I will depart tomorrow."

Jean-Luc and his girlfriend arrive and join the conversation. He'd anchored his 75-foot yacht, *Teva*, outside the pass for two days until the wind calmed down; only then had he taken it in.

Smart.

Barbara, owner of *Nootka Rose*, has arrived, balancing a tray of assorted snacks and salmon pâté from Canada. She contributes an unusual tale to the conversation: She and her husband had sailed down the American and Mexican west coasts to Puerto Vallarta. He was ready to call it quits. She wanted to go on.

Barbara captivates us with her sea story that took place near Kadavu:

"The winds were strong, the compass was swinging wildly, my crew was terrified, and then the fog rolled in like an Alfred Hitchcock thriller. I had to heave to for the night. The locals told me that spirits living there can suck up a boat and it can disappear from the globe. It's an area of the world similar to the Bermuda triangle."

One advantage to giving these parties: The sea stories are never boring!

Tina and Dennis make a grand entrance. Dennis wears the T-shirt that Günter gave him. The front says *Cannibal Café. We'd love to have you for dinner.* Tina brings a chocolate cake for the occasion. She plants it squarely on the table directly in front of Günter.

"Whose birthday is it?" Günter asks.

"It's a Halfway Cake for *Pacific Bliss*," Tina answers.

"Thanks!" Günter uncorks another bottle of champagne, and we all toast once again, this time to Günter's mistress, *Pacific Bliss*.

More stories. More champagne. More laughter. The evening passes gloriously!

The next morning I wake up with sunlight streaming through *Pacific Bliss* and pleasant thoughts about the party. The salon is heaped with dishes (all nicely washed, thanks to Tina and Barbara).

Günter and I talk about what we should do differently for the second half of our circumnavigation. We're determined to proceed much more slowly, staying to enjoy people and cultures we like. Following that plan, we decide to stay in Fiji for another season. We plan to obtain a permit to sail to Fiji's remote Lau Island Group.

⚓

October 14: As the sun sets at the entrance of the marina, we sip cold beers and munch on taco chips, waiting for the taxi that will bring our friends, Toni and Ingrid, from the Nadi airport. Soon they arrive, pulling two enormous duffels. Toni rolls his up the gangway, eyes twinkling, moustache twitching. Ingrid—tall, solid, and capable, with dark blonde hair—follows behind. She lets her duffel and huge carry-on bag drop onto the deck. We smother each other with great bear hugs. We've been good friends forever, it seems. Günter's friendship with Ingrid predates mine, going back over thirty years to the German Enzian Ski Club, after he first emigrated from Munich to Malibu.

Our friends stack piles of stuff on the galley counter: newspapers and magazines from their stopover in Sydney, German coffee and chocolate, honey, curry sauces, cheeses, and even salami from Trader Joe's in California.

After catching up on personal news, the talk turns to the latest terrorist attack, this time in Bali, Indonesia. Car bombs have exploded near the Kuta beach area where Günter and I spent part of our honeymoon.

I am so relieved that I didn't have to view all of this on TV!

At night I lie awake in my bunk with frightening images of Australian rugby players racing through my

Cruisers attend our halfway celebration.

Mother and son, Yalobi Village, Yasawa Group, Fiji.

head. Men in the prime of life. Youngsters cruelly and forever changed, with arms and legs and body parts strewn over the streets, their corpses burned beyond all recognition. These horrible images sear the soul and present a shocking, dramatic contrast to the peacefulness of the sea.

Highs and Lows in Yalobi Village
Yalobi Village, Waya Island, Yasawa Group, Fiji
17°18.6´S, 177°07.4´E
October 23

"*Bula!*"

Friendly Fijian children on the beach greet us as we pull *Petit Bliss* onto the sandy shore above the tide line. *Pacific Bliss* remains anchored far out in the bay off the island of Waya, the southernmost island in the Yasawa Group. A burly, woolly-haired man soon arrives and walks alongside us on the beach as the children traipse behind. He introduces himself simply as John.

"Where is the house of Tui Waya, the chief?" Günter asks, following the advice given in the *Lonely Planet* guide. "We want to pay our respects with a *sevu sevu* ceremony."

"His brother, Navalu, interim chief now. Elections in 2004," John answers. "Tui Waya died in 1989. I take you there."

The yaqui root is used in the South Seas to make *kava* for almost any occasion. "*Nogu sevu sevu gor. Nogu sevu sevu gor,*" Günter mumbles under his breath, practicing what he will say when, finally, he presents it to the chief.

John leads us through a little well-kept village toward the chief's hut. We pass a mix of woven and wooden homes. The doorways are framed with colorful ti plants and flowering frangipani. The four of us (Toni and Ingrid have joined us) troop single file, following John through the village's "Main Street," a simple dusty path lined with plants. We pass an impressive monument that dwarfs a nondescript wood church. Towering dark green mountain peaks form a majestic background to the drop-dead gorgeous landscape. But I dare not take photos—that is, not until we have presented our gift and have been officially welcomed into the village.

"You never know, we could be rejected and asked to leave the village," Günter cautions as we trudge along in the tropical heat.

"I doubt they'll kick us out!" I say. We file through a narrow door into the chief's hut. There sits the chief, wearing belted khaki shorts and a blue checked shirt. It is open at the neck, revealing a white T-shirt underneath.

No sulu (skirt) for him!

He orders us to sit.

Ingrid and I adjust our long skirts and sit cross-legged on the floor in front of him, muffling our mirth, as Günter and Toni try to sit in the proper knee-length *sulus* that they've worn in deference to the chief!

As it turns out, Günter doesn't get the chance to say the words he has so diligently practiced. John says everything for us in rapid Fijian. It's a very long speech. Apparently John is saying all the things that we conveyed to him along the way.

Günter places the root on the floor in front of the chief. According to tradition, the chief can either accept the gift by picking it up or reject it by simply letting it lie there. Finally it is the chief's turn to talk. He turns to all of us, and in a low, clear voice, says a few sentences in Fijian.

John translates: "You now have permission to go anywhere you want in the village."

Our relief is palpable. We all smile.

"Do I have permission to photograph children?" I ask. "I would like that."

John talks with the chief in Fijian and then replies, "Yes, you have permission to photograph chief; but, he says, only with the men."

Obviously, they misunderstood my request. Already John is arranging Günter and Toni on either side of the chief. I unpack my Nikon, focus quickly, and manage to take one photo in my flustered state. Fortunately, I discover later, it turns out well!

We walk back with John along Main Street. The monument near the church, John explains, had been erected as a tribute to the village's having been spared a measles epidemic that had devastated nearby islands. The entire village had prayed for divine mercy, and their prayers, they believe, were answered.

John invites us to a *kava* ceremony at his home at 4:00 p.m. "Not Fijian time," he warns. "California time," I promise. After a wonderful lunch at Adi's backpacker resort, we dinghy back to *Pacific Bliss*. There I download and print a few full-size photos to take back to the village as gifts. We return quickly, hoping to be there for school adjournment, but the children have dispersed all over the playground by the time we arrive. (The school in Yalobi Village serves as an elementary boarding school, so most of the children travel there from other villages and islands, returning to their homes only on weekends.) As soon as the children realize that they can see themselves in my digital camera, they crowd around, almost knocking me over, while they pantomime for my Nikon. Some even follow us to the beach and collect shells to give to us.

We barely make it to our *kava* ceremony on California time (ten minutes late). John and his wife Doris have made a supreme effort to make the ceremony special. They own a complex of three huts: one for cooking—where they wash the dishes outside; a second for guests; and a third for sleeping. They invite us into their sleeping house. A mat covers the floor of the large room; a pile of *sulus* occupies one corner; clothes hang neatly on nails. John places the family's orange plastic *kava* bowl in the middle of the room; he surrounds it with four coconut shells. Doris hangs freshly made gardenia leis around our necks. The strong scent wafts through the room. After we exchange pleasantries, we take our positions, sitting cross-legged on the floor around the bowl.

We had brought another yaqui root as a gift. Because that takes a long time to grind, John uses a packet of commercial *kava* instead.

"I see that Fiji now has instant *kava*," Günter quips.

John laughs. "Yes, now tourists can buy this to take home. Costs $1."

John explains the ceremony to Toni and Ingrid: "*Bula*. Slap your hand on one knee, if you are the one holding the shell. The rest of you, clap once. Drink it down in one long gulp. *Bula bula*. Clap, clap, clap." He fills each shell in succession and leads us through the routine. Ingrid and I decline a second round, but the men and Doris have two.

John's grandsons, Matthew and Little John, stare at us while they edge closer to Doris. Little John fondles the lace on her dress. After we give them candy, coloring books, and crayons, they overcome their shyness. The entire family plays with the newfangled four-at-a-time soap bubble machine we brought them. We also present gifts of T-shirts, lotions, and perfumes to Doris and John. Then I offer to take a portrait of the family. "I will give the photo to you tomorrow."

As the family stands woodenly in front of their thatched hut, they remind me of the sepia photographs of my grandparents. I laugh and shout, "*Bula bula!*"

Doris breaks into a big grin, and I quickly snap the photo.

Back on *Pacific Bliss*, a golden glow floods the cockpit. The four of us enjoy rum punch sundowners to mask the mud-hole taste of the *kava*. The novocaine-like feeling in our mouths has slowly disappeared, but the euphoria of our wonderful day in Yalobi Village remains far into the evening.

That day is the high of our stay in Yalobi. We never suspect that the next will be our low.

I so wanted Toni and Ingrid to experience the full orange moon of Fiji, rising like a flattened pumpkin from the sea, but luck is not on my side. Instead, dark clouds race furiously past a sooted globe, which sits between the shadowy peaks that surround us. All night the winds (we call them williwaws) scream from the mountaintops and blast into our dreams—so loudly that Günter has to reach over me to shut the window completely.

At 0400, unable to sleep, I go up to the nav station to check the instruments. The wind is only 20-plus knots, but it seems like more. I open the cockpit door. The williwaws are pushing and spinning *Pacific Bliss* around like a toy top—from one end of her tether to the other. I have had enough. I want to leave this bay and the so-called "protective" peaks that cause these screaming winds.

⚓

Günter and I snuggle into the comforter in our cozy master berth in the morning, Knowing there will be no sunrise, we are not eager to face the elements.

"I'm *so tired* of this howling," I complain.

The gloomy skies turn darker still. Lightning cracks in the distance. And then the tropical deluge begins.

"Guess it's hunkering-down time today," Günter says as he closes the salon door to shut out the noise. However, by mid-morning we spot patches of blue in the sky, and by noon we decide to go ashore to deliver the full-size prints I'd made of the chief's brother. Also, we want to say our goodbyes.

When I give her the family portrait, Doris hugs me like a long lost friend. We stay less than an hour, but tears of joy fill my eyes as we make our way gingerly down through Yalobi Village for the last time. I am carrying a gigantic apple strudel cake that Doris made with her own hands, allowing me to take a precious part of this little village with us on our voyage back to the mainland of Viti Levu.

It is almost 1600 when we return to *Pacific Bliss*. Ingrid and I head for the galley to make dinner before darkness sets in. Toni is out in the cockpit waiting for Günter to help him lift the dinghy onto the davits. Sailing out first thing in the morning is no longer an option. It is now a must. Our guests have weekend flights to catch from Nadi to Los Angeles. The weather, for a change, seems to be cooperating.

Suddenly, Toni shouts an alarm. "Günter! You know that Swiss monohull in the harbor? It seems to be pulling away from us…no, I think *we* are the ones who are moving!"

We all rush to the stern. *Pacific Bliss* is, indeed, drifting silently and inexorably—right toward the reef on the opposite shore of the bay!

Günter rushes to start the engines. I dash up to the bow to grab the handheld windlass control. I bring up chain and more chain. We had put out a 3:1 scope in 40 feet of water—that's 120 feet of chain, plus the bridle. As the chain comes up, I should feel the weight of the anchor at the end…but I don't.

Something isn't right.

Suddenly the rest of the chain comes rushing through and wraps around the windlass.

"There's no anchor," I shout. "It's gone!"

"Can't be!" Günter calls back. He is still at the helm, idling *Pacific Bliss*.

Rolf, the owner of the other yacht in the harbor,

Kava for the *Chief*

1. Adi, manager of the backpacker resort; 2. Günter and Toni wear appropriate *sulus* to bring *kava* to the chief; 3. John and Doris with their grandchildren; 4-6. Yasawa Island school children are entertained by seeing themselves on the digital camera screen; 7. Toni and Günter pose with the island's chief, who is wearing shorts!

Adi's backpacker resort is nestled below the high mountains that cause the williwaws.

approaches us in his dinghy. "You've been dragging," he yells.

"We know," Toni shouts back. "Come on board."

All of us go up to the bow. Günter examines the swivel connector at the end of the anchor chain, rolling it back and forth in his hand as if he cannot believe what he sees. Indeed, the part has broken, sheared sideways from the force of the williwaws. Our anchor is probably buried deep in the sand. "Do you have a spare anchor on board?" Rolf asks.

"Yes, two of them," Günter answers. "But we're too close to the reef. Let's get out of here."

We motor deeper into the bay. Once there, Günter retrieves the spare Fortress anchor from down deep in the port sail locker. It had never been assembled. The night turns black as pitch. I direct a flashlight beam, while Toni and Günter lay the parts on the bow, along with the instructions.

"You guys look like parents assembling the kids' toys the night before Christmas," I joke.

No one laughs. It begins to rain. Huge drops soak the instructions. We have to move the entire assembly underneath the hardtop bimini. The level of frustration increases. Civility decreases. One and one-half hours later, we're ready to scream at each other. I, too, have lost my sense of humor.

Finally the task is completed and Rolf loads the second anchor into his dinghy to set it out. It isn't an easy task, but when it's done, we are all in a better mood.

We had invited Rolf to dinner hours earlier. Now, before eating, we thank God that His angel is still watching over us, and we pray for milder winds this evening.

"It could have happened while we were ashore today..." Ingrid begins.

"Or worse yet, while we were sleeping last night," Günter adds.

In the morning, I give Rolf the coordinates of where we had lost the anchor. The spare anchor is like a spare tire on a car: okay for temporary use, but not reliable for the long term. Then we say goodbye and head off for Mana Island. But the wind shifts! We'd motored here to Waya Island with the wind right on the nose and had anchored in a harbor protected by mountains on three sides. And now we will have to motor to Mana Island with the wind on the nose again.

And I thought only children could be that contrary!

Günter apologizes to Toni and Ingrid: "Normally, South Seas sailing would not be this bad, but this is an El Niño year...."

Despite the choppy seas and slow going, we finally reach our destination, but dual-anchored off Mana Island, we don't dare leave the boat. The next morning, though, with *Pacific Bliss* safely tucked in a

Ingrid and Toni relax for a few hours at the island's resort.

beautiful lagoon behind the barrier reef, we breakfast comfortably at the island's resort. Then we set sail for Vuda Point Marina.

Fortunately, *Pacific Bliss* has an opportunity to shine during her last sail of the season. She slaloms between the reefs and past Navini Island, a paradise of sand and palms, making 8 knots on a broad reach. Her sails are full in the 17-knot SSW wind—and Toni and Ingrid are in heaven. At the helm, Toni scans one shining island after another through his binoculars. The sun glints on the occasional whitecaps. Bright cumulus clouds float against a pale blue sky.

"You see, there *is* another kind of sailing…" Günter begins.

"The way it's supposed to be," I finish his thought.

The following day, at Vuda Point, we hire a taxi to drive Toni and Ingrid to the Nadi airport.

Now, much has to be done to get *Pacific Bliss* ready for her seasonal storage. Despite brutal heat and humidity, Günter and Dennis, who has left his air-conditioned condo to help him, make great progress: They take down the main and jib and fold these sails neatly for storage on land; they remove the anchor so that the chain can be readily hooked up to the lagoon's center buoy; and they fasten heavy chains to lines at the stern port and starboard cleats. With marina help, the entire Med-moor system is fastened to vertical railroad ties dug deep into the bank. The guys also cover the dinghy and outboard motor with canvas and shield the instruments.

As for me, there's no more luxuriating in the sunrise with my coffee while I catch up on my journaling. I'm taking preemptive strikes to protect *Pacific Bliss* and its contents from heat and mildew while we're back home in California. I go through every food locker and compartment on the boat—and there are dozens of them! First I empty each unit completely. Then I disinfect and wipe it, using hundreds of sheets of Bounce® to (hopefully) prevent moisture and to repel insects. That done, I tackle the stove and galley utensil storage areas, with all their rust stains; then I empty and clean the fridge.

"Now, let's have a nice dinner at First Landing, where it's cool," I suggest to my soul-mate.

"Yes!" he agrees quickly. "And a giant cuba libre, while we're waiting for our food!"

The next morning I'm up bright and early. And I feel great. Before my morning coffee, I walk around the entire marina circle, including the turning bay and the inner bay, taking photos. There's the yellow center buoy where they chain all the yachts, bow toward the center, in case of a big blow!

Snap.

I walk to the embankment built up around the "hole." It holds rail ties, dug into the bank like fence posts.

The inner basin of Vuda Point Marina is a protected "hurricane hole." The yachts are Med-moored stern-to and attached to railroad ties pounded deep into the ground. The bows are attached to a center buoy.

Snap.

I see the chains attached to the stern dock lines of our *Pacific Bliss*.

Snap.

Crews of Fijians are water-blasting and bottom-painting boats.

Snap.

A travel lift is constantly in motion, groaning as it pulls one sailboat after another from the water.

Snap.

I take photos of the "buried" yachts: *Astrolabe, Nicole-Spain, Adventura*—all of them surrounded by tires against their hulls, which lie now in a long trench dug into the bank. It's quite a sight!

Snap. Snap. Snap.

Return of the Anchor
November 1

A thin, wiry man with wild black hair, wearing nothing but grimy denim cut-offs, trudges up the gangway onto *Pacific Bliss*. Stooped shouldered, he is burdened like Atlas. Draped around his neck is a heavy piece of curved rusty iron. The man grins as Günter and I rush to meet him.

"Rolf, you've brought our Delta anchor back from the sea!" Günter gently relieves him of his burden and clasps his arm around the man's shoulders.

"Yes," Rolf answers. "When I contacted the divers in the village, they insisted they would have to search the entire Yalobi Bay to find where the anchor is buried. That might turn into a multiday project. So I told them, 'No, you will *not* search the entire bay. We know the *exact* GPS position, the depth and length of the chain, and the wind direction. You will look there.' Sure enough, we could see the path in the sand where the chain was dragged away. And your anchor was buried up to the hilt. It was easy to find."

"Lois is always so particular about putting everything in the logbook when we arrive at an anchorage," Günter continues. "It pays off. I have a good navigator." He gives me a proud look. "And I'm glad to end the season this way. We are safe. *Pacific Bliss* is in good shape. And now I even have my anchor back!"

Later in the evening, Günter refuses to settle in until he writes this analysis into our log book:

> Swivel Analysis:
>
> The swivel connector was attached directly to the anchor. If the anchor is set firmly and does not move when the boat swings, then a bending force is applied to the swivel connector. This reduces the strength of the connector by at least a factor of 3 (e.g., from 2500 lb to 800 lb) as I saw on the technical specs. I think this was the case for us because the diver saw the anchor solidly embedded. To avoid this, a foot of chain must be inserted between the anchor and the swivel connector. Not knowing what they call them here, we referred to the variable winds coming down from the peaks of the Yasawas as williwaws. We had read about williwaws as the downdraft effect of the wind from the Andes as it cuts down to the Chilean coast.

Our Last Night on *Pacific Bliss*
November 2

Tonight will be our last night on board. *Pacific Bliss* is looking like a vessel being put to bed for a good, long rest. The three salon seats inside are protected with sheets and afghan throws, the pillows are stripped of their cases, and one final batch of laundry will go over the lifelines before we leave for breakfast at The Hatch.

Both of our rolling duffels are on the salon seats—almost packed—full of computer manuals, backup photo CDs, the journals for my book-in-process, and very few clothes. We are leaving almost everything here, except for a few swimsuits, shorts, and tops to take with us to the resort.

We have mixed feelings about leaving *Pacific Bliss*. On the one hand, we'll miss our nice, peaceful mornings, coffee in hand, the sun rising while we sit in the cockpit looking at our current surroundings. On the other hand, we look forward to seeing our family and friends again. We also know that we won't be gone long—only a few months. At the end of cyclone season in Polynesia, we shall return. We want to see New Zealand, the most southern Polynesian country, and we realize that we've only had a taste of Fiji. Next year, we will complete the South Pacific segment of our circumnavigation that will take us all the way to Australia.

First Landing Resort
Beachfront Unit #305
November 3

"I feel like I'm King of the World," Günter says as he looks toward the beach and the sea beyond from the comfort of our bure. "*Wunschlos glücklich,* wishlessly happy. I am blessed."

"And I morphed from a hot-and-haggard, cruise-worn boat-frau to Queen as soon as I walked into this luxurious thatched hut yesterday afternoon. Do you realize we hadn't had a tub bath in eight months, and we've had no home, not even a temporary hotel room, other than *Pacific Bliss* on our entire Voyage 2?!"

Günter nods and smiles. He is wrapped in a navy-and-white striped beach towel, having just returned from a refreshing dip in the pool.

We are seated side by side on green canvas deck chairs, sipping our morning coffee. Birds chirp cheerily, and we are bug-free within a screened porch.

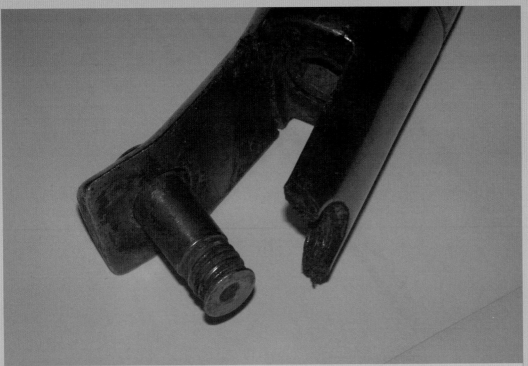
Williwaws blowing into Yalobi Village Bay spun our yacht like a top and caused this swivel connector attached to our anchor to break.

Günter is deep into his new book, *Dandil,* which reveals Arab life as a violent and cruel society.

I begin a new journal. The birds continue their loud chorus. A pair of them walks along the little flower garden that is just outside the screened porch. They have brown heads and bodies, gold masks around their eyes, and golden beaks. As they take flight, I notice a ring of white in their tail feathers. Other feathered wonders hang out by the pool, and these I call "Christmas birds" because they have velvety green bodies with burgundy heads.

I look out at this Pacific Ocean we have crossed. I think of our yacht, *Pacific Bliss,* sitting safely in the marina, all prepared for the cyclone season. A peaceful feeling washes over me. I turn to Günter. "I was just thinking," I murmur.

"That *this* is another Moment of Bliss?" He has finished my thought.

The Longest Day: Coming Home for Our Winter
November 6

Back in our air conditioned room at First Landing, I never want to leave! A sweet and charming Indo-Fijian, Primaya, gives me a manicure and pedicure inside our screened-in porch. Later, in mid-afternoon, Günter and I enjoy a light seafood curry at the shaded bar. And then we saunter back to our room for a decadent afternoon of reading in bed.

By 7 p.m., we are packed and ready to leave. Our taxi shows up promptly at 7:45 to drive us to the Nadi airport. Check-in is fast and easy, despite a thorough examination of our luggage on the U.S. side.

After eight months in the South Pacific, we enjoy our first American fast food at a Burger King near our designated gate. It tastes great! Then we board our plane for the 11 p.m. flight to Los Angeles. Enduring this 10-hour flight in coach isn't so bad: We have four middle seats on a 747 for just the two of us; after all that tropical heat, the plane is refreshingly cool; we enjoy a hot meal with wine; we curl up in our cozy *Pacific Bliss* jackets and then sleep most of the way over the Pacific. But crossing the international dateline makes this seem like the longest day we have ever experienced. Our sense of time is warped beyond all comprehension. At customs, the lines are fast and efficient, and soon we are on a shuttle flight to San Diego.

The view from the smaller plane is spectacular. "Look!" Günter nudges me, "Catalina Island."

I see a long, thin stretch of land that appears to be floating in a vaporized, golden glow, and I see surreal formations of a type of cloud I can't identify. "It must be an optical illusion," I answer.

"Or perhaps it's smog…" Günter suggests. "No matter. It's gorgeous."

On our approach to the tarmac, the sun breaks through the cloud cover and turns the ocean into a stream of liquid gold. As we land, it descends farther into the horizon. And later, just as our taxi arrives at our doorstep, the bright orange globe settles gently into majestic Mission Bay.

Home! How sweet it is!

Vuda Point Marina protects yachts stored "on the hard" during the cyclone season by placing them into holes dug in the ground.

One can find most of the attractions in New Zealand somewhere in the United States: rugged, snowcapped mountains; rolling hills; great beaches; geysers; glaciers and adventure sports; but one would have to travel to Florida or California to find the sun-kissed sands; to the Rockies to find the high mountains and to the Appalachians to find the low ones; to Alaska to find the glaciers; and to Yellowstone to find the geysers. In New Zealand, one can see it all in less than three weeks by touring both islands in a camper van.

That is what we decide to do.

Milford Sound, South Island. Photo by Sabine Hofmann

Chapter 9
New Zealand Adventure

Back on Bliss
Vuda Point, Viti Levu, Fiji
March 7, 2003

I unpack my Fiji Journal from November 2002. I notice that the last entry records our mutual vow to keep bliss on *Pacific Bliss*. Looking around me, I find that pledge ironic. Günter is overwhelmed by all the tasks remaining to be done on our yacht. He trips over huge boxes we brought back from the States. His *Mistress Bliss* now has backups for Ray, parts for the head, extra zincs, and galley supplies. Everything is unpacked and strewn around the salon. And Günter abhors disorder!

"Cool it," I reason with him. "We must have order up *here*," I point to my head, "even though there seems to be disorder *on the boat*. Look, *Pacific Bliss* will be out of commission for five more weeks of the rainy season. We can't even take down the tarps, make the beds, or unpack our library. So let's just make a realistic plan on what we *can* do during this one week before we leave again."

Günter tentatively buys into my solution, although his face is still drawn. "That's why I need you," he says, hugging me tight. "To set me straight."

So we leave everything and check into our seaside bure at the First Landing Resort. I'm relieved to see his face beginning to lighten up.

Bliss Is Back.
First Landing Resort, Room #306

In the morning, Günter makes a pot of coffee and brings it to our screened porch. I follow him with the cups. Birds are already singing, greeting the arrival of dawn's first light. The tide rolls in, lapping against the rocky shoreline less than 60 feet away. We take it all in, pleasantly ensconced in our seaside retreat. We are delighted to be back in Fiji. As we sip our coffees, we talk about our failure to keep this atmosphere of peace, harmony, and bliss—which is so ubiquitous in the South Pacific—an integral part of our home back in San Diego. It was not for lack of trying.

After returning to San Diego from Voyage Two, we had marveled at the view of Sail Bay from our condo in Pacific Beach. We remember how we had planned to be home each day in time to maintain our sundowner tradition, purposefully facing the Pacific Ocean each time the sun's orange rim disappeared below the horizon. We traveled to Texas, to Germany, and on to France, visiting family and friends. We enjoyed it all, except for catching miserable colds during the harsh winter of Europe. Then, after the holidays, our spirits were dampened with the death of Günter's 90-year-old mother. He returned to Germany for the funeral. As it was for me when my parents died, it took him months to recover.

Now we are the matriarch and patriarch of our respective families. What a sobering thought!

As a disturbing background to all of this, the threat of war with Iraq had dominated the news, and we had spent many anxious hours glued to cable news programs and internet sites.

But here in Fiji, there is no CNN or Fox News to interrupt our peace. Gone are the sound bites and flashy visuals of global conflict. In their place, we wake to the sounds of the chirping birds and incoming tide. And in the evening we watch the sun drop into the sea and the moon rise over the Mamalucas as we slowly sip our sundowners.

Bliss is back.

Pampas grass waves in the wind at the sand dunes on North Island.

Drenched!
First Landing Resort
March 10

    It is raining. In fact, it has been raining for three days. Torrential rains. The kind that give the word "deluge" a special meaning. Not like the wimpy showers we experience back in San Diego. Viti Levu, Fiji's largest island, is hostage to a weather pattern set up by the latest cyclone. Günter and I sit here with our coffee, safe within our screened-in porch. We joke about the scare we had yesterday when we visited *Pacific Bliss*. We repeat the story to each other and laugh, but when it happened, it wasn't so funny.

We trudge along the yacht basin quay with our umbrellas protecting us from the worst of the downpour. As we round the section where *Pacific Bliss* resides, Günter points and turns to me, white-faced. "She's listing!"
    I can see that the bow is below the "water line" marker painted on her hull. Yet her stern is right up where it should be.
    Is she taking on water? Günter rushes onto the gangway. I follow closely. Quickly, we climb over tarp lines and up to the bow. Once there, the problem stares us in the face: The tarp we had placed over the trampoline is full of rainwater—gallons and gallons of it.
    Günter rocks his body from side to side, trying to create enough momentum to slosh off some of the water. But nothing happens. I rush to the bow to help. We swing our bodies in sync, first one way, then another. Still nothing. He decides to try another approach: to untie the tarp. He squats at the front of the fiberglass bow. Meanwhile, the downpour continues to drown us.
    "G-r-r-#*+@^##!!!!" he curses. "I can't work these lines loose."
    He pulls out his pocket knife and opens it.
    "I'll just *cut* the rope to the tarp."
    Just then, he loses his footing—and slides right into the center of the trampoline…and directly into the deep pool of water.
    I shout a meaningless warning.
    Drenched like a drowned rat, Günter scrambles to safety and grabs the mast. He's still holding the open knife.
    He lifts a corner of the tarp and cuts the rope that holds it. Suddenly, the dam of water bursts and, for a moment, swallows him as *Pacific Bliss* becomes level again.
    "You could've stabbed yourself with that knife." I try to maintain a stern face while willing myself not to

laugh. "Why didn't you drop it?"

"I was worried it would cut the new trampoline as I fell," he says as water pours off his clothes. "Can you imagine having to replace *that*?"

Always thinking of Pacific Bliss *first. What can I say? She is his mistress!*

"*I* was worried about replacing *you*."

Günter ignores my comment. "Fortunately, we were here to rescue her when the rains came."

A 747 Goes Better to Weather.
March 12

Wanting to touch all corners of the Polynesian triangle, we had planned a three-week excursion to New Zealand, a vacation with no concerns about wind, currents, and mooring problems…just traveling around seeing things like ordinary tourists.

At 0700 there is a knock on our door. The Kids are here already! Our son, Markus, and daughter-in-law, Sabine, have just arrived from Santiago, Chile. After beginning their adventure in Alaska, they have been backpacking around the world. They have traveled throughout North, Central, and South America, reaching the continent's southernmost tip before backtracking and hopping a plane to meet us. Their objective here (other than spending time with us) is to reach the northernmost and southernmost tips of New Zealand.

One of *my* objectives here (other than spending time with them) is to continue my research into the exploration feats of the early Polynesian navigators. This trip to New Zealand will complete our travels to the three points of the Outer Triangle that encompasses Polynesia, the lines that embrace Hawaii, Easter Island, and New Zealand.

A Maori historian and anthropologist, Te Rangi Hiroa, also known as Sir Peter Buck, called his ancestors the "Vikings of the Sunrise." They had begun their explorations in these islands of the Western Pacific, voyaging eastward in their double canoes—predecessors of the modern catamarans—in search of new lands. They left from Samoa to eventually discover the Marquesas. And from there they had dispersed through the tropical islands of the Eastern Pacific, even reaching remote Easter Island. Buck describes New Zealand as their last great migration: They had changed course and headed back towards the setting sun.

Imagine the challenge of reaching New Zealand on board an ancient, Polynesian sailing vessel! As a modern navigator, I marvel at the audacity of these mariners in undertaking such complex and dangerous voyages across the prevailing southeast trade winds, into a southerly belt of unpredictable winds, and then into latitudes of prevailing westerlies. Even today, such a voyage is hazardous, and *we* know exactly where these islands are.

We on Pacific Bliss *are wimps. We chose to sail in the tropics but fly to New Zealand!*

As Günter is fond of saying, "A 747 goes better to weather."

From Skytower Scream to Maritime Museum
The Park Towers
Auckland, New Zealand
March 13

After experiencing the beautiful islands of the tropics, I am amazed to find that Polynesians are still migrating to other worlds. Even today, migration and upward mobility are parts of the Polynesian spirit. For example, with over 60,000 immigrants from various Polynesian islands, Auckland has become the largest Polynesian city in the world; Hawaii is now the home of more than 16,000 Samoans; there are more Cook Islanders in New Zealand than on Rarotonga, their own largest island; and, by a recent census, at least 16,000 Polynesians reside in Los Angeles. Apparently, despite the laid-back lifestyle of the South Pacific, "you can't keep a good Polynesian down."

Günter and I still view as Paradise the islands some of the Polynesians are leaving behind. We are pleased with our decision to spend another year exploring the South Pacific. But now, with The Kids, we are eager to explore New Zealand, the southernmost part of Polynesia.

Two days in Auckland so far and the four of us are having a blast! The guidebooks emphasize that New Zealand is *the* country for adventure tourism. One thing is certain: An enterprising tourist business has bent over backwards to think up any way to have fun, seek thrills, and enjoy new adrenalin-packed experiences. Not to be outdone by The Kids, Günter and I declare that we are game for anything—well, almost anything.

It begins with the Skytower, a mere downhill urban walk from The Park Towers. The Skytower is New Zealand's tallest structure at 328 meters—taller than the Eiffel Tower's 300 meters (984 feet). We ascend in the elevator, a fast 40-second ride, to the observation deck and walk around its 360-degree perimeter, taking dozens of photos of the city.

Markus notices a platform that extends from the glass walls of the tower. "You can bungee jump from here!"

Gulp. What did we say?

We watch the jumpers standing in line at the platform. Do Grandma Lois and Grandpa Günter still have it in them? Günter picks up a flyer. The cost is over $100 U.S. This, for less than a minute of seeing the cement pavement of a downtown city street racing toward your face. Such a deal!

"I could treat you to a very nice dinner and drinks

for that price," says Günter.

So he has cold feet, too.

As we walk through the main floor of the tower, Günter comes up with a solution to our dilemma. He spots a photo booth where tourists can have souvenir photos made of a simulated jump. We pose for the photo, pay for a copy, and *voilà!* We send it via e-mail to our friends and post it to our website. A few unsuspecting souls even congratulate us on our jump!

The next day we all stroll over to America's Cup Village. New Zealanders are still smarting from their recent 5-0 loss to Switzerland. Twice they had dropped out of the race due to problems. On TV, we had watched their mast break during fateful Race #4. What a blow to Kiwi pride—especially since many other New Zealanders were paid mightily to crew on the victorious Swiss yacht.

What we've seen so far gives us a positive impression of Auckland.

Forget the heat of the tropics! We could live here.

The following day, we walk through all 14 buildings of New Zealand's excellent Maritime Museum. I find stirring displays and hear mesmerizing stories of how New Zealanders have been depending on the sea for centuries. Over 99 percent of imports and 99 percent of exports (by volume) travel by sea to and from New Zealand. How ironic that in our modern era we claim the term "globalization" even though it was actually achieved centuries ago by the European sailing ships!

As we traipse from a gigantic shed housing an old Maori double-hulled canoe and onward to a replica of an ancient masted schooner, I'm reminded that all this tells the story of brave seamen: It begins with the Polynesians, but progresses with the European explorers, such as Abel Tasman and my personal inspiration, Captain James Cook.

During the evening, I cannot resist reading a few sections from the books I purchased at the museum. I learn that exploration of "the lands down under" gained fresh impetus when Anthony van Diemen was appointed Governor General of the East Indies in the 17th century. He devised a Grand Plan for a new voyage of discovery: He would send ships as far south and east as possible to attempt an outline of a supposed new continent to be known as New Holland. The voyage was to determine whether or not this continent was connected to Antarctica. To this end, in 1642 van Damien commissioned Abel Tasman to lead the expedition. In time, Tasman landed and named an island after himself––Tasmania. He then sailed eastward, sighting "a large, high land, with mountaintops covered in dark clouds." He called this *Staaten Landt.* Later, when he discovered this was not connected to the Southern Continent, he

DID YOU KNOW?

NEW ZEALAND

There are almost 12 times as many sheep as people in New Zealand—approximately 50 million. Sheep farming is a two billion dollar industry.

New Zealand was the first country in the world to give women the vote, in 1893.

By the end of the 19th century, New Zealand colonists called themselves "Kiwis," whereas the British were called "Poms." Kiwi is the name for New Zealand's native flightless bird. Kiwis call the fruit, also known as Chinese Gooseberries, "kiwi-fruit."

Bungee jumping was born in Queenstown, New Zealand, known as the country's "thrills capital." The sport was pioneered by New Zealand daredevils A.J. Hackett and Henry Van Asch in 1988. They took a 143-foot (43-meter) head-first plunge off the Kawarau Gorge Suspension Bridge, the world's first bungee site.

Picton actually lies north of Wellington, New Zealand's capital. The ferry that crosses Cook Strait from Wellington to Picton sails north from North Island to reach South Island.

Doubtful Sound was so-named by Captain Cook because he doubted that it was a sound when he first saw it.

The annual rainfall in Milford Sound is 300 inches—more than any other one place in New Zealand. The Sound is actually a fjord carved out by glacial action.

Queen Elizabeth II is officially Queen of New Zealand.

A New Zealander, Ernest Rutherford, is known as the Father of Nuclear Physics for his orbital theory of the atom.

The first man to climb Mount Everest is Sir Edmund Hillary, born in Auckland, New Zealand. His face is depicted on New Zealand's five-dollar bill.

Both Australia and New Zealand were once governed by Britain as part of their territory of New South Wales. When Australia became independent, she offered New Zealand to become one of her states. New Zealand refused. Both Australia and New Zealand are part of the Commonwealth.

In contrast to Australia, which was principally settled by convicts, New Zealand began with ready-made families pre-selected by immigration agents and the New Zealand Company. Most settlers had been rural farmers in Britain and Ireland; they transported and then adapted their culture to New Zealand's dense bush, heavy rains, strong winds, and lack of infrastructure. The result of this process is a resilient, energetic, and resourceful people.

Lois and Günter participate in a staged photo at the Sky Tower in Auckland.

Markus and Sabine crowd into their overhead berth in the camper van.

renamed it *Nieuw Zeeland*.

Tasman successfully mapped the west coast of New Zealand as he continued northeast. Eventually he reached Fiji and Tonga. But since his voyages returned nothing for the stockholders of the Dutch East India Company, interest quickly waned and further exploration became of little or no interest to the Dutch.

A hundred years later, sailing from Tahiti on *HMS Endeavor,* Captain James Cook opened a sealed packet of orders from the British Admiralty. They told him to sail to 40 degrees south in search of a land mass called the Great Southern Continent. As Cook pushed on to 40 degrees without sighting land, it became so cold that his men were literally freezing. Fearing the worst, he turned and headed north and west, to the coastline that Tasman had charted over a century earlier.

Cook finally sighted land in October 1769. Although skeptical that this was the Great Southern Continent, he made a thorough survey of what turned out to be the two islands of New Zealand, one of which had been entirely missed by Abel Tasman. Immediately he claimed both of them for King George III. By the time he arrived back in Britain, Captain Cook had dashed the hope of a great southern continent, established a life-long friendship with the local Maori, and charted 2,400 miles of coastline—all in fewer than three months of sailing!

Cook was an amazing man! I feel honored to be in some small way following his footsteps.

Touring, Dune Surfing, and Reaching the Northernmost Point of North Island
March 15

We load our own luggage and all The Kids' backpacking gear into a taxi and set off for United Campervan near the Auckland airport. After the first few days of touring, we adjust to our new procedure, just as we adjusted to taking the dinghy to shore each day when we anchored *Pacific Bliss* in a bay. Each evening, Günter and I lower the table to make it into a bed that fits across the back of the camper, using the seat cushions as the mattress. In the morning, we massage each other's stiff necks. Then we stash the bedding into its cubby and set up the table for breakfast.

Markus and Sabine have more challenging sleeping arrangements. They have to climb to the bunk over the cab, without handholds. Since there is so little headroom, they must lie down and roll to their sleeping spots. Markus, with his 6'4" frame, takes the inside. Once there, he cannot sit up in his bed. Sabine has to leave the bunk for him to move.

Uh, oh. This "camper for four" must have been intended for parents with two small children…and I am the one who ordered it.

Fortunately, everyone laughs and no one complains…yet.

To get to the town of Russell, we drive the camper onto a ferry that crosses part of the Bay of Islands. Before us stretches a breathtaking view: lush islands in all

Markus rolls down a hill in a large ball partially filled with water. This is called Zorbing.

We walk through the Waipoua Forest to see the ancient, graying Tane Mahuta, Lord of the Forest, the world's largest living kauri tree.

directions as far as the eye can see.

Now I understand why this is a favorite cruising grounds, despite the ordeal of sailing here.

Our Top Ten campground is near the town. The concept of Top 10 Holiday Parks—a chain of campgrounds found throughout New Zealand—is well thought out. The design fits this outdoorsy country.

Our first day's travel totals 154 miles—similar to a 24-hour passage on the boat. So far, we are enjoying this method of travel. It is quite a convenient way to see New Zealand.

The next morning, Sunday, rains pummel us sporadically. It is an ideal day for exploring the Russell Museum. Russell, formerly known as Kororareka, was the first permanent European settlement in New Zealand and dates from the early 19th century.

Afterwards, whenever I can risk it, I take the camera out from underneath my rain poncho to photograph the old church and cemetery nearby. As Günter and I walk past, the congregation booms out a song that lifts our souls. Heavenly blue morning glories climb a fence and roses bloom as big as pie pans.

We meet The Kids at Jolly's, a waterfront café, for lunch and then amble back to the campground. In the cafeteria, where other campers are cooking, we sit in the lounge to watch the TV. We have been so remote from the news. The war drums are beating loudly now; a conference is scheduled in the Azores tomorrow for the "coalition of the willing" to fight Saddam Hussein in Iraq. The world seems so far away here. Except for the blowing up of a Greenpeace ship by French saboteurs back in 1985, New Zealand has played a small part on the world stage.

The following day we have no time for a leisurely cup of morning coffee. The four of us leave the campground at 0630 to walk to the ferry that leaves Russell at 0730. We are off on the Dune Tour. At the ferry landing, a tour van picks us up to meet the Dune Rider, an air-conditioned four-wheel-drive converted military vehicle, of the type last used by the New Zealand government in East Timor. The vehicle's design is ideal for wet dunes and mud, but not for passenger comfort. We endure a 50-mile ride along the seashore to Cape Reinga. The seats become harder by the mile.

A welcome stop along the way is Puketi Forest. Similar rainforests covered most of the land from Auckland to the north of North Island. With the coming of the Europeans, the hardwoods were taken for shipbuilding, and large swathes of forest were cut for farmland. Only a few protected areas of native forest remain today.

One of the protected species is the kauri. Some of these trees are 1000 to 2000 years old! Once there, we hike on a convenient boardwalk to the site of *Te Tangi o te Tui,* Puketi's giant. It stands 50.9 meters high (that's about 16 stories) and is almost 4 meters in diameter (around 12 feet). Despite its hugeness, it is only the fourth biggest kauri in the country!

How awesome, yet humbling, to stand before this ancient tree, knowing it took root here many, many centuries before any human being ever set foot on these shores.

Back on the truck, we head for the Cape. But there is one important stop along the way: the Te Paki sand dunes. The sport here is to surf on boogie boards provided by the tour company. If the surfer can go fast enough down the highest dune, he or she can manage to land in the stream at the bottom to cool off. I make it almost to the stream and then dig my feet into the sand to brake. I don't want to get wet. Sabine stops dead in the middle of the hill, laughing as she pushes her board to get sliding again.

The tour continues, and finally, Markus and Sabine meet their first objective: to reach the northernmost point of North Island, Cape Reinga. We all tramp to the lighthouse to watch the waters of the Pacific Ocean and the Tasman Sea collide. Whitecaps foam and froth from crest to crest.

I would not want to be sailing out there!

The next morning, Markus drives the camper van up a high hill overlooking the town of Russell. I walk around the town park with the others, but I gravitate toward the massive sundial. Its surface is made of inlaid tile and depicts a flattened globe. I walk around it again and again, taking photos from every angle.

I turn to Günter. "I'd like to have a garden with such a sundial some day."

"In your dreams," he says.

What was I thinking? We live in a condo. We don't even have land for a garden.

Günter and I feel obligated to visit the Russell radio station before leaving the area. Why? This non-profit operation provides extremely valuable weather forecasting to sailors on all South Seas shortwave radio nets. It is run by two retired gentlemen, who personally guide seafarers to destinations throughout the islands, especially from Tonga and Fiji to New Zealand and back. We and all sailors in Polynesia are indebted to them, and, in a personal and direct way, Günter and I want to express our appreciation for what they do.

They greet us warmly. With justifiable pride, they show us around their small station. They are obviously happy to receive our visit. And we are happy, as we leave, to make a needed financial donation to this necessary and free cruiser service.

As we drive south from Russell, I realize that Northland, New Zealand, is a story of two coastlines. Both remain unspoiled. The east coast north of Auckland is sophisticated and urbane. Its pristine beaches are white-sanded and tranquil, places of relaxation and activities—golf, swimming, sailing, and diving. They cause me to think. But the west coast is rugged, soulful, and simple. Its scenery sets me to dreaming.

The Lord of the Forest

I cannot get those giant kauri trees out of my mind. They say that even the redwoods of Big Sur, California, cannot compete with the kauris' ancient appearance and aura. I must have another look.

We take the West Coast Road (also called the Kauri Coast Road) south. We follow signs posted for Tani Mahuta Track and the Waipoua Forest. There, we have been assured, we will find Tani Mahuta, Lord of the Forest, the world's largest living kauri tree, guaranteed to take our breath away. This great work of nature was discovered in the 1920s by surveyors who had been contracted to build Highway 12 through the forest. They called it Tani Mahuta after a god in Maori mythology. Tani was the son of Ranginui, the Sky Father and Papatuanuku, the Earth Mother. Being a jealous child, he separated his parents and then, out of love for his mother, created the living forest to clothe her. As a result, even today, all creatures of the forest are considered to be Tani's children.

Walking the short track that leads through the cooling shade of the forest canopy, I flush with

anticipation. Not far into the walk, we sweep around a corner and I stop dead in my tracks. There he is! Suddenly, I'm brought face to face with the Lord of the Forest. I stand perfectly still. I stare. My first glimpse of this magnificent tree takes my breath away! I can sense Tani Mahuta's ancient presence and animal strength. He dominates the forest.

Almost 2000 years old, he, too, is almost 16 stories high, but he has a circumference of over 45 feet. He is the giant of giants! An enormous growth that dwarfs everything else.

A wooden fence protects him. A viewing bench surrounds him. I sit in silence. Awed. I wonder at the centuries that have come and gone under the spreading branches of this primeval forest patriarch. Then, I stand and move back…farther…farther…farther. I must fit this entire majestic being into my camera lens. I must…I must….And, finally, I rejoice…because I have him!

Zorbing, Sheep, and New Zealand History
Rotorua
March 20

On our first full day in Rotorua, we head for the Agrodome Park. We have purchased a combination package that combines zorbing, sheep, and history..

There's no question that the inventive New Zealanders have come up with more adventure tourist schemes than any other country we have visited. The revolutionary Zorb™ at the park is the world's first

1. We take the Dune Tour to Cape Reinga, the northernmost point of New Zealand; 2. The Cape Reinga lighthouse; 3. Sabine surfs the dunes; 4. Markus and Sabine are exhilarated after their mountain hike in the cool, fresh air of South Island.

At Picton, we take the ferry across the Cook Strait.

ever globe riding site. It is relatively new, operating commercially since 1997.

The Zorb globe is an 11-foot-high inflatable transparent sphere. Only one tourist at a time can ride inside the globe, which is cushioned by a two-foot layer of air that supposedly protects the rider from the ground while the Zorb rolls downhill at high speed. Markus is eager, but Sabine, Günter, and I are skeptical. We head for the sales office. The "wrangler" explains that there are two types of Zorbing—dry and wet. Markus chooses the wet version based on the description: "In the Zydro™ ride we add water so you can run, tumble, flip or slide inside, as the globe hurtles downhill at speeds of up to 30 km/h. We have cool water in summer and warm water in winter so you're not an ice cube at the bottom!"

Markus changes to swim trunks and heads up the high hill. Soon he is hurtling down. It doesn't look like fun to us, but he exits the Zorb with a grin.

The Sheep Show is a must because New Zealand is all about sheep. Approximately 50 million sheep occupy New Zealand, almost 12 times as many sheep as there are people. It is a two billion dollar industry.

The show is an action-packed hour called "farming entertainment." An energetic presenter promises to take the audience deep into the world of New Zealand farming by introducing us to 19 breeds of sheep. The show includes a sheep shearing demonstration and even gets the audience involved in bidding on sheep during a lively auction.

For me, the dogs are the best part. Huntaway dogs and Heading dogs demonstrate their ability to respond to commands and keep those sheep in line; in fact, a big Merino sheep at the center top row of sheep just stands there calmly with a dog standing on his back. Booths are set up around the seating area where participants can feed the lambs or even hand-milk a cow!

No thanks. Been there, done that!

A quick tour of the geysers, part of the package, is disappointing, but the day ends on a high. The evening's activities at the Rotorua Cultural Center depict Maori life, with a focus on warrior traditions.

First, we are treated to the Maori war chant and challenge, called the *haka*. The warriors, wearing loin cloths and sporting tattoos over most of their bodies, march toward our group chanting fiercely, much like the Marquesan warriors. They flail their arms and stomp their feet, but there the resemblance ends. We're startled when they stop in front of us and angrily stick out their tongues, their eyes bulging.

Fans of rugby union football (soccer) know one

version of the *haka* that is customarily performed by the All Blacks before major games against non-New Zealand teams. This version begins with the chant "*Ka mate, ka mate.*" ("It is death, it is death.") This *haka* is said to have actually originated when one of New Zealand's last great warrior chiefs, Te Rauparaha, was fleeing from his enemies. He hid in a sweet potato field one night, and by morning awoke to be told by a hairy chief that his enemies had gone. He then performed his victorious *haka*:

> *Ka mate, ka mate*
> *Ka ora, ka ora*
> *Tenei te tangata puhuruhuru*
> *Nana i tiki mai whakawhiti te ra*
> *Upane, upane*
> *Upane kaupane*
> *Whiti te ra.*

> It is death, it is death!
> It is life, it is life!
> This is the hairy man
> Who caused the sun to shine again for me.
> Up the ladder, up the ladder,
> Up to the top
> The sun shines.

As the sun sets, Günter, the "chief" of our group, is accepted by the warrior chief with a *Hongi* (greeting). They do not shake hands. Instead, the two chiefs press noses to share the breath of life.

Now we are allowed to wander through the village. In various buildings, Maori dressed in traditional costumes re-enact weaponry handling, flute playing, and carving. Afterward, we are treated to a traditional concert followed by a *hangi* (feast). The food has been prepared the traditional Maori way on hot stones in an authentic wooden oven.

The day's experiences have whetted my curiosity. Back in the camper, I delve into the history of the Maori, the takeover of these islands by the British, and all those New Zealand sheep.

New Zealand received its first flock of 100 sheep in 1834. Over the following decades, great swathes of forests fell to create grazing land. European domestic animals, pests, birds, and plants ravaged the indigenous forests by the end of the century, far exceeding the extinctions initiated by the Maori about 500 years earlier.

European settlement increased dramatically with the founding, in 1837, of the New Zealand Company. The purpose of this company was to establish a British colony in the South Pacific. The company sold land at above market prices to would-be immigrants, and then used that profit to subsidize further immigrant passages. Migrants were allowed to work off the cost of passage to their new home. The scheme was so successful, it brought settlers by the thousands to North Island's Wellington, Wanganui, and New Plymouth regions, and to South Island's Nelson area. Such success was too good to be ignored. Consequently, Britain decided to annex the country. All lands, henceforth, would become a monopoly of the British Crown. Britain's Colonial Office sent William Hobson to New Zealand to negotiate a treaty with the Maori chiefs. He arrived at the Bay of Islands in January 1840 and presented his written treaty—in both Maori and English—to 500 Maori chiefs.

The treaty specified that the Maori were ceding their sovereignty over North Island to Great Britain; that any future sale of land would supersede the original title and all further claims; and that all sale of land would transpire only between Maori chiefs and representatives of the Crown. In exchange, the Maori were guaranteed proprietorship and full use of their lands, protection by the Crown, and all the rights and privileges of British subjects.

But there was a catch….

The Maori language version of the treaty guaranteed *te tino rangatiratanga*, full chieftain authority; the English version had the Maori chiefs subordinating this ancient right to British law and government. The chiefs who had signed the treaty were totally unaware of this deception. And in May 1840 William Hobson officially proclaimed Britain's sovereignty over North Island "by virtue of cession" and over South Island "by right of discovery."

What followed were two decades of war and bloodshed.

Britain named the conflict the "Maori Wars" and, of course, insisted that the Maori were the aggressors. Losses on both sides were formidable. The British had an organized army of 14,000 professional soldiers, with an efficient supply infrastructure, and could stay in the field for extended periods of time. Maori warriors had no such supply structure and, needing food and water, could sustain battle for only a few days at a time. By the mid-1860s, the war had dwindled to intermittent, local skirmishes. But the final peace agreement was not concluded until 1881. After that, great tracts of the best Maori lands were confiscated by the British and sold to settlers. And by 1890, British colonists owned 22 million of the 26 million hectares that are New Zealand.

By 1900, all those sheep had replaced hectares of pristine forests, and Maori with no land became tenant croppers and day laborers. Their villages gave way to shanty towns. New Zealand had become British in soil and blood.

Glowworms and Craters
Waitomo
March 22

>Shine little glowworm, glimmer, glimmer!
>Lead us lest too far we wander.
>Love's sweet voice is calling yonder.
>Shine little glowworm, glimmer, glimmer...

I hummed this song as a child, but today I realize that I had no idea what a glowworm was, even though I had seen a firefly many times.

The Waitomo Glowworm Caves Tour tops any New Zealand vacation wish-list, so says our guidebook. The tourist brochure we picked up proclaims that the species of glowworm here, *Arachnocampa luminosa*, is unique to New Zealand. We must go!

After we climb into a small craft, our Maori guide takes us through a cave complex that glows with the luminescent light of thousands of magical glowworms.

While we explore, our expert teaches us about the caves: The Waitomo Glowworm Caves were first explored in 1887 by local Maori Chief Tane Tinorau. He was accompanied Fred Mace, an English surveyor. Local Maori people knew of the subterranean caverns nearby, but this cave had never been thoroughly explored until Fred and Tane went to investigate. They built a raft of flax stems. Using candles for light, they floated into the cave where the stream goes underground. As they entered the caves, their first discovery was what is now called The Glowworm Grotto. As their eyes adjusted to the darkness, they saw a multitude of lights reflecting off the water. Looking up, they discovered that the ceilings were dotted with the lights of thousands of glowworms.

In 1889, Tane Tinorau opened the cave to tourists. Chief Tane and his wife Huti escorted groups through the cave for a small fee. But visitor numbers soared, and in 1906 the administration of the cave was taken over by the government.

Almost 100 years later, in 1989, the land and the cave were returned to the descendants of the original owners. Many staff employed at the caves today are direct descendants of Chief Tane Tinorau and his wife Huti.

It's good to know that justice has come to some Maori—even if it was 150 years late!

Impressions of Wellington and On to the Ferry
March 24

In the morning, we leave Turangi for Wellington, a five-hour drive. Wellington, the capital of New Zealand, is the southernmost capital city in the world.

I have mixed feelings about Wellington. The adage, "You never have a second chance to make a first impression," can apply to a destination as well.

My first impression of the city of Wellington, unfortunately, is negative: I'll never forget images of New Zealand youth marching through the streets of their capital to the American embassy, where they burn the American flag and chant anti-Bush and anti-American slogans. On the other side of the street, a lone, elderly gentleman peacefully holds a pro-Bush sign out in front of him. A young demonstrator crosses the street, tears the sign from him, knocks him over, and breaks his little sign in two.

So much for democracy! In this nation, it is dangerous to take the path less traveled (or chosen). I don't look forward to touring this city.

The next morning, Günter and I take a cable car to Kelburn, overlooking the city. The views of the bay are stunning and my impression of the city turns positive.

Günter and I walk back down the hill via a path that winds through a botanical park and ends in an English style rose garden. In a contemplative mood, we sip coffee in an indoor tropical greenhouse and café.

We have one errand in the city: attempting to find a waterproof shower switch for *Pacific Bliss*. It seems logical to shop at the seaport, so we catch a taxi there. But we strike out.

Two days later, we rise early to drive to catch the *InterIslander*, the ferry that we have reserved, from Wellington to Picton, South Island. We drive onto the car platform and leave our camper for the duration. The 15-mile crossing will take three hours. We grab breakfast there, but I spend most of my time taking photos and movies as we cross Cook Strait. After all, it was my hero, Captain Cook, who realized that these are two islands, not one! I want to capture it all.

We drive on through lush Marlborough Sound to Nelson, a delightful town where we head for the marina to have late lunch/early dinner. I order a fish plate; Günter orders *cockles* (clams) in a delicious wine and cream sauce. To top it off, we find our boat part in the marine store there.

Tramping Tasman
March 27
Abel Tasman National Park, South Island

We decide to, as the locals say, "tramp" South Island's Abel Tasman Park, the smallest of New Zealand's national parks, but the most visited. A water taxi takes Günter and me to the most scenic section. This begins in Marahau and continues all the way to separation point in the north of South Island. The driver takes us ashore at Bark Bay and drops The Kids off at Big Tonga.

Our own walking time is expected to be about two to three hours to walk a 7.8 kilometer section of the trail, about right for us. Before long, we are on the most beautiful part of the Coast Walk. Campers can stay at

NEW ZEALAND'S GREENHOUSE GAS

We think of New Zealand as clean and green. In fact, the country's ad campaign is called "New Zealand Pure." Yet CHG emissions per capita rank 12th highest in the world. Why? Four million New Zealanders share their land with 50 million sheep and eight million cows. In addition, each year about 2.2 million visitors tramp, wheel, wine, and dine across this small country, adding to its ecological burden.

Livestock produce methane from rumination. Methane is a more potent greenhouse gas than carbon dioxide. This gas can trap 20 times the heat of an equivalent volume of carbon dioxide. New Zealand does not have many mineral resources. It must depend on its "solar economy," in essence, turning sunlight into exports. Because sunlight is free and inexhaustible, the economic basis of the New Zealand economy is in principle sustainable.

Here's how it works: The sun shines on the sea, making plankton grow that feeds the fish. New Zealand exports fish. The sun makes the crops, dairy cows and dry stock grow, so New Zealand exports produce, wine, milk, butter, meat, hides, and wool. Where exotic forests have been planted, the sunlight makes these grow and New Zealand exports timber. Finally, sunlight evaporates water that rains down to fill the hydro lakes, from which drinking water and electric power are derived.

huts (cabins) along the way. Trails are well marked and outdoor toilets are provided at each hut.

We follow a well-worn path that winds and climbs through the forest. Huge tree ferns open their delicate arms wide as they take in the sun and spread lacey shadows in front of us. Every so often the bush clears to permit a peek of the vista below. An emerald sea contrasts with spires of blue-gray rocks on the shore. Black cliffs rise dramatically. The backdrop is the deep blue sea beyond, meeting mountains on a distant shore that fade into pale purple against the horizon. We walk silently holding hands. I hear the squish of our Tevas® against twigs and stones as the sea laps the shoreline.

Words would wreck this wonderful walk. It is a Moment of Bliss.

April Fools
Wanaka, South Island
April 1

We three sit at the camper table, having our usual breakfast of muesli, yogurt, and honey. Günter arrives at the door, a newspaper folded under his arm. "Want to hear the good news and the bad news?" he asks.

I assume that the good news is that he managed to locate a newspaper. Despite the onslaught of negative news, we still like to read the paper with our morning coffee. "So what's the bad news?"

"We are ordered to leave here before the checkout time of 1000."

"What? But what about the hike we planned for today?"

Günter's face is serious and solemn. "Someone reported that we have been peeing behind the camper rather than walking all the way to the facilities during the night." Sternly, he looks at each of us in turn.

"Guilty as charged," answers Sabine, shifting her wiry frame on the bench.

Günter laughs. "Gotcha. April Fools!"

I am so relieved that we can stay here another night. These are gorgeous grounds, with three levels of campsites. At our top level, our van is backed up to a fence. We overlook rolling hills that reach all the way to Lake Waneka, framed by mountains. The tallest of them is called Mount Aspiring.

After breakfast, we follow the directions on a flyer, "Diamond Lake–Rocky Mountain Walking Track," we picked up at the office. It is a 20-minute drive, then a 775-meter climb.

At last, a tour we don't have to pay for!

We walk up a road to Diamond Lake, a pond that sits in idyllic pasture land with reeds and cattails on three sides and a sheer cliff on the fourth. We trudge up a cow path, around the pond, and up through a forest. We enter a clearing with a full view of the pond below.

It does indeed sparkle like a precious diamond!

Higher up, the view becomes even more stunning. Rolling hills contrast with the flatlands of the valley. Far below, the long, winding arms of Lake Wanaka come into view, the lake such a deep navy blue that it almost looks purple. The sky above is royal blue—what a perfect day! As we climb, the mountain ranges ahead go on and on, fading into pale purple at the horizon. I want to keep looking up, but hygiene concerns force me to look down. The path is dotted with shiny chocolate-colored sheep turds and common cow pies! Hearing unfamiliar animal noises around us, we realize that the cows here howl rather than moo. Strange!

Farther up, we encounter a group of shorn sheep. "They must be cold," I call to Günter, who is always leading the way.

Then, standing proudly on top of rocky ledges, we see some large, wooly creatures. They stand still and look at us, posing while I take their pictures. The trail winds up and around sharp rocks and cliffs. Every turn provides another spectacular view.

We walk up to a prominent ledge overlooking the lake and mountains below. This must be our designated Viewpoint C pointed out in the brochure. (Viewpoint D, the farthest, is the one Markus and Sabine have headed for.) We set out our lunch, granola bars and mandarin oranges, and sit there, all alone. It isn't until we pack up and prepare to walk back that we notice that hikers ahead of us have gone on past. We realize that another rocky outcrop is the real Viewpoint C; many hikers are resting there.

"It's okay," says Günter. "In this fully marketed land, I appreciated the solitude at our very own viewpoint!"

Southland—A Harsh yet Wondrous Land
April 6

After spending a day in Queensland, we continue our tour of South Island at a quicker pace. Finally, we drive across the suspension bridge to Bluff, the southernmost town in New Zealand. After lunch at the historic Bluff Restaurant, with a spectacular view of the rocky islands off the rugged shore, we walk to the lighthouse. Then we check in at the Curio Bay Camp.

This camp turns out to be the least hospitable site of our three-week trip—a true adventure in the cold. Of course, our heater chooses this moment to run out of propane. During the long, frigid night, all four of us make use of Sabine's technique to avoid having to walk down the path to the outhouses, which are about a block away.

How I yearn for the tropics! Never again will I complain about the heat!

In the morning we hike down a trail to Slope Point. At 46°47' south, this is the southernmost point of South Island. The scenery reminds me of photos of the Scottish

New Zealanders claim (and *Guinness* agrees) that Baldwin Street in Dunedin, South Island, is the world's steepest city street, a 38 percent grade.

highlands overlooking the sheer cliffs of the North Sea. It is not a land for the meek. One must be tough and strong-willed to live here. No wonder it is filled with Scottish immigrants!

We head to the point at the end of the bluff that overlooks the sea. Stewart Island is a speck way out there, 19 miles (30 kilometers) southwest of Bluff.

As I stand there, shivering in the wind, I search for words to describe this godforsaken country. Awesome. Powerful. Stark. Rugged. Wild.

What trees remain are bent over, decrepit, and old before their time. The swamp grass runs untamed, waving in the cruel winds. The angry, fierce sea rushes in at high tide to swallow the gray rocks and slam against the stark cliffs. It is time to head back north—away from this hostile, yet wondrous, land.

I could not live here.

Heading Back to Auckland
April 11

Our drive north takes us through the charming cities of Dunedin and Christchurch. We have now reached Picton, where we will spend our last night before catching the *InterIslander* back to North Island. What a pleasant surprise! Barbara and Jerry of Nootka Rose contact us, and we arrange for them to visit. This is the first time we have talked with other cruisers in weeks!

"You're doing what many cruisers do," Barbara informs me. "Many of them touring here left their yachts in the Bay of Islands. Now they're seeing New Zealand by car or camper van…like you."

"See?" Günter turns to me. "Why risk storms sailing to and from New Zealand? I told you a 747 goes better to weather!"

Barbara laughs. "You're right. Cruisers have no desire to take any more chances…once they've survived the weather along the way. They don't want to venture into those dangerous southern seas with their boats."

"They hire a camper van," Jerry adds. "That's what we did."

After crossing to North Island, we stay at the campground in Lower Huff, near Wellington, again. I'm happy to be in a warmer climate. We spend a few days enjoying the cities and parks on the way back to Auckland.

Frankly, after three weeks, we're tired of the touring life and the man-made thrills of New Zealand. We are cruisers, and our hearts are still in Vuda Point, right on the deck of *Pacific Bliss*. We've seen and learned a lot; we've had fun with The Kids; and now, we're ready to go back to sailing. The real thrills and challenges of the sea await us.

Fiji, here we come!

DID YOU KNOW?

THE ART OF THE TATOO

The English name for this body decoration comes from the Tahitian word *tatau* and has been incorporated into most European languages. Joseph Banks, the naturalist aboard Cook's ship *The Endeavour*, was the first to record this practice in his journals while in Tahiti in 1769. All Polynesians excelled in this artistic expression of their culture. But it was in the Marquesas Islands and New Zealand where tattoos had the greatest social significance. Although women were less tattooed than men, both were expected to adorn their thighs, hands, and feet. In the Marquesas, the geometric designs were the most popular.

The wealthy could afford the best tattoos. The tattoo artist was the *ta'ua patu tiki,* "expert in hammering images." He and his entourage of helpers had to be fed and housed. The artist received his final payment in pigs and war clubs. The right hands of women had to be adorned by the age of twelve so that they could prepare *popoi* from bread-fruit and anoint corpses with coconut oil. Of course, no self-respecting woman would consent to marry a man who was not tattooed. The greater a man's tattoos, the greater was his wealth, sense of style, and ability to endure pain.

The process of tattooing a boy could be spread out over three to four months; further designs could be added in adulthood. Before the first tattoo, the father would build a special house. A *taboo* was declared, during which the father could have no sex. Only a virgin woman could assist him in preparing the powder used as the dye. He would heat the shells of the candle-nut tree, called *ama,* until they opened. Then he would spread the kernels over the fire so that thick soot developed on the underside, which was then placed on a banana leaf to dry. The black powder was then mixed with water in a coconut shell. (This same type of soot is collected and used on the Lau islands of Fiji to make the black dye for their traditional bark-cloth designs.) The intricate geometric patterns used for tattoos mimic the designs used on Lapita earthenware found by archeologists in Fiji. It is possible that over thousands of years and thousands of miles the art form was transferred from clothing and pottery to the human form itself.

The *opou* (patient) would try to contain his pain as a sign of bravery. As the tattoo progressed, the assistants chanted and played the flute. The more the coverage, the more assured the son would be of attracting admiration. It would be worth the pain. For days after the application, the patient would experience inflammation, swelling, and fever, sometimes fatal. No wonder the patients of traditional tattoo artists were often referred to as victims!

Application of an ointment called *paku*, made from the juice of banana stems, hastened healing, and the application of hibiscus leaves relieved inflammation. The most effective medicine was made from the fruit of the nono tree, called *noni*. Fruit juice made from this tree is now sold worldwide as a health drink.

Abel Tasman is the smallest of New Zealand's National Parks but the most visited.

Hiking trails and campgrounds along the bays allow one to easily tramp Abel Tasman National Park, South Island.

A Tribute to Captain James Cook

Ambition leads me not only further than any other man has been before me, but as far as I think it is possible for a man to go. James Cook, January 30, 1774.

Captain Cook has been my hero for most of my life. In New Zealand's Maritime Museum Bookstore, I purchase three more books to add to my collection: *Captain's Log: New Zealand's Maritime History*, by Gavin McLean; *The Explorations of Captain James Cook in the Pacific, as Told by Selections of His Own Journals,* edited by A. Grenfell Price; and *Captain James Cook* by Richard Hough.

I continue to peruse them during the remainder of our South Pacific voyage.

I revere Cook because he was the consummate explorer and the original hard-core adventurer—and because his legend lives on in popular culture. Few men in the history of the world possessed such a variety of skills necessary for a career in exploration. Captain Cook had self-confidence, superb navigational talents, geographic curiosity, a fascination with science, knowledge of shipboard diseases, and an understanding of indigenous peoples. To Cook, adventure was more than risk-taking; it was a calling, one that bordered on art and required courage and class. And Cook has never disappeared from the public consciousness. His ambition "to go as far as I think it is possible for man to go" became the starship Enterprise's mission, "to boldly go where no man has gone before." Captain Cook became Captain Kirk.

Cook's reputation does not relate to his rank, however: He held the rank of captain for just four of his fifty years on this earth. I want to know more about what it was that turned this humble man—an introvert, a commoner—into the legendary figure he became.

In 1728, England was still an agricultural society when Cook, the second of eight children, was born. In a day when young men were trained to follow in their fathers' footsteps, young James aspired to a world that was limitless and free. He began to distance himself from his farming family, sought approval from a series of surrogate fathers, and copied their traits: notions of honor, duty, and country. One of these surrogates took note of his intelligence and paid for him to attend elementary school, a great honor in an illiterate society. Cook was known as a loner, yet respected by his companions. At 17, he left school and ended up in Staithes, a small fishing village on the North Sea, apprenticed as a shop boy. There, he listened to herring fishermen tell tales of their days at sea, sprinkled with references to the workings of the sun and stars and currents. James was intrigued. At night, he pored over books on mathematics, astronomy, and geography, ignoring anything unrelated to the sea.

When he was ready, Cook left the life of a shopkeeper behind, slung his few belongings over his shoulder, and trekked the 12 miles to Whitby, the shipbuilding and cargo transportation center for the entire North Sea and Baltic. Cook gaped at the international armada of cargo ships—their billowing yards spreading wide like the arms of God. For the first time, he heard the sounds of foreign tongues. He had wandered to where he belonged.

A few days later, Cook stepped on board the *Freelove*, signed the muster book, was issued a hammock and blanket, and began "learning the ropes" as an apprentice. As the years passed, he was transferred to other vessels and began open-ocean passages across the North Sea. He was promoted up the ranks, yet he continued to teach himself mathematics and astronomy by candlelight.

Sailing became Cook's passion. He learned the logistics of loading cargo, how to balance weight in the hold, how to order supplies, and how to oversee refurbishment of masts and hulls between voyages. He learned what sail combinations worked best in which winds, how use a "lead line" to measure sea depths, and how record speed and distance. And he learned the fundamentals of navigation, determining latitude with a sextant. (Measuring longitude was still an inexact science.)

By 1752, Cook had worked his way up from apprentice to seaman to first mate. At 26, Cook was offered the position of Captain of the *Friendship*, his employer's best commercial vessel. Cook turned it down and instead set sail for London, where he enlisted in the Royal Navy, throwing away nine years' seniority and advancement and starting all over again.

After just a month, Cook was promoted to master's

mate. He then boarded the *Eagle* bound for the wilderness of Canada to fight against France in the Seven Years' War. Once in Canada, Cook trained as a surveyor and cartographer and was soon promoted to warrant officer. When his master was promoted to another command, and after passing a written exam, Cook became a full-fledged ship's master. He had risen from the lowest rank to the highest available to a noncommissioned officer in just 2 years and 12 days. He proved himself as a master surveyor in the battle of Quebec and was making a name for himself.

When the war ended, Cook was laid off with a nice sum from His Majesty's war chest. He now turned to a new adventure, love, and began courting Elizabeth Batts, a merchant's daughter. She soon became his soul mate. She believed in James and supported his dreams. The happy couple said their vows a mere two weeks later and bought a three-story brick row house on the main thoroughfare leading from London to the coast. It was a great marriage and a continuing romance. Cook would never be unfaithful—even when the ocean took him away for three years at a time. Elizabeth would never remarry even though she would survive James by 60 years. She and James had eight children. Before she died, she burned James' dozens of love letters, making sure that the world could never know their most intimate secrets.

In the spring of 1763, the Navy recalled Cook. Britain had been given control of Canada and needed to chart the new acquisitions. Cook was given a small schooner, *Grenville*, and an added title, "the King's Surveyor." His work during the following years was so exact that it would be used well into the 20th century.

But back in England, the aristocratic world was planning an expedition, a circumnavigation that would change the world forever. *Endeavor* would carry out this mission. And James Cook, assisted by the political scheming of Lord Sandwich, would become the ship's master.

A ship's master had never been chosen for command. And never in the history of the Royal Navy had a sailor risen through the ranks and been awarded a commission. When given command of the *Endeavor* in 1768, Cook was not even a lieutenant, let alone a captain. But Cook was an astronomer who was also known for his superb navigational skills, an ideal balance of seaman and scientist.

Cook's Voyage of Discovery on the *HMS Endeavor* was ostensibly launched in order to observe the Transit of Venus, when the disc of Venus would pass over the face of the sun. Based on the length of time it took to do this, astronomers could calculate the distance between the earth and the sun, which it was thought would help to gauge the size and scale of the universe. In reality, sailing under the pretense of science, the Royal Society's vessel could prowl the South Pacific without raising French or Spanish suspicion. They would locate the mythical Southern Continent, once and for all—or not—and chart any islands along the way, claiming them for England.

For most of its voyage, the *Endeavor* would sail through unplied waters, symbolic of the untraveled path the Apollo15 spacecraft would take on its mission to the moon. *Endeavor* pushed south from Madeira, raced past Africa, swerved south-southwest toward South America, rounded Tierra del Fuego, and headed toward the Pacific. With its 30 sails hoisted by 20 miles of line, *Endeavor* logged an average of 100 miles per day. Being the man in charge was not easy. The crew could collapse into their hammocks after four hours of watch, but Cook was constantly on call, never able to totally relax. Cook knew that he was being studied, his actions compared for better or worse with other captains the crew had sailed under. Throughout the voyage, he handled his new-found power better than most.

Upon entering the Pacific, the *Endeavor* was the only British ship in that vast ocean. With no superiors within thousands of miles, Cook could roam as he pleased. As we cruisers know, the prevailing winds here in the Pacific blow east to west, then rotate counterclockwise up the coast of South America towards the equator. Typically, tall ships would go with the prevailing winds up the coast of Chile, then "go where the wind blows" toward Tahiti. But Cook indulged his craving for adventure by pointing due south, attempting to discover Antarctica. After five days heading south into cold rain and roiling seas, he gave up and headed to Tahiti.

Tahiti was perfectly positioned in the Southern Ocean to observe the Transit. The Transit observations proved disappointing, so Cook used his remaining time to survey the Society Islands. After that, he opened Admiralty's orders that sent him south again in search

of the elusive Southern Continent. He failed again, dispelling the myth, but what he did find was New Zealand. According to historians, when Cook found the country Tasman had sighted, it was no more than a line on a map, but because of his superb charting skills, he left it an archipelago.

I continue to follow Cook's explorations throughout our circumnavigation, as we sail on to Australia in the wake of the greatest explorer the world has ever known. We enjoy a reenactment of Cook's landing in a place now called Cook Town. We climb a hill on Lizard Island to Cook's Lookout, where Cook searched for a way through the Great Barrier Reef.

After charting the eastern coastline of Australia, Cook continued on to New Guinea and Java and home. He returned in June 1771 after 2 years and 11 months, having sailed 30,000 miles and having charted over 5,000 miles of coastline.

Cook's second voyage of discovery, on the HMS *Resolution* and accompanied by *Adventure*, was another search for the Great Southern Continent. He crossed the Antarctic Circle for the first time in history, then crossed it twice again. He finally reached 71°10´ latitude, disproving the continent's existence. The Antarctic Circle would not be crossed again for nearly half a century. *Resolution* returned to England after 3 years and 18 days. As the first man ever to have circumnavigated the world in both directions, Cook was honored as England's hero by King George III.

Cook finally received the rank he deserved. He was promoted to Post Captain. He set sail on his third voyage of discovery with *Resolution* and *Discovery* for further exploration of the Pacific and to find an exit from the Northwest Passage. The expedition re-visited New Zealand, Tonga, and Tahiti where he was welcomed like a king. He came to see the Pacific as his kingdom, where he could do no wrong.

After leaving Bora Bora and discovering and naming Christmas Island on the way to the North American coast, Cook was flabbergasted to see tropical islands off his port bow. He had stumbled upon Niihau and Kauai, two of the Hawaiian Islands. The date was January 18, 1778. Cook stayed two weeks, replenishing his stores, and then hurried north.

Because the Pacific coast of North American reminded Cook so much of New Zealand, he named part of it Queen Charlotte and another part after his beloved Ship's Cove. Cook had surveyed Newfoundland much earlier in his life; now he was setting foot again on North American soil. He then sailed in and out of the wide inlet leading to Anchorage but failed to find the Northwest Passage. He continued through the Aleutian Islands and into the Bering Sea, while on the other side of the continent, the Revolutionary War raged on land and sea. Cook maneuvered through ice and fog, frigid seas, and summer blizzards, sailing back and forth between North American and Asian landmasses, trying to find a gap in the ice. He was above 70° north, as far into the northern high latitudes as he'd ever sailed into the southern. Without knowing it, Cook gave up just 50 miles southwest of the Beaufort Sea, entrance to the Northwest Passage. Then he returned through cruel gales and storms, reaching the Hawaiian Islands at November's end to wait out the winter.

In Kealakekua Bay on the western side of Hawaii, the Big Island, Cook was treated to the welcome of his life. The bay's name meant "pathway of the gods," and at first the locals thought Cook was one of their gods.

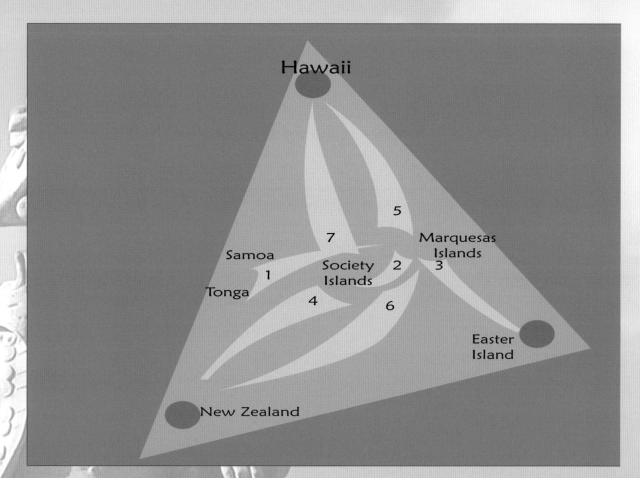

By coincidence, his ships had sailed into the bay during an annual festival to pay homage to Lono, the god of plenty. The natives, who had never seen monstrous sailing ships with billowing white banners, thought that, for the first time, their god was paying a personal visit. For three weeks, Cook was treated to feasts and celebrations. But the behavior of his crew began to grate on the natives. For one thing, their insatiable sexual appetite was making the women's mates jealous and angry. For another, the natives wondered why divine beings needed so much sustenance—hogs, vegetables, and fruit. Eventually, when an old seaman died and was buried ashore, the natives found out that Cook's crew was not immortal. The Hawaiians became fearless and began stealing knives and iron goods from the ships. They cheered when the ships left.

Unfortunately, Cook was forced to return to repair a broken mast. Tensions increased. The natives continued to steal and were punished. Then one of the chiefs was killed in a confrontation. Cook was ambushed going ashore. He was set upon and cut with the very knives he had given to the islanders, his body and that of four dead marines set upon a litter and brought to an emu used for roasting pigs. Later, Cook's bones, skull, arms, and hands were delivered to *Discovery*.

Günter and I have visited the Hawaiian Islands, the northern point of the vast Polynesian Triangle, many times. But after researching the life of Captain Cook, I turn a tour of Big Island into a special quest. South of the Kailua Kona airport and the town of Kailua Kona, we drive through a village called Captain Cook. We head toward the shore and park near a sign that points to Cook's memorial in Kealakekua Bay close to where Cook met his death. I stand and stare at the Pacific lapping against a rocky lava shore. Underneath those waters, Cook's roasted remains are buried in a coffin weighted with cannonballs. An obelisk commemorating Cook rises from a clearing in the water, on a small square of land that was deeded to Britain from the United States in homage to Cook, the greatest adventurer of all time.

James Cook's reputation lives on. During his lifetime, he discovered more of the earth's surface than any other man in history. He had a prophetic vision of the world that was realized centuries later when Neil Armstrong took his first step on the moon. In fact, his three epic journeys are equivalent in distance to sailing to the moon!

Martin Dugard says, "It was Cook who began knitting earth's cultures one island at a time. Two centuries after Cook, the Internet finished the task, creating a global village. It's sweet irony that Tuvalu, a collection of islands in Cook's beloved South Pacific, has overcome its remote global locale by basing its entire economy on the Internet."

Usually a man with such a global vision wouldn't pay close attention to detail. Yet Cook's maps of the South Pacific were so accurate that his input is still being used in paper charts that we have on board *Pacific Bliss*. I'm comforted to know that as long as we sail the South Pacific, we'll have Captain Cook sailing right along with us!

Hindu temple, Nadi, Fiji.

Chapter 10
Fiji: One Country, Two Cultures

Easter Sunday Panic Attack
Vuda Point Marina, Vitu Levu, Fiji
April 20, 2003

0600: Günter awakens me by gently tickling my feet. "Would you like to see the sunrise? Did you get enough sleep?"

"Yes." I rub my eyes and reach for my pareu. I reach the cockpit in time to see the marina's inner bay turn blood red. The reflection lasts only a moment before it changes to the typical amber. A waning moon highlights the dark blue sky as the sun breaks through on the opposite shore of the circular quay. Birds chorus the dawn as they flit from tree to tree along the shore.

Günter, wearing his black-and-yellow lap-lap, hands me a coffee. We talk about Easter Sundays past and how, last year, we celebrated this holiday on *Pacific Bliss* as we sailed from San Diego to the Marquesas; how I had set out a basket with green grass and chocolate eggs for our crew. This year, we will play Handel's *Messiah* here and then meet the van at First Landing Resort to attend a Fijian church in the village. Ma, a cook at The Hatch, the marina's restaurant, has invited us.

After coffee, I go down to the galley to boil potatoes and eggs for potato salad. That heats the inside of the boat while the sun continues to bake the outside. First mistake. Already sweaty, I pull my zipperless blue sheath over my head and realize that it is too tight with the bra I'm wearing. I try to pull it off. No luck.

"Dear, you'll just have to wear this one," Günter says. "There's no time for you to change anyway." I pull it down and smooth it out. After fluffing my hair, I grab my hat and sunglasses.

"Hurry!" Günter calls. I rush down the gangplank to meet the van without my usual bottle of water. Second mistake.

The church is beautiful, larger than I expected, and arranged in the typical Methodist style we'd seen in the Cooks. Three sections of seats face the pulpit, with the choir to the left, the children to the right, and the rest of the congregation in the middle. The women are not wearing hats, so I keep mine in my bag. We take a seat in the back near the door.

With the sun already beating down, the day promises to be a scorcher. An usher motions us to the front. "We want to catch any breeze that might come up," Günter whispers.

"I'll turn on the fans," the usher says as he leads us to the front of the church. He's barefoot, yet he's wearing a white short-sleeved shirt and necktie with a white sarong. Ceiling fans begin to whirl. I take out my hat and use it to fan my face. My chest feels constructed in the tight dress. I feel short of breath and force myself to relax.

The service begins. The preacher dons his jacket over his shirt and tie. Just looking at him makes me sweat even more! When I notice that the entire congregation is barefoot, I motion to Günter. We slip off our shoes. Wiggling my toes makes me feel cooler, but that doesn't make up for the pressure on my chest.

We stand silently as the congregation belts out spirituals in Fijian. A little girl, about seven years old, brings us a hymnal so that we can follow along. She mouths to us in English the page number of the next hymn, and the next, as we attempt to decipher the Fijian words.

Ma, a cook at The Hatch, with Gunter.

All the while, I feel as if I could collapse any minute.

After we sit and the sermon begins, the church warms even more, and the fans cannot keep up. Since I can't understand Fijian, I try to cool off by imagining how good it would feel to rip off my dress and jump into the cool pool at First Landing. My mouth goes completely dry, and then a piercing headache begins. I'm suffocating. Panic sets in.

I'm going to pass out right here. I'll fall to the floor. I'll come to with a terrific headache and the entire congregation looking down at me. At least, someone will put a glass of water to my lips.

I imagine stories of survival, of sailors on rafts sucking the flesh of fish, sucking rubber, anything to get a drop of water.

Stop it! Don't make it worse!

The preacher drones on. The little girl looks over at me as if to ask, "What's wrong?"

I motion her to come over.

"Water," I whisper. "I need water. Can you help me?" She goes back to her seat.

"You're asking a lot," Günter whispers. "She doesn't understand you."

But she *does* understand. When a break comes and the congregation stands up, she comes and takes me by the hand. I follow her out the side door of the church. Right there, protruding from the foundation, is a pipe with a handle. *Water!* I cup my hands as the girl turns it on. After drinking only a few handfuls, I feel my strength return and my headache recede. I splash the refreshing water on my face and arms.

I follow the girl back into the church, fan my face with my hat, and sit it out to the end, another hour. The choir rises to sing again. All the women are dressed in white frocks with full-length white satin underskirts.

How can they take it?

I leave the church with a new respect for these Fijian islanders.

We take the van ride back to First Landing where we stop at the bar for a cold smoothie. That gives us enough energy to walk to The Hatch. I'm still wearing the sheath dress, but it feels okay now.

Back on *Pacific Bliss*, Günter lifts the dress over my head easily—it's not necessary to rip it off after all! But from now on, I'll be wearing a loose tent dress or Hawaiian-style *muumuu* to church!

Stuck in the Anchor Locker *
Vuda Point Marina

I am way forward in the starboard hull of *Pacific Bliss* when I hear a distant, "Lois…help."

I rush topsides to the cockpit. Then I hear another muffled, "Lois…help." I can barely make out Günter's words: "I'm stuck…up here…in the anchor locker."

Crawling under the sunshade lines, I make my way to the bow of the boat. I see Günter's legs flailing in the air. He is head-first into the anchor locker—all the way to his waist. He's wearing shorts, and his bare torso is squeezed tightly in the square opening. With his hands down, he has no way to right himself.

"Put…put your hands under my stomach," he grunts. "And pull."

I try again and again to grip his sweaty skin. No luck. I scrape my arms against the sharp edge of the hatch until they are bruised and blue. But I cannot yank him out.

Time is getting short. Blood is rushing to his head.

What if he loses consciousness? He will be dead weight. Take a few deep breaths, Lois. Keep calm. Think!

Suddenly, I realize that we are not alone! We are in a marina at midday. Some yachties or boat workers must be within earshot. I rally what strength I have left and take another deep breath. "He-e-e-lp!"

Now Günter shifts his weight enough to make a small opening.

I pull desperately on his legs. Out he pops like a cork from a bottle! We both fall onto the deck.

Clearly disoriented, Günter lies there breathing hard. Then he stumbles to his feet just as a burly Fijian worker bounds onto the gangway. A yachtie follows a few steps behind him.

*This story was first published in *Latitudes and Attitudes* in their "*So you think that was dumb?*" section.

"Are you all right?" the yachtie asks.

"I th-think so. I feel a little dizzy."

I had expected Günter to emerge red-faced; instead, he is ghostly pale. Rivers of sweat pour down his face and drip onto his bare chest. He is shaking. I lead him to the galley and dress the superficial wounds on his belly.

"Let's go to the showers," he gasps, still drenched with sweat.

We stand together in the bamboo-enclosed unisex showers a few yards from the yacht basin, letting the cold water refresh our bodies.

"What happened?" I ask as we walk back to *Pacific Bliss*.

"A shackle pin dropped as I was working on the anchor. I tried to reach it. But it had dropped all the way to the bottom. You know how deep that locker is!"

We walk up the gangway to our Med-moored yacht as Günter continues his story.

"I kept thinking I could reach it. I managed to touch it. Then, all of a sudden, my equilibrium shifted, and I was stuck in there, head down. What a horrible, suffocating feeling!"

"Don't you *ever* do that again!" I order, trying to put on a stern face. "Ask *me* the next time. I'm so short…I could probably have *stood* in there. Maybe I could have grabbed it with my toes."

Günter hangs his head with uncharacteristic humility. "Yes, it was very foolish of me."

I seize on the rare opportunity. "And don't you do anything else foolish. I need you! How else am I going to sail around the world?"

We hug each other tight. Then we turn on the fans and collapse into the master berth. Later, too exhausted to cook, we stagger to The Hatch for Bula Burgers and cokes.

When we return to *Pacific Bliss*, Günter has an idea. He opens the lazaretto in the cockpit. "No worries," he looks up at me. "*This* locker is wide and shallow." He begins to throw things out onto the deck like a squirrel digging for nuts.

"What are you doing *now*?"

"I'm looking for something." After a few moments, he straightens triumphantly. "Look here." My chagrined captain, a loyal connoisseur of the San Diego West Marine store when we're not cruising, holds an impressive mechanical gripper with an extra long handle. "I forgot we had this. This is *exactly* what I bought it for." His mouth droops. "And now, I'll probably never have another reason to use it!"

The price tag is still on the tool.

That "Glimpse of the Underglimmer"

We need a break from boat chores, so we designate Saturday as "date night." Our regular taxi driver, Sen, drives us to Lautoka. In his late twenties, Sen is a lanky, dark-haired Indo-Fijian with a shy, pleasant personality. Last year, he picked me up many times at Vuda Point Marina and drove me to Lautoka or Nadi for all my shopping needs. One time, on our way back, he stopped to show me the colorful Hindu temple on the outskirts of Nadi. We had become fast friends.

Indo-Fijian is the official term the government for Indians living in Fiji. Most of their ancestors were brought from India to Fiji by the British during the colonial era to work the sugar cane fields. Many still work them today, but only Fijians can own the land here. It is the Indians, however, who make the economy work; they own and run most of the banks, shops, and services.

In just a couple of weeks, Günter and I, along with only one other cruiser, will be honored guests at Sen's wedding to Shelly; he has asked me to be their official photographer.

We take in a movie at the Lautoka Cinema, followed by dinner at the Lautoka Hotel. We enjoy the Steve Martin comedy *Bringing Down the House*, but it's the laughs in the theater —full of Indian and Fijian children—that please us the most. When we leave, though, we notice that the children are divided into their own racial cliques.

Despite what we've heard and read about easing racial tensions, we note that there is actually very little integration. The Indian children attend their own schools where they learn English, Indian, and also Fijian; the Fijians attend schools where they learn English but never Indian, even though Indians comprise 40 percent of the population.

The following Saturday, we attend an Indian Fire Walk. We watch two men spread out a pile of coals with the longest-handled rakes I'd ever seen. They cordon off a 6-by-12-foot rectangle with ropes, leaving only one opening for the walkers to file through. Another man in a long-sleeved, muslin shirt sets up and lights small altars of incense, charcoal, and flowers. Drums sound and cymbals clash. Then a barefoot man with a long white beard, wearing a sleeveless natural-colored tunic and sarong, marches through the coals. Right in the middle, he stops! He lays a large red flower over the red-hot coals, then continues his march to the end.

Günter gasps. I am mesmerized.

Following the first man, two men wearing high hats march through side by side. Then the entire group of marchers, about ten, files through. No one runs. There is a pause, and then the leader marches through again, picks up the flower, and continues on to the temple.

That's the end. Everyone rises. Slowly and silently, they vacate the grandstands.

Amazing! We never expected to attend an Indian Fire Walk in Fiji.

⚓

We continue to prepare *Pacific Bliss* for cruising by day, and to solidify our plans for the season by night. We're especially interested in visiting Fiji's remote Lau Group.

During Pizza Nights at First Landing Resort, we talk with other cruisers who have been in this South Pacific area for years. They claim that no cruising permits are given for Lau, and that the only way to get there is through a personal invitation. Mr. Mora, the current President of Fiji, lives there and does not want visitors, they tell us, because the island's residents want to keep it undeveloped and natural.

Undaunted, Günter and I decide to pursue all methods, through the government and also though the marina's owner, whose family reputedly has land there.

Now our battle with bureaucracy begins.

On April 28, we take a taxi to Lautoka, a Fijian point of entry, to obtain a permit for cruising the Mamalucas and Yasawas, just in case we need it. This is a simple three-month renewal. While at the customs office, we explain that we want to cruise the rest of the Fijian islands—and the Lau Group as well. "That's easy," the constable says, "I will give you a letter to take to the Office of Fijian Affairs in Suva."

I am surprised but pleased that it could be so simple.

"Here is the letter you will need," the constable says as she hands it to me.

But of course, nothing is ever easy in the islands.

A few days later we take a taxi, following King's Road all the way to Suva, Fiji's capital. The trip takes about four hours. We check into the Peninsula Hotel.

The next day, the bureaucracy battle intensifies. First, we head for the Office of Fijian Affairs as directed. This office directs us to another office, which directs us to a third. In this office, we finally obtain permits for every island we want to visit except for the elusive Lau Group. Then we go to two more offices to present our paperwork and pay.

The following day, we arrive for our scheduled appointment for the Lau Island Group with a bureaucrat named Salote, only to find that she has called in sick. The day after that, she calls in sick again. We are referred to the Lau Provincial Office in the Arcade.

Our taxi drops us off behind the shopping center. It seems like a strange location for a government office, but we know by now that such offices sprawl throughout Suva. We've been to five of them so far! We search for and find the name on a door.

Inside, a group of Fijians, most of them wearing sulus, are just hanging out around a massive desk in the corner of the room. One of them motions us in, and another fetches two chairs.

We sit and a burly Fijian wheels his chair toward Günter. "What is your story?"

Günter carefully explains our desire to visit the Lau Group for our research into Polynesian sailing and migration.

"I am writing a book," I add. "We understand that your Lau Group is where the Polynesian and Melanesian societies intersect. Our marina told us that we need a letter of introduction from a landowner. But that apparently is not the case."

"No, we go through procedures now. That is why they directed you to our office." He straightens his shoulders and wheels his chair up to the desk.

Günter hands him the typed letter of introduction.

"Ah! Now we will process the permit and have it typed." He calls for a clerk, then rolls his chair back from the desk and slouches again. "So you're Americans," he begins with a big smile. "We in Fiji support Americans. U.S. allies since World War Two. We Fijians, we are warriors." He pounds his chest. "We went to fight in the Solomons so that our own country would not be invaded. And our soldiers fought hard."

"I know. I read James Michener's books. He writes about brave Fiji fighting men."

"Yes, the Fijians back then would have eaten those Japs…" he says with a straight face, "…but those little guys were too tough, not good eating."

I stammer…at a loss for words.

Then the big man's face breaks out in a satisfied grin.

⚓

While the bureaucratic wheels turn, we make use of down time to have a drink and a meal at the Suva Royal Yacht Club, to tour the Fiji Museum, and to conduct research at the USP (University of the South Pacific) library. The most interesting stop by far is our visit to the Fijian Parliament where, from the visitors' gallery, we are able to observe the Fijian government in action at their impressive Parliament Building.

After we return to Vuda Point, we go to First Landing for dinner. I ask Maggie, the resort manager, whether the Fijians built the magnificent building and grounds through their own funds or foreign aid. "The Germans and Americans paid for it," she informs me. "In fact," she continues, "it was the Americans who forced them to resolve the last coup."

"Why? I thought Britain might have interceded."

"No," she responds. "The American embassy essentially said, 'You solve this hostage crisis quickly and return to a democracy or we pull out.' And if the Americans pulled out, the British, Australian, and New Zealand embassies would have quickly followed. Fiji couldn't exist without foreign aid."

"So what happened? Do they have a new

constitution now?"

"It seems that the indigenous Fijians now have the majority of the seats, and that they will always have the power now," she replies. "They had to write a new constitution after the 2000 coup because U.K. would kick them out of the Commonwealth—again—if they didn't. Financially, Fiji must be part of the Commonwealth. The Fijians need the Indians though. They have organizational ability. It would be a very different country without them."

Maggie goes to attend to business and then returns to our table. "The next generation of Fijians might be different," she continues. "Those with education might be just like whites—solely interested in business and profit. And then they would lose the basic nature we have all grown to love. Would you like to visit Fiji then? The friendliness would be gone."

By night, I continue to read books about the coups I purchased at the USP library; one is written from the Fijian perspective, the other, from the Indian. Both sides agree that Fijians must learn business and entrepreneurship. Then, they believe, things will change.

But can Fijians ever become entrepreneurs? Business goes against some of their inherent values; for instance, they believe that all wealth belongs to the family and the community. When a relative—no matter how distant—comes to an entrepreneur's place of business, that proprietor cannot turn down a plea for help; he must share the goods from his store. That's not a formula for business success.

⚓

Every morning, Günter and I read *The Fiji Times* together over breakfast—often at The Hatch, where we are now. "The second case in three days of domestic violence where a man beats his woman to death," he reads out loud.

We whisper about the Fijian waitress here at The Hatch who has come to work with a black eye and bruises.

She stops at our table and sees our paper open to the headline. "I'm leaving my man before that happens," she confides. "Who needs a man anyway? I just do all the work while he spends his afternoons drinking *kava*."

Live in a place long enough and one discovers its ugly underbelly.

At First Landing, I stop in for a manicure from my charming Indo-Fijian friend, Primaya. We talk about that coup of May 2000 when Fijians, backed by the military, took over the government after an Indian Prime Minister was duly elected. Primaya emphasizes how bad it was for the Indians in those areas where the Fijians looted and burned stores and homes. "You can bet the Indians here will be kicked off the Fijian lands when their 40-50-year leases expire," she adds.

I'm learning firsthand about the tough problems in Paradise. It makes me sad. Because I find Fijians to be among the friendliest, most hospitable we've met of all the South Seas islanders.

I love them all, Indians and Fijians alike.

Beaching the Cat
Denarau Anchorage, Viti Levu, Fiji
May 20

The maintenance of replacing the zincs must be performed every one-to-two years, or whenever the plates are damaged by the electrolytic process. They are inconveniently located on the bottom of each propeller shaft. To get to them, we must lift the craft out of the water or beach the boat on an incline.

At 1000, we had pulled anchor and headed for such an incline. Now *Pacific Bliss* bobs gently in the still bay, waiting patiently. Her instruments show Force 0 wind. The sky is baby blue with white fleece clouds, as serene as the scene on a toddler's pajamas.

Nevertheless, Günter and I watch the clock with trepidation. We are waiting for a certain moment: *exactly* 45 minutes after high tide. Then we will motor to the mud bar and attempt to glide our catamaran onto the mud without sinking her too deeply into it. Though we have sailed over 17,000 miles, this will be the first time we've ever attempted this procedure. We ask God to make sure that our Guardian Angel is still on duty.

The moment arrives. Waving our hands above our heads, we let loose a primal scream: "A-a-ah!" Günter starts the engines. Events now unfold in slow motion. We snake through the Denarau Marina channel. We pass two excursion yachts, *Captain Cook Cruises* and *Whales Tale*. Their passengers wave at us. I see a pair of moon jellyfish gliding along our hull: one floats flat like a purple-rimmed plate, the other puffs open its bell, trailing translucent tentacles. We motor slowly toward a row of posts where workhorse vessels are tied. *It goes against my grain to have to inch forward this way.*

But I caution Günter, "Nice and easy now…easy does it."

He's in perfect control of the boat. Inch by inch, slowly, carefully we move forward. Finally…we kiss the bank. No scraping. No scratching. Just a gentle settling-in. We are beached.

Günter deploys the dinghy. He checks the depths at the props, the dagger boards, the rudder. I record his measurements. "She's resting on her belly," Günter says.

"Two bellies," I contribute. "Like a pair of beached whales."

"Piece of cake, this Beaching a Cat," he boasts, grinning.

But beaching our catamaran is only part of the story…the worst is yet to come.

Günter calls David, the mechanic at Denarau Marine. He arrives with his assistant in a small powerboat. They get out at the same time and promptly sink into the oozy mud up to their knees. It sucks as if it wants to claim them. David reaches back into his boat for a tarp and lays it lightly over the mud to catch anything that might fall into the water.

They know what they're doing.

Getting to the zincs is no easy matter. First, the propeller must be removed, and no matter how hard they struggle—and they struggle mightily—it won't come free.

I hold my breath.

It's a race against time. The tide will rise soon. If it does before the job is done, water will flood into the shaft and ruin all the electrical wiring there. For a while, it looks like we're in serious trouble, but in the end all goes well because with one final heave David and his assistant slide *Pacific Bliss*'s blades from the shaft and finish the job. All work completed, they take off with a wave of their hands.

Now we're alone and must stay here overnight. We have to wait for the tide to rise, for the right moment to free our Cat from the deep mud that holds her.

Unbeaching the Cat
Denarau Island

I awaken at 0600 after a fitful sleep. I go to the helm seat with my morning coffee. The sun breaks dramatically over the highlands of Viti Levu. The tide is rising nicely. *Pacific Bliss* shifts a bit in her muddy cradle, adding a little more weight toward the stern. I see this as a good sign. Perhaps she will float off all by herself at high tide! We should only be that lucky!

Captain Günter is not persuaded. His apprehensions kept him awake most of the night. He's afraid we have miscalculated.

"We couldn't have," I object. "We beached *Pacific Bliss* at the exact hour that will allow the next high tide to float her free."

"Here's the problem," Günter explains. "Every day, after a full moon, the peak of the next tide becomes steadily lower. Remember, the evening tide that we stayed up for was even lower than the daytime tide when we beached her. And when we walked around the top deck last night, she was clearly not floating. With each day's tide becoming lower at its peak, we may be stuck in this mud too deeply now to float free."

Waiting for the next full moon and the highest tide that accompanies it is not an option.

Günter continues, "If worse comes to worst, we'll hire some workmen to dig two channels to pull the hulls out. *Pacific Bliss* may have settled in with all her weight. After all, she didn't budge at high tide last night."

We wait and watch.

The tide rises slowly—much too slowly. Günter takes a measurement at the swim ladder. It is 3.1 feet versus the 3.5 feet when we beached. The bottoms of the dagger boards are stuck tight into the mud even though Günter has lifted them up as far as they will go.

"Let's just give it a little test," he says. He starts the engines. *Pacific Bliss* doesn't budge. The situation does not look good.

"See that barge over there!" I point. "Maybe he could help."

Günter talks to the barge captain, who agrees to deploy his powerboat at 1015, exactly 15 minutes before peak of high tide. It has a 30 horsepower outboard motor. If that fails to work, he says, he'll use the big barge itself. "But I don't think that will be necessary," he adds.

For a long five minutes we agonize over potential damage to the dagger boards, or worse yet, the rudders. Then we pray again for the safety of *Pacific Bliss*.

Now it's time for action. Günter readies a heavy line to use, if necessary, as a towline for the barge. Promptly at 1015 a man motions to me from the barge. I signal for him to come over. We fashion a bridle to the powerboat and cleat it at each stern hull of *Pacific Bliss*. Günter begins to rev both of our 40hp engines in reverse. The men in the boat pull their line taut.

It is 1030, high tide.

"Let her roll!" Günter yells.

Engines scream. The reluctant mud makes terrible sucking sounds, fighting to hold onto its prey. The tug-of-war continues. Tight line. Roaring engines. Moments of dread. Then, suddenly, after one giant sucking sound, *Pacific Bliss* leaps and she is free again! Her engines purr. She is happy to be out of that disgusting mud!

After all, she's a Cat, not a pig.

But it's never over until it's over. I'm always amazed how quickly a positive situation can deteriorate on a boat. The barge crew fails to watch the towline. They let it go slack, and it begins to drift to our prop. Thank God our engines are in neutral now! Günter quickly dons his mask and fins and dives beneath the hull. The line is around the propeller, but after a struggle, he's able to untangle it.

Günter gives the barge captain and his crew $50 Fijian for their wonderful help in setting us free.

We have arranged to berth on Denarau Marine's dock, next to the mega yachts.

But first, we anchor in the bay, wash down the *Pacific Bliss* decks with our salt water hose and share a can of ice cold Fiji Bitter. "To no…more…adventures," I toast.

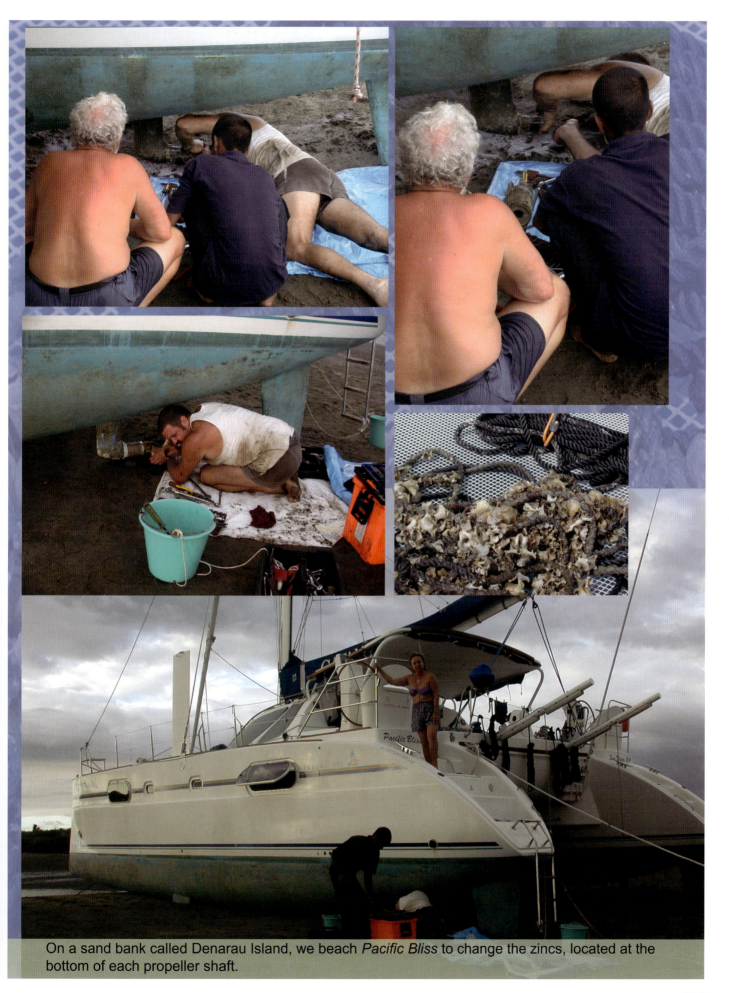

On a sand bank called Denarau Island, we beach *Pacific Bliss* to change the zincs, located at the bottom of each propeller shaft.

Helmut and Lydia join *Pacific Bliss* as crew.

"Yes, to no more adventures for a very long time… but I know they'll come," Günter adds.

Reef Encounters of the Worst Kind: Attempting To Circumnavigate Fiji
Denarau Marina, Viti Levu, Fiji
May 30

Lydia and Helmut Dueck are an adventurous German couple who decided to backpack around the world before they marry and have children. We first met them through our website. Helmut's dream has always been to sail around the world when he retires. He is a sailor, but Lydia, his fiancé, has never been on a sailboat. Crewing for us is an opportunity to find out whether his dream will work for them. Only in their twenties, they are wisely thinking ahead!

Last season, they flew from Australia to Fiji to interview with us. Lydia is a pert, fun-loving blonde. Helmut is dark-haired and serious, yet I suspect that he can be fun, too.

We had arranged for a taxi to meet the couple at the Nadi airport and to take them directly to *Pacific Bliss*. They appear relieved to see a berth freshly made up for them and towels and washcloths in their own port head. Frugal backpackers, they find *Pacific Bliss* luxurious. We find them to be a refreshing, happy couple and look forward to spending time with them.

I awaken to hear Günter offering Dave, the mechanic, a cup of coffee. He has brought our dinghy and motor back—now it starts immediately with one gentle pull of the starter rope. That is the end of the fixing—finally, so Günter is in a great mood. Helmut and Lydia sleep in.

We spend the afternoon planning our route: We hope to round the entire north coast of Viti Levu and then island-hop the east coast as far south as the island of Ovalau, Fiji's original capital.

Now that we have crew, there's one more maintenance procedure to do: climbing the mast to check for loose fittings. With Lydia taking photos, Günter hoists me up our 60-foot mast for the first time. I am relieved that nothing is loose; it's mighty scary aloft, almost to the top!

The next day we all rise early and eat breakfast together on board. Helmut and Günter hose down *Pacific Bliss* and fill the water tanks one last time while Lydia and I batten down the hatches, straighten the inside, then wait—forever it seems—for the marina to be unlocked so that we can take one long, last shower. Our leaving is not without anxiety: At the marina we learn that the benign weather forecast has changed to "rough to very rough seas" with a strong wind warning. The southeast trades have set in with a High over the entire Fiji Group. While paying our bill, Günter overhears that a supply barge cannot make it into Musket Cove due to strong winds.

"Navigator, it's your decision," Günter says.

"Let's go. The bay we're heading to, Vitogo, should be sheltered from the southeast by Viti Levu hills."

"We could pull in at Lautoka if we have to," Günter says.

"Except that I don't want to anchor in the sewer outflow again," I answer.

By 1015 we reverse smoothly from the dock, and we're off. It turns out to be a perfect day. *Pacific Bliss* loves wind, and she delights in prancing ahead on her favorite point-of-sail: a beam reach. We all work together to single-reef the main and let her go. We pass Saweni Bay, on past Lautoka, and wind through an island and reef system that looks much more difficult on the chart than it actually turns out to be. It is well-marked.

So far, so good.

We arrive in Vitogo Bay at 1445 and anchor easily with our new crew working in unison. We enjoy a *brotzeit*, a swim, and a siesta. Later we sip cold white wine as the sun dips below the reeds on the reef nearby. We are the only vessel in the bay.

"This is the way life should be," Günter says. He holds me tight as we sit together on the cockpit seat.

Later in the galley, Lydia and I chop beef and veggies

for a pasta stir-fry while listening to Bula 100 "oldies but goodies." A breeze wafts into the galley through the salon windows. What a relief to cook without heating up the boat! Helmut and Günter sit nearby at the salon table discussing the details of our sail up the coast. The pungent smell of Trader Joe's Summer Curry Sauce builds up our appetites.

After a delicious dinner, we all go up in the cockpit to watch the stars light the sky with no city lights to interfere. Helmut and Lydia are in their element. They are truly amazed by it all.

The dawn is overcast, but I see faint golden streaks behind a rounded hill with a few scraggly trees. A low fog hugs the sea directly ahead of *Pacific Bliss* while a brisk trade wind ripples the surface of the bay. We are sailing along at 8 knots already. I am happy to be here, finally on our way toward new adventures after so many weeks of fixing.

A mist hangs in the air for hours, causing the reeds among the reefs to look surreal, like an oriental painting. Rounded hills fade and turn purple as they recede; other hills, other bays, taking their place. High cirrus clouds swirl in paisley patterns, signifying stronger winds above.

Off watch, I head for the galley to make Bilge Pasta Salad, one of Günter's favorites. I'm just about to drain cans of peas and mushrooms when suddenly the cans slide off the counter. A 20-knot wind, right on the nose, comes up from nowhere. Lydia is shocked to see the sea change so fast. Helmut just continues to fish off the stern.

It's time to return to my navigator duties. Looking at the route we're on, I note that rounding the northwest point of Viti Levu has put us out of the sheltered lee of the island. Now easterly winds are hitting us with full force. Our nice-and-easy sail of yesterday is but a pleasant memory. Günter turns on both engines to power through the whitecaps at 7 knots.

We are all on lookout now as we navigate through the reefs. Fortunately, they are well marked. They are shown on the electronic MaxSea charts, and the chart we've laid out on the salon table even gives compass directions. To make the turns, I take the nav station inside, Günter takes the helm, Lydia takes the pulpit seat, using our powerful binoculars, and Helmut takes the other bow seat. The wind remains at Force 5, but as we round the northwest point of Viti Levu, it lessens a little. Strong gusts hit as we slowly approach Tomba Naloma, our anchorage. We know that this bay is full of reefs close to the shore, but because it's not low tide, we can't see them.

We motor in slowly. I take up my position at the bow with the anchor windlass control. "Don't worry," Günter says. "I'll bring you right to the

Helmut catches a trevella along the north coast of Viti Levu, Fiji.

anchor symbol we put on *MaxSea*.

30 feet, 28 feet, 26 feet...we should be there in five minutes."

We creep cautiously. The wave heights gradually decrease, but the wind keeps blowing.

"24 feet. Drop anchor," Günter commands.

I drop, but the wind blows us backward rapidly. The windlass won't release the anchor chain as fast as the wind is pushing us back. Then all of a sudden the anchor catches and jerks the boat.

"Let out more chain," Günter shouts from the helm.

"I'm letting it out as fast as I can," I shout from the bow back into the wind. "I've got 120 feet out and she's still pulling."

Günter comes forward. "Let's deploy the bridle with a short leash this time. Let out some more."

He sets the bridle, but now the entire chain has payed out. At the anchor locker, I can see the rope, all the way to the bitter end. I try to bring some back in by reversing the windlass control. The rope binds and bends the chain stripper (the device that pulls the chain from the chain wheel and lets it fall, pulled by its own weight, into the chain locker). Helmut helps me straighten out the mess.

Now we have a "broken boat" again. Until it's fixed, we'll have to haul the anchor up hand over hand, which is not only physically strenuous but can also be

223

dangerous when timing is critical. We brainstorm the next port where it can be fixed—Tonga?

But only if we manage to get there by sailing against these trades to the Inner Triangle of Samoa, Tonga, and back to Fiji. That plan is not looking good.

"I know David at Denarau Marina could fix it," Günter says.

"Do you want to head back there?"

"No."

"Neither do I."

"We'll just have to be careful. After all, we made it from the Marquesas to Raiatea before we could repair it the last time."

Our sundowners are gloomy. I fix strong cocktails: rum with Diet Pepsi and limes. We need them. "I feel so bad," Günter says sourly. "It was a lousy anchoring job."

The Captain heads below for a rest, but I know he will not sleep. He will continue to brood.

I sip on my drink as I watch the sun dip behind the haze on the horizon.

Welcome to another typical cruising season with its typical ups and downs.

We three congregate in the salon watching the weather and listening to the wind howl through the rigging. When Günter comes into the salon, he orders the wind reports via Sail Mail. They predict 25 knots today and 30 tomorrow and Thursday.

Not good.

We decide to set anchor alarms: Lydia, at 1200, Günter and I at 0200, Lydia again at 0400 if it hasn't calmed down. This reminds me of the windy San Blas Islands of Panama. I feel sorry for Helmut and Lydia. This is all new to them.

We all go to bed early and read.

⚓

One wouldn't know by the peacefulness of this morning that this is the bay that I had grown to hate only yesterday. From the cockpit, I watch seabirds soar over still waters; they fly by me in pairs. Golden light breaks through low lying clouds hugging the bay. Hills hug us on three sides, purple-gray, silent, protecting.

Yes, yesterday I wanted *out of here*, never to return.

How quickly and easily the sea changes its face! One minute brooding, the next minute inviting. One minute savage and threatening, the next, calm and pristine. Like she is right now.

Will this be yet another cruising day that points out our vulnerability out here, how simple mistakes can lead to dramatic and immediate consequences?

This morning, *Pacific Bliss* faces west, pushed by a gentle SSW Force 2, 7-knot breeze. The hills brighten as the sea wrinkles.

How long before the high trade winds roar in from the southeast again, turning the sea into a monster?

By 0815, the sun is high enough for us to see the reefs and sail on. Upon leaving Tomba Naloma, we are all convinced that we are rounding the marker for Davy's Rocks, a hazard called out on our charts. I appear topsides to announce that I'm turning *Pacific Bliss* to follow the path on the electronic chart, just as we had the day before.

Surprise! There is no passage between the reef and the marker.

"Slow down," I warn Günter.

He had both engines revved, prepared to make the passage quickly before the wind and waves pick up. He cuts back the throttle.

"Looks like a reef straight ahead!" I shout.

Lydia dashes to the stern from her bow lookout. "Stop! Reef!"

The boat comes to a sudden halt. The depth meter shows less than 10 feet!

Now we know that we can no longer rely on these reefs being marked. All alone out here, we can't afford to take chances.

We creep along the reef, following the dotted line on the chart called the Northern Passage. The passage snakes from Sali Sali Reef, where we come too close for comfort, into Tavua Bay, past Namuka Reef on our south, between Thakau Moi Reef and Mathuata and Tovu—tree-covered hill islands—and on through an open stretch where the east wind howls. Then we close in on Thakau Tanua Reef and creep through another narrow passage between it and Malake Island. As we exit that channel, we see the two islands of Nananu-I-Ra and Nananu-I-Cake. The first is touristy, but the anchorage is small. With a 20-knot wind, we're afraid of dragging anchor. We head for a big bay instead and set the anchor with 140 feet of chain, in 41 feet at low tide. It's deeper than we'd like and not very sheltered, but at least we won't swing into anything.

Lydia and I fire up the breadmaker to bake wheat berry bread while Helmut continues to fish. Toward dusk, he hauls in a trevalla. We gorge on warm bread while the fish marinates, then fry potatoes and plantains. The high wind gusts cool the salon, so we sip on hot Good Earth tea spiked with rum.

Life isn't so bad after all!

As we let down our guard and begin a leisurely dinner in the salon, the day falls apart. It begins slowly—this falling apart—as one event careens into the next.

First, Günter notices that the anchor alarm shows that the boat has moved 500 feet. "Can't be!" His face pales. "Must be a mistake—it didn't go off. Helmut, let's check our calculations."

It's a repeat of our experience in the Yasawas: The computer shows that we have drifted halfway into the bay! We quickly clear our half-eaten dinner. I tell everyone to shut the hatches, in case we end up on a reef today, after all. Then Günter calls us all into the cockpit for instructions.

The night is pitch black.

"Lois, go to the nav station. Follow our MaxSea track back to our original anchoring location. I'll just motor slowly. Helmut and Lydia, after we pull anchor, you'll use the flashlight and spotlight to warn us when we're near shore."

Pulling anchor is difficult now with the stripper broken, but our new crew makes fast work of it. Günter inches toward shore while I direct our autopilot carefully, using plus or minus one degree, until we are a few boat lengths from our original anchoring spot. Fortunately the wind has died, and the anchor sets easily.

I never want to see this Nananu–I–Cake Anchorage again. Our crew wanted a learning experience; well, they're certainly getting it!

June 4: We set a watch schedule overnight: Lydia until 1230; me until 0300; Helmut until 0500, and Günter in the morning. When I join Günter in the cockpit after his watch, he asks, "Are we getting too old to be doing all of this? I'm tired of this living on the edge."

Déjà vu. We've been there before. We didn't like it then. And we really don't like it now.

I don't want to escalate Günter's mood with a response. The morning is gloomy enough as it is. I already know we won't be moving on. Without the sun, we won't be able to see the reefs.

I bring him a second cup of coffee. "I can tell you what Mom used to say when I groused about gloomy days."

"Ah! Your mother, sweet Sigrid. What did she say?"

"Lois Joy, just remember, there's always sunshine in your heart."

"I'm so glad I really connected with her the last time I saw her. She was the most gentle person I've ever met."

I think about her and the sun breaks through!

Günter's mood improves.

As the day drones on, the strong wind returns. It whistles through the rigging, swinging our little home around as she pulls tight on her two anchor chains. We all know that it's a given that we stay here until the weather cooperates.

While the men focus on boat maintenance, Lydia and I bake up a storm, creatively using ingredients we have on board. We realize that we will need to provision soon. But how?

We jump into the bay to cool off after cooking. The current races so fast between the hulls that I dare not let go of the swim ladder. The dinghy goes wild, bouncing on the waves.

The wind blows so hard that we have our sundowners inside. Lydia compares her expectations with how she feels about sailing now. "I thought we'd be sitting outside, in a calm anchorage, sipping piña coladas in the sunset," she says, discouraged.

"Did you expect to have wind for sailing?" I ask.

"Of course. I dreamt about sails billowing in the wind, pulling us along."

"But then when you wanted to sip those piña coladas, the wind would suddenly disappear?"

"I didn't think of that…in fact, now I wonder whether I should buy into Helmut's dream of sailing around the world."

The next day, the bay is still too rough to deploy *Petit Bliss*, so we order a pick-up from Safari Lodge nearby. Günter opts to stay with the boat.

The three of us take off in the skiff. It turns toward Ellington Wharf, where we receive the brunt of the east wind racing through the channel. The spray comes over the high sides of the launch. Helmut's T-shirt is sopping, but he laughs.

"It's good I brought a spare," he shouts over the shrieking wind.

When the launch stops at Ellington Wharf, I'm amazed. I cannot imagine *Pacific Bliss*—or any large boat for that matter—pulling up to this dilapidated structure. We disembark. On the wharf, angry brown froth smashes against the jetty. Palms bend over in pain.

Wind-dried and salty, we hike toward the bus stop. After a mile or so, an Indian cane farmer with thick black hair and dusty clothes offers us a lift. We pass field after field of sugar cane.

He drops us off at the farmer's market. What a scene! Colorful blankets cover the grass. Fijian mothers hold the babies and toddlers, while older children play games together in the shade trees across from the market. Under the shade of a banyan tree, men drink *kava* and gossip. The produce is laid out in mounds. A mound of limes: $1 Fijian. A mound of oranges: $1. A bunch of bok choy: $1. One green papaya: $1. Soon our canvas shopping bags are full, with a $1 bunch of bananas topping it off.

"*Bula!*" Women wearing colorful *muumuus* greet us with wide smiles. They even smile when we don't buy from them. They do not cajole, like Indian vendors.

We find three grocery stores containing everything else we need, including a *Fiji Times* and lots of chocolate to placate Günter. After catching a taxi back to the wharf, it's another wet ride back to *Pacific Bliss,* where the high winds have continued unabated.

Finally the next day the sun shines, and the wind decreases enough that we dare to leave the bay. We navigate the reefs past Ellington Wharf and through the narrow Navelau passage to Viti Levu Bay. The process is horrendously slow. Our disturbingly inaccurate electronic chart shows us going over land in many places. We are thankful to have sharp lookouts on board. By the time we anchor twice in the bay, we are all tense and tired.

The following day, we motor for five hours and are forced to pull in at 1315. The skies turn dark and foreboding; ominous clouds line the entire horizon. Navigating through the reefs had been tricky with full sun; no way do we want to take this route under an overcast sky. We anchor in a muddy area south of the Natori Ferry Terminal. Then we set a second anchor as well. Appropriately, Günter plays Pink Floyd's *Dark Side of the Moon,* one of his favorites.

We come topsides in the morning, overjoyed to see a flotilla of 12 sailboats passing by the bay's outer limits. This makes navigation easier; *we'll* be following *them.* Even so, navigation is extremely tricky. By the time we anchor again, I collapse into my berth while Günter takes The Kids to a nearby reef to fish and snorkel. I'll have my chance to snorkel in Leleuvia, a small sandy island that is touted as a backpackers' paradise.

Pacific Bliss Goes Snorkeling.
Leleuvia
17° 48.5' S, 178°43' E
June 11

Yesterday, the four of us snorkeled through colorful coral in crystal clear waters dappled with the refracted light of a beaming sun. We swam from our anchored dinghy to the palm-covered islet of Leleuvia in a sea of teal glass. We ambled around the islet, digging our toes into the sun-baked sand. Every so often, one of us stooped to examine a shell, a piece of driftwood, or one of the delicate pink-and-white magnolia blossoms that had wafted onto the shore.

Perhaps *Pacific Bliss* had become jealous. After all, we left her anchored in the bay while we went off in *Petit Bliss* to explore. Perhaps *Pacific Bliss* was determined to go snorkeling as well. Why else would she allow herself to be pulled into a current and blown onto a coral bed?

Today, before 0500 and still pitch dark, I am rudely awakened by a thumping sound.

I head topsides to check it out. It has just begun to rain, so the sky remains ink-black. I take the torch (flashlight) and check the anchor chain. It is pulling tightly; the wind has returned. I check the stern. *Petit Bliss* is bobbing furiously, pulling on the painter and occasionally hitting the swim ladder. Much ado about nothing.

So she is the one making all the noise! No worries.

Then I notice the pale teal color of the water highlighted in the torch's beam. My pulse quickens. Something is not right. Pale means shallow.

I rush back into the salon to turn on the instruments. Yes, the depth meter shows only 3.8 feet! I check the wind direction. South. It was from the northeast when we anchored here. Then the weather turned calm for one glorious day of sea and sand.

Günter comes up from the starboard hull, and I fill him in. "We have over 90 feet of chain out, but the wind has shifted almost 180 degrees, pushing us toward the reefs."

"We'll have to take in some more, he says."

We pull in about 8 feet of chain by hand. Besides the chain stripper being broken, our up/down windlass control only functions intermittently.

During breakfast, we discuss re-anchoring with our crew. We are not comfortable in this small anchorage with reefs on three sides.

The seas are benign and the wind calm as we head for another anchoring location that allows us more swing room. We proceed to a familiar, sandy area that is farther out to sea from our snorkeling area of yesterday. Before we can drop the hook, a wind comes up.

"Now we have wind and it begins to piss," Günter complains as he grabs his rain gear. "We should have done this before when it was calm."

Men! Monday morning quarterbacking.

He motors and stops at our selected spot. "Drop anchor," he commands.

The crew complies as the wind pushes *Pacific Bliss* toward the reefs. Then we all realize that by the time the anchor hits bottom, we will be too close to these new reefs to allow for swing room if the wind changes direction again.

"Pull anchor," the Captain Günter commands. This time, the windlass control doesn't work at all. Helmut has to pull up the anchor with all that chain hand over hand. Both engines are in neutral.

Then things happen at warp speed—too quickly for us to analyze. A fierce gust of wind appears out of nowhere. And we think we've hit the dangerous area of strong current that the Fijians on shore have warned us about. *Pacific Bliss* is pushed out of control, and the entire anchor chain begins to pay out. Helmut had not cleated it off. Now he cleats it, but we can't pull it in. It is probably caught in the bottom—and not where we want it.

"Go forward, Günter," I yell, but the wind swallows my words. Günter comes up to the bow to evaluate the situation, with the engines still in neutral. "No. Take

The sun sets over the long reefs of Leleuvia where *Pacific Bliss* went snorkeling.

the boat forward so that we can pull the anchor loose!" Günter rushes back to the stern, but it is too late.

Pacific Bliss, stubborn as she can be sometimes, has stopped right in the spot where we had gone snorkeling the day before! What audacity! What obstinacy! Her bottom is sucked into coral, and she is not budging!

Helmut and Lydia jump into the water with their snorkeling gear. They find no damage anywhere—so far. But the bottom tip of the starboard dagger board has snagged a coral head. Günter helps me winch *Pacific Bliss* forward since the anchor is still out and holding. No luck. Helmut is still in the water, trying to push *Pacific Bliss* off the coral head from the starboard hull. That doesn't work either.

Then we get lucky, very lucky.

A dive boat is returning to the islet because of the inclement weather. I wave frantically. The passengers all wave back, nice and friendly.

"Come here! Pull us!" I yell from our bow. Immediately—no questions asked—the Fijian boat roars closer. The driver throws me a long towline, which I tie to the bow cleat. The boat pulls, Helmut pushes, and *Pacific Bliss* is coerced into deeper water while we pull in all that chain. Her snorkeling escapade is cut short.

They say that there is always a first time for everything. This is the first time during our circumnavigation, though, that *Pacific Bliss* has gone snorkeling. In over 17,000 miles of sailing, halfway around the world, she had never kissed a coral head. Until now.

And if I have my way, she will never kiss one again!

Later we sit around the salon table sipping hot chocolate and munching cookies, attempting to nourish our shaken souls. Captain Günter has finished beating himself up. Now he sits there, glum and dejected. "I don't need this," he says. "Lois, what do you think we would be doing if we were back in San Diego right now?"

"Thinking about snorkeling in crystal-clear waters near a sandy palm-covered island somewhere in the South Seas?"

Levuka—Fiji's Ancient Capital
June 13

When I record the passage from Leleuvia in the logbook, I realize what day it is: Friday the thirteenth. No wonder it was one wild ride! Thankfully, the passage was short and we're here, although Levuka is on a lee shore, the windward side of the island.

This morning at 1100, the sun appeared just in time to make the passage. It continued to shine while we navigated the Moturiki Channel, then disappeared for good as we sailed up the east coast of Ovalau to Levuka. We experienced 20-knot winds all the way, with occasional gusts to 25. The waves were 3 meters high. One of the huge waves splashed into the cockpit, drenching Helmut.

The main street of Levuka, Fiji's original capital, on a rainy day.

Lydia did not have a good passage. She spent it lying on her stomach on the cockpit bench, queasy and frightened. These were the highest waves she had experienced because, until now, we had been protected by Fiji's reefs.

After a well-deserved siesta, the four of us dinghy to the wharf. We walk the length of the town until dusk. We pass by groups of women and children in flowery frocks chatting underneath shade trees lining the seaside promenade. From the sidewalk, we can see *Pacific Bliss* bobbing in the background. It dawns on us that anyone on Main Street can see her. They all know who we are. Tourists are rare in Levuka.

We pass three lively pool halls—that's where the men and boys hang out. We amble into the expansive lobby and past the charming curved bar of The Royal Hotel, the oldest continuously run hotel in all of the South Pacific. No one knows when it was built, but records show that this historic building has existed at least since the early 1860s. Reportedly, ship's masters, plantation owners, and even the notorious blackbirder, Bully Hayes, frequented this hotel.

A plaque provides the history: In the 1830s, Levuka had been a small whaling and beachcomber settlement. It was virtually lawless; ships followed a trail of empty gin bottles through the passage into port, and the town was a haven for escaped convicts, ship jumpers, debtors, and other ne'er-do-wells. The Royal was the finest place in town and *the* place to stay. The front rooms faced the sea, so that the captains could keep an eye on their anchored vessels, just as we look out at ours now. A crow's nest still stands atop the hotel's top floor.

The next day, after a night as bumpy as if we'd been on a miserable passage, we venture to Ovalau Holiday Resort, a 3-kilometer taxi ride over rutty blacktop roads. We skirt around potholes and gulleys washed out by last night's high tide at full moon. In many areas, the high seas had taken sections of the road out to sea and left debris behind.

This is the same full moon and strong surf that battered Pacific Bliss. No wonder I couldn't sleep! God has, yet again, sent His guardian angel to watch over us.

The casual resort contains about a half-dozen bures. We have chicken curry with rotis, pepper steak with rice; and a family-size cole slaw salad. The food is wonderful—especially because we don't have to cook on board with the rain pelting the cabin roof. We talk about what we've seen in Levuka so far.

"It's the land time forgot," says Günter.

"It's a wild west tumbleweed town transposed to

Helmut, Lydia, and Gunter wait in Levuka for the customs office to open.

the Pacific," says Lydia.

"Don't forget the fish factory," adds Helmut. "PATCO employs 1000 of the 1800 people who live here."

We call for a taxi back. The rain continues into the night.

The new day begins with more rain. We've signed up for Epi's Lovoni Highlands Tour. We decide to take it despite the rain. Back on Main Street, we pile into the canvas-covered back of a truck, and off we go, bumping and slip-sliding along the muddy roads to the village of Lovoni, built on the crater of the extinct volcano at the island's center. At the outskirts of the village, we pick up a well-known tour guide, Epi Bole.

Epi leads us past tiny homes made of western-style weatherboard. At the community hut, he tells stories of his ancestors who first settled this land. The villagers of Lovini, he tells us, are a proud people. They are descendants of the strongest tribe in Fiji, the Cakobau, who were never defeated. In fact, they showed their displeasure with the European settlement of Levuka by burning it down three times. Men from Lovini demonstrate their superiority by wearing hats in other villages, including in the chiefly village of Ba.

From what Epi tells us, the political climate in Fiji is depressing, and the future of the sugar industry does not look good.

Epi has the typical Fijian opinions on land ownership (it should all belong to the Fijians; he is pleased that even the former Crown land is being returned) and on Indians (the Queen should have taken them all back when Fiji became independent).

"Don't the Fijians need the Indians?" Günter ventures. "We see them working the land owned by the Fijians…we see them running the stores, and even most of the tourist operations. Seems like a symbiotic relationship to me."

Epi nods slowly. "That's true," he admits. "Lots of Indians left Fiji during the 2000 coup—mostly the professionals—doctors, lawyers, businessmen."

How can they reconcile the two positions? They want the Indians gone, yet they like them to do all the work they don't want to do. They're not realists, they're dreamers. Too much kava *in the blood?*

"Do the people here want large families?" Lydia asks.

"Yes, they want as many children as possible," Epi replies.

I know that the Indians, when asked, will respond similarly. Both ethnic groups want to increase their own numbers—this without regard for the quality of their children's lives, the cost of their education, or the hazards of pregnancy.

We watch a relative of Epi making our lunch on a one-burner hotplate in the corner. Two little boys, two and four, hang on her *sulu*. Another child is clearly on the way.

"Where will she deliver?"

Epi explains, "She will deliver in Suva. The Levuka hospital lost five babies in last month. No ultrasound here. No Cesarean either."

I imagine life in Lovoni Village. A one-room, weatherboard house. Hotplate in the corner. Washing dishes outside from water out of a bare pipe. Two beds at the edges of the mat-covered room, one for the children, the other for the parents.

No wonder the educated young people go to Auckland to find work and dream of going to America.

Back in Levuka, I ask to be let out of the truck at the ATM on Main Street. After I nonchalantly insert my credit card and pull out a pile of Fijian $20 bills, I turn to see a group of Fijian teenagers close behind me. Curious, they want to see how this new money dispenser works. Later, I would read the headline in this morning's paper: "Westpac launches Ovalau's first ATM." The article explains how this is "launching the old capital into the electronic banking age." Obviously, this ATM has quickly become the pride of the town!

On Tuesday the port captain is finally on duty after his Monday holiday. We check in and check out on the same day. We're ready. It has been a very long weekend under mostly rainy skies. We all walk into town with our bags to provision. Then next morning, we turn *Pacific Bliss* around in the small wharf, and we're on our way. We look back to see the entire island of Ovalau shrouded in gloomy, low-lying clouds. We can't even make out the highlands in the center. No wonder they changed Fiji's capital!

We sail on, with a full main and jib, along the island's eastern shore, beyond its northern tip, and on to the Makogai channel 17 miles away. As we enter a deep bay and anchor in 50 feet, next to us is *Velele*, a small sloop-rigged monohull from Seattle, Washington, U.S.A.

What a small world!

The Largest Clams in the World
Makogai Island, Fiji
June 20

0630: Roosters crowing. Birds gossiping. Fish splashing. What an idyllic morning! As I sit in the cockpit, the only sound of civilization is the generator from the research station located farther into the bay. We will visit that facility today. The coffee pot whistles. As I turn to the galley, I notice fountains of cumulus clouds at each of the bay's entrances. Palms fringe the mountain tops, rimming the dawn. It is the type of morning I love.

Makogai is one of these rare jewels that few know about. It's not listed in the *Lonely Planet*. The only way to get here is to sail as we did or hitch a passage on boats visiting the government aqua-culture operation and sheep station. This island, transferred over to Suva in 1979, has a history as a leper colony. Now it's a spawning area for an exotic species of giant clams called *Tridacna gigas*.

Our snorkel over the reefs is perfect. The spawning beds are specially marked. The giant clams bred here are the largest I have ever seen—humongous mollusks with lips of cobalt blue, emerald green, and mottled brown. They are set in corals covering every color of the spectrum. Fan coral in shades of amber and taupe wave at me while iridescent reef fish dart in and out of the coral. A huge sea slug that looks like a fat crooked finger lazily makes its way over the sandy sea floor.

What a wonderful day! We enjoy a glorious sunset, sipping cold white wine in the cockpit while we admire the western sky at the opening to Dalice Bay. I feast my eyes while Lydia excitedly snaps one photo after another.

The next morning, we snorkel through the two reef gardens again before heading for the fishery. We learn that the fishery plants hundreds of baby clams along the reefs throughout Fiji and exports some to Tonga and the Solomons.

A supervisor there gives us a tour of the giant clam incubation tanks. He tells us that this species are the largest of the bivalve mollusks. In ten years they can be measured end to end with outstretched arms. They have a 100-year lifespan and can weigh up to 500 pounds. With their shells wide open, they bask in sunlight so the symbiotic algae living with them can produce their food. Interestingly, hundreds of tiny eyes dot their skin, allowing them to sense sudden changes in their environment. The shells then close defensively. The man says that the adult clams here are incapable of slamming their shells completely shut because of their massive bulk. Still, no one volunteers to put that to a test with an arm or foot!

Back on *Pacific Bliss*, I ask Helmut to help me plot our course to Savusavu. We talk on the VHF to a couple on a Swedish Ketch, *Lorna*, who sailed out earlier. They warn us not to take the western passage out of this bay. Apparently, another catamaran was hung up on a coral head for weeks after taking that route. Based on their advice, we'll go back out the way we came—even though its 5 miles farther and will add an hour to our passage.

It's a pleasant night, but by 0430 I'm wide awake. The mighty East Wind has returned. "Relax and try to get

Molakai is a spawning area for an exotic species of giant clams.

another hour of shut-eye," Günter says. "It will be a nice sailing day."

Sailing to Savusavu and Settling In
17°20.8' S, 178°59' E

The sailing is great. *Pacific Bliss* is in her glory, comfortably sailing along on a beam reach at 8 knots SOG (speed over ground) in a Force 4 ESE wind at 17 knots. Twelve miles into our trip, Makogai's coastline fades behind the stern as we head for Vanua Levu, Fiji's second largest island. We cross the Koro Sea with a full main and jib. On a beam reach at first, the ride is rather lumpy, but later, with a following sea, it turns pleasant. We grab a mooring in the bay right in front of the town. I log our trip: 56 miles in 8 hours at an average speed of 7 knots.

Sleepy Savusavu, located on the peninsula that divides Savusavu Bay from the Koro Sea, is Vanua Levu's second largest town. The tourist slogan here is "the hidden paradise." Because the town is a Port of Entry and a natural cyclone hole, it is a popular gathering spot for cruisers. It reminds me of Neiafu in Tonga's Vavau Group.

Already I feel safe here!

As soon as chores are done, we go ashore to acquaint ourselves with our new surroundings. We tie *Petit Bliss* at the dock at the Copra Shed. Eventually we find our way to the Planter's Club where, we've heard, there is a contest going on between the planters and the yachties.

In operation for 46 years, the Planter's Club is a revelation of how colonial life here must have been. Copra production was this area's main business during the second half of the 19th century, but then profitability began to decline. The farmers are still struggling to remain viable.

We enter a compound with a massive, colonial-style building in the back, surrounded by a white porch and picket fence. To the right, we see a small shed with a sign, "No alcohol allowed." Through the open door we can see men drinking *kava*. To the left, we see two lawn bowling fields, side by side. Customers with cocktails line the porch, loudly cheering on the teams.

We go inside the building and order rums and cokes. Everyone is friendly. All the "planters" we meet are Fijian—the best-dressed and most cosmopolitan Fijians I've ever seen! No fraying 1950s-style *muumuu* dresses for these women: I notice that one wears a black silk top with black-and-white vertically-striped pantaloons. Her hair is straight, cropped short, and swept behind the ears. *Smart!* Günter can't help but notice how a full-length sarong wraps another lady's curvaceous figure; she wears a modern stretch lace

From the trampoline of *Pacific Bliss*, I look up to the high pier and Main Street of Levuka.

op cropped at the waist. The men wear long pants or pressed jeans and *bula* shirts with short sleeves. There are no T-shirts in sight except among the few white yachties who are here, like us, to observe.

I'm happy to see such apparently well-to-do Fijians. I want to learn more about this different world of Savusavu. But for now, we need to go back to *Pacific Bliss*. Soon our crew will be leaving.

Saturday goes by in a flash with usual frenzy of packing and goodbyes. Helmut and Lydia will continue their own adventure before returning home to Germany. As we always do, Günter and I have mixed feelings about crew leaving. On one hand, the enthusiasm, optimism, and energy of youth has left *Pacific Bliss*. We feel sort of blah and alone now. On the other hand, we enjoy our solitude. Schedule becomes less important, as does wearing clothes on board! And now we will have the opportunity to explore this island and others at our leisure. We will cook only when we're hungry—much easier on our waistlines.

Sunday in Savusavu at the Lighthouse Church
June 22

I sit on the helm seat with my coffee, watching all the boats in the anchorage swing east to southeast and back again in the wind, all lined up and in step, like obedient soldiers. Thirteen yachts swing behind us, another dozen in front of us. Günter joins me. We sit together at the pulpit seat, watching the picturesque town wake up.

On the spur of the moment, we decide to attend a church service. We remember a sign pointing to "Lighthouse Baptist Church" above a store on Main Street. We're not sure when the service will start, so we're there early. That gives us the opportunity to meet the pastor and his family; he has a wife and five children with another on the way. Darren Purdy is an outgoing man of medium build, mustached, with a dark complexion and receding hairline. Jane is quiet and gentle; she reminds me of the missionary wives who visited the church of my childhood. The Purdys have served 5 years in Fiji, 15 months of those in Savusavu.

Later we would invite this family on our yacht for a coffee klatch and have a wonderful prayer session with them. Darren asks God to help us determine the best routes going forward. We still plan to realize our dream of sailing the Polynesian Inner Triangle: to Fiji's Lau Group, to Tonga, to Samoa, and back.

Decisions…Decisions: Polynesian Paralysis or Going with the Wind?

On Tuesday, *Fidelio*, a red-and-white yacht we recognize from Tonga, plops down alongside *Pacific Bliss*. Ian has sailed here from New Zealand. Many cruisers know his voice from his shortwave weather net.

We are relieved to have the weather expert "next door." We dinghy over to get his advice.

I tell him our dream of sailing (or motoring during a calm) directly to Tonga from the Lau Group and on to Samoa: "I'm concerned…the weather charts show sometimes two days in a row of calm, settled weather, occasionally three…never more."

Ian's advice does not impart confidence. "This is a rather tricky triangle," he warns. "The seas are angry there…and the wind is often gusty and unpredictable."

Back on board, Günter and I discuss what to do. "Why ask for trouble?" I rationalize.

"We get into enough tricky situations as it is," Günter says.

We take some time to reflect on our prayers with Darren. We had explained how we left France going west, always west, and when we changed our original plan to sail northeast for part of the voyage, it just didn't work out.

"Do you know going west is scriptural?" Darren had asked. "The Tabernacle always faced east to west. First the entry, the sacrifice, the washing area, then the holy of holies. Also, all major revivals have proceeded east to west."

Perhaps that says something about God's will for our voyage. We leave it all in God's hands.

From then on, events seem to take over. We know we want to go to Taveuni, Fiji's Garden Island. A local travel agency gives us some suggestions for transportation there and places to stay. We also check on ways to get to the Lau Group without having to sail there.

The next day, we are invited to a cruisers potluck at the Waitui Marina. We enjoy the potluck immensely but return confused and conflicted. The marina manager informed us that we had to take *Pacific Bliss* out of Fiji for three months. Conflicting stories and rumors abound about the weather, navigation, and bureaucratic difficulties of sailing to the Lau Group.

The confusion continues on the Savusavu VHF Net The next day. By mid-morning, Günter has thought it through. "Why speculate? Let's go to customs today and hear it directly from the horse's mouth."

Mark, at the customs office, looks efficient and crisp in his white uniform. I'm encouraged. "Yes, it *does* say only three months on the forms. But I guess that's been on there for about ten years. I don't know how *that* wording got on those forms, but I *do* know that you have to leave Fiji before the 12 months is up."

We're relieved. Now we have options again. The continuing bureaucracy issues, however, turn us off on our plan to sail as far as the Lau Group and then to double back. And the weather dissuades us from sailing what some are now calling "the dangerous triangle." We

Churchgoers line up at the storefront on Savusavu's Main Street. Their church is located on the second floor above the shops.

decide that we want to end this Polynesian Paralysis.

"Some things are not just meant to be," I begin. "You can feel when they're not right."

"Gentlemen never sail to weather," Günter quotes.

There's a point where persistence does not pay, and flexibility means going with the flow. The sea has taught us that.

The next day during our 0900 SSB call, we inform our cruising friends Tina and Dennis, who left Fiji a month after we'd arrived here, that we'll join them in Vanuatu. We'll fly to Lau out of Suva. Then, instead of attempting to circumnavigate Viti Levu, we'll take the northern route back, reverse-navigate through those reefs, proceed to Lautoka, make repairs again in Denarau, rest in Musket Cove until we have a weather window, then take off with the trades, going with the wind. But first, we must see Fiji's Garden Island.

Taveuni Bound
June 30

Our taxi drops Günter and me at the Savusavu bus station in plenty of time; our bus is due to arrive at 8:30. As we watch the buses arrive, load passengers, and depart, not one of them sports a sign for Taveuni. Günter has been pacing around. This time his impatience pays off: He discovers that our bus is not parked at the station, but out on the main street.

"Hurry! People are already lining up to board. One hour early and here *we* are—late!"

We grab our luggage and run for it. We climb the steps into the bus to find every seat already "saved" with backpacks, satchels, or duffels. We stand in the aisle for a while, then we select a couple of seats anyway.

A cross section of humanity piles onto the bus: children with dripping ice cream cones in one grimy hand and sticky candy in the other; mothers smothered with babies, diaper bags, and pillows; and fathers with huge duffels, rolled up mats, and packages of *yaqona* (a root used for making *kava*). There are no luggage racks and no under-bus storage, even though this is the only commuter bus that meets the ferry bound for Taveuni. Luggage fills the aisles. Those who set their luggage on seats in the back rows to reserve the space simply climb over the other seats to get to theirs!

It's sheer bedlam. My senses are overloaded. I hope that the passenger who left the daypack on the bench seat I am now occupying will be small—to match the size of the pack.

A skinny young boy sits down next to me.

Ah! I'm in luck.

But then a wooly-haired Fijian mother with the widest hips I have ever seen appears at our bench. She is holding a toddler, a humongous shoulder bag, and a blanket!

This is not going to work!

I decide to follow the example of those passengers who climbed over the seats. I hoist myself, over each row, one by one, daypack and snorkeling bag hanging around my neck. I settle in among a group of young boys at the back.

Günter stands in the aisle, red-faced and fuming, surrounded by heaps of luggage. He can't find a seat. He pushes forward to talk to the driver. "I have a ticket but no seat."

The driver scowls. "If you want a seat, come back on Wednesday."

"Just take that aisle seat," I mouth and point. The two passengers on the bench scrunch over toward the window without a word. Günter piles our two duffels in the aisle on top of a heap that is already four duffels high. The bus groans up the hills along the Sunshine Highway, burdened with its heavy load of Fijians, Indians, food, and luggage. We are the only white people. The town of Savusavu fades behind us as the stench of human sweat fills the sweltering air.

The bus clatters along on the Sunshine Highway. Mothers nurse their babies. Toddlers squirm and whine.

Fortunately, the sea breeze continues to blow through the bus.

We bump along—past jungles, copra plantations, and villages of corrugated iron—on a washboard road that shakes every joint of my body. After three long hours, the bus finally rounds a teal, picture-perfect bay and grinds to a halt at the Ferry Landing. Families spread their blankets on the grass and sit down together to wait.

When the ferry can be seen around the bend, chaos ensues. The teenagers run onto the dock first, followed by the families with all their gear. Günter loses his cool. "Rush to the front!" I run to the ridge overlooking the ferry landing and down the path to the rickety dock. A Fijian teenager in a blue woolen cap rushes by, swinging his huge duffel. It hits me; I weave and almost lose my balance.

"Go. Run. Save us a seat!" Günter yells. The ferry eases to the dock. Near the front of the line, I am stopped dead behind a massive Fijian woman who is seeing off her young son. After he embarks, she just stands there, and I cannot get past her without falling off the narrow dock.

Günter, farther behind me and caught in the crowd of families, makes a pushing motion. It's not in my nature to push. Instead, I sneak underneath the matron's vast arms and leap inside the ferry. As short I am, I have to duck to enter the low passenger compartment. I manage to save a spot on the bench for Günter, who follows with our luggage. The benches fill fast. But families calmly spread out their blankets on the floor. By the time every surface is filled to capacity, the ferry leaves the dock.

I look around for life preservers. I don't see any.

This ferry is probably double-booked: Those without seats seem to equal those who have them.

We settle into the ride. Fortunately, the waves are not high, that is, until we turn directly into them as we approach Taveuni. Then the sea splashes into the open "windows" of the ferry. The passengers seated on the benches next to the windows calmly reach over to pull down the tarp.

No panic. No worries!

But now I feel claustrophobic. In the darkened compartment with the windows covered, we cannot see the horizon. I turn to Günter. "What a setting for seasickness! I would not want to take this voyage during high winds. Imagine the catastrophe in a severe storm."

"I wonder whether they have such a thing as a life raft. Let's check that out when we get off."

As we leave the ferry, I spot the "life raft" strapped onto the roof. It consists of two flat sections of boards nailed together.

It might be sufficient to hold one of those families. If it even floats.

We decide to take another, much larger, ferry back, directly to Savusavu. That will eliminate the bus ride as well. With this change in plans, we'll have to cut short our stay in Taveuni since that ferry only comes here twice a week.

That's okay. We didn't sail halfway around the world only to drown on a ferry.

Island Intrigue: The Saga of Susie's Plantation
Taveuni, Fiji's Garden Island

After Günter and I disembark from the ferry, we look around for our promised ride to Susie's Plantation. All the passengers have left the wharf. Other than the nicely frocked Fijian lady wearing a large-brimmed hat, we are the only ones without a ride. The lady turns to us with a friendly smile. "Where are you headed?"

"Susie's Plantation," Günter says. "They were supposed to pick us up."

"I'm Susie's aunt." The lady offers her well-manicured hand.

We introduce ourselves and share the next available taxi.

"I'm confused," I begin. "I thought Susie's is now run by a Swiss couple."

"That's true—to a point. But Susie is back." The lady clasps her hands and looks out the window. Obviously, she doesn't want to tell us more.

After we arrive at the plantation, we find that the Swiss couple story is true—partially. The manager is Viola—originally from Frankfurt, Germany—but her partner, Roland, is Swiss. While Viola runs the resort, Roland runs his own dive operation on the premises. Both are blonde, tan, and fit.

During dinner that evening, Viola explains: "Susie owns the Plantation. It has been in her family for generations. But I've been managing it for three years. I've put a lot of effort into it."

"It shows," I answer. "I love the landscaping. And all the flowering hibiscus trees—red, orange, and yellow—I can tell that they've been pruned and taken care of."

I won't tell her what else I noticed this afternoon. Thatching blown off the roof; the generally run-down nature of the bures; the Plantation House showing its age and neglect.

"We tried to buy the resort," Viola continues. "Susie has unrealistic expectations. She doesn't understand how much money needs to be put into it."

"I run the diving operation," adds Roland. "You cannot really run a profitable resort here on Taveuni without diving. Viola has done a lot, with little money. But so much more needs to be put into it to make it a good operation. It was a backpackers' place when she took it over; she's upgraded it to *budget resort* status."

Taveuni, Fiji's Garden Island, is overrun with lush vegetation.

Günter and I exchange glances, curious about how Viola ended up here.

After a glass of wine, Viola seems eager to tell us her story: She had moved from Germany to Santa Barbara, California. She met Roland on a vacation to Fiji; they had a nice fling, but neither could let it end there. Back in California, after racking up a $5000 phone bill, she decided it was less expensive to just fly back to Fiji to sort it out. It worked. Love-struck, Viola returned to California to quit her job and sell her home.

"I sold my collection of high heels and business suits and moved to Taveuni."

"Now she has a collection of flip-flops," Roland interjects. "A pair in every color."

"First, I moved into Roland's bachelor bure. I cleaned and organized it stem to stern."

"Then she started on my dive shop. At that point I told her, 'I think you need something else to do.' That's when she checked into managing Susie's."

An entire string of failed managers had preceded her, but Viola *was* making the resort work. Until now.

Viola has not only fallen in love with Roland; she has fallen in love with the Plantation, as well.

In the morning we meet the waiter, Patrick, at the Plantation Dining Room. The well-built Fijian, who has plucked a giant red hibiscus bloom and placed it behind his ear, informs us that it will be a while before he will have coffee ready. "Meanwhile, you can take Boxer here for his morning walk."

Boxer's brown and white tail wags expectantly. He follows us eagerly. We walk down the main road encircling the island, much of which winds around the Plantation property: 300 acres that have been in Susie's family for generations. Coconut groves give way to fields, uncultivated now. Tangled vines fight their way to the tops of spreading shade trees. Exuberant wildflowers line the roadside; their hues range from white to yellow to blues and purples. Bright butterflies dart crazily across an abandoned taro field. They land in a yellow mass under a wild hibiscus tree with matching yellow blossoms. The sun rises from behind the purple mountains of Taveuni, placing a yellow halo around the tops of coconuts palms.

It feels like God is setting up a wondrous photo op just for me.

That afternoon Günter takes advantage of the island's main activity by participating in a refresher diving course taught by Roland. I settle into a lawn chair on a bank overlooking the sea. I write to the music of the tide lapping and gurgling against the shore. Whenever I need a break, I walk partially down a ladder where I can view from the shore the fish swimming among the coral. The perfect creative environment, it's a welcome change from writing on board *Pacific Bliss*.

While Günter and I bask in the serenity of the Garden Island, a real-life drama unfolds around us. For the players on stage at Susie's, this week is far from relaxing. The next day one of them, Josephine, a Fijian who is a "Jill of all trades" at the resort, fills me in during my massage.

"You're probably the last customer I will have here," Josephine informs me.

"Why? Are you not busy?" I ask.

"I was earlier this week, *four* massages," she answers. That seems a large number to her.

"But Viola is leaving. She gave us all notice." I can hear the deep sadness in her voice. "I have been working for this resort for the last ten years, cooking, cleaning, waiting on tables, and now massages," she continues. "I fill in whenever someone doesn't show up for the job."

Dinner seems strangely subdued that evening. I can tell that the servers, including Patrick, are not their usual exuberant selves. Viola never appears at all. We ask Roland about her.

"She'll be okay tomorrow. Perhaps too much sun or dehydration."

I suspect emotions play a large part in her failure to appear.

Susie and her in-laws have arrived. The in-laws have moved into one of the guest rooms in the Plantation House, and Susie has moved into the Big House edging the Resort.

The plot thickens.

The next day, after a nice walk, we return to find the Plantation bustling with activity. Workers are scouring the grounds and woods across the road for banana leaves, palm fronds, red ginger, and hibiscus. An elaborate setting for a grand buffet is being staged inside the Plantation House. The bar area has two giant pots filled with banana leaves standing on either side. Outside, workers are preparing a *lovo* (a feast cooked in the earth like the New Zealand *hangi*). Piles of *dalo* (an edible root similar to taro) and *kumera* (sweet potato) have been stacked on the grass; a group of men are lining the earth oven with stones and kindling. By evening, the inside dining area had been cleared for the *meke* (dance), and tables for the diners have all been placed outside on the patio.

During the dinner, Günter and I sit next to Susie's in-laws. Her mother-in-law is a feisty 85-year-old, making plans for her husband's 95th birthday. She does most of the talking.

Time for the flashback. We now learn the back story.

"Susie was been born into an aristocratic Fijian family. Her father, who's dead now, was Ratu (chief) of Taveuni. So Susie was brought up on this 300-acre plantation much like royalty. You must understand: *Everything* was done for her. They brought in a tutor from New Zealand to teach her English and other subjects. They threw huge parties on the Plantation grounds."

"Like this?" Günter asks.

"Harrumph! This is nothing! There were so many guests some of them had to be housed at the Grand Pacific Hotel in Suva. Do you know that hotel?"

"Yes, we saw it when we went to the capital for cruising permits."

"Well, it was one of those times when Susie was in Suva, meeting guests, that she met our son, Brian… He's Australian…from Sydney. He first saw her on the plane landing at the Nausori Airport near Suva. She was the most beautiful girl he had ever laid eyes on!"

"Then what happened?" I ask.

"Brian never expected to see her again. Imagine his surprise when he met her in the hall of the Grand Pacific! This time, Brian was determined to follow up. Susie was enthralled. And from then on, they were together constantly."

She leans over the table, as if confiding in me. "Luv, do you know Brian married Susie right next door at the Big House—27 years ago! There were 70 invited guests. The reception spilled over into the Lodge…that's demolished now. My mate here helped build this very house for the newlyweds…didn't you?" She doesn't wait for her husband to respond but keeps talking as we eat our diner.

We find out that during the following years, copra production waned. Prices fell. The natives no longer wanted to work the Plantation's coconut groves and taro fields for a pittance. Susie tended to the house and her flowers. Though she had been brought up a Princess, she discovered she liked to cook.

"She was a mighty good cook, too," the mother-in-law went on. "In later years, she turned their house into a resort. Then she hired one manager, and another, and another. They started with the simple backpackers' dormitory. But now you see many buildings here.

"Then Susie's parents—Fijians from here in Taveuni—passed away; they are buried in plots, with huge limestone gravestones, near the Big House."

The buffet table is being cleared and desserts set out. The conversation fast-forwards to the year 2000. Brian became ill with leukemia, we learn. He went back to Sydney for treatments. Eventually, he became too sick to return to Taveuni. He died in Sydney, with Susie by his side. And for the past three years, she lived there with her in-laws.

Günter gets lei'd.

During a break in the program, we meet Steve, Brian's brother. He tells us more of the family story: "We've tried since Brian's death to make Susie an Australian citizen. We hired attorneys—must have written about 40 letters in all. If she had applied even *one day* before Brian died, they tell me, it could have worked, but now they have officially deported her."

"That's sad," I offer. I don't know what else to say.

"Well, not really," he says, surprising me. "In the end, it's better. Here she's a princess, and always will be. In Australia, she doesn't really fit in. Why not be some place where people look up to her?"

Now the pieces come together. Susie will live here, fix up the Big House, and run the resort.

The *meke* is about to begin. As the "Master of Ceremonies," Viola performs her role perfectly. She is exquisitely dressed for the occasion, but her face shows her stress.

It doesn't help that the generator conks out, stopping the recorded music for the dancers. The generator failure reminds me of something Viola had told me earlier: Requirements for a successful resort are good wine, hot showers, and internet access. Well, the generator has been on the fritz for almost two days now, the phone lines have been down for another two. We've had no hot showers or internet access all week.

I feel for her.

We see Susie in the audience, encouraging her two daughters. One is blonde with European features; the other has Fijian features, but with dark, straight hair. As they take center stage, Susie rises from her chair on the sidelines and loosens the brown girl's ponytail, letting her locks drape across her shoulders.

This is the only time I see Susie actually do something!

"Susie plans to get her children and all her cousins, nephews, and nieces here involved in the *mekes*," the mother-in-law, my new confidant, whispers. The *meke* ends. Günter and I carry our charged lanterns back to our bure. "Do you think this will be the last *meke* for Viola?" I ask Günter.

"Probably. This appears to be her last hurrah."

Thursday morning, we are on the patio enjoying our last breakfast at the Plantation. The staff is friendly, despite working late the evening before. One woman hangs flower wreaths—made especially for us—around our necks while the others gather around our table to watch. My eyes are watering. Farewells are always hard. Roland and Viola stop by to say goodbye. They are leaving sooner rather than later. We're not surprised.

We have been invited to the Big House. After packing, we rush over. My eager octogenarian confidant invites us in. She leads us through the massive dining room with its huge wooden table and hutch to a screened porch that she calls "the parlor." There, she introduces us to Susie. The Fijian lifts her head, says hello, and puts her head down again.

Is she a cold person or merely shy? I can't figure her out.

We follow our elderly leader through the porch and outside where her husband joins us for a walk through the unkempt garden. "It needs a lot of fixing up, but Susie will get it done," she continues. "She has relatives here to help her. That parlor is just where Susie's father used to sit when he ran the plantation. He would ring the bell, and then all the plantation hands would scurry to meet him there to take their orders.

"Here was the big kitchen," she points to a typical Fijian outside cooking area, constructed as a lean-to in the back of the house. "This plantation was built in the 1800s. It was the only one on all of Taveuni. It was a hoppin' place in its time. Susie will fix it up again."

I sense ironic foreshadowing in my guide's optimism. I don't have much confidence in Susie's relatives. They have been gathering around the gigantic kava *bowl in the yard since Susie came back.*

I would love to talk with this spunky couple some more, but we have to excuse ourselves to catch the ferry. Our driver foretells the resolution of what Günter calls *The Saga of Susie's Plantation*. "I give Susie three months," he says. "She's a Fijian."

So is he, I notice.

"They don't have a head for numbers. Her relatives won't help, either. They'll just hang around."

For the remainder of the way to the ferry I can't shake the deep sadness I feel at the Fijian drama we've brushed up against. So much of the South Pacific's culture is dying; I wish that this story would end happily with this small slice of Taveuni history being preserved.

The Islands That Do Not Want Tourists—Fiji's Lau Group
July 6

We'd flown from Savusavu and stayed overnight at the Raintree Lodge in Nausori, near Suva and the airport. Now the Twin Otter prop plane rises through the early morning darkness. As it levels off, a thin line of orange rims the eastern horizon ahead.

"The crack of dawn," Günter quips; he is seated across the aisle from me in the small 20-seater.

The flight beyond Suva is breathtaking. Fiji's far-flung reef system stretches below me—shades of lime and teal and copper. I look down at islands we had sailed to from a different perspective. I see Makogai surrounded by sugary sand and coral reefs. I can make out the small passage we took through those reefs to enter Dalice Bay. Ovalau is obscured by clouds,

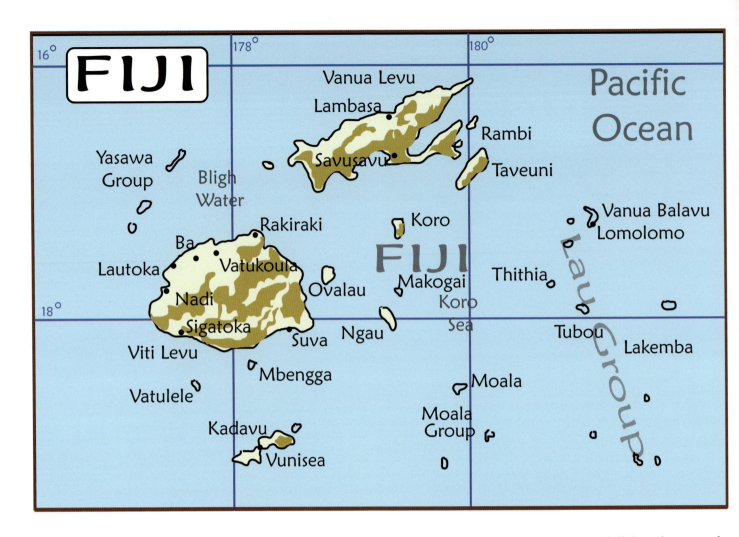

its typical state. Leleuvia shines like a little gem, an emerald isle set in iridescent blue.

From high above, though, the network of reefs looks more challenging than ever, a maze that we had somehow managed to survive so far.

How can we possibly make it back to the west coast of Fiji through all that? Some say that these reef systems are the most difficult in the world to navigate.

After we pick up our luggage directly from the plane's belly, Günter hails a truck with a red canvas-covered bed. He turns to me and shrugs. "Looks like an island taxi to me."

"Where to?" the driver asks.

"We're not sure. We need a place for a week. We tried to get through to Moana's, but couldn't."

"That'll be $20 Fijian," he says.

We bump along a dirt road, across a bridge, and through a few villages, while I worry about how we will obtain accommodations with no reservation.

"Trust me," Günter says. "This reminds me of my backpacking days. They'll have room or they'll find room."

After we pass through Lomaloma and onto a single-lane, two-track road, we turn into a little clearing near the sea, across from the bush, and stop. We see four primitive bures, a mangled volleyball net, and a rickety wooden lean-to piled with pots and dishes that must be the kitchen.

A white woman with glasses, straggly hair, bad teeth, and dirty Capris approaches us. She looks surprised.

"Do you have a bure for two?" Günter asks.

"We do have one available…" she hesitates. "I just have to get it ready."

I explain that I had tried to call but couldn't get through.

"How do you know about us?"

"You're mentioned in the *Lonely Planet* and *South Pacific Handbook*. One of them said you're from New Zealand.

"Yes, I am. I'm Carolyn. My husband, David, is Fijian."

We wait outside until the room is ready, then unpack and settle in. The bure is larger than the one in Taveuni. We check out the bed; it is firm and fairly new, better than the lumpy one we endured in Taveuni. Mosquito netting hangs from the four corners of the canopy. A lone window, with wood shutters and no screens, faces the sea to catch the eastern breeze.

The accommodations are basic: The guests share one toilet, wash area, and shower. We have electricity only when the generator is running (usually afternoons).

Lois and Gunter stand next to the huge wooden *kava* bowl at Susie's Plantation. The largest *kava* bowl in the world?

At night we will take the charged lanterns, one per bure, back to our room. There's water pressure in the evening till 8:00; this is the only time one can take showers (cold, of course).

We spend most of the day sitting outside our bure in camp chairs, quietly reading, while we listen to the incoming tide lap the stony shore. We are only 30 feet from the shore at high tide. I look up from my book. "This reminds me of camping in Minnesota, except it's the sea instead of a lake. There, I also had to spray constantly for mosquitoes—although we didn't have these no-see-ums."

"It's not camping," Günter retorts. "It's just life in Lau."

Later David stops by with their only child, Moana, a pretty girl about nine years old. She has dark skin and brown eyes, with straight thick brown hair. David—wearing a T-shirt and shorts—is broad-shouldered and stocky, yet fit.

⚓

At breakfast David greets us cheerily. "Eat light, because you have to save room for the feast after the church service," he says, looking up at us expectantly. "I'm going ahead. You can come later."

It's only our first full day here, but how can we turn him down?

We change clothes and follow Carolyn and Moana along the single-lane road, more like a path, to Lomaloma. Coconut trees and bush line both sides. After a mile or so, we reach the outskirts of the village. Soon we come upon a Tongan-style church with its characteristic bay-windowed front, surrounded by a grass lawn and a picket fence. Carolyn informs us that it was built in the 1820s. The congregation is standing and belting out songs in Tongan as we find our way to a pew.

We're surprised to see David walk up to the lectern. He looks great! He has changed to a gray long-sleeved shirt with a gray *sulu* to match and a natural-colored *tuvalu* (mat) around his middle. Over it all, he wears a tropical beige suit jacket. Carolyn whispers to us that he is filling in for the pastor, who is visiting in Tonga this week. The entire service is conducted in Tongan. It ends about 10:30, and then the feasting begins. And what a feast it is! A long runner has been spread on the floor over the center of a large empty bure next to the church. Mats for seating have been placed at the sides and ends. Huge platters at the center contain piles of mackerel, coral trout, and barracuda. . Heaping bowls of curry sit alongside the typical South Pacific side dishes of dalo and yams. We are all invited to take our places. After

The Bay of Islands in the Lau Group contains numerous round islets like these, similar to those in Thailand.

the blessing we all turn our plates over. Then the family hosting the event (they take turns every week) waits on the congregation. They pour lemonade as dishes are passed around until everyone has eaten. Then they serve dessert to everyone individually—large bowls of chocolate cake smothered with lemon pudding. I can't finish half of it. How these Lau folk can eat!

During the walk back, I swear I'll never eat for the rest of the day.

Back at Moana Resort, Carolyn and David have strung hammocks for us from trees lining the shore. They invite us to take a welcome siesta. Later they call us for dinner. They have a guest whom we must meet: the local doctor—an Indian.

He has brought lots of food: a fish pie, chicken with soy sauce, taro, and lobster curry.

With basic foods and no alcoholic beverages here, I'd expected to lose weight here. This is so not happening!

⚓

Our infamous oyster catching trip comes about quite accidentally. During breakfast, David invites us to go fishing with him.

The sea is calling. The four of us hurriedly change to swim suits and pack our snorkeling gear. Soon we are purring through the reefs surrounding the shoreline, beyond the colors of lime and teal to the deep blue sea.

David explains where we are: "We're heading into a larger lagoon now. It's 37 by 16 kilometers. Tongans call it Rarirari. *Palangis* call it Emerald Lagoon. It's still within the main reef system."

I'm reminded that the island's name, Vanua Balavu, means "long land."

"How long is the entire barrier reef?"

"The reef is 131 kilometers long," David answers.

"About 80 miles or so," Günter converts.

We pass palm tree islets with perfect sandy beaches for picnicking. We motor past tiny dome-shaped islets rimmed with sheer limestone cliffs that remind me of the Vavau Group in Tonga.

As the bay opens up, the view becomes almost indescribable. The scene is different from anything in all of Fiji (or the South Pacific, for that matter). It most resembles bays in Thailand—dozens of rounded islets topped with coral, bushes, and even a few bonsai-like trees. We behold a fairy-tale wonderland. I can imagine a setting that includes dwarfs and elves and strange animals—all miniatures. We come upon a different, more awesome view around each bend. Then David takes us to an area filled with mangroves. The water is murkier here.

"Unfortunately the tide is coming in now; otherwise you could see oysters from here. But they are still here, stuck to the tree trunks under the water. You just have to snorkel for them. Want to try?" He heads the boat to an area where the water is clearer.

We all jump in. The guys have the heaviest tools; they continue to chip away, scraping the oysters off the tree trunks and throwing them into the boat. I help Günter for a while. Then Carolyn and I return to the boat while the men continue. "They are the hunters and gatherers," I tell her. "We are the Queens."

Günter keeps on long after David comes back. He gathers his catch in his shorts, swims back to the boat, hands them to me one by one, and then returns to the mangroves for more. "I love this!" he yells back.

The pile of oysters in the bow keeps growing.

"Enough," David says finally. Günter climbs back into the boat. Carolyn has thought to bring limes. We all feast on raw oysters, still salty from the sea, until half the pile is gone. We decide to save the rest of them for dinner.

David motors to a sandy beach where we disembark and walk to a pristine saltwater lagoon called Turtle Lake. Patches of lime-colored sea grapes glow below the shallow water.

But we're done exploring. Face down on our beach towels, we fall fast asleep in the sun. When we return, we're still so mellow that we take a sun shower and soon fall fast asleep again in our bure.

This day we have arranged to go to Mualevu Village, to the family home of our Fijian friend Vasenai, a single mother who works in Vuda Point. When she found out that we intended to visit the Lau Group, she gave us a box of empty glass bottles to bring to her parents to use for packaging and selling their coconut oil. They are raising her daughter.

We take a car loaned to us by the Indian doctor. When we stop at the police post to ask directions, they tell us that her mother is there, filling out a report. Excitedly, she talks to David in Fijian, and we follow her home.

The villagers are shocked to see us arriving by car.

"They were expecting you," translates David, "but by sea. Vasenai called her mother just last weekend, asking whether they'd seen your yacht yet. The news of your coming has spread."

We explain why we came by plane instead.

While the villagers gather around, Günter presents the box of glass bottles to Vasenai's mother. She sends one of the children to get the father from the taro fields. Viliame returns in coveralls, dirty and unshaven. Even so, he looks handsome and too young to be a grandpa already.

We meet Vasenai's three-year-old daughter. She is cute as a button with curly hair and fiery eyes. I suspect she is quite a handful.

"Are you adopting her?" Günter asks.

The grandmother nods. We learn that is common when there is no husband involved. Usually, even if the girl later marries, she leaves the child with the grandparents. I show the girl pictures I took of her mother, then give them to the grandmother for safekeeping.

The village children crowd around—they probably don't see many *palangis*. At a table underneath a shade tree, I open my backpack. Taking out a set of crayons and colored paper, I hand it to one of the girls. The kids are well-behaved. No one tries to grab her crayons. After she begins coloring, I unpack a second set of crayons and hand one colored paper to each child. The kids occupy themselves, drawing pictures of bures, palm trees, and suns with smiling faces.

Meanwhile, Günter talks with the men. They answer his questions in short phrases.

"They understand English quite well," David explains. "But it is difficult for them to speak it."

Günter hands an oversized postcard of San Diego Bay to Viliame.

"Big city you come from," he remarks and grins widely.

Later Viliame takes David, Günter, and I on a walk to explore the village. We walk past round Tongan houses interspersed with square Fijian bures.

"Why did the Tongans build theirs rounded?" I ask.

"To stand up better to cyclones," he answers. "The wind just goes around them."

We walk down a long path leading to the sea. A large powerboat lies on the shoreline, underneath a stand of palms, its hull cut through by a reef. Palms bend before the fierce wind; the sea foams against the shore, and farther out, the whitecaps rage.

I cannot imagine a landing a dinghy near this village. Anyway, we could have never left Pacific Bliss at anchor in these waters!

Viliame seems to understand. "Too rough," he points.

We turn and walk back to the village. David takes us aside. "The village people, they do not know what to do; they were not prepared for your visit."

"We don't want to interrupt their day," Günter says. "We should leave now."

David explains to the villagers that we need to return the doctor's car, that we must leave now because we borrowed it only for a few hours. The group seems relieved. "I will call Vasenai soon," her mother informs me. "I will tell her that you came."

Carolyn brings us coffee in bed this morning. How nice

The church in Lomaloma sits high on a hill in Fiji's remote Lau Group. The services there are conducted in Tongan.

Flying in a small plane to the remote Lau Island Group is a fantastic way to to experience a bird's eye view of Fiji's colorful network of reefs.

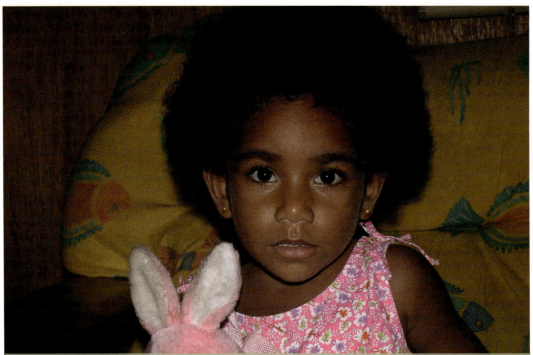
Vasenai's daughter is being brought up by her grandparents in the Lau Group. Even if she marries, the daughter will continue to live with them, not with any new family that Vasenai might begin.

Zealand. Carolyn had been one of his students. She's been in Lau now for nine years. We are her first guests at this seaside location this season, although they have others in their guesthouse in the village. There is only one other white woman on Vanua Balavu. She is also married to a Fijian. Despite the hardships, Carolyn likes it here.

Women like her amaze me!

After dinner, the wind blew so hard that I had trouble walking against it back to our bure. The tide came thundering in, an extreme contrast to its gentle lapping against the sand only a few days ago. We went to bed, relieved not to be "out there" in the angry seas, worrying about our anchor dragging us toward those dangerous reefs.

to be waited on like this! We awoke at dawn as usual, but after a trip to the outside toilet, we retreated back into our cozy bed to read. It is not a morning to greet the sun. A big black cloud is coming our way.

"It may not clear up all day," Carolyn warns us as she turns to leave.

"A good day to stay in bed," says Günter, buried in another detective novel. Carolyn brought up a stack of paperbacks yesterday—Günter is in heaven. He goes through them so fast!

The East Wind is back in all its fury. It arrived yesterday toward dusk. At first, it brought refreshing, cooler air through our little bure. We propped open the window and opened the double doors wide. Then it became stronger. For the first time, we could not have dinner outside. We retreated into our bure, closed the doors, took the sticks out of the windows, and closed the wooden shutters so that only slits of light came through. Then we read by the lone florescent bulb of the lantern.

"Scuse me," little Moana called outside our door in her sweet voice. "Dinner is almost ready."

We sat in the enclosed dining area, cozy with the warmth of an open fire in the corner. The floor was sand (unfortunately filled with no-see-ums). Carolyn was barbequing lamb chops and sausages from New Zealand. David was in another room sitting on a mat and drinking *kava* with two of his friends from the village. This gave Carolyn an opportunity to talk about her life and how she came to live in Lau. She and David had prior marriages. David taught martial arts in New

I spend much of my day writing in my journal—about "the simple life" and what a contradiction that is.

Because the more simple life is, the more complex it gets. Simple things—like fire, water, and electricity—are no longer givens.

Take fire, for example. David keeps worrying about the fire for his *lovo* (underground barbeque) going out for the feast and *meke* tonight.

Take water. I had planned to take a shower and wash my hair this morning, thinking that the water pressure would be on until 8:00 as usual. (Since there is not sufficient pressure for all the villages here at once, the next village usually gets water pressure after 8:00. But this morning, the village "powers-that-be" turned it off at 7:00.) Daily, Carolyn fills barrels of water so that they last until 4:00 when the village turns the water back on. The resort also collects rain water.

Take electricity. Daily, David lugs the battery to charge it from the solar panel on the generator. The resort has no refrigerator because it would take too much battery power.

Günter interrupts my journaling about the simple life. "Write down how I see beauty in your soul," he says.

I couldn't imagine being married to some egotistical corporate honcho who is playing golf at some five-star resort while I maintain my image as his trophy wife. How plastic! <u>This</u> *is real.*

During breakfast, David relates how the children would peek into the windows of their house in LomaLoma after he brought Carolyn to the island. David would reach out of the open window and pat them on the head. "No looking at the *palangi*," he would warn.

"They thought I was a ghost," Carolyn adds. "The small children were afraid of me. Then a few years later, during a wedding when I invited white guests, the children said, 'Lots of Carolines here today!' Fijians have Caroline as a name, but not Carolyn."

Despite the weather, the *lovo* is still being planned for tonight. Carolyn and a hired lady from the next village are already husking coconuts.

Günter and I walk to the village and on to the General Store that doubles as a bank. The store is basic: unpainted, wooden shelves with supplies behind the counter, a storage area stacked with boxes of supplies, and a front area with benches where customers wait for rice, sugar, and flour to be weighed. The Indian matriarch wears an elegant blue-and-violet sari with a sheer mauve scarf covering gray hair swept into a bun. Günter goes up to the old-fashioned teller window to change money. We would learn that the doctor and the merchant's family are the only Indo-Fijians on the island; that the Indians in Moana's school seem well-accepted by the other children; and that the Indian matriarch has lent over $150,000 to Fijians here. Although very little of it has been paid back, she continues to be kind to them and to give out more loans.

As we return to the resort, the wind increases and the rain begins. Even inside this reef system, I estimate the wind to be about a Force 7. Carolyn dials a weather forecast: strong wind warnings for eastern Viti Levu, Vanua Levu, and all of Lau, decreasing on Thursday.

Surely, the Littles, a family that Carolyn invited, will not be arriving for the lovo *in this weather!*

We take refuge in our bure.

The rain stops, and although the sky is overcast, wind continues to blow. We venture out to check on the preparations.

"We prayed that the rain would quit," Carolyn says.

"So did we," Günter answers.

"Fortunately, my fire did not go out," David says. He has purchased a pig, hoping the Littles will show. It is still cooking in the *lovo*.

Good news! As preparations continue, the Littles arrive: 70-year-old Grandfather Colin, his sturdy wife, two daughters and sons-in-law, and a months-old baby. They had braved the angry seas in a small boat piloted by an Indian man who seemed confident about getting them to their destination. They hugged the reefs at low tide, venturing out into open waters only when necessary.

"How high were the waves in the open?" I ask.

"About two feet higher than the roof of this dining area."

I'm shocked. "You must have gotten soaked. What about the baby?"

"The baby was fine, slept all the way," the grandfather replies. "We had an old air mattress. "We ripped it open to make a tarp to cover the baby, and it kept us partly dry. Took us seven hours to get here, with two stops at islands to rest and eat."

"We came over the roughest part in the morning; I think the wind built during the day," his wife adds.

"We were singing 'Amazing Grace' and hymns about sea and rescue all the way," the sister-in-law says. "And we prayed a lot."

What a courageous family!

As we sit talking with the Littles, we enjoy *palangi kava*, vodka-spiked tropical punch they brought.

Carolyn and her helpers set out heaping plates of side dishes on three tables shoved together under the roofed dining area with its back closed to the sea. The East Wind lessens. The pig, miraculously, is crisp and done. David carves it on a separate table, then brings over plates of pork, along with two roasted chickens, potato salad with sausages, Indian curry brought by the doctor, and mackerel caught today.

The entire village of Narotivo has seated themselves on the lawn outside dining area. As we near the end of our feast, David introduces the chief of the village, a hefty gray-haired patriarch who looks the part, wearing a grass *sulu* and leis. The village had assembled quietly in the dark. Now a fluorescent light strip is turned on. The chief introduces the dancers and they perform exuberantly, despite the weather.

Although we have seen many dances by now, this one is special because it has become a village affair. David has been working with the chief all year, convincing him to make the villagers practice their dancing. He has given the village $130 for this night, collected from all his guests. David hopes this will encourage the villagers to be ready for more such performances. He trusts the proceeds will go to something to benefit the entire village, such as a new generator.

Surprisingly, it turns out to be a lovely night. The wind dies. The moon—fuller now—peeks out occasionally. Even the Southern Cross breaks through. David cuts off the head of the pig and presents it to the chief to take home. The women and children of the village leave to take their babies to bed. But the men stay late. They pound and squeeze the *yaqona* root to make the traditional *kava*. Then they form a circle in the yard and conduct their ceremony. Inside, the servers sit around the tables, munching on the leftovers. The Little family says their goodbyes and leaves for town. Günter and I join the *kava* circle for awhile. Then we join the group still sitting at the tables, talking and enjoying everyone's company far into the night.

Moana stares in wonder while David, her father, steers the skiff through the gorgeous bays of Vanua Balavu, in Fjii's Lau Group.

Miracle over Makogai
Makogai Fiji
July 20

The week after we return from our adventure in Lau goes by in a flash. We clean *Pacific Bliss* and provision for the passage from Savusavu back to Denarau. Many things on the boat are broken and will need to be fixed there. The up/down anchor control works only sporadically. We can't trust it. We're afraid we won't be able control the chain's release and it will all come rolling out. So we decide to use our back-up French anchor with its 180 feet of line. With only the two of us to haul it in, hand over hand, we know it won't be easy. Navigating through reefs without crew will be difficult as well. Günter spends much of the week working with a Savusavu technician to repair our laptop. Now it works, but intermittently—the worst—and it takes a half-hour to boot. Life is not perfect, we admit, but we decide to limp back anyway.

The first day, we sail back to Makogai, using our outgoing track from our earlier stop to enter the difficult channel. Then it rains for two days.

On the third day, the rainbow over Makogai is stout and solid-looking. We take it as a clear sign from God that the relentless, driving rain is finally over. The rising sun sneaks between the clouds, casting her beam toward the stern of our catamaran. Günter turns toward me as I clear the breakfast dishes from the cockpit table. "Quick! Let's get out of here before this bad weather system moves back in."

I stack the dishes in the galley sink and rush to the bow to haul anchor. "The anchor line is wrapped around a coral head!" I yell back to Günter. "Gun the engine forward. Maybe we can work it loose." We go back and forth, round and round. It doesn't come loose.

"I don't believe it," Günter groans. "This is…was…our best chance to get out of here, and now we've got an anchor problem. I'll dive down."

He's already donning his snorkeling mask. I hand him his fins. He jumps off the stern ladder and swims forward to the anchor. Fortunately, it's not a serious problem and, experienced at this by now as he is, he frees it within minutes.

Soon we are motoring through Dalice Bay toward the dangerous pass, the only safe exit through the Makogai's protective reef.

The pass is deep enough—20 feet. No problem. But, in places, it's less than 32 feet wide. With her 24-foot beam square in the middle, *Pacific Bliss* will have less than four feet leeway on either side. One mistake and it's all over. We are the only yacht in this area. Occasional workers do arrive by boat to the fishery here, but I doubt that they would have the equipment to pull us off, should we dash into the reefs. We are on our own.

To make matters worse, our computer completely died while we were waiting here for the weather to clear, the last of a long list of equipment malfunctions. I am forced to navigate the old-fashioned way—by sight—without access to our incoming GPS track. If ever navigation demanded absolute concentration, this is the time.

We slow down to enter the passage, with the sun at our back. Perfect! I'm on lookout at the bow, calling directions to Günter at the helm, as *Pacific Bliss* painstakingly winds her way through the reefs. I stare at them through the clear water; they are zigzagged and sharp—gigantic saws that could cut our hulls to smithereens.

We continue to inch forward. I lean over our bows, looking from one side and then the other as Günter carefully guns the two engines. My tongue is as dry as sandpaper. My heart pounds like I'm running a 10K.

About halfway through, I straighten to direct Günter the rest of the way.

Suddenly my stomach knots.

No! We have lost the sun. The clouds have closed in. I can no longer make out the reefs. Too far to the left or to the right, and it's curtain time.

"Stop!" I shout.

"I can't!" Günter shouts back. I'm going as slow as I can. If I stop now, completely, we might turn sideways. All 43 feet of us. We're longer than the channel is wide!"

Things happen quickly at sea. Any lapse in judgment could cause our boat to break on the reefs. There is nothing to do now but pray. But I know that any answer from God must come quickly. There's no time to kneel—no time to plead. Only time to ask and believe.

"God, please move those clouds…those over there, blocking your sun. Now!"

Incredibly, the answer is immediate. God parts the clouds as clearly as He parted the Red Sea back in Moses' day.

Yay, God!

The sun is back over my shoulders again, nearly overhead now, showing the way.

Through my polarized sunglasses, I see that *Pacific Bliss* is still positioned exactly between in the middle of two reef walls—they are separated like an underground chasm. And jagged rocks and coral still threaten her on both sides.

Ever so slowly, while maintaining steerage, Günter nudges *Pacific Bliss* forward, as I shout warnings and directions: "A little to the port…straighten her, straighten her…that's it…coral on the starboard now…careful…careful…." Every foot is treacherous and uncertain but, after what seems like an eternity, we finally make our way through the remainder of the channel.

Back into safe seas again, there's no need for a lookout. I breathe a deep sigh of relief and walk back to the cockpit to stand next to Günter. "It is a miracle…a real miracle…"

Günter nods. His face relaxes, releasing its frown and furrows.

I look back toward our wake. White froth over

DID YOU KNOW?

FIJI

Fiji is an archipelago of 333 islands encompassing 7,056 square miles, about the size of the U.S. state of New Jersey. The country's main sources of income are tourism and exporting sugar.

Indigenous Fijians live throughout the country, while Indo-Fijians reside primarily near the urban centers and in the cane-producing areas of the two main islands. Most Fijians are Christian; two-thirds are Methodist. About 77 percent of the Indo-Fijians are Hindu; 16 percent, Muslim; and 6 percent, Christian. The total population of one million, with a median age of 25 years, is 51 percent Fijian, 44 percent Indian, and 5 percent European and other Pacific Islanders.

Fiji's geography, smack in the middle of the Pacific Ocean, has made it a destination and a crossroads for many migrations. Archeologists tell us that the Lapita people, ancestors of the Polynesians, settled the islands first. Austronesians settled the Fijian islands around 1500 B.C. Melanesians followed 1000 years later, coming from Southeast Asia via Indonesia. Oral history in both Africa and in Fiji refers to a great ship, *Ratu*, sailing to Fiji and landing at what is now called First Landing, near Vuda Point. This contradicts the East Asian migration story and modern day beliefs.

The Dutch explorer Abel Tasman visited Fiji in 1643 while looking for the Great Southern Continent. In the 1820s, European settlers and traders founded Levuka, the first modern town in the Fiji Islands. In 1871, the nation state of Fiji was founded, and Ratu Cakobau was crowned as its king. Fiji was established as a constitutional monarchy. Lavish spending saddled the kingdom with so much debt that, in 1872, it offered to cede the islands to the United Kingdom. Despite the annexation of Fiji as a British colony in 1874, Levuka remained the capital for another three years before the administration was moved to Suva. In 1970, Fiji attained independence, ending 96 years of British rule.

Relationships between ethnic Fijians and Indo-Fijians have often been strained, and this tension has dominated politics in the islands. In 1987, the military staged a coup to prevent an Indian coalition party from taking power. The new constitution of 1998 provided for a multiracial cabinet and a coalition government, and Fiji's first ethnic Indian Prime Minister, Mahendra Chaudhry, took office a year later. But ethnic tensions plunged Fiji into a nightmare in 2000 when a group of armed soldiers entered Parliament and took three dozen people hostage, including the prime minister. Although the coup was foiled, the democratically elected government was not restored to power. Instead, the military and the Great Council of Chiefs, a group of 50 traditional Fijian leaders, appointed an interim government dominated by ethnic Fijians. Elections were held in 2001, but no party achieved a clear majority. Democracy during the following years was messy, and in 2006, there would be yet another Fijian coup!

navy blue. That means deep water. Slowly I gaze at the sky, up toward the clouds. Those clouds have closed in again, as tightly as a one of Makogai's giant clams.

The sun has disappeared!

"Thank you, God," I murmur. "Thank you."

We unfurl the jib and sail onward, content with our speed of five knots on a beam reach, too overcome with joy to bother with the main. The sky remains overcast. Four hours later, we anchor near the sandy beach of Naigani, well beyond a patch of coral.

After our chores, we sit in the cockpit, sipping our sundowners and enjoying the light show. Pinks and mauves deepen to reds and maroons. The sun slowly slips into the waves like a squashed golden gourd.

Günter turns toward me. "Do you think we'll see a green flash?"

"Nah, the sun is pressed too flat. I've seen the flash only when the sun is full and round, with absolutely no clouds on the horizon."

"Could happen. There's no haze now. That might lead to a refraction of light *because* of the squashing."

Günter is right, as usual. He's a physicist, after all. Green flash! For a fraction of a second, an iridescent green light surrounds the gold, right after the sun sinks into the sea.

"Thanks, God, for sending your angel yet again to watch over us." I raise my glass to the glowing horizon. I'm truly grateful.

And yet, I'm beginning to have a few misgivings.

Were today's events just another example of God watching over us, as we'd asked Him to do when we began this world circumnavigation? Or were they warning signs to "cool it?" Perhaps God is telling us that sailing halfway around the world is enough, already. Is it right to ask Him to protect us for yet another 18,000 miles?

I think back to conversations with our cruiser friends. Here in Melanesia, many of them have decided to end their voyages by sailing north from Fiji to the Marshalls, then back to the west coast of the U.S., settling for a Pacific circumnavigation. Others are planning to ship their yachts back to the U.S. from Australia. For the past two seasons, we have been sailing the Coconut Milk Run. This is easy compared to what's ahead. The passages beyond Australia will be fraught with danger: threats of pirates, terrorism, and anti-Americanism adding to the omnipresent fear of turbulent seas and equipment failures.

Dare we ask God for the strength to go on?

Kissing Another Reef and Limping Back to Denarau
Naigani Island, Fiji
July 23

We wait for two days for a weather window to sail to Viti Levu Bay. Whether we dare the inland passage or take the Vati-Ra channel, it makes no difference. Either way, we will need five to six hours of sun to make it. Six hours of sun seems a difficult proposition in Fiji these days!

We use the time here to move our navigation route over to the JoyBook, the computer I use for my writing and digital photography. We're fortunate to find a computer expert on *Itchy Feet*, amazingly anchored right next to us. Ray troubleshoots our HP laptop and coaxes it into working again.

Finally, the third day looks promising. We leave Naigani behind us in stark relief. Makogai shines in the sun, and even farther behind we can see the cloud-crusted island of Ovalau. By noon, the massive reef system at the entrance to Viti Levu Bay comes into view. It is 3.5 miles to our old anchoring spot, one hour to get there, another to get out. We have no incoming track to guide us. During the process of dealing with the recalcitrant computer, Günter had mistakenly clicked "erase all tracks." Knowing that markers are missing in this bay, we opt to continue on. That means we'll be anchoring at Nananu-I-Cake, a place I'd rather forget.

"Better the anchorage you know than the one you don't," says Günter as he motors over to our old spot.

We're the only boat here. After anchoring, we jump into clear water and swim to the bows of *Pacific Bliss*, relishing the freedom of swirling water over our naked bodies. We swim back under our boat's belly, between her two hulls, to the swim ladder. We air-dry and gaze longingly at each other….

"I'll fix some drinks," says Günter. "Then I have an idea for another kind of adventure…."

He pours a cold wine for me and a rum-and-coke for himself. "Cheers." We clink our glasses and look each other in the eyes, drinks forgotten….

We're heading for the master berth as I glance back toward the stern. "The boat has turned all the way around!"

"What? How can that be?" Günter looks at the depth meter. "Two feet, three inches!"

"And there's coral."

"No!"

"Yes! We've drifted into a coral bed, right below the swim platform. We're not touching it—yet—but I could step right onto it."

Günter turns on both engines. I take the helm while he goes forward to pull the anchor line. After taking up 10 feet or so, *Pacific Bliss* drifts and the depth meter changes to 36 feet. With next to no wind, we had drifted around to a coral shelf.

"We could re-anchor here, just a little deeper."

Günter is upset and determined to leave. "No! This place is bad luck. We're outta here."

"Where to?"

"The resort."

"But there are four yachts there now, there won't be any room. Remember? We discussed this on the way in, when we decided *not* to go there."

The anchor is all the way up. Günter takes back the helm and turns into the bay.

"Just check it out on the charts. Find us a spot. And get some clothes on."

I turn on the computers in the salon (we're using two now for navigation, just in case…) and while they're booting, I check the paper charts for a suitable anchorage and throw on a sarong.

As I head topsides, I hear a terrific bang-bang, clash-clash. The dagger boards are bouncing wildly. I look over the side and can't believe what I see!

Günter has cut the corner to the resort—not much, but of course, any peninsula juts out more underwater than one can see on the surface.

He had taken off in a huff, at 6 knots, without waiting for me to report on what he'd just asked me to do! No talk, just action! I'm frustrated, angry, and ready to explode. But that will only make the situation worse. An ugly knot forms in my stomach.

Control, Lois, just keep your cool…and think.

We both see the approaching motorboat at the same time. It's a Fijian woman, probably fishing. We hail her. She keeps going.

I cup my hand, motioning for her to come toward me. She turns, slows down, and appears to hesitate. "Help! We need your help to get off this reef," I yell.

"She's coming," I tell Günter.

"Throw her the port bow line," Günter commands.

I loop it carefully while she motors closer. She motions for me to throw it. I motion her closer. I do not want to miss my throw.

The waves are pushing us farther onto the reef. Every second counts now.

The woman motors up to the bow. I throw the line. She grabs it but obviously doesn't know what to do with it.

"Cleat it to your boat, then pull." I show her what I mean by pointing to the cleat on our boat. Her clouded face breaks out in a smile.

Taking orders from another woman is giving her some confidence. I think she will help us out!

She secures the line, guns her engine, and pulls us out easily. We weren't hung up after all! It must be soft coral because there's no scraping sound as *Pacific Bliss* floats free.

The woman pulls us out into open water, then turns toward us to hand the line back. I ask her to simply drop it. She doesn't understand that I can just pull it in. She comes right to the bow of our boat with hers. Then she finally uncleats our bow line and hands it back. We're off!

At the resort, of course, we cannot find a suitable anchoring spot with the four yachts taking up the space. Reefs line both sides of the anchorage and run halfway along the front of the resort. Any wind change, and even those boats would be on the reefs.

No thanks! We've had enough of reefs for one day.

We motor back to our original spot but nearer the dock. We anchor in deeper water, 45 feet, with 120 feet of line and allowance for a 180-degree wind change! We are taking no more chances on this passage back to Denarau.

Out here, anything that can happen, will happen!

July 24: We are relieved to leave this accursed anchorage of Nananu-I-Cake for Vitongo Bay. Another 46 miles of painstaking reef navigation, and we're there. We use both computers: one with close-up views of where we are and the other for macro displays of where we're going. As we head into the muddy mangrove-lined bay, the sugarcane fields of Lautoka are burning, sending up plumes of smoke. It's a custom to burn them at the end of the harvesting season. The wind gusts to Force 6, with angry whitecaps. All night, *Pacific Bliss* rolls with the waves, making us feel like we're still at sea.

This morning, a pale orange light sneaks over the mountains of Viti Levu, Fiji's largest island. A bank of fog rises over the mangrove swamp. Hunks of burnt sugarcane cover the boat. We pull anchor and motor off. By evening, we're back to Denarau and civilization.

The return trip from Savusavu has taken us only one week, but the intense focus and navigation through the reefs has taken its toll. We're clearly "Fiji'ed out," ready to leave Fiji's reefs and politics and problems. We've learned more than expected about Fiji's two adversarial cultures. We've had our "glimpse of the underglimmer." And now it's clearly time to move on.

Farewell, Fiji! Hello, Vanuatu!

A mangrove tree such as this one is typically underwater at high tide. Oysters cling to its roots.

What a contrast! Back near Denarau Marina on Fiji's main island of Viti Levu, water lilies burst forth from a manmade pool at a golf course.

Local women of Waterfall Bay in Vanuatu's Northern Bank Islands walk along the shore at low tide collecting shellfish.

Chapter 11
Vanuatu's Remote Northern Banks Islands

Passage to Vanuatu
At Sea, 17°54´S, 172°56´E
August 20, 2003

For two days, our passage from Fiji is fun. Günter and I enjoy the ease of sailing to the wind, using our autopilot's TRACK setting. But now, only our second night away from land, things are already going wrong with the boat. We can no longer get the GPS feed from the B & G display, a problem we thought we had solved back in Fiji's Denarau Marina. We have to switch to the little Garmin GPS, with its "highway" graphics, and adjust Ray, our autopilot, a few degrees when needed.

At the beginning of my 0900–0000 watch, I rouse Günter with more bad news. "It's Ray again. He gave out. Come up. Quick! I've got to go back to the steering wheel."

A grumbling Günter comes up to troubleshoot the problem. He turns the salon into a war zone: Seats of the settee are scattered over the floor; the stuff underneath the nav station is strewn about. He checks all the connections while I hand steer—until midnight. Eventually he finds and fixes a loose connection, and he puts Ray back to work.

In the morning we speculate about what more can go wrong. Our biggest fear is that Ray will fail again and we will be forced to hand-steer all the way to Vanuatu. Not fun!

But I drum up my courage.
We can do it, if we have to!
Losing sleep while we dealt with Ray's breakdown has upset our usual passage rhythm. Our watches are tedious and tiring and come much too quickly.

On my first watch, I find it difficult to determine whether the radar is showing squalls ahead or just low rain clouds. And on my second night watch. I return topsides to find that the weather has worsened. Bullets of rain pummel my face. I squint through the inky blackness. Then I freeze….

Günter is not in the cockpit! Where is he?
Frantically, I bend over the empty helm seat, grip the metal railing, and peer into the abyss. Nothing!
I must find him!
I head for the bow. Once there, I see…nothing. The misty void sends chills up my spine. I shiver. Shaking, I turn around to the cabin roof. I think I see a shadowy form. Yes! It's moving! It's coming down the wooden safety steps. Then the shadow slips.
Oh my God! Did he fall overboard?
Suddenly, his figure emerges. His right hand is gripping the safety straps alongside the cabin. With excruciating slowness, he makes his way toward me.

I've been holding my breath. Now my fear turns to anger. I gasp, "We promised… never…go forward… when underway…without informing the other person!"

We hug each other tight. His sailing jacket is cold and wet against my cheek.

"I'm sorry," he whispers. "It won't happen again."

It is 1700 on Wednesday, this third day of our passage. About this time on land we'd be thinking about sundowner time. But we don't have our usual sundowners during a passage. I have just made an entry into the logbook before turning to talk with Günter in the cockpit: *Sunny skies. 310 nautical miles into the passage. 206 to the waypoint off Efate, Vanuatu. Then only another 20 nautical miles to the entrance.* I record the wind at 11 knots, mostly on the nose; we are motoring along at five knots, using one engine. One would think our dispositions would be as sunny as the weather.

But, no! We are sitting together in the cockpit, talking about shipping *Pacific Bliss* back to the States when we reach Australia. Usually, when one of us wants to quit, the other wants to continue. This time, though, we are both dead serious.

"I feel out-of-command," Günter gripes. "I don't feel in charge of the boat, and I have no sex drive to boot."

"Well, it's not as if we *have* to complete the circumnavigation. We don't have to prove anything to anyone. Except maybe to ourselves...."

"I don't know *what* I want anymore." Günter leaves me in the cockpit and paces in the salon.

After dinner I read until it's time for my first evening watch.

I turn to a section in *Oceans to Cross*: "Life is about how you respond not only to the challenges you've been dealt but the challenges you seek."

Well, we sought all this. Does that mean we will let ourselves down if we don't complete it?

I sit for while and stare into space.

Then why continue? If we are not going around the world, is there a book here? Is there such a thing as partial-circumnavigation? A Pacific circumnavigation, perhaps?

At this point, I'm not sure what *I* want.

Would our souls die if we didn't continue? We've both conquered so many obstacles in our lives. Isn't that enough?

Of course, I wouldn't be doing all this soul searching if we were having a great time on this passage. But we're not. What should have been a blissful sail with the wind has become drudgery as we motor against the wind. And the hassles with boat maintenance are wearing us down. I wonder if someone up there is trying to tell us something. I thought God was smiling on us. Now I'm not so sure.

Is it really decision time? Enough already?

Exploring Port Vila, Vanuatu's Capital
Port Vila, Vanuatu
August 22

We are safe on a mooring in Port Vila Harbor and, almost instantly, our attitudes change. Attached to *Pacific Bliss,* our dinghy floats calmly and yanks on her tether. Surrounding boats swing silently at their own moorings, their names reflecting the dreams and aspirations of owners we have yet to meet: *Shoreline Song*, the neat little monohull, flying a commonwealth flag; *One Day*, a white catamaran with blue trim. Günter pours me an arrival drink, a cold glass of my favorite Sauvignon Blanc. "Here's to new adventures," he toasts.

"To new adventures," I raise my glass. Then I detect a twinkle in his eye, and I become suspicious. "Uh-oh. Exactly *what* adventures?"

"I was talking to Rolf on the VHF about accompanying *Yelo* as a buddy boat. To the Solomons."

"The Solomons!" Ugly newspaper phrases spring to mind. "Political dissidence... Cauldron of Unrest."

I pour myself a second glass of wine. I need it.

"Just a couple of days ago, you talked about shipping *Pacific Bliss* back from Australia, about hanging it up. Now you want to add another dimension to our boat problems?"

"Yes. This Coconut Milk Run is becoming mundane... boring. I'm talking about *real adventure*."

I'm too tired to answer him, let alone argue. We sit for awhile, silent in the serenity of our mooring. Finally, I re-start the conversation. "Rolf's a crazy man."

"I know. That's why this idea intrigues me."

"You need a crazy man for a buddy boat captain?"

"Yes."

Finishing my second glass of wine, I'm mellowing by the minute. Well, Rolf's a fellow Catana owner. *Yelo* is almost a sister boat to ours, the same model, built only six months later. That has some advantages... maybe. At least Rolf, like us, has experience fixing a Catana. "Perhaps it *would* be a good buddy boat."

⚓

It's Friday, and after a few days here, we've become familiar with Port Vila. We're sitting in Hannah's Café, admiring condiments from all over the world. When it comes, lunch is delicate risotto-spinach turnovers with refreshing iced coffees. This is a level of sophistication way beyond what I expected from an undeveloped country like Vanuatu.

After lunch, we stroll through the huge outdoor market. They will be closing it for the weekend, so we rush to Bon Marche´ and buy the last of their baguettes, cheese, and liver pâté.

We have invited Rolf, and his sailing partner, Daniela, for sundowners. Daniela is Swiss. She is thirty-something, lithe, blonde, and fun-loving. We all laugh a lot and get along well. We share dozens of Catana stories. The two arrived about 5:00 p.m. It is 10:00 when they leave.

Now, that's a great sundowner!

The days turn into weeks as we spend our time just "messing with boats." We leave our convenient mooring to anchor near a shipyard, which is called simply 17°44

Pacific Bliss is docked in Port Vila, the capital of Vanuatu.

South. There Günter puts *Pacific Bliss* through a list of repairs and improvements that must happen before we can leave with *Yelo*.

Yes, we now have a plan that will take us through the remainder of Voyage Three. We will sail north to the remote Banks Islands of Vanuatu. The staff at the Port Vila Visitor's Center has informed us that, beginning September 15 on the island of Vanua a festival will be held to celebrate the installation of a new chief. This is just the type of cultural experience we were looking for! A *Port2Port Rally,* sponsored by the Port Vila Yacht Club, will begin on October 20. This will be our first cruising rally. Joining it will cause us to skip New Caledonia, another French territory, but it will allow us to sail to Australia in the company of other yachties. Yes, Voyages Two and Three have taught us to be flexible and to sail with the wind, but not to be so whimsical that we would give up our plans for Australia to sail now with Rolf to the Solomons.

Günter and I are mission oriented, after all!

While we're Messing with Boats, always our first priority, we do take some time here and there to acquaint ourselves with Port Vila.

The variety of stores in here is amazing! Why are there so many Vietnamese and Chinese store owners? we wonder. We learn that their ancestors had been brought here originally as indentured laborers to work the coconut and sugar plantations. Now they have all become shopkeepers.

We lunch at Hannah's again, and afterward we discover a used bookstore where Günter buys a pile of Wilbur Smith books for fifty cents each. We enjoy Tuskers at the Waterfront Bar and Café; the brew is not as good as Fiji Bitter, but it is welcoming and ice cold.

The next day we lunch at the Waterfront Café. The burgers surpass the Bula Burgers in Fiji, but nothing can come close to the burger with pineapple rings and beets in Aitutaki. Next we attend a Cruiser's Book Swap. Towers of paperbacks cover an eight-foot table. We bring 15 books to exchange, and we take 13 back. What a great idea!

A favorite stop when provisioning in this port is Jill's Café, also called The American Way. I love sitting at the brightly painted blue-and-yellow picnic tables on the patio. I devour an old-fashioned hot-fudge sundae. Günter favors iced coffee in a tall milkshake glass with two scoops of vanilla ice cream. The setting is a step back in time—all the way back to '50s Americana.

Imagine finding this in remote Vanuatu!

On August 29, when all repairs on *Pacific Bliss* have been completed, we take her across the bay and back to our old #25 mooring ball. We're happy to be in familiar surroundings again, near *Dawn's Light, Sojourner,* and all the other yachts. Friday is the big party night in Port Vila. We take a water taxi with Rolf and Daniela to a tiny island in the bay called Iririki. There I sip on my first tropical drink in Port Vila—piña colada in a half-coconut shell, but made with ice, not blended. We watch our first "snake dance," a common must-see tourist attraction in Port Vila. The dance originated in the island of Mota Lava in the Banks Islands, where the snake is a humorous phallic symbol in their fertility rite.

I've read about this dance, so I know that the presentation here has been "sanitized" for tourists. The all-male troupe now wear black briefs, instead of going naked, and each dancer swings a long decorated stick, representing his "snake."

Günter takes a photo of Daniela and me posing with the dancers. Then the program changes to '50s and '60s music played by a six-piece band. By this time other yachties have arrived, and all of us dance late into the night.

On Sunday I'm up early, and I decide to take a 7:00 a.m. photo walk. The absence of traffic allows me to stand in the streets to photograph some of the wonderful murals on this capital city's buildings. The usually bustling market is hauntingly empty; its stalls have been cleaned, and its tables are topped with benches. I walk through it silently, remembering the chaos during the week. The bay along the waterfront is glass-like, smooth, and green.

At the top of a hill that overlooks the city, I stop at the Winston Churchill Avenue sign and turn toward Independence Park. Joint rule was proclaimed there in 1906, with the ceremonial raising of the British and French flags. A daily check was made to ensure both flags flew at the same height. Apparently, the British and the French consulates were each terrified that they might be upstaged!

I had learned some of the history of this strange Condominium government from museum displays: Australian planters settled in the islands of Efate and Epi to grow coconuts for copra trading. Other settlers came over from New Caledonia with the dream of seeing the New Hebrides annexed to France. The only way this rivalry between the French and the English could be resolved was to establish the Anglo-French Condominium of the New Hebrides, formalized in 1922. Amazingly, the people of Vanuatu had the British queen and the French president as joint heads of state! Many of the "manbush" (simple island people) believed for a long time that the queen and president were married and that the country was ruled by this couple.

A favorite story of the islands is about how they determined on which side of the road to drive. The government was at an impasse. Both French and British cars were coming off the ships, with steering wheels on either the left or right side. Finally one wise politician figured out a way to solve the problem: "Let's watch

The snake dance is common in the Northern Banks Islands.

Rolf swims with a dugong in Lamon Bay.

for the very first car to come off that ship tomorrow," he pointed at the harbor. "If the steering wheel is on the left, we will all drive on the right, and vice versa." The first car off the ship was made in France; its steering wheel was on the left. Consequently, to this day, all driving in Vanuatu is on the right side of the road.

I pass a church with open doors where I see workers inside, setting up rows of chairs for the Sunday service. They smile and wave as I walk past them. Farther on, I stroll past the imposing Port Vila town hall. It has a French design, complete with a drive called Ave de General de Gaulla.

The building now housing Vanuatu's Supreme Court is the former "Joint Court of the Condominium." As I walk along, I remember reading how that court arbitrated disputes between the British and the French. *The Lonely Planet* provided an example of its eccentric judgments: A French man who murdered an Australian in front of witnesses was permitted to remain at large on his home island. But a French woman who dared to insult a magistrate was rewarded with one month in the lockup.

I walk down the cliffs east of Port Vila to view the yachts quietly nestled in the harbor. I wonder what the parliamentarians on the hill, running their country and looking down from their office windows, think of the lifestyles of these sailors. Do they imagine them adventurers exploring new worlds? Or do they merely think of them as rich foreigners? Are they envious?

Hours have passed. I turn back toward the Yacht Club, the Waterfront Café and *Pacific Bliss*. She is looking very pretty, gleaming in the morning sun. "You're finally fixed. Soon, *Miss Bliss*, you'll be off sailing again. And with *Yelo* as a buddy boat, I guarantee…you'll be sailing fast."

I pat her hull as I climb on board.

Build-Up to the Banks

On September 1, Labor Day in the States, Günter and I labor through a long To Do list. After the boat is ready, we dinghy to the markets for one last time. At the butcher, we pick up previously-ordered beef and veal, vacuum-packed and frozen. We buy staples for ourselves and also food and used clothing to give to those in need. We send postcards and final internet messages. Then we say heartfelt goodbyes to the cruising community gathered here, to old friends and new. By noon, we are sailing north under a full main and jib.

Despite beauty and culture that rival any of the islands in the South Pacific, the Northern Banks of Vanuatu attract very few tourists. Those who do visit are usually yachties. Now, *Yelo* and *Pacific Bliss* are becoming part of this select group, heading north to experience a way of life that most people only read about in adventure magazines. In fact, most of *us* have never been to such a remote part of the world!

Our excitement has been building since we first found out about the Cultural Festival. Now, the program is also being promoted on the Namba Net, the cruisers' SSB net here. (To explain, a *namba* are penis wrappers, or sheaths, made from dried banana or pandanus leaves, dyed red, purple, or green. They are worn by Ni-Vanuatu males during traditional, or *kastom,* ceremonies. Some men from very *kastom*-oriented villages wear them all the time.) I eavesdrop on the joyful banter. Other yachties are saying they want to see this ceremony, too!

We may be taking different routes, but we know where we'll all end up: at Waterfall Bay for the beginning of the Cultural Festival.

Searching for Dugongs
Esema, Havana Bay
17°33′S, 168°17′E
September 2

Moo-aa-n.

It is 0615. We walk around the decks in the heavy dew, our bare feet soaking it up.

"That's the dugongs moaning," Günter says.

"I don't believe you. Those sounds are coming from land. I know the moo of cows and the cockle-doodle-doo of roosters. Remember, I grew up on a farm!"

We've already researched Havannah Bay in Nicole Rhind's *Vanuatu Yacht Guide*. It told us there are dugongs, tiger sharks, and dolphins in various parts of this huge bay; in fact, a school of dolphins had joyfully escorted us into this anchorage. But enough of dolphins. I'm looking forward to seeing my first dugong.

Dugongs and their manatee cousins are the world's only herbivorous marine mammals. The dugong, or "sea cow," feeds on sea grass, which tends to grow in the calm, shallow bays of coastal islands and coral reefs. It has a thick layer of fat, giving it a rotund shape. Small paddle-like flippers are positioned far forward on its body, and it has a broad, flattened, powerful tail that resembles that of a whale. Feeding on sea grass and, occasionally, on marine algae, a dugong can grow nine feet (three meters) long and weigh up to 924 pounds (420 kg)! Vanuatu's dugong population may be increasing, but worldwide the creatures are being overhunted and are dying in great numbers from pollution, loss of adequate food, and entanglement in fishnets.

I want to see one before they become extinct!

My thinking is interrupted by singing. At first, I imagine it's Daniela; after all, *Yelo* is anchored next to us. But then I recognize a girl from the village. She is in her dugout canoe, bright and early, because I'd asked her to bring "paw-paws" (mangoes) today. Before she leaves, I question her about the dugongs.

"Not here. Deeper out." She points toward the entrance.

We pull anchor and sail 50 miles north to Epi, along with *Yelo*. After we anchor in Revelieu Bay, Rolf and Daniela invite us to share a tuna that they'd caught along the way. It is a pleasant interlude.

But as we turn in for the night, the weather turns ugly. Confused seas rush over the reefs and a roiling surf pounds the shoreline. The wind shifts and gusts to 20 knots. It whistles through the screens so hard that I have to close the windows. *Pacific Bliss* pulls at her anchor and rolls from side to side. Günter pulls me toward him in a spooning position and hugs me tight to

DID YOU KNOW?

VANUATU

Vanuatu is made up of some 80 different islands in the shape of a "Y" on a northwesterly slant, located right on the Pacific Rim of Fire, on the subduction zone of two tectonic plates. The islands of Ambrym and Tanna have active volcanoes. The northernmost islands, the Torres Group, are about 900 km from Aneityum at the southern tip. The entire land mass takes up only 7,574 square miles (12,189 square kilometers). Port Vila, the capital, is located on the island of Efate.

Vanuatu does not have the ethnic strife observed in Fiji. The government wants development to benefit everyone equally, while preserving the nation's age-old customs and traditions.

The majority Melanesian population is about 174,000, with 45 percent under the age of 15. This population declined from about one million in the early 19th century. The infection-ridden vessels of the sandalwood traders and the blackbirders brought new diseases that wiped out entire villages.

Vanuatu's Melanesians came with a wave of migration from Southeast Asia, moving through Indonesia and the islands of the New Guinea chain towards Australia and the Solomon Islands. A subsequent wave finally crossed the seas from the Solomons to the Vanuatu archipelago about 3000 BC. Between the 11th and 15th centuries AD, Polynesian voyagers from the center of the Polynesian Triangle brought new skills and customs.

The first European to visit this island group was Pedro Fernandez de Quiros, a Portuguese mystic who arrived in 1606 and christened it "Terra Australia del Espirito Santo," hence the name Espiritu Santo for the nation's largest island. Quiros soon left. Then, 160 years later, Louis Antoine de Bougainville arrived and named a few more of the islands. In 1774, Captain James Cook discovered Vanuatu on his second Pacific voyage on board his ship the *HMS Resolution*. He mapped the islands for the first time, christening them The New Hebrides. Cook stayed only 46 days. After that, many navigators and whalers came and went.

In the 1880s, France and the United Kingdom claimed parts of the country, and in 1906 they agreed on a framework for jointly managing the archipelago as the New Hebrides through a British–French Condominium. An independence movement arose in the 1970s, and the Republic of Vanuatu was created in 1980. The nation's name was derived from the word *vanua* (meaning land or home) and *tu* (stand).

Vanuatu claims the highest concentration of languages per population of any country in the world! There are at least 105 local languages as well as the more widely spoken English, French, and Bislama. The national language is Bislama, a form of Pidgin English. In French, the Republic of Vanuatu is called République de Vanuatu; in Bislama, it is *Ripablik blong Vanuatu*.

put me to sleep.

I won't be swimming with dugongs here!

We experience a fast sail to Lamon Bay, a.k.a., the *Bay of the Dugongs*. By evening, the wind has calmed. The Southern Cross shines and a half-moon gleams. We have a great time partying with other yachties who are anchored in the bay, but we never spot a dugong. "I give up," Günter says. "Let's face it. We'll never see a dugong anywhere in Vanuatu if we don't see one here."

However, the next day, anchored in Banam Bay, our adrenaline kicks in, big time.

I hear Rolf's outboard revving at the swim steps.

"Dugong! Right in front of *Nikita,* about 30 meters!" He has dinghied over to pick us up.

"Get in! Hurry,"

I grab a camera; Günter grabs some diving equipment. We jump into the dinghy and head toward the dugong.

We see the creature below the surface. Günter's snorkel and mouthpiece have been left behind, so Rolf lends him a mouthpiece. I try to take a photo from the tossing dinghy, but my digital camera is too slow. No matter. When Günter returns, he says this is another experience he'll never forget. The huge animal, about 500 pounds, just ignored him when he patted his hide. He just continued to graze on the ocean grass, sucking it up like an industrial vacuum cleaner.

"You can find them on Ambrym," a local tells us later. "But there are none that are this friendly and gentle. They don't let you touch 'em like this one did."

I leave the bay satisfied and contented. *I may not have petted a dugong, but I've seen one in the wild!*

Life at Anchor and Cruiser Camaraderie

Some days, knowing that we will just take off again, we don't even bother to lower *Petit Bliss*. I take my shower at the swim ladder and rinse by swimming around the boat. Then I stay on board. But that doesn't mean the day is lonely. People come to us.

In Lamon Bay, three Vanuatu children, ages 11, 12, and 13, all brothers, stop to see us. "We have 15 in our family," the oldest informs me proudly. They are well-mannered kids. They jump on the trampoline, sit at the helm, and ask politely whether they can see the inside of *Pacific Bliss*. Seeing the interior, they are silent and wide-eyed. I serve them juice in the cockpit while Günter talks with them in Bislama, a form of Pidgin English. It has a very small vocabulary of about 5,000 words, and one word may be used in place of five to ten English words, making it easier to learn. One can pick it up in a few weeks.

The brothers speak Bislama at home but English in school, and they will learn French when they go to high school. Here are some phrases Günter learns:

What is your name?	*Wanem nem blong yu?*
I'm from…	*Mi blong…*
Do you like…?	*Yu ting you likim…?*
I like it very much.	*Mi likim tumas*
I don't like	*Mi no likim*
Do you know	*Yu save*
I do not know.	*Mi no save*
I am very happy.	*Mi glad tumas*

"How would I introduce my husband?" I interrupt, putting my arm around Günter.

"You would say, '*big man blong mi,*'" one of them says. They all laugh.

But the strangest Bislama phrase is the one for helicopter: *mixmaster blong Jesus Christ.*

That evening, cruisers in the bay show up for a party; it's spontaneous—the best kind. Word travels quickly throughout the anchorage, and everyone brings food and drinks. I spread it all out on the cockpit table, buffet style.

We meet Michelle and Tam, who have lived on their yacht in the Bay for about a month. Michelle is teaching art at the High School and working on a project for her BA thesis. She is also writing a book, and she sells native art on a website. Tam, a sturdy, quiet, blue-collar sailor, is a mechanic; he repaired *Yelo* while spending the last cyclone season in New Zealand.

The talk turns to how missionaries have "wrecked" the native lifestyle. Discussion rages, pro and con. Was life in Vanuatu idyllic, or brutal and short? By the end of the evening, we have defined that "lifestyle," and we realize that it hadn't been that great—especially for

Our buddy boat, *Yelo*, sails along Havana Bay north of Port Vila, Vanuatu.

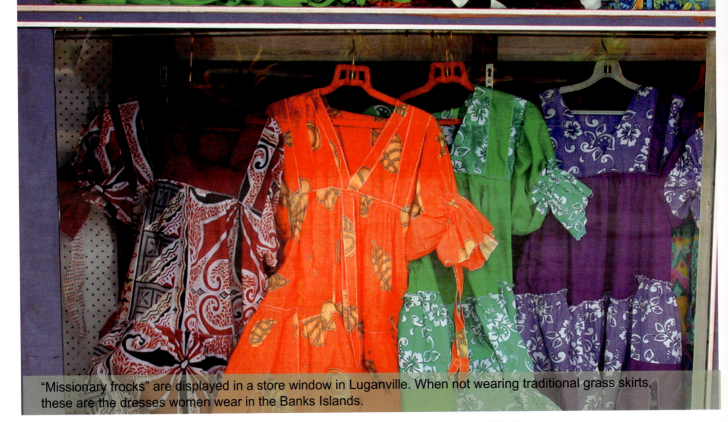
"Missionary frocks" are displayed in a store window in Luganville. When not wearing traditional grass skirts, these are the dresses women wear in the Banks Islands.

women. Before the missionaries came, female value was less than that of a prized pig, which could be used, at least, to increase a man's rank. Women fed the pigs, made the family's clothes, gardened, and cooked. Like pigs, but lower in status, they were considered part of a man's wealth. And, often, they committed suicide.

No wonder!

But now, women no longer work the fields or do hard physical labor, and their marriages are more of a partnership.

The conversation drifts to the practice of circumcision. Michelle had recently attended the circumcision ceremony of a pre-pubescent boy, and she tells us about it. She didn't see the actual surgery, but with food, music and dancing, the entire ceremony was treated as a great celebration. She informs us that female circumcision (sometimes called female mutilation) is not practiced in Vanuatu.

While washing the dishes, Günter and I talk about the evening's conversations. We agree that cruisers are far more interesting than most landlubbers. Their sailing and adventure stories are fascinating, of course, but equally intriguing are their perspectives on history and culture. Cruisers love to read and have considerably more time to analyze and discuss what they've read. They don't just sit on their boats and stare at the horizon. Devoid of communication with the outside world, they become thinkers. They probe. They reason. And they come to fascinating conclusions about life, people, and the world in which we live.

Sailing Fun and Challenges
September 7

The sky is overcast as we slowly sail along. Island shapes of monochromatic gray bleed into a gray sky. Behind us, Lamon Island looks foreboding. No wonder the locals there called it the home of ghosts and spirits! We've been day sailing, island-hopping north from the main island of Efate, to Shepherd, to Epi, and now we are underway to Malekula. That means we will miss Ambrym, the Volcano Island. But as we pass by, its peak comes into view, gloomily puffing white and gray smoke.

By noon, the wind picks up, and we raise the main to gain some speed on *Yelo*, sailing alongside, but it doesn't work; the main steals wind away from the jib, and we have to pull it in. With a fickle wind on the aft starboard quarter, Ray protests again. I've been seeing this from him off and on throughout our Vanuatu passages. Whenever a gust arises, *Pacific Bliss* is pushed to starboard, and Ray cannot handle it. He beeps and demands attention. I tire of babying him, so I hand steer for awhile. I want Ray to pull his weight. He used to be so steady. Is this a warning?

By late afternoon, while I'm at the helm again, thick, gray clouds hover over the hills of the long gray-green island of Malekula. We are headed toward Port Stanley, following the faint profile of *Yelo* with her billowing spinnaker. *Pacific Bliss* is sailing wing on wing at a leisurely 4.5 knots. She is balanced in precise rhythm; Ray hasn't complained once. The wake rustles gently behind the stern and the wind brushes my cheek as I turn to feel it. We have an almost perfect following sea.

The typical ups and downs of a sailing day. We love the highs but lament the lows. But isn't that the nature of life? Even an EKG has an up and down rhythm.

We douse our sails as we close in on the entrance to the Uri anchorage, and we motor easily through the pass between islands. They are surrounded by long outstretched reefs, clearly distinguishable in teal and brown. Then the Anchor Dance begins. We crowd in behind three yachts that are taking the shallow waters. But we're too close to them and have to pull back to the 62-foot depth. This means that we are anchored on a shelf—a little dragging and we're in trouble. We set our anchor alarm, and within hours it beeps. So we reset the beep range from its present 250 feet to 500 feet. We have 120 feet of anchor chain and bridle out. This makes things a little safer, but it's still difficult to relax.

I burn nervous energy by baking. It will be Günter's birthday tomorrow, and I have a chocolate cake to bake. But my cooking is interrupted again and again by vendors and curious locals who paddle up to *Pacific Bliss* in their dugout canoes. Sometimes entire families arrive in two or three canoes. They tie up to the stern hulls. One boy climbs out of his canoe and up onto the steps to the cockpit! We trade one bag of rice for three pamplemousse (grapefruit). We trade a T-shirt for pawpaws. We have come so far north that *vatus* (Vanuatu coins) are never mentioned here; our visitors either want handouts or want to trade. I hand out one lollipop after another before each family leaves.

Then we dingy to *Yelo* for a mahi-mahi dinner. The fish was caught by Rolf as he and Daniela came through the pass into Stanley. They serve it with rice and fresh octopus. *Hmmm...absolutely delicious.*

We've been racing *Yelo* throughout the island chain, but we are no match for her multiple headsails or for Rolf's knowledge of sailing tricks. Truly, he is the Catana expert. One trick he describes to us explains his procedure for bringing down the entire mainsail quickly. We call this Rolf's Rapid Dousing Technique.

On September 9, the two buddy boats are sailing along in a 10-knot wind with gentle following seas. The sky is 50 percent overcast; the other half is filled with fluffy white clouds. *Pacific Bliss* is finely balanced, wing on wing, doing 6.7 knots. We leave the island of Malekula behind and head for the next island, Espiritu Santo. The Port of Luganville can be seen as we approach Espiritu Santo. Opposite the port, and within the harbor, is a tiny island called Aore, which boasts a resort for yachties.

Provisioning in Luganville

We moor safely close to the Aore Resort's dock. At 24 feet, the sea is perfectly clear—right down to the coral bottom. Günter and I drop bread crumbs to feed reef fish, watching how they form in schools to follow the crumbs. Günter observes that if he drops a crumb out of their feeding frenzy, it goes unnoticed by the school for some time; then, eventually, one lone fish will venture from the school and find it. Whereupon, the entire school will swerve swiftly to join him. "Just like human behavior," I remark.

In all of nature, there are many followers but few good leaders.

"Let's join them," Günter says. He dons his snorkel and jumps in. I follow. At the swim ladder, he takes my hand. "I'll lead you to the dock. I like to swim holding your hand. I like to show you things."

"I like that too. I have no sense of direction, once my head is under water."

I don't know how Günter keeps his orientation without popping his head up. Holding Günter's hand, I glide over purple staghorn coral with blue tips. I love snorkeling among reef fish with incandescent shades of yellow, blue, and gold!

Günter points his index finger at a fish who aggressively heads right for his mask; the fish turns away. I point my finger. But another fish darts straight toward my mask. I point my finger at it. It turns sharply, swims to my backside, and nips me right behind my knee! Ouch! This has never happened to me before!

After our swim, we take the island ferry across the channel to Luganville. The ferry lands on an unattractive, cluttered beach. We disembark through stones and shallow water and follow steps up a hill that leads, surprisingly, to a group of old WWII Quonset huts

Before World War II, this area was a scattered collection of modest buildings separated by coconut plantations. Then the Americans came and changed its face forever. Japan's lightening advance through the Pacific reached the Solomons by 1942. Vanuatu's settlers were convinced that invasion was imminent. However, in May of that year, a U.S. fleet arrived and began constructing bases, first on Efate, Vanuatu's main island, and then on Espiritu Santo, Vanuatu's largest island. Over 100,000 U.S. servicemen were garrisoned around Luganville, tripling the population almost overnight. In all, half a million Allied soldiers passed through this archipelago on their way to war.

With Japan's defeat in 1945, the Americans withdrew as quickly as they had arrived. They abandoned huge quantities of equipment and sold some at bargain basement prices. The Americans had asked the condominium government and planters to buy the rest for eight cents on the dollar. But believing the U.S. would just pull out and leave the equipment behind, the Vanuatu government refused. Furious, the U.S. chose, instead, to dump everything into the sea near Luganville—airplane engines, bulldozers, trucks, jeeps, even crates of Coca-Cola and canned food. The pile created a jetty and a vast underground tourist attraction called Million Dollar Point, which is now a major diving mecca.

Greed and spite…waste and wonder!

A dirt road brings us to a dusty main street that must be the widest in the South Pacific—probably built to carry those American tanks. Luganville is a throwback in time. Lining each side of the street is a long straight row of staid storefronts, many with Chinese names. Missionary dresses, flowered and flowing like Hawaiian *muumuus*, appear on mannequins in shop windows. Rolls of printed cotton fabrics are piled alongside. Other shops carry an amazing variety of hand-woven baskets.

The entire town is sleepy and dilapidated. Vacant lots with concrete slabs remind us of busier times. We walk the entire main street in about 20 minutes. Near the end, we come upon a large playing field and a lovely old grandstand. A plaque tells us this is where the Condominium was proclaimed in 1906, with the ceremonial raising of the British and French flags. Another plaque proclaims Vanuatu independence in 1980.

We head back and criss-cross the wide street a few times, first to place our order with the butcher, then to the market, to the chemist (drug store), to a few supermarkets, and finally to a ladies' handicraft store. Our big finds in town are chocolate bars and brie cheese. Weighed down with shopping bags, we trudge back to the ferry to cross the channel to the more contemporary Aore Resort.

The Tale of Two Birthdays—and Killer *Kava*
Aore Resort
September 10

"Let's go to Island Night at the resort to celebrate my birthday," Günter suggests.

I tease him. "I thought we celebrated that last night, with Rolf and Daniela. I distinctly remember the-rum-drinks-that-had-no-rum. And have you forgotten the special Double Dutch chocolate birthday cake I made, the two symbolic candles you blew out, and the port wine, *on the house*?"

"Yes, but that was my Vanuatu birthday. The time zone makes today my *real* birthday, since I was born in Germany."

"What an excuse to party. But…why not?"

So, we dinghy to the dock and celebrate at Aore Resort for the second night in a row.

Before dinner, we are invited to the side patio for *kava*. Wow! One little one-half coconut shell full of *kava* numbs my lips immediately! It is a direct hit to the senses.

"Another one?" the server asks.

"No way!" I shake my head.

We learn that Ni-Vanuatu make *kava* differently from the way it's prepared by Fijians: Here, they include the green part of the root. That doubles the potency.

We hear stories about cruisers who were invited to a feast on a Vanuatu beach. *Kava* flowed, and the last thing they remembered was how they wobbled as they stood up. They had been drinking *kava* like the natives. First, their legs felt like jelly; then they went numb; then they had to be carried to their dinghies. The next morning, they didn't remember getting back to their yachts or anything that had happened the night before. *Kava* in Vanuatu can wipe a person out. It is a devastating drink!

One Sweet Day
15°02.085′S, 167°04.867′E
September 12

We sail for seven and a half hours up the east coast of Espiritu Santo under sunny skies with winds ranging from 10 to 15 knots. Having *Yelo* as a buddy boat forces us to stretch. We learn new sailing techniques. For example, we experiment with the snap shackle to let the jib hang way out. This allows us to capture more air and gain speed. And before rounding Thion Island and heading into Orly Bay, we douse our sails, using Rolf's Rapid Dousing System. It works like a charm!

We drop anchor, the only yacht in the harbor. An hour later, *Yelo* arrives. The two yachts are centered in this bay of beauty, so quiet, so secluded. The tide is coming in. It gently laps the reefs far to our bow. Cows moo on the shore to our port. Birds twitter in the bush. Günter and I enjoy an early sundowner; we sit side by side at the cockpit helm, enjoying the ambience of this special moment.

After dinner, I access the Tusker CD handed out to cruisers in Port Vila. I find that Thion Island, near our anchorage, is a cattle ranch, owned by the Japanese to grow their own special beef. "You will be left alone in the anchorage," says the guide.

And so we are. We see two dugout canoes as the sun disappears over the hills. But the men in them keep a discreet distance.

I wake up early to a full moon. No wonder I cannot sleep! It's magic, and it beckons me. I leave my bunk and head topside. The moon perches high above the hills to the west; it traces a path down to the mangroves lining the shore and across the bay to *Pacific Bliss*. The stars twinkle overhead, but their light becomes fainter by the minute as an amber streak of dawn makes its

During the second day of the festival, yachties learn how to weave and make kakai (island food), and laplap, the national dish of Vanuatu, similar to pizza.

way through the heavens. Light creeps subtly over the black hills, outlining the palms and, later, silhouetting them with a pink glow.

Pacific Bliss rolls gently over rippling swells. My eyes follow her long anchor line. Beyond it, I see islands on either side of the channel. I sit on the cockpit bench, holding a flashlight as I write. I barely move. I don't want to disrupt the drama of this new day unfolding around me.

By 0535, the stars have disappeared, but the moon still shines bright through a mauve-blue misty haze. Rocky, tree-covered outcrops now stand against the shore and sky in stark relief, with a stretch sea between them. They remind me of the myriads of little outcrops in the Bay of Islands in New Zealand and the remote Lau Group in Fiji.

How blessed are we, to compare one remote area of the world to another! I think of Mom, how she encouraged me to see this world as long as I am here.

How wonderful is this world God has created! I cannot praise Him enough.

Making Water Music in Gaua
Pweterat, Gaua, Banks Islands
14°18.768´S, 167°25.9´E
September 13

After sailing eight and a half more hours, we're anchored in Pweterat, Gaua. The four of us have joined a group of other cruisers on shore. We have been invited to participate in a demonstration of the island's claim to fame: making music with water. This custom is only found in the Banks Islands of Vanuatu. The women perform a series of synchronized fast clapping and slapping both under and over the water to produce music. One has to see and hear it to believe it. After watching and listening for while, we can detect not only a "water melody" but a background harmony as well. We have all been watching the performance from shore. Now the chief asks the yachties to go into the water to join the women. A few of us do. The women show us how to clap and slap the water, but our efforts fail dismally. We realize how difficult this is!

The older women are wearing grass skirts; their bosoms are bared. Now the chief asks the younger women to bare their breasts as well. Many appear to be in their late teens or early twenties. They are shy; they shake their heads and look down. The chief asks them a second time.

Daniela whispers to me, "Should we take off our own tops? Maybe they'll feel less embarrassed." I nod, ready to do anything, but the women comply before we can help them out; they remove their tops and throw them on shore. We continue our lesson with them for a while. Though we never do make any water music, trying has been great fun.

The Making of an Island Chief
Waterfall Bay, Vanua Lava, Vanuatu
13°49.6´S, 167°23´E

I drop the hook after a pleasant sail from Gaua to Waterfall Bay. The anchor drags along the hard, rocky bottom. Günter, at the helm of *Pacific Bliss*, pulls back again and this time, it holds.

A black-bearded young man of medium build, solid and fit, waits patiently in his dugout canoe until we complete the Anchor Dance. Then he introduces himself merely as Kerely. Soft spoken and gracious, he welcomes us to the Bay on behalf of the three large families who live here. He explains that there is no village, only a primitive compound that he built here three years ago. Since so few visitors come to the island, the families have no need of a public outhouse; however, the locals have just completed one during the past week for use by the yachties to be used at the upcoming installation ceremony. They have also erected bamboo food and souvenir stalls. He expects the crews of at least fourteen yachts to attend the three-day event. Most are already here.

"What a nice, gentle man!" I turn to Günter, still in the cockpit. Together, we watch Kerely paddle off. It is only later that we learn it is *this* man, with the modest demeanor, who will be installed tomorrow as the island's new chief.

Within the hour, Captain Jouke of *Freya*, a Dutch-flagged monohull anchored in the bay, dinghies over to hand us a schedule he has printed out that covers the next three days—sort of. There are no times noted, just a starting time of 0800 for each day and a list of activities. Events will unfold, he says, on "Vanuatu Time."

"This place has been a beehive of activity," Jouke continues with his Dutch accent. "You wouldn't believe all the pounding and sawing that has been going on over there! Most of the bamboo structures you see now weren't there a week ago. Some are just being finished today."

⚓

On Monday morning, September 15, we dinghy to a boulder-filled shore where a group of young men, designated as "Security," pull *Petit Bliss* to safety across the black volcanic beach and above the high tide line.

The first entry on the program is called "Waterfall Walk." We are led along a stony, winding footpath to the base of spectacular falls, as dramatic as any we'd seen in all of New Zealand. This natural wonder, twin waterfalls, is obviously the pride and joy of the locals.

"If these falls were *there*, they would be *fully marketed*," Günter quips.

I'm enchanted by the sight and sound of dual rivers, rushing over a precipice, tumbling over giant jutting rocks, and crashing into a deep, inky pool near the sea.

I turn to watch the long line of yachties following, single file, along the winding path from the dinghy landing. Seventeen boats are now anchored in the bay.

The Lonely Planet's description of how to get here is anything but encouraging:

> From Sola you can do a three-day return walk around the South Coast to Sarah Falls, overnighting at Vureas Bay where there's a small guesthouse above a black swimming beach. This place charges 2000VT for a bed and all meals; you pick up a guide here for the falls. Villagers say it's a reasonably easy, one-day return walk from Vureas Bay to the falls, where there's no camping, so aim to spend two nights with them. It's a half day walk from Sola to Vureas Bay.

The guide also warns: "In 1998 none of these places were providing mosquito nets." It is an area of malaria and dengue fever!

We see no tourists, no backpackers. No wonder!

Our guide escorted us back to the festival grounds. Curious children steal furtive looks at the line of white yachties who traipse down *their* waterfall path; they hide behind their mothers' skirts when we smile back.

We reach a clearing of black volcanic sand, swept hard and clean. The locals have felled trees and halved the trunks to provide seating for us. Around the clearing are structures made of bamboo stalks with pandanus and palm leaves. A local man takes us aside and points proudly to the results of their hard work: the community house, the changing house, and the speakers' dais. He asks me to inspect one of the two outhouses with newly poured concrete floors (and the requisite keyhole-shaped hole in their centers).

As I come out, I give him a thumbs-up. Truly, it was more than I expected.

The clearing begins to fill. To be here, families have trekked through the jungle from the villages to the south, near Vureas Bay. They still carry baskets of fruit, *nangae* (nuts-on-a-stick), coconuts, and many varieties of *laplap*, which resembles pizza. They plan to sell their food in the five hastily-constructed stalls positioned along the path to the waterfall. Other families from the south have arrived by sea. They squeezed into their community fishing boat with its failing prop and aren't sure whether their unreliable "water taxi" will get them back.

The drums roll. We take our log seats. The omnipresent Snake Dance, which will commence each day's program, is about to begin. Naked except for skimpy black thongs, the Ni-Vanuatu males prance around the grounds carrying striped sticks adorned with feathers. Their entire bodies are painted black with white stripes. The drum beat increases. Faster. Faster.

DID YOU KNOW?

CANNIBALISM IN VANUATU

Cannibalism was a common practice throughout all of the South Pacific. While in Fiji, we often saw Cannibal Café T-shirts; in Vanuatu, the subject is more sensitive. This hesitancy to joke about cannibalism might be because Vanuatu was reportedly the last country to give up the practice. In fact, the last recorded act of cannibalism was in 1969 among the Big Nambas tribe on Malekula, the last tribe to convert to Christianity. That was the year man walked on the moon! There are unconfirmed reports of cannibalism on the island of Efate as late as 1987.

Cannibalism was part of the tribal culture. It was practiced between tribes, and there is a history of eating white missionaries. The government tends to treat cannibalism a tabu subject. Because people who have eaten human flesh are still living, it is a sensitive issue. Only the islands of Banks and Torres never practiced it.

Contrary to popular cartooning, people weren't put in huge pots surrounded by vegetables. They were cooked in underground ovens. Two reasons are given for the origins of cannibalism: Some tribes believed that consuming human flesh would give them magical powers; others sacrificed people if pigs weren't available. After the sacrifice, they were eaten.

Apparently the meal was tastier and more tender than pork, so pigs were sometimes swapped for humans. On the island of Tanna, the Ni-Vanuatu ate people who had died of natural causes. On most of the other islands, the victims were killed. Most cannibalism was a result of tribal warfare.

The Kastom Ceremony

1. A choice pig is selected and tied to a specially-constructed platform.
2. The pig is tied, its neck shot through with an arrow, and then bludgeoned to death with a club.
3. A snake dance begins all Kastom ceremonies in the Bank Islands.
4. The man chosen to perform the pig killing dance dons a long, Rasta-like beard that extends below his waist. While the tam-tams pound in an ever-increasing beat, the fierce dancer stomps, grunts, and groans, turning faster and faster.

In the northern part of Vanuatu, status within the clan was earned by males through the *nimangki* system. Many rituals and feasts were held to promote the adult male's rise up his village's social ladder. Each grade meant a step closer to achieving chiefly status. On a supernatural plane, the more grades a man had earned, the more powerful would be his defenses against sorcery while alive, and the more potent would be his spirit after death.

INSTALLATION OF A VANUATU CHIEFTAIN

. Kerely sits on his throne atop the platform, waiting to be installed as the new chief.
. The qualities and abilities of the new chief are recounted to the audience.
. A triton shell is used to assemble the family.
. The blood mark is applied to the face of each member of the family in the new chief's blood line.

And the dancers match the beat to a frenzy.

We had already seen what was billed as a "Snake Dance from the Banks" (costumed dancers cavorting on the cement surrounding a pool during cocktails) at the Iririki Resort near Port Vila. Also, we saw a much livelier version at the Aore Resort. Those tame, tourist-centered performances pale in comparison to the wild and furious action of *the real thing* we are witnessing now! No women enter this dance. It's a passionate display of masculinity. Forming a line, they weave like a striped snake. Bent over, and pumping their legs vigorously, the men whoop, holler, and wave their snake sticks crazily.

After this opening dance, Roger, the official Head of Security, approaches the bamboo speaker's dais. Smartly dressed in camouflage fatigues, he raises the red-and-green Vanuatu flag—ever so slowly—on a bent bamboo pole. A group of bare-breasted women in grass skirts sing the Vanuatu national anthem a capella, harmonizing in sweet, melodious voices.

The festivities have barely begun, and already I am dazed by sensory overload.

This dramatic kickoff is followed by a series of welcome speeches given from the speaker's dais, which is festooned with plants and flowers.

I sense anticipation building. The audience fiddles impatiently. Everyone is eager for the main event to begin: the infamous Pig Killing Ceremony.

Finally, the speeches end and the ceremony starts. This is the traditional pig-killing dance. The dancer wears a white-banded headdress of springy sticks, tipped with white feathers. His blackened face is half-covered by a long Rasta-like black beard that hangs below his waist. His muscled biceps are ringed with flowers and plants, and his blackened ankles with tufts of woven grass. A fiber pouch, hanging around his waist, bounces over his grass skirt. In his left hand, he holds a wooden bow; in his right, a freshly-sharpened arrow.

Off to the side, a group of grass-skirted men pound their tam-tams in a steadily increasing rhythm. In the middle of the clearing, the dancer stomps, grunts, and groans, all the while whirling faster and faster.

This is the wildest Pacific island dancing I have seen yet!

Suddenly the drums go silent and all dancing stops abruptly. A hush falls over the crowd. Attention turns to a platform at the other side of the clearing. At one end of the platform is a stone altar. It is where a pig will be sacrificed. Kerely sits calmly on a makeshift throne near the rear of this platform. He has been transformed from the gentle man we had met two days earlier. Now his cheeks are marked with white stripes and his bare chest is a mass of red-and-white geometric designs.

Many in the crowd leave their log seats for a closer look. Günter and I follow them. Two warriors tie the legs of the pig and hold it on the ground. Another warrior charges toward the unsuspecting animal with bow and arrow in hand. In one swift motion, he pulls the string back releases the arrow straight into the pig's neck. Immediately, the warriors holding the animal bludgeon its head with a huge carved club. They gut the pig while he's still alive and bury the intestines in front of the platform. The family being installed is called to form a line before the pig. The retiring chief turns to the audience; he delivers a long, fiery speech in his native dialect. I have no clue what he is saying as he waves his arms dramatically, but I'm mesmerized by his passion. He ends his speech with a flourish and turns his attention back to the family. His fingers dip into the pig's blood. Then, with great formality, he dabs small smudges on the temples of every member of the new bloodline. This act of royal ascension concludes the formal installation of the new chief.

Kerely—now the new chief—gives a very eloquent speech with far less arm-waving. Apparently the speech is very well received. The locals nod and smile. At the end, in Pidgin and in English, he invites everyone to lunch. The crowd disperses toward the food stalls for a wide assortment of dishes and desserts.

After lunch, Günter and I wander again to the spectacular waterfalls.

As we loiter, a crowd of schoolchildren surrounds me. Although it is a weekday, they have obviously been excused from school for the Installation Ceremony. They are happy, fun-loving, and very curious about our lives. And their English is surprisingly good. They want to know how we live in America and why we would leave such a "rich country." I turn the tables on them. "What are your hopes and dreams?"

"I want to go to America some day," one answers. And all the others nod and grin.

A village elder urges the yachties back to the clearing. The next event is about to begin. Again, we sit on the logs. A dozen men, wearing grass skirts and woven arm and ankle bands, dance wildly again, while pounding their tam-tams and shaking bags of nuts. It's not a sedate dance, but its movements are far less ferocious than those of the frenzied snake dance. Later even women join in and, eventually, the dancers urge the audience to join them. I am hesitant at first, and I attempt to shrink back into the crowd.

It's one thing to walk around with a camera on my neck. It is quite another to get up close and personal, holding hands, inhaling sweat, attempting to match their rhythm.

But the friendly, encouraging smiles eventually win. The Ni-Vanuatu laugh, cheer, and clap as all of the yachties kick up the dust. By the time dusk falls and the security boys help us drag our dinghies over the stones and launch them, we are coated with black volcanic sand and thoroughly exhausted. We will definitely sleep soundly tonight!

Tuesday's festival program opens with the standard snake dance, which is followed by demonstrations of *kastom* (traditional) activities. Locals dressed as clowns show us popular pantomimes; others demonstrate how the meat is removed from a coconut. One activity reminds me of a colonial-style Virginia Reel, except that it is performed only by men. Some older women demonstrate their own hand-clapping game as their bare breasts and grass skirts swing to the beat of the omnipresent tam-tams.

Yesterday Pat of Aldebaran, our spokesperson, had explained to our hosts that yachties usually take a siesta after lunch. The organizers have dutifully inserted "rest time" into the day's events so that we can dinghy back to our yachts for a midday break.

Ah, the blessed flexibility of operating on "island time!"

The afternoon is devoted to demonstrating the preparation of various kinds of *kaka*i (food). My favorite demonstration reveals how the islanders prepare *laplap*, the national dish of Vanuatu. Round stones had been heated the day before, then allowed to cool overnight, so that they will not crack and fly apart. Women have gathered piles of seashells, which they use to peel manioc, taro roots, and yams. That done, they grate the root crops into a doughy paste, after which men knead the mixture by pounding it with large clubs that resemble baseball bats. When it's ready, the dough is spread, like a pizza, on a flat, circular piece of wood. They then carefully lift the mixture and place it on taro leaves. Next, men with machetes slash ripe coconuts into halves, from which women scoop out the white meat. Then they squeeze the meat through tightly clasped hands and fingers until its juice covers the dough. Leaves from the laplap plant (similar to banana leaves) are wrapped around the doughy mixture and bound with strands of vine. Finally the packages are placed into the heated stone oven and covered with more stones.

When the *laplap* is satisfactorily cooked, women distribute it among the yachties. It's not a dish that Westerners find appealing. It is bland and tasteless, but nevertheless very filling.

During *kakai* preparation, many of the men have been busy making *kava*. (Here it's called *aelan bia*—island beer.) I cross the waterfall path to watch them prepare it, expecting to see a fascinating primitive process. And what do I find? Surprise! They're grinding the yaqona root in a Western-style meat grinder! They place the mush into a container, add water, and work the ingredients around with their hands. Then the mud-colored liquid is filtered through coconut fibers. Once the liquid is ready for drinking, it is poured into a half-coconut shell, which is used as a cup. (For this reason, a draught of *kava* is known as a shell.) As in Fiji, etiquette here requires that each participant drink his or her bowl of *kava* in a single gulp.

After the feast, we yachties are invited to participate in a *kava* ceremony; however, the organizers point out that it is not mandatory. I respectfully decline. After my *kava* experience at Aore Resort, I know that Vanuatu *kava* is considerably stronger than the Fijian variety—and certainly much, *much* more than my American system can tolerate.

⚓

On the third day of the festival, a few of the local men and boys guide the yachties to the mountain ridge that overlooks Waterfall Bay. They are proud to show off the gardens—primarily root crops—that they tend way up here on the ridge. No wonder these men and boys have such muscular bodies—it's quite the climb just to go to work, let alone weeding and digging up root crops! I am drenched with sweat just getting here. I could not imagine engaging in hard, physical labor afterwards.

The excellent view of our yachts nestled far below is worth the effort. We take a circuitous route back down to the waterfalls. And while a few hardy cruisers hike to the top of the waterfall, Günter and I relax with the others at the bottom.

We lunch at the food stalls again and talk to the locals, many of whom we now know by name. I can't get enough of the children! I have become enthralled with their cute faces, curious eyes, and cheery dispositions. They remind me how much I miss my own grandchildren this far into Voyage Three.

I'm amazed by how happy these people are. With no modern conveniences, they are content with what little they have. I have not seen one manufactured toy here—not even a doll. The older children play simple games and sports; the younger children keep themselves occupied with a minimum of adult supervision—they chase each other, push stones around with sticks, or climb naked among the dugout canoes on the beach. Many of the babies are obviously in that frustrating age we Westerners call the "terrible twos." Yet I have never once seen or heard them whine, complain, or throw a tantrum.

As the sun beats down upon the clearing, we're treated to more dancing. The weather on this third festival day is the hottest so far, and even the bare-breasted and bare-chested old timers are dancing lethargically. I slump onto a tree stump, fanning my face with my giant sunhat. When the time comes for audience participation, very few yachties join in.

Suddenly the tempo picks up: A choir, composed of young men and women who have been trained at the local mission, takes to the dais. They sing Sunday School songs and spirituals that lift our spirits and bring us new energy. After this, closing ceremony speeches are warm and touching.

Günter has to stoop to enter this Uriparapara home.

Evelyn, a teacher, is the most educated resident of Uriparapara.

The choir returns for the closing songs, composed especially for this festival. Two are quite dramatic, with graceful hand and body movements, to represent Waterfall Bay, their very special place. But it is the closing song, "We Are Friends," that will remain etched in my memory forever. Tears run down my face as one performer after the other steps from the group on the dais to sing a poignant solo: "My name is Martha and I love you; my name is Robert and I love you; my name is Jimmie and I love you...." After the song, we are all hugging each other, and no one has a dry eye.

Security helps us drag *Petit Bliss* over the stones and launch her one last time. One of the young men says goodbye and places a gentle kiss on Günter's cheek. As we motor back to *Pacific Bliss* in our dinghy, tears begin to flow again when we look across the bay toward the buildings that were built especially for us.

Families are still waving to us from the shore.

Uriparapara, the Village in a Volcano
Lorup Bay
13°32.43´S, 16°72.04´E
September 20

Dawn breaks over the hills of Vanua Lava and *Pacific Bliss* bobs gently in the bay. I look back on the three days of the Waterfall Bay Cultural Festival with fond memories: the warmth and friendliness of the villagers as they shared their customs with us; the shy smiles of the *pikinini* (children) as they stole furtive glances at fair-skinned yachties; the tearful farewell. Waterfall Bay still tugs at my heartstrings as we haul anchor.

But we are destined to move on to new adventures. The idea of sailing into the breached crater of an extinct volcano has convinced the four of us to sail *Pacific Bliss* and *Yelo* to an even more remote part of the Banks Islands. Today we set sail northwest to Uriparapara, the northernmost island of Vanuatu. Yes! Lorup Bay has one of the most geographically spectacular entrances to be found anywhere in the world. The old volcano blew out a northeastern wall, allowing the bay to form, and we will have the adrenalin-packed experience of sailing directly into its center. The adventure continues.

After a fast four-hour sail during which experienced the full gamut of weather, we face fierce winds as we enter the bay. We can't afford to focus on the spectacular entrance—we have to concentrate on controlling the boat.

Now, listening to the gusts screaming like bullets as they race down the cliffs of the caldera, Günter has second thoughts about this adventure. Not only is he not looking forward to sailing out of this broached crater, but the thought of sailing back south makes him extremely anxious.

Pacific Bliss swings like a wild woman on her long tether (almost all of 180 feet of our chain are out). She's within 80 feet of the nearest reef. Ominous clouds hover over the rim of the cauldron. Angry strips of cloud race across the three-kilometer bay.

"We *must* calm down and just take this one day at a time." I try to soothe Günter as we sit in the cockpit after breakfast. "We have it so much better than these villagers. Even if we're stuck here, and cannot make it south in time for the Port2Port Rally to Australia, you know we'll survive."

"Yes, yes, you're just humoring me. I just want to get to shore today to meet some of these villagers. Then I'll get over this mood."

"The weather does appear to be clearing...Look! Children!"

Children are already heading from the beach to our boat, paddling three dugout canoes.

"Dangerous. They look too young to be out here alone."

"I see their mother in another dugout, near the shore; she's keeping an eye on them."

A small, tough girl paddles furiously, then grabs the swim ladder to stabilize her canoe. Two boys follow her. I greet all three, talk with them awhile, and then hand them lollipops. I select a set of hairclips for the girl. She paddles back to show her mother, who is still hanging back, holding a toddler. I motion for her to come to our boat. Meanwhile, the older boy hands me a paper fish made of construction paper. "Trade?" he asks. I hand him a box of matches. The mother arrives, and, clearly, she is proud of her children's ability to trade. Trading means survival. The family has five canoes, she tells me. They always come out to trade with yachties.

The weather improves, allowing us to launch our dinghy and go ashore. The village boys who meet us help pull up the dinghy. Günter strikes up a conversation about the kids' talent for trading. "We trade for matches, kerosene, batteries, lots of things…" says one of the boys. "But we already have everything we need here on this island."

"So what would you do if you ran out of matches?" Günter asks him.

A man joins the conversation and introduces himself as Hunan. "No one goes hungry in Uriparapara. If we don't have matches, we can still make fire."

"Show me," Günter says.

"Follow me."

We walk with him along the beach, then turn into the village. A naked toddler sits on a mat in front of his home. He tries to walk, and I have to smile. I encourage him, as his mother beams; she has a friendly, angelic face. We watch the smoke curl from a small log in a fire pit, and we sit around the pit with the family. Hunan demonstrates how to start a fire without matches. With his hands, he digs into the sand, shaping a small bowl. He places small twigs into it. He cuts two sticks, sharpens the end of one and makes a groove in the other, after which he spins one into the other faster… faster…faster. A small spark appears. He blows on it, and then continues the process; rub, blow, rub, blow…. Children gather to watch. About five minutes later, they clap and cheer as the spark bursts into flame.

We take our leave to walk through the village. People are not shy about approaching us and asking questions, mostly about the Waterfall Bay event. "We can do better *kastom* dances than them," one man says. There's no question that they are assessing the money such an event would bring them.

Later we join other yachties on a tour of the school. We meet Evelyn, the schoolmistress. She is 19 years old! Usually she shares first through eighth grades with another teacher, who is off now on maternity leave, but now she is teaching all the children. There are two one-room buildings, one for grades 1-4 and the other for grades 5-8. One assignment for 10 to 11 year olds was to write a story, complete with pictures and English text, about what they did during their one-week holiday. Everyone mentioned a yacht, and there are numerous drawings of yachts under sail on the schoolhouse walls. Other yachties have donated paper, pens, and pencils to the school. We do the same.

This is a village and boarding school. Children who live over the mountain ridge stay here during the week and walk for hours back to their homes on weekends. The school has its own garden, which Evelyn must manage as well. Her sister and family help her with that, she says, but the children must work in it after school. With so many students to care for during the day, Evelyn often goes to the school at night to prepare lessons and grade papers by the light of a kerosene lantern. There is no electricity on the island, so she often takes the lantern home with her to read in her bed. Most of the villagers do not have that luxury, she tells us; they can't accomplish much after sundown with their small fires.

I can see that Evelyn is a practical person. Her haircut is short and shaped like a bowl. "My brother cuts it for me," she says. "I ask my schoolchildren to cut their hair short, too…so that they are not distracted by picking off head lice while I'm teaching."

I'm impressed with this articulate young teacher and want to know more. I invite her to dinner on *Pacific Bliss*. Rolf and Daniela have already agreed to come.

As we walk along the beach toward our dinghy, we attract a crowd of followers, so there's no problem finding someone to answer our many questions.

A decrepit powerboat sits back from the shore in some weeds. "Are you using this?" Günter asks.

"German couple left it here. We *were* using it to go to Sola," one of our followers answers. (Sola is located in Vanua Lava, the Banks administrative capital.) "But now, no gas for motor."

"Too bad. We have lots of diesel, not much gas."

We pass by a solar-powered telephone installed by Telecom of Vanuatu for emergency use. It had been kaput for a year. A yachtie fixed it just a few days ago, we learn, by merely connecting a loose cable.

Yachties aren't just curious onlookers in these islands; they are necessary cogs in the commerce system of the Northern Banks. Other than the copra boat that comes once or twice a year to trade, yachties are the only vessels to visit these islands. Their help, and the supplies they bring—flour, sugar, rice, matches, batteries, candles, and clothes—make a huge difference in the lives of these islanders.

In a few hours, Evelyn, Daniela, and Rolf arrive at *Pacific Bliss* for sundowners and dinner. Quizzing Evelyn takes up most of the evening. This capable, intelligent young woman amazes us. She is miles apart from her counterparts in the South Pacific. She tells us she likes island life. But she admits that traveling has taken her only to Port Vila.

Evelyn is indispensable to the life of this village. Having completed all of her secondary education, she is the most educated person in Uriparapara. Consequently, she has assumed a three-fold responsibility: She is one of two teachers for 42 schoolchildren; she is Secretary to the Chief, taking notes at meetings and recording laws and resolutions in English; and she is the accountant for the village store. We wonder what life has in store for Evelyn.

Günter dares to ask the questions we're all thinking: "What about your future? Will you marry?"

"I will find my husband on another island," she says carefully.

Her enunciation and locution are perfect; she speaks as if she's giving a lecture. When we ask her what gifts she would like for herself and for the school, her answer shows no sign of begging or complaining. She is not only smart, but savvy. She is more than intelligent; she is wise, curious, determined, and ambitious as well.

I love this young woman! I want to take her home!

As I observe her watching me cook a simple pasta-cheese dish—her curious eyes wide open—I imagine what it would be like to take her to Texas, to a Thanksgiving dinner with my extended family. I imagine her eyes taking in *that* scene, a huge table filled with turkey, dressing, potatoes, and gravy; cranberries; sweet potato and string bean casseroles; and pies galore. I can see her staring at my sister's modern kitchen, the opulence, the dazzling—and embarrassing—mountain of children's' toys. But then I have second thoughts: Her people need her here, and I should not tempt her.

I soon discover that I'm not the first yachtie who would like Evelyn to visit. During dinner, she tells us she was offered a ticket to Melbourne by an Australian yachtie couple. She was to contact them by phone from Port Vila, where she was pursuing a college degree. But tragedy struck her family. Her father collapsed and died after working in his garden. As the oldest child, she was summoned home.

Evelyn has not been allowed complete her college education. "You're needed here at *this* school," she was informed. In return for teaching on this tiny island of Uriparapara, the government of Vanuatu will pay for her education, when she decides to continue it. "Perhaps," she says, "I'll do that when the other teacher returns as headmistress."

After dinner, Günter and I give Evelyn a solar-powered calculator, an alarm clock, a flashlight—and a *huge* hug.

I'll never forget this amazing girl.

Western Style Laplap for Tea
Waterfall Bay
September 22

At 0800 Sunday, *Pacific Bliss* leaves for Waterfall Bay, and *Yelo* takes advantage of a HIGH to blow her to the Solomons. Rolf and Daniela will have a fast sail, but we find ourselves struggling. We motorsail hard on the wind, which increases to F6 and F7, 18-21 knots, with the DRIVE /STOP readout occurring again and again. For four hours, we beat against boisterous, confused seas. It is an uncomfortable passage of 29 miles. Finally, we're relieved to be back in Waterfall Bay, where the water is calm and the sea behind the reef glistens in the sun. Even though we miss *Yelo*, now out of VHF range, we're not alone. We talk with *Freya*, who left Uriparapara directly for Vureas but had to turn back to this bay, and *Aldebaran,* who arrives here a few hours after we do.

We don't plan to launch our dinghy here because we intend to leave early to sail south. However, within an hour after we anchor, Chief Jimmy stops by to invite us to his home for dinner. Günter explains why we cannot take him up on his offer. "Please understand," says, "we must sail when we have the right wind and it is not too strong." So we invite the chief and his wife, Lillian, to tea.

I prepare a double-sized loaf of cinnamon-raisin bread in the breadmaker. It bakes while I join Günter for a short siesta. I am awakened by a tap on the hull.

"They're here already." I rouse Günter.

Lillian climbs up the swim ladder steps from their dugout canoe, carefully balancing a small plastic bowl filled with four cherry tomatoes and four eggs. I'm touched. I know how precious this food is to her!

It is far too hot for tea, and the timer on the bread machine shows 20 minutes left, so I serve cold juice out of cartons, and we talk in the cockpit. The breadmaker beeps. Both visitors rush to see the machine. They had never seen a breadmaker before! The chief makes that loud, whistling sound, common to all Ni-Vanuatu when they're impressed. We allow the bread to cool while we attempt to continue the conversation, but Jimmy is distracted. He just stares at the loaf on the breadboard. I slice half of the loaf and place one slice on each of the small plates, along with knives to spread butter and jam. The jar of raspberry jam is labeled "Made in Port Vila, Vanuatu," but our guests have never tasted anything like it. It goes fast. I ask Jimmy whether he wants another slice. Of course, he does!

"Go ahead, slice it yourself," says Günter.

Jimmy cuts a thick slice. No tea-sized portions for him! As he slathers on the butter and jam, he says, "Very good. American *laplap*." He devours that slice and cuts even more. Before long, the entire loaf is gone!

Our pleasant visit ends, but before they return to their village, I give the couple a large vacuum-packed container of yeast. It should help them through the entire year.

Günter asks Jimmy to send Nika to us. Nika is one of the security team that had befriended us during the festival. He had helped us land *Petit Bliss* on the rocky shore and carry it up to the beach numerous times. Günter had taken a special liking to his gentle nature and shy, engaging smile.

Nika comes to the boat as the sun is setting. He has been fishing all day. Günter astounds him by giving him a small pair of binoculars. "To use for hunting in the bush," he explains. "Or to be the first person to sight a new yacht coming in." Nika is so amazed and grateful he hardly knows what to say.

The following day, as we prepare to pull anchor, Nika paddles to *Pacific Bliss* and calls to get our attention. He holds out a water-filled plastic bag with fresh prawns—still alive and squirming—and a brand new "prawn-catcher," an intricately woven basket with two sections. Lured by bait, prawns enter the first compartment and then become trapped in the second.

I already know that this special basket will never experience seawater—it will hang on our wall at home as a daily reminder of Nika and the other wonderful people of Waterfall Bay!

The Propeller Thank You Party
Vureas Bay, Vanua Lava
13°55.54′S, 167°26.77′E
September 23

We left Waterfall Bay and its fond memories behind at 0630. Three hours later, we are anchoring in Vureas Bay. As soon as we are settled, rowers come to welcome us. We recognize many of them from the

Vanuatu is known for its deep, freshwater blue holes. We dinghy down Forest River to find this one.

festival. Most of them had walked the rocky and hilly trail to Waterfall Bay, but some had gone by boat and had to leave early because of a faulty prop. Günter had looked at it then and tried to fix it, as had other cruisers. Now Günter asks about the prop.

"Still broken. We cannot trust it to go out to fish," one man says.

We're touched. A setback like this can be disastrous.

Günter offers them *Petit Bliss*'s spare prop. When he takes it from the storage locker, the villagers are surprised to see it is shiny, black, and brand new.

"Such a good prop, just for us?"

"We will not need it. Soon we are going to Australia," Günter tells them.

"Then we will make a party for you today," insists Graham, the "water taxi" driver.

The party is given at the home of Graham's uncle. When we arrive, we're amazed at the setting. A fish line has been strung between two trees and a post. Draped over that line is an abundance of tropical flowers and long plant leaves. Inside this boundary lies a western-style rooster-print tablecloth covered with many mats and numerous containers, all bursting with food: manioc with nuts, yam *laplap*-and-coconut, baked papaya with coconut, chicken with vegetable greens, and prawns.

"Sit," Graham's aunt commands us. She is a large, plump woman, wearing a flowered *muumuu* housedress. We settle onto the grass. About a dozen villagers gather around, but they all remain standing. I motion for them to sit on the grass, too. They shake their heads no. None of the locals—including the children—will take their own food until we begin to eat.

I say grace and then they pass the food to Günter and me. We receive glass dishes and spoons. "Sorry, we don't have forks," Graham apologizes. The village nurse, another guest, is offered food next, followed by a couple of men. Our host and hostess and the ladies who prepared the food all stand to the side, smiling. They say they will eat later. After we've eaten, Graham and the two men tell us how much they appreciate the new prop. The nurse makes a speech telling us how much she and the village appreciated the bag of prescription glasses and sunglasses we had given them during the festival. Then she hands us a huge hand-woven basket filled with six eggs, one coconut, two pumpkins, and a huge green cabbage. "For your return voyage. Thank you from all of us."

I'll never forget this precious moment!

Tomorrow we'll face the elements and whatever else is in store for us. But tonight I glow in the happiness and joy that flows from this wonderful group of islanders.

We talk with them about our goal of sailing around the world. Graham asks, "Why would you want to do this?"

"To see how different people live around the world, and to experience happy moments like this moment you are giving us today," Günter says.

They smile warmly and nod in understanding.

Forest River Blue Hole and Hotel California
Oyster Island's Outer Anchorage
15°22.7′S, 167°11.7′E
Peterson Bay Inner Anchorage
15°22.5′S, 167°11.4′
October 2

We drop anchor in the outer anchorage. I think it's pretty here, but Günter hates it. He had been forced to snorkel a couple of times, to check the anchor, and, because we had flaky winds for sailing and two showers along the way, he had already arrived in a grumpy mood. "I want to cruise one season in Australia, fix all the things on this bucket that don't work, then sell *Pacific Bliss* there." This time, he seems serious, determined to carry out his plan.

Günter thinks the Inner Anchorage will be better, so first thing in the morning, even before the Namba Net comes on, we launch *Petit Bliss* and motor through the pass to check its depth. A few hours after low tide, we find spots of less than 3.5 feet. The turns are sharp and tricky. Günter stares at me and I stare back at him. Slowly, in unison, we shake our heads. Uh, uh. Neither of us is willing to risk grounding or damaging *Pacific Bliss* at the last anchorage we will see before leaving for Luganville and Oz.

We return and talk with Rolf.

"Chicken," Rolf taunts us. "I'd do it."

But we don't change our minds. We already know that *Rascal Too* admits to running aground in the Southern Pass. That pass won't work for us; its width is 24 feet. That's our boat width!

On Friday morning we dinghy across South Peterson Bay and enter Forest River. We motor slowly for a few miles until we are in the river's heart, called the Blue Hole. The water is crystal clear with a white, sandy bottom. Emerald leaves reflect on its cobalt surface like dots on a Seurat painting. Stunning! I peer into the jungle to find even more shades of green—from apple, mint, and lime to olive and pistachio. I watch a parrot with electric green wings dart across the river in front of us. We cut the motor. The warbling of birds fills the air.

We are all alone back here. We drop the dinghy anchor and jump in. The water is so dark it's almost navy, and it's deep, fresh and icy cold—a fantastic reprieve from the inescapable sultry climate. As we dinghy back, the evaporating water cools our skin, and we're refreshed all over again.

This trip to the Blue Hole puts us into better spirits. We've regained our confidence, so much so that we decide to take *Pacific Bliss* through that pass after all! I stand at the bow and direct Günter, who is at the helm. We make very slow progress, holding our breath at each sharp turn. Surprisingly, the trip goes exactly as planned and in time we're anchored safely in the delightful calm of Inner Bay.

It's a perfect morning. I sit in the cockpit of *Pacific Bliss*, listening to birds calling from a thick stand of trees that line the shore. I can make out the mainland of Sanko Island through a narrow strip of coconut palms. The sun rises higher, causing the bay to sparkle like crystal. I'm happy we came here to this peaceful retreat.

I close my book to see what Günter is up to. He sits at the computer, toggling back and forth between our Max Sea TRACK, tide tables, and the Tusker Vanuatu CD, which delineates the waypoints out of this inner anchorage.

I look over his shoulder. "The passage through the reefs reminds me of the 'Hotel California' song by the Eagles. You can get in, but you can't get out."

"It's not that bad," Günter reassures me. "We'll make it through. The question is *when*."

"You mean we won't be stuck here forever, like in those commercials for the Black Flag roach motel?"

"Be serious. We managed to get in; we'll get back out. The problem is that we wanted to leave for Luganville on Monday morning. Look at the colors in this tide table: gold for daylight, black for night. From 0600 till 1800, it appears that there will be a dual low tide all day; the high tides are in black, meaning they'll be when it's dark."

Nothing is ever easy!

"I'm afraid to go through that pass in the middle of the night," I confess. "But I noticed this morning that some yachts that had been anchored *inside* our paradise are now anchored *outside*, over by the reefs." Günter explains, "They wanted to be able to leave in the morning! That's an option we have. We can wait till morning's light, leave at 0600 at the end of the high tide. There will be a faint light, but no sun at our backs to help us actually *see* the reefs. We could follow our Max Sea TRACK back out, but that would be difficult since then I'd need to steer by the autopilot instead of hand steering, and Ray doesn't respond so well when we're creeping along. It's a problem, but I'm not concerned: we'll get out."

So we enjoy a relaxing Sunday, listening to music, reading, and writing. But nothing this good can last

MESSING WITH BOATS

Corroded Rollers
by Günter

Rolf and I spent most of our first Sunday in Port Vila fixing Ray, our autopilot. We found that when my new HP laptop is plugged in (not even turned on), the displays to the Raytheon multis from the GPS *do* work. Go figure.

Then we began to troubleshoot the problem with the rollers. (The topping lift needs electric winch force to pull it up; the main halyard also sticks). It turns out that all the gook from cleaning the cockpit ends up in the roller compartment where all the reefing lines go through. When we removed the covering, we found that the aluminum rollers were badly corroded with pockets of salt. Rolf also discovered that the door and door jam to the port aft cabin came ajar during the passage. No wonder it had made so much noise during the passage with only a 15-knot wind, albeit hard on the wind.

On Monday, Lois and I contacted the shipyard with a plan to bring *Pacific Bliss* by after lunch. We had a brief siesta in the port hull, the side with a refreshing breeze, then motored to the boat yard called simply 17°44 South. After picking up one of their moorings, we dinghied in to talk to Jean-Pierre. He came back with us to look at our roller situation and could begin work at 0900, right at the mooring. Yay!

Two days later, we were still in the shipyard anchorage, waiting for Jean-Pierre to complete fixing our roller part. (He usually arrives at 1000. I guess Vanuatu time is even slower than Fiji time.) He had to take a blowtorch to it to get rid of the built-up corrosion on the aluminum. I was afraid of him breaking the part, and then what would we do? What a can of worms I've opened up! But it is dangerous to go off sailing with that axle ready to freeze (jam) up at any time.

The next day, the workers at the yard took a hacksaw to our axle part, the only way they could get out the crud. Scary. But we knew they could weld it right there if necessary, so we crossed our fingers.

By Friday, though, one week after we arrived in Vanuatu, John-Pierre came to take the braces off the wood in the forward port cabin that need repairing, and to get paid for his work, including the roller re-do: $350 US, 35,000 Vatus. We returned to the Port Vila anchorage and picked up our old mooring #25, successful on the first try.

A young boy in Uriparapara plays his ukelele for us.

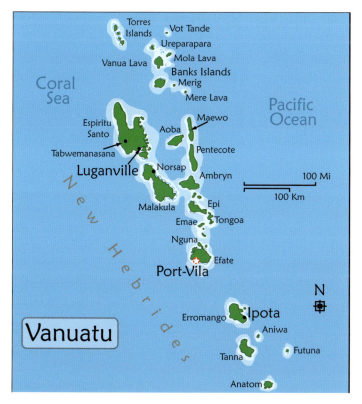

forever.

I never cease to be amazed at how fast things change out here.

While I'm engrossed in writing about the Blue Hole, Günter goes to the starboard engine room to change the gear oil. As he works, he notices a nut that has worked its way loose from a bolt on the alternator that had been added to *Pacific Bliss* in San Diego. His face pales as he tells me what could have happened if it had shaken loose the rest of the way during a passage: The entire alternator could have fallen off, doing who-knows-what to the engine.

What other dangers are hidden somewhere on Pacific Bliss, waiting to surface at the worst possible moment?

At 1400, *Freya* calls. "I just looked at my tide tables," Jouke tells us. "We're already into a falling tide. We need to leave for the outer anchorage right now."

They had made this excursion a few times before, so, to follow them out would be the safest move we could make. I haul anchor just as they motor past. We catch up with them, then snake through the pass, the sun behind us, still high, the reefs perfectly visible. Piece of cake! We anchor on the inside where it's shallower, close to *Quo Vadis* and *Freya,* and we position *Pacific Bliss* where we hoped we'd be, exactly in the center of the three surrounding reefs.

Then the anchor drops too quickly, jumping the gypsy (roller) and feeding the rope almost to the bitter end. We struggle to bring up the anchor with the windlass control, but of course the rope at the end catches and jams. This time, I feel like swearing right along with Günter! Slowly, we pull up the rope, and we manage to free it from the roller—just as a pissing rain begins.

Janneka, on nearby *Freya*, notices something wrong and sends Jouke over with their dinghy. With the two strong men, Günter and Jouke, at the bow, I gun the engines to create slack when needed, while they pull up the slack and cleat the rope off, foot by foot.

Sweaty and discouraged, Günter snarls, "I'm replacing this entire *G-r-r-#*+@^##!!!!* system!"

Why did this happen? We look up the specs for the anchor rope. They say our rope should be 16 mm, but the factory has given us 20 mm. Our stripper fits the profile for the chain instead of the rope—no wonder it sticks! Now we are both swearing at Catana engineering. They had specified the system incorrectly. In Oz, we will simply replace the entire anchor rope.

To thank them, we invite Jouke and Janneke for sundowners. Günter goes on and on complaining about what is wrong with *Pacific Bliss*. Could the port rudder be going out of alignment because the starboard rudder has too much pressure on it? The French often used nylon as a material for bearings versus the preferred Teflon, which doesn't swell up in the tropics. Finally, the discussion is resolved when the guys settle on a plan to "drop the rudder" at Aore Resort. (Greg had already offered to help.)

How good it is to have such experienced and helpful cruisers as new friends!

An Uneasy Passage Back to Luganville

The next morning, we haul anchor right after listening to the Namba Net. It's a difficult process without the stripper. While I take the helm, Günter has to manually pull the chain over the roller at the chain locker so that it won't bind up. I set the course on autopilot, and we turn south toward Luganville. The first part of the passage is inside the reef system. The wind is mostly on the nose, but the waves are reasonable. Even so, Ray is *not* holding the course. *Pacific Bliss* weaves like a drunken sailor, back and forth. My mouth goes dry just thinking about sailing all the way to Australia like this.

But that's not the end of trouble. At the Aore Resort, there is no buoy for us, even though we had one reserved. We have to anchor across the Segundo Channel in an anchorage called Beach Front, only a mile away.

A Grand Arrival
Aore Resort, on a Green Mooring
October 8

Thank goodness, our reserved mooring is ready. I call the resort on the VHF, as instructed.

"Do you want us to pick up that green ball we're heading for?" I ask.

"Yes," Jody, the manager, says. "and, everyone is watching you."

I can hear laughter coming from the deck of the Aore Resort where an entire group of cruisers has gathered. From the sound of it, they are either into an extended lunch or an early happy hour.

There's nothing like knowing you're the center of cruiser attention to knot your stomach and prepare you for a mooring performance. I know I must not fail!

So, very carefully, I follow Günter's hand commands. When we come close to the green ball, I ease both engines into reverse; *Pacific Bliss* stops smartly, and Günter reaches down, picks up the ball and cleats it off.

A rousing cheer comes from the deck.

"That was a masterful touch at the engine," Günter compliments me.

I feel like I'm floating on a cloud.

We dinghy to the dock and join a group of a dozen or so cruisers, all sitting around in a semicircle facing the moored yachts. They're celebrating Glenda and Dan's 3rd anniversary (*Dawn's Light*) and Pat and Greg's 36th anniversary (*Rascal Too*). The big blowout progresses from beers to tall, green midori lemonades with lots of ice to wine and pizzas and, finally, to delicious crème brûlée! By the time we leave, about 9 o'clock, 20 cruisers are still holding down the fort, and I feel like I never want to eat or drink again!

The Rudder Party
Aore Resort Island
October 9

It's a new day; we've recovered. Günter finishes his coffee and goes through his To Do list. Methodically, he sets out all the tools and manuals he will need. Jouke and Greg arrive on board to help. Greg brings all his own tools. He even brings his own hookah diving system. First, the guys lower the rudder about 20 cm, then grease it with lanolin, which can be applied under water. Then Jouke checks out the engines and adjusts the fan belts. All three men seem to be enjoying the challenge. Believe it or not, there is no swearing, which surprises me. Tina and I assumed that went along with every "fix-the-boat" project!

Meanwhile, I decide to make use of the huge pumpkin we'd been given in the Banks. This will be my very first pressure-cooker pumpkin soup. I modify *Amanda's Galley Companion* pumpkin-orange soup recipe by throwing in a few carrots. As the guys work, I cut and cube and pare.

By the time the wives, Pat and Janneke, arrive a few hours later, the pumpkins and carrots have turned to mush, and I'm busy mashing them with a fork. I invite them into the salon, and we chat while I continue working. The women page through my cookbooks and discuss recipes. Then we discuss the Port2Port Rally and go over the entry forms. Janneke says *Freya* plans to sail straight to Oz as soon as the weather permits. But Pat tells us that *Rascal Too* is interested in staying behind with us and joining the Rally.

The talk turns to our husbands. I share with them my surprise that fixing boats can actually be a pleasant undertaking. However, in fact, with the six of us all working together, this is turning into a veritable rudder party!

"They *do* enjoy this. It puts them in their element," Pat says. "Greg would always troubleshoot mechanical problems in his engineering business, although he usually told his workers what to fix. He loves to get his hands dirty."

"And Jouke ran a construction equipment business. Knowing how to fix machines was critical," Janneke explains.

"Günter likes to invent and solve problems," I contribute, "but he prefers to manage others who get their hands dirty doing scientific experiments."

We are obviously proud of our men, as they work for hours. It's still morning, when the guys—full of dirt and grease—wash up to take a beer break. I'd kept a few bottles on ice for them, which I serve, while we women share ginger beers.

By lunchtime, the rudder is fixed, the starboard wheel turns like a dream, the engines purr, and the men declare *Pacific Bliss* fit for the final passage of the season. Then the six of us sit around the salon table and talk. Janneke raves about all the space on a Cat: "A toaster that just sits there all the time!" she exclaims. "And a separate shelf for your microwave!"

I smile to myself. *I wouldn't trade a catamaran for any other boat.*

Pat brought a loaf of French bread; she uses it now to make a platter of salami, cheese, onions, and tomatoes. I serve my pumpkin soup, with thick slices of toast. It brings rave reviews. Everyone asks for seconds, and before long, the entire batch is gone.

Günter compliments me on the lunch: "I'm so glad you decided to make that soup. It turned out to be a real gourmet treat. Don't forget that recipe!"

But for me, the best part of the rudder party occurs when *Rascal Too*, who has made the passage twice before, decides to buddy boat with *Pacific Bliss*.

Günter is just as elated as I am. "Now we can have you within *pan pan* distance," he tells Greg.

Yay, Rascal Too!

Pacific Bliss Goes Walkabout.
Aore Resort
October 10

The sun is high and hot. By mid-afternoon, Günter and I escape below. We lie naked on our bunks as the whirring of the fan numbs us to sleep. "Lois!" says Günter sharply, breaking into my tropical dream. I sit

up. He had been asleep next to me, but now he is gone. Somehow he sensed trouble and went up to the salon.

I throw a sundress over my head and follow his voice. Then I hear Jody's voice on the on the VHF, calling from Aore Resort. *"Pacific Bliss, Pacific Bliss."*

We can't make out the words that follow—she has her "squelch" turned up too high. But it takes only one look outside to see what's wrong. *Pacific Bliss* is one boat length away from crashing into *Delight.* That yacht's captain doesn't appreciate the visit. He is already in his dinghy, preparing to knock on our hull.

It appears that while we were enjoying our afternoon siesta, *Pacific Bliss* became lonesome and decided to go walkabout, visiting other boats in the mooring area! She drags the green mooring, which suddenly has an amazing ability to stretch. Did she get tired of being tethered and try to break away? There is no wind, a small current—as usual here—and a high tide. Oops! Did I just say *high tide*? We had pulled the bridle tight to give the mooring line a short leash at *low tide* last night. Perhaps the chain that attaches the mooring to the block on the sea bottom couldn't take the strain.

Fortunately, another yacht has left their mooring. This mooring is heavier, and it's farther out, in 80 feet of water. We grab it, and soon we are secure again.

On the resort deck, yachties are obviously watching and laughing. Günter knows that he'll need to think up an explanation before we join them at cocktail time. When we come ashore later, Günter lets *Pacific Bliss* off the hook and defends her honor: "She was just getting ready for the *Port2Port Rally*," he explains. "Because she has two hulls, she fears that she will be classified as a 'double yacht' and be forced to drag a drogue anchor as a handicap. She was just practicing!"

Preparations, Parties, and Another Setback
October 12

The week leading up to the Rally will go fast, we hope. Our lists contain new projects every day. Günter's major project is refueling. Each morning, he takes jerry cans we borrowed from Greg on the 0700 ferry to the gas station across the channel. The ferry brings him back at 0800. He can only make one trip per day because the resort doesn't want jerry cans on the later ferries. So, this process will continue through Tuesday. Then on Wednesday, Günter will take the ferry again to refill the propane tanks, which I need for cooking.

While he's doing this, *my* major project is navigation. I file away our Vanuatu charts and take out those needed for the passage. I copy a few of Greg's more detailed paper charts. Then I enter waypoints into the log book for Chesterfield and other reefs, and enter the route into my Max Sea computer program. That done, I go back

A Uripara man demonstrates how to make a fire without matches.

to the resort to send e-mail messages to a long list of friends and relatives.

All the while, tropical heat weighs us down like a suffocating blanket. The sky is a dull gray. On *Pacific Bliss,* the barometer reads 1000mb. The weather is deadly still. Vanuatu is situated in a low, between two highs. We have enough diesel fuel to motor the whole way, but some yachts in the Rally can only motor for a 300-mile range. So everyone sits and waits for the weather to change and the wind to come up.

Meanwhile, we are invited to parties, parties, and more parties…life isn't so tough here after all. Many of the partiers are Aussies. We wonder whether these parties are intended to harden our livers for even heavier partying in Oz. But then how will we withstand the shock to our systems when we abstain during the passage?

Vanuatu seems to hold us in her clutches; first with no wind at all, then with howling winds, then with furious torrents of rain. But that's not all—Günter decides to test the engines, and we are stunned when the starboard engine won't even turn over. Lack of any response when he presses the switch again sends him into a deep despondency. What will we do if *Pacific Bliss* can't be fixed in time to leave with the rally? What if she can't be repaired before the cyclone season sets in?

"I don't know any place in Espiritu Santo where we could leave her safely. She'll be sitting here for months, crippled, and who knows what will happen to her before we can get back here to reclaim her?" Günter worries. "I have to call Greg to take a look at the engine." Günter dinghies anxiously to *Rascal Too.*

Hours later, two dirty men emerge from *Pacific Bliss's* starboard engine room. Their faces are wreathed in smiles. That's all I need to know.

Rain and Richard
October 19

A week has passed; we're still at Aore Resort. It's pouring so hard and continuously, we might just as well be moored under a waterfall. It's the heaviest rain we've seen in Vanuatu.

Dampness pervades *Pacific Bliss,* but it fails to dampen our souls. The engine has been repaired. God has answered our prayers, and we are all set to head safely for Oz! One of these days, hopefully Tuesday, the skies will lighten, the sun will shine, *Pacific Bliss* will slip her mooring, and we'll be off, free of the spirit of Santo at last.

Despite the downpour, Richard arrives from Yucca Valley, California, to crew with us again. He is looking fresh and rested.

"Looks like you brought us the same weather we had when you left us in Tonga," Günter quips.

Richard grins. "Yep, I never change."

I enjoy having another person on board, especially Richard. After breakfast, he helps me chop vegetables for soup while we listen to the Namba Net. Yachts that had already left experienced two days of ideal conditions, covering close to 200 miles each day under fast SE winds of 20-25 knots; but now they are getting hammered. One of them, 40 miles north of Chesterfield Reef, is being hit with torrential rains and 50-60 knot winds. *Freya* is anchored on the reef, waiting it out, experiencing 25-30 knots. The gamble didn't pay off for those who had taken advantage of the HIGH instead of waiting for the rally! I turn off the Namba, pleased that we made the right decision; the GRIB files we received today show only ten knots for our kick-off on Tuesday.

Anticipation builds.

Soon, very soon, we will be off to the World of Oz!

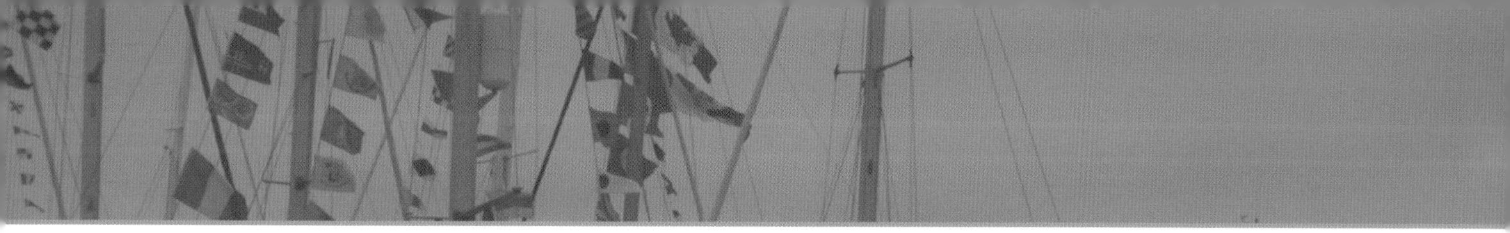

CHAPTER 12
AUSTRALIA: THE LAND OF OZ

The Last Passage
October 22, 2003

The moon rises surely and slowly, a glowing apostrophe in the diamond-studded sky. That other glow, far ahead of the starboard bow, is *Rascal Too*, our buddy boat in this Port2Port Rally. As I leave the helm seat to make coffee, the moon fills in like a luscious white melon. I return with my coffee to see it shine directly into the cockpit; it is my friend for this first night watch of our passage. How lucky I am to have the 0300-0600 for the entire week! If every night watch is like this one, I will arrive blessed and renewed.

Now as the moon rises smack in the center of a triangle formed by three surrounding stars, I feel that the show is just for me, even though billions have seen it before. It continues to rise, snubbing out all but the most stalwart and determined stars.

I check the instruments and update the logbook. We have sailed 18,000 nautical miles since we departed from Canet, France. November 7 will be the third anniversary of that departure. Now, here we are, over halfway around the world, about to enter the Land of Oz.

In Our Own Cocoon
At sea, 20°42′S, 155°26′E
October 26,

Oh the stars out here! And the galaxies! At 0300, when I take over the watch from Richard, he points out two puffs—similar to the Milky Way—called the Large Magellanic Cloud and the Small Magellanic Cloud. A mere 160,000 light years away, they are the closest galaxies to Earth. Between these, the three stars of Hydra glimmer. Awesome! During my watch, I gaze at these new-found friends while I continue to delight in the constellations I've befriended before: the Southern Cross, resting on her side in the wee hours of the morning, and Orion, still high above the mast, his belt sparkling like diamonds.

Pacific Bliss motorsails serenely at 5.5 knots in light winds of 7-8 knots from the northeast. slip-sliding away under an umbrella of stars. We could go faster, but we are deliberately holding back because we want to meet *Rascal Too,* our buddy boat on this passage, and then arrive at Hershey Bay together. This is a rally, not a race, so the pace has been nice and easy. At 0430, we reach the Kenn Reef turn, and I change the TRACK function to our waypoint to off Wreck Reef.

Gradually a faint orange glow rims the eastern horizon and the galaxies slowly disappear, followed by Hydra, Vela, and Pyxis. The horizon turns a deep red-orange, then lightens to a subtle pink-orange behind wispy mare's tails.

I refill my coffee, prepare toast with jam, and return to the cockpit for a ringside seat during the second act of the Nature Light Show, which is always dramatic but never the same. The sun, a bright orange medallion, pops out of the sea. An intricate, filigreed gold edging surrounds the nearby clouds. Golden rays fan out to touch the farthest clouds, stretching, beaming. Wisps of cirrus all around the horizon are bathed in the warming light and begin to shimmer and glow. The sun's rise this morning is not subtle. It is shattering—a Creation Sunrise, bursting with all the life and energy of God.

Lois and Pat model their entries for Melbourne Cup Hat Day, only one of the many contests held during Bundaberg's Welcome Week.

Günter hums as *Pacific Bliss* continues to swish through the gentle seas. We three are in our own cocoon, a private world within an outer world of sky, clouds, and deep blue sea. During sundowner time (this time, with sundowners, a Captain's Special because the sea is so benign), Günter and I dance on the deck to songs from the play, *Forever Plaid*. Richard joins us when we sing "Waltzing Matilda." We dedicate this song to Phyllis, who will meet us soon in Australia.

As I take my first evening watch, *Pacific Bliss* continues to glide in her own little world—a world of her own making on this blessed passage to Oz.

I wonder if *Pacific Bliss* is trying to make it up to us for all those problems we had with her rudder; perhaps she overheard what Günter said about selling her in Australia. "I can tell you now, *Pacific Bliss*, he didn't really mean it. He is one happy man on this passage. He'll fix you up like new—no, better than new—and we'll continue on around the world. After all, you're part of our family!

"You'll like Australia, *Pacific Bliss,* I know you will. And Günter says next year, he'll never have you three days away from a good ship's mechanic.

"You'll always be his mistress, *Miss Bliss*. He can't get along without you. You'll see!"

Pacific Bliss Arrives in the Land of Oz.
24°45′S, 152°23′E

The next day, when I come on watch at 0300, I can see the lights of Bundaberg glimmering on the horizon, as if the town is expecting us.

Australia, the long-awaited Land of Oz!

I make a pot of coffee. Then I sit at the helm taking it all in. A shooting star streaks across the sky. Surprisingly, a white tern appears from nowhere; it circles the bows and then lands on a pulpit seat for the ride on in. I view both events as signs of good luck. Ahead—to our starboard—the running lights of *Rascal Too* bounce through the waves. Our new Aussie friends, Greg and Pat, are magnanimously leading us into their country.

Never before have I felt such a sense of elation and destiny upon arriving at a foreign port.

Our engines drone along at 6 knots. I enjoy a second cup of coffee and feel even higher. I wake the guys when we reach our waypoint for the Burnett River. Günter takes the helm. Richard is the lookout, and I take control of the nav station. We follow the buoys in; navigation is easy, not the way it was in the islands. Here, not one of the buoys is missing!

We change our clocks to Australian time; I log that we've dropped the hook at exactly 0500, at dawn's light.

It has been a passage of a little less than seven days—at a nice-and-easy average speed of 6.24 knots.

As I said so often, passages are not my favorite part of cruising, but I can't complain about *this* one. It's been perfect!

Blatant Bribery
24°45′S, 152°23′E
Bundaberg, Australia
November 2

What a study in contrasts! In one day, we cruisers have been transported from the serenity of life at sea to the frantic hustle-bustle of The Big Tent. A huge white structure has been erected on the grounds of the Bundaberg Port Marina to house the Port2Port Rally events. An aging rock 'n roll group shouts lyrics of the 1950s; dancers swirl about between loud announcements of winning raffle tickets and prizes. And buffet tables are crowded with ever-hungry yachties.

At first, I am flying high. But later, din and activities become just too much, and I yearn to escape to the peace of my cabin, with ear plugs to silence the raucous party. One day after our arrival, we greet Phyllis at the airport. She arrives excited and ready to party, and she infuses the three of us with renewed energy. We find our second wind and keep going.

Sandwiched between events are many contests. Contests of every kind imaginable. Eagerly, I enter the Passage Story, the Brain Strain, and the Lethal Bundy Rum Drink competitions. Entering the Best ETA (estimated time of arrival) competition is automatic, because all yachts had to provide this information to the Port Authority. Of course, *Pacific Bliss* has already won the "fastest multihull" contest; now she has a plaque to show for it. But, to be honest, that's not really much to brag about—we were the *only* multihull in the rally!

After a few days of this wildness, some of the more sedate cruisers say they've had enough Aussie partying. "No more tent," they say. But the majority of us Port2Port participants have more stamina, and we are determined to stick it out through the entire week-long program.

In the Best Dressed Yacht competition, the four of us go all out to dress *Pacific Bliss* like the *grand dame* she is. It's the most team fun I've had since decorating the St. Croix Falls High School homecoming float in 1959. But back then, I didn't realize that one could bribe a judge blatantly and get away with it.

Our blatant bribery begins innocently enough: Since combining new signal flags with our courtesy flags from countries we have visited would be a good start at dressing our yacht, I visit the Ships' Chandlery and consult with Merris, the manager, about purchasing a set. Not only is she out of stock, but the only marina in Australia that has them is in Melbourne, far across this vast country on its southwest coast.

"If I place the order today, what are the odds of the flags arriving here in time for the Best Dressed Yacht

The town of Bundaberg welcomes the yachties during week-long festivities following the Port 2 Port Rally.

Blatant Bribery
in the Land of Oz

1. Bribing the judge; 2. Richard, Phyllis, Lois, and Günter; 3. *Pacific Bliss* wins first place for Best Dressed Yacht; 4. Richard, Günter, and Greg; 5. Jouke and Janneka of *Freya*.

contest?" I ask.

"I'd give it less than 10 percent," she frowns.

I turn to leave.

"Perhaps you could borrow a set from one of the yachties at the docks here," Merris calls after me as I open the door. "Or I could loan you these display flags from our store."

How nice! What store in the U.S. would do this for a yachtie?

I walk back to the counter, smiling.

"Also, I'm a judge, and I can be bribed." Her face lights up and her eyes twinkle.

"This is becoming very interesting," I joke. "What kind of wine do you like?"

"White and very cold."

"Chocolates?"

"Swiss."

As I saunter on my way back to Gray Dock and our #14 slip, I have an idea….

The next morning, we rush from store to store in Bundaberg to get the supplies we will need: a box of chocolates; a bottle of white wine; 25 large balloons—red, white, and blue for the U.S.A., and green and gold for Australia—and one giant heart-shaped balloon for good measure. Also, we buy file folders in red, white, blue, green, and gold; and a zillion streamers in the same colors. The crowning purchase, however, is an Aussie barbeque apron flaunting the figure of a beautiful woman with very huge breasts. It's rather gross, but right in line with the Aussie humor we've encountered so far.

Phyllis and I call the apron "Miss Bundy Boobs." We decide to make her the centerpiece of our décor, along the port side of *Pacific Bliss*—exactly where the judges tend to walk the dock.

The yacht *Freya* kindly lends us their signal flags, and Richard hangs them high along with all the country flags.

Contest Day arrives. I letter the red, white, and blue file folders to say: WE LOVE YOU and the green and gold to say: AUSSIES, and I hang them over the lifelines; Phyllis and Richard inflate the 25 balloons. Günter unpacks his treasured California Republic bear flag and fastens it opposite Old Glory. We festoon the stern with red, white, and blue streamers and balloons, and we blare an assortment of Aussie rugby tunes from our cockpit speakers.

But our scheme doesn't stop with this U.S.A./Aussie love fest. We are now ready to set up the cockpit table, where the most blatant acts of bribery will be performed.

Judging is scheduled for 2:00 p.m. By 1:30, *Pacific Bliss* is ready to be viewed. Phyllis and I walk the docks to check out our competition.

"I think we have a chance, I guess."

"No contest," Phyllis crows. "We'll take it."

Right before 2 p.m., we see the judge walking a dock, the one farthest from our slip at Gray Dock. We rush back to *Pacific Bliss*.

Then, we wait. And wait. And wait. A stiff breeze comes up. Miss Bundy Boobs' streamers are being pulled free from her nipples, where they had been pinned.

Finally, close to 4:00 p.m., Richard scouts the situation. He hurries back, panting. "They forgot we're here, on Gray Dock," he gasps.

"What?! What a letdown!"

"Yes. The judge has already gone back to work at the chandlery. I tracked her there. She says if she can find someone to mind the store, she'll be right down here."

"That doesn't look too promising," I say. "More than likely, the winner has already been chosen."

"But even if that's so, it was before seeing Miss Bliss and Miss Bundy" Günter counters hopefully. "And it can be corrected."

"There she is!"

Merris greets us and apologizes profusely. Then she walks alongside the dock studying our display. When she spots Miss Bundy Boobs, she stops dead in her tracks and begins to laugh—and the laughter doesn't stop until tears come.

We invite her to board. Günter has "Waltzing Matilda*"* blaring from the cockpit speakers to greet her.

Then Merris sees the bribery table. She is stunned. "Oh, this is too much! The red roses, the heart balloon, the white wine and—wow!—even the candy."

"If that's not enough," Günter jokes, "there's a card, and I can even throw in a few Aussie twenties to make sure we win."

"You've already won!" She jumps up suddenly. "I have to get my husband to take a photo of this."

Merris rushes down the dock and soon returns with her husband, who carries a large professional-looking camera, the kind news reporters use. Günter takes her arm gallantly to board *Pacific Bliss* and leads her back to the bribery table. There, she poses with the heart balloon and points to her chocolates. Günter pours wine for her with a flourish. She takes it to the cockpit bench and squeezes in next to her husband. She opens the card with the big red heart and reads the gushy romantic prose out loud. Then she turns toward her husband accusingly: "I haven't received this many presents at one time from YOU in the ten years we've been married."

We all laugh until our sides ache.

After the couple leaves, we ask each other, "What do you think? Did we really win? Or was she joking?"

The following day, there is another gathering in the Big Tent. Contest winners are being named. I don't win

the Best Passage Story—our passage to Oz was simply too benign. I'm not even close on the Brain Strain, and our entry of Richard's favorite rum drink recipe doesn't win either—even though we'd added the lethal Bundy Rum.

Then the emcee calls out the winners of the Best Dressed Yacht competition. And *Pacific Bliss* wins the Gold!

I walk forward to collect a $100 gift award certificate from Merris. She hugs me tight and whispers, "Make sure to spend that at *our* store—maybe those signal flags?"

The sea has taught us many lessons while sailing the South Pacific, among them, how to be flexible and, whenever possible, to sail with the wind.

But in Australia, I have learned the most enjoyable lesson of all: Bribery will get you everywhere, and blatant bribery, in this wonderful Land of Oz, will get you there *fastest*! It will take a week to prepare *Pacific Bliss* for storage in Bundaberg, as it did in Fiji at the end of Voyage Two. And then we'll say our goodbyes and return to our home in San Diego. However, we will leave knowing three important things for sure: We *will* be back; we *won't* sell *Mistress Bliss*; and, while we wait for our return, we eagerly look forward to seeing and enjoying much, much more of Australia.

What we added to the card we gave to Judge Merris was brief and simple, but to this day, we mean every word of it:

WE LOVE YOU, AUSSIES.

EPILOGUE

Pacific Puddle Jumpers Class of 2002 at their reunion 10 years later.

The Pacific Puddle Jumpers held a ten-year reunion in Puerto Vallarta, Mexico in March of 2012, hosted by *Latitude 38*. It was attended by 30 cruisers who sailed to the Marquesas Islands in the spring of 2002. Some of us gave a seminar to the "class of 2012" in La Cruz. At the close of the seminar, here's what we said to the new crop of Puddle Jumpers:

This voyage will change you. You will NOT come back the same person you were when you left. You will stare death in the eye…and survive. All of you will face fear and each of you will come back a better and stronger person. You will get closer to God and the universe. You'll become extremely grateful for the opportunity to have taken this voyage. From now on, you will become more appreciative of all you have and for your many blessings. You'll come back happy, and most likely, remain happy for the rest of your lives.

Of course, we 2012 Puddle Jumpers had our own events. One was a sundowner, and what a magnificent sundowner it was! Plans were to attend another event at the Yacht Club, but once the stories got going 'round and 'round, no one wanted to quit telling them! So we all stayed far into the night telling sailors' tales, and we laughed and laughed until our sides ached.

We keep in touch with numerous crew, buddy boats, and cruisers who sailed parts of the South Pacific with us:

- Doug resides in Idaho and Arizona and keeps a sailboat on the Pacific Coast in Seattle. He still dreams about undertaking a multiyear sailing voyage.
- Claudie and Jean-Claude caught up with *Pacific Bliss* sailing in Thailand and now keep *Makoko* in the south of France.
- Tina and Dennis reside in Washington State; their yacht *Alii Kai* is moored on the Pacific Coast.
- Suzy and Clark live in San Diego with their yacht *Final Straw* moored nearby.
- Susan and Keith own a ranch in California and moor their yacht *C'est la Vie* in Puerto Vallarta.

- Paul and Janice live in San Diego; their son Luke completed college and enjoys a fine career.
- Lydia and Helmut settled down to careers and children; they now have four.
- Phyllis and Richard live in Yucca Valley, California.

We find that most of the sailors have settled down, with two exceptions:
- Elaine and Richard returned to the west coast of the United States and lived on board *Windarra* while working and putting their son Jesse and daughter Sarah through college. Now they plan to continue their sailing adventures by rounding Cape Horn.
- Daniela and Rolf sailed north as far as Japan and then south as far as Mauritius, east of Madagascar. They plan to round The Cape of Good Hope.

Following book presentations, I am often asked the question, "What is your favorite South Pacific island?" My usual answer is Aitutaki. Evidently, Steve Davey agrees with me, because in his book, *Unforgettable Places to See Before You Die,* (2004), he writes: "No artist's palette could ever conceive of a more perfect, more luminescent turquoise than that of the lagoon of Aitutaki, arguably the most beautiful in the world." In 2008, One Foot island nearby was awarded "Australasia's Leading Beach" at the World Travel Awards held in Sydney. And in 2010, Aitutaki was nominated "the world's most beautiful island" by Tony Wheeler, founder of *The Lonely Planet* Travel Guide.

Spoiler Alert: Günter and I did sail on to complete our circumnavigation. It took us 8 years and 34,000 nautical miles to circumnavigate the globe, and to return to our starting place, the same dock at the marina in Canet, France. After achieving this goal, we returned to our home in San Diego, where I enjoy writing, speaking and photography. Günter has found fulfillment in tutoring inner city children; he brings science, physics, and math to life for them in the "Kids at Heart" program of UPLIFT, a local charity. I'm proud to serve on UPLIFT's Board of Directors.

And what of *Pacific Bliss?* We sold her to a U.K. family, who continue to take good care of her. She enjoys sailing with children on board. She has repeated our passages through the oceans of the world and, at the date of this printing, she is somewhere in the South Pacific. Being family, she also suffers from "wander-thirst." She continues to follow the path of her first circumnavigation. But for us, once around is enough!

Surprisingly, Günter and I found "those rolling hills of Bavaria," where Günter was born, in Polk County, Wisconsin, within 30 miles of *my* birthplace! There we purchased a lake home we call *Northern Bliss*, where our respective families from Munich, San Diego, and Minneapolis gather for family reunions. After completing a world circumnavigation, we both feel that we have indeed come "full circle," back to our roots. Mementos of our travels grace our California and Wisconsin homes. One of our favorites is a coffee table and fireplace mantle made of ancient kauri wood that had been preserved for thousands of years in a New Zealand bog.

We hope you've enjoyed reading about our circumnavigation so far. If so, you will want to follow us through the final phase of our grand adventure. More excitement—including sailing through dreaded Pirate Alley—awaits you in the next book of this series: *In Search of Adventure and Moments of Bliss: THE LONG WAY BACK.* And be sure to join us on my author website, www.loisjoyhofmann.com, our sailing website, www.pacificbliss.com, and my sailing-and-travel blog, http://sailorstales.wordpress.com/.

Appendix A:
Specifications for *Pacific Bliss*

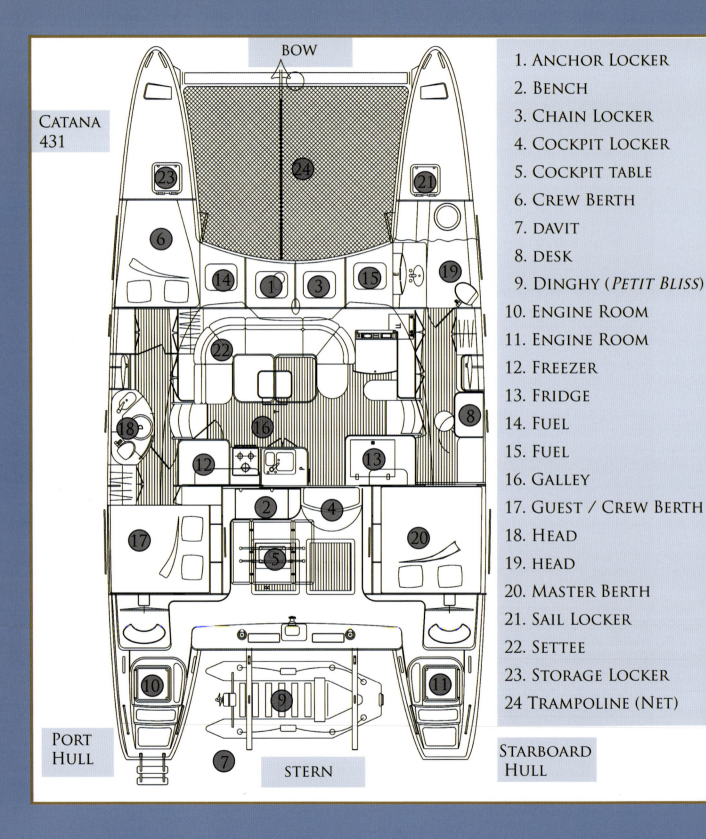

MAIN SAIL

JIB

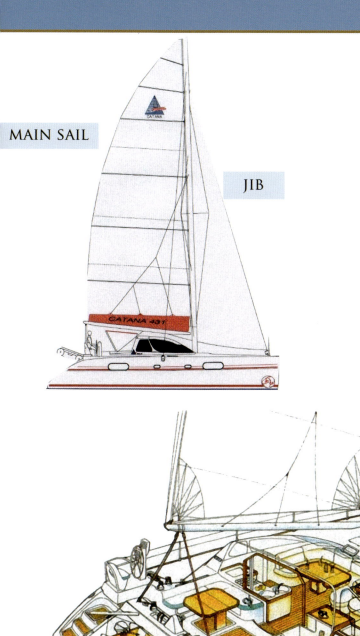

REEFING & HALYARD CONTROL AT STERN

CATANA 431 LAYOUT

Appendix B: Glossary

Aft towards the stern or after part of a boat
Anti-fouling paint bottom paint that deters the growth of algae, barnacles, etc.
Apparent wind the velocity of air as measured from a moving object, as a ship
ARC *Atlantic Rally for Cruisers*, first organized by Jimmy Cornell, a sailing legend
ASA navigation exam a test given by the American Sailing Association to certify navigators for sailing or cruising
Autopilot electro/mechanical steering device for automatic course keeping
B&G a manufacturer of marine instruments and displays; we used the term to refer to our display at the nav station
Amidships toward the center
Anchor Light a white light always displayed at night when the boat is at anchor, six feet off the deck of the bow
Backwinding; aback when the wind catches a sail in the opposite side of its working purpose
Beating sailing a boat to windward by tacking or zig-zagging at an angle to the wind (since a boat cannot sail directly into the wind)
Beam the breadth of a ship at its widest part
Berm a land barrier separating two areas of water
Bilge the space underneath the floorboards of a yacht
Bilge pump a pump placed in the bilge set to pump out water when it reaches a pre-determined level
Bitter end the tail end of a line
Bimini a protective cover of cloth, wood, or fiberglass
Bimini shades on *Pacific Bliss*, canvas sides that are zippered to attach to the central, hardtop bimini and can be unrolled and attached to the lifelines
Boat speed There are two types of boat speed: speed relative to the surrounding water and speed over ground (SOG). If the water is completely still, the two speeds are the same.
Bollard a short post on a quay or boat used to secure a rope
Boom a spar to which the bottom edge of a sail is attached which pivots at its forward end, allowing the angle of the sail to be changed
Bosun's chair a board or canvas seat with a rope attached that allows a person to perform work aloft; the seat is hauled up the main mast using a halyard
Bow the front part of a boat
Bowsprit a pointy projection from the bow from which the lower end of the jib is connected as well as the bobstay underneath (this does not apply to *Pacific Bliss*)
Broach or death roll a sudden and hazardous veering of a boat, as when it is out of control going downwind. The boat can swing sideways allowing waves to roll over it.**Buddy boat** a companion boat to keep one safe when underway, like a buddy swimmer or diver
Brightwork wooden parts on a boat which are varnished
Bula a Fijian greeting meaning "hello" or "welcome"
Bulkheads load-bearing walls that keep the boat together structurally
CAD (computer-aided design) the use of a computer with sophisticated software graphics to design products or systems
Careen to place a boat on her side so that work may be carried out on her underwater parts. (This term applies to a monohull, not a catamaran.)
Catamaran two-hulled sailing vessel
Chandlery a marine store that sells all kinds of boat-related products—needed and unneeded—to make a hole in one's wallet when cruising
Ciguatera a toxin accumulated in reef fish that is poisonous to man
Cleat a T-shaped piece of wood or metal to which a rope can be secured by taking two or three turns over and under the arms (ears) but only *after* making one complete turn around the base
Cleat off to secure a line or rope to the boat and to a stationary fixture on shore
Close-hauled all sails pulled in tightly when sailing into the wind; the same as beating (see Points of Sail in Appendix D)
Cutter a sailing vessel with one mast rigged with two foresails
Cockpit a recessed part of the deck containing seats and the steering station
Crest of a wave the top of a wave
Dagger board an adjustable centerboard that acts like a keel when lowered. When raised, it allows a

catamaran to surf. *Pacific Bliss* has two dagger boards, one at each hull.
Davits spars that extend over the stern of a boat to raise or lower the dinghy
Day sailing sailing only for the day, with the intention returning to port before dark
Depthsounder an instrument that measures how deep the water is
Dinghy a small boat that is towed behind or carried on a larger boat; also called a tender
Dogwatch the typical mariner's day is divided into six watches, each four hours long, except that the 4:00 to 8:00 p.m. watch may be "dogged"; that is, divided into the first and second dogwatches, each two hours long, to allow men on duty to have their evening meal. In pleasure sailing, dogwatch has come to mean whatever the crew decides it to be. On *Pacific Bliss*, we called the 12:00 to 3:00 a.m. watch our "dogwatch."
Downhaul a line that pulls something down to the deck, e.g., the spinnaker had *downhaul* and *outhaul* lines on each side
Doldrums an area with no wind or light variable winds just north of the equator in the Atlantic and Pacific oceans, situated between the trade winds
Double-reefing the main putting two reefs into the mainsail
Draft the depth of water below the keel (in the case of *Pacific Bliss,* the draft was the depth below the hulls, or the bottom of the dagger boards when down)
Dry dock the storing of the boat out of the water
EPIRB Emergency Position Indicating Radio Beacon. A dictionary-size device that communicates directly with a satellite in the event of an emergency, relaying the position of the ship in distress. Ours identified *Pacific Bliss* and whom to contact (our sons).
Fathom six feet
Fetch the distance wind or waves can travel without obstruction
Fender a bumper slung over the side of a vessel to prevent damage to the hull when moored on a dock or rafted (side-tied) to other boats
Foot the bottom edge of a sail
Freeboard the height of a boat from the surface of the water to the deck
Furling the method of stowing a sail on a spar
Forces 1-12 wind states on the Beaufort wind scales (see Appendix C)
Genoa (jenny) the large triangular front sail on a boat; we used the term alternately with jib; when partially furled, it served as a smaller foresail
GMT Greenwich Mean Time. Can also be called UTC (Universal Time Zone) or Zulu Time
Go to weather to go toward the direction of the oncoming wind (see no-go zones, Appendix D)
Halyard rope or line used to raise (haul) or lower (douse) sails
Hand steer steering by hand instead of by the autopilot
Hank to attach a sail to a stay
Hatch a square opening on a deck that has a hinged cover or lid
Harness Think of a dog or horse in a harness. Sailors wear these to attach themselves to jacklines that run the entire length of the boat to protect them from falling overboard.
Head the toilet and/or bathroom on a boat, or the top of a sail
Helm the means by which the rudder and hence the direction of the vessel are controlled. *Pacific Bliss* has two helms (which we call the steering wheels). A tiller used instead of a wheel can be called the helm.
In irons The boat is pointed too close to the wind for the sails to generate any power (unless they are backwinded; see above). The sails will be luffing (flapping) in the breeze and making noise, like a flag.
ITCZ, or Intertropical Convergence Zone (the doldrums) the area encircling the earth near the equator where winds originating in the northern and southern hemispheres come together. The location of the intertropical convergence zone varies over time. Over land, it moves back and forth across the equator following the sun's zenith point. Over the oceans, where the convergence zone is better defined, the seasonal cycle is more subtle, as the convection is constrained by the distribution of ocean temperatures. Sometimes a double ITCZ forms, with one located north and another south of the equator. When this occurs, a narrow ridge of high pressure forms between the two convergence zones, one of which is usually stronger than the other.
Jib a small triangular sail in front of the main sail
Jibe (gybe) a maneuver that changes the mainsail from one side of the boat to the other when the wind is blowing from behind
Keel the lowest part of the boat, weighted in a monohull to provide stability
Ketch a two-masted sailing ship with the steering station located astern of the aft mast (mizzen)
Knot meter Indicates how fast the boat is moving in the water, in nautical miles. The actual progress influenced by factors such as current and leeway (as opposed to the absolute geographic movement determined by a GPS).
Lanyard a piece of rope attached to something for easy retrieval
Lazy jacks lines to contain the mainsail while it is being lowered

Lee the side that does *not* have the wind blowing on it, as in "the lee of the wind"
Lee shore a coastline on which the wind blows (which is to the lee side of the sailing vessel)
Lee cloth; lee board a board or canvas rigged to prevent a person from rolling off the bunk in high seas (not necessary on a large catamaran since it does not heel more than a few degrees)
Leech the aft edge of the sail
Lifelines safety cables stretched along the entire deck *Pacific Bliss*
Lines ropes on a boat
Lying ahull sails down and just drifting at the mercy of the seas
Luff 1. the part of a sail closest to the mast; 2. allowing the sails to flap in the wind
Mahi-Mahi a delicious fish, also called dorado or dolphin fish
MaxSea a computer navigation program
Mole a massive wall, usually made of stone, that extends into the sea and encloses or protects a harbor
Motu a Polynesian reef islet
Monkey fist a weighted ball secured to the end of a casting line
Monohull single-hulled vessel
Multi-meter any instrument that reads out multiple parameters
Nav (navigation) station the brain area of a boat occupied by charts, radios, laptops, and navigation instruments and aids
Navteq® a weather forecasting system
Noqu sevu sevu gor a greeting spoken when presenting the *kava* plant to a chief. If the chief accepts the gift, he will solemnly pick it up and then bestow his blessing on your family, crew, and home country.
Old salt a sailor who has years of experience at sea
Overfalls a turbulent surface of the sea caused by conflicting currents or the wind moving against a current
On the hard when a boat is put up on land, usually for storage or repair in a shipyard
On the hook at anchor
On the nose wind in one's face; heading into the wind
Painter a rope attached to a dinghy for towing or mooring
Points of sail direction of a vessel in relation to the wind (see Appendix D)
Port left side (think "port wine" and "port," each word equals 4 letters; the longer word for right is *starboard*)
Port bow front of the boat on your left as you face forward from the stern
Puddle Jump Cruiser slang for crossing the Pacific Ocean
Reach sailing ninety degrees to the wind; the most comfortable point of sail
Reinforced trades strong trade winds
Reef to reduce the area of sail (see Appendix D)
Rhumb line In navigation, a rhumb line (or *loxodrome*) is a line crossing all meridians of longitude at the same angle, i.e., a path derived from a defined *initial* bearing. Upon taking an initial bearing, one proceeds along the same bearing without changing the direction as measured relative to true north. A rhumb line appears as a straight line on a Mercator projection map. On a plane surface this would be the shortest distance between two points, but over longer distances and/or at higher latitudes great circle routes provide the shortest distances.
Rig to fit out a boat or its mast with sails and rigging
Rode a rope or chain, especially one attached to an anchor
Rogue wave an unpredictable, abnormally large wave that occurs on a seemingly random basis in the oceans
Roller furling rolling up the sail into the headstay like a window shade
Run, broad reach, and beam reach these define points of sail. Refer to Appendix D.
Salon the living room area of a yacht (also called saloon)
Scuppers the narrow space between the bulwarks and the deck through which seawater or any other water on deck may run off
Seacocks valves which open and close pipes going through the hull of a boat
Seamounts underwater mountains
Settee a seat or sofa on a boat
Sevu Sevu a formal Fijian ceremony where *kava* is usually drunk
Sheet a line (rope, cable, or chain) used to control the movable corner(s) (clews) of a sail. The *mainsheet* is attached to the boom and is used to control the mainsail. The *jib sheet* attaches to the clew of the jib and controls it. The *spinnaker sheet* attaches to the clew(s) of the spinnaker.
Side-tie to fasten alongside another yacht or a dock
Shackle A u-shaped metal connecting link with a straight pin closing the u. The pin has an eye at one end and a short screw at the other.
Shoal a shallow area with banks of sand, mud, or rock; a bubbling and swirling sea in this area warns one of rocks below the surface.
Shrouds the main lateral supports of the mast standing rigging consisting of strong wires that attach to the deck

Spar any stout piece of wood or metal used as a pole to support sails and rigging on a ship; thus the boom, main mast, and jib pole can all be called spars
SOG (speed over ground) the movement of the boat relative to the bottom of the ocean
Step the mast erect a mast and attach the standing rigging
Spindrift spray that blows from the surface of the sea; spindrift begins with a Force 7 sea state (see Appendix B)
Spinnaker a large triangular sail set at the front of a yacht for running before the wind
Spreader support that holds the shrouds away from the mast
Spring line a line used when the boat is docked to keep her from moving forward and aft
Standing rigging cable securing the upper part of a mast (shrouds and stays)
SSB (single side-band) radio a method of long-range radio communication
Starboard right side
Starboard bow front of the boat to your right as you face forward from the stern
Stays wire supports for fixed spars. The headstay also serves as an attachment for the jib.
Stern back end of a boat
Stink potter a derogatory term that sailors use to describe a motor yacht
Surf to ride the waves on a catamaran
Tack to change a yacht's course by turning through the wind, so that the wind then blows on the opposite side of the yacht
Tachometer a gauge that shows the RPM (revolutions per minute) of an engine, thus indicating its speed
Toerail a small wooden edge which surrounds the deck of a boat to keep sailors' feet from sliding off
Topping lift the rope which controls the height of the outer end of the boom
Topsides the act of being on the outside deck of a boat relative to a person "down below"
Trampoline, net a fabric deck stretched on the braces connecting the hulls of a catamaran, resembling a gymnastic trampoline
Transom the horizontal portion of the stern of a boat
Traveler a sliding fitting to which the mainsheet is attached, keeping the boom in the same place as it is moved in and out
Triangular main sheet system type of sail rigging used on a Catana catamaran
Trimaran sailing vessel with three hulls
Trough of a wave the lowest part of the wave between crests
True wind speed and direction of the actual wind as if the vessel is not moving
Warp a line attached to the stern of a boat to slow down the speed
Watermaker a machine which through reverse osmosis creates potable water from seawater. Ours is a Spectra® brand.
Windlass a device which hauls up the anchor. On *Pacific Bliss*, ours was electric.
Wind states Beaufort Force states (see Appendix C)
Wing on wing opening the foresail and mainsail to maximum amount of surface to capture all of the wind available
World Cruising Routes "The Bible for Cruisers" by Jimmy Cornell
Yaw to erratically deviate from a steered course as when struck by a heavy sea
Yawl a two-masted sailboat with the steering station forward of the aft mast (mizzen)
Zulu Time Greenwich Mean Time. Zulu is used in the military and aviation.

Appendix C: Beaufort Scale of Sea States

Admiral Francis Beaufort was a 19th century British tar in the days of the old wooden tall ships. The scale he developed has been ridiculed by mariners for being patternless because there is no apparent uniform progression in the scale. Force 2, for example, describes winds from 4 to 6 knots, Force 3 from 7 to 10, and Force 4 from 11-16. Then Force 5 covers only from 17-21. The wind differences vary from 2 knots to 3, then 5, and back to 4.

Our *Pacific Bliss* Ship's Library contains a book called *Mariner's Weather* by William P. Crawford. He claims that the lack of symmetry was not part of Beaufort's plan, and defends his damaged reputation by saying that the Admiral was not referring to wind speed at all! He says that what the esteemed Admiral had in mind was the number of sails that should be furled as the wind strengthened. In light airs, just one would be taken in, whereas in a gentle breeze might require three. In a near gale, seven would come down, and in a violent storm, eleven.

There is now a tendency to express wind value in knots instead of Beaufort scale. The *Pacific Bliss* multi units mounted throughout the boat allow the user to choose whichever he or she wishes as a display. We tend to use the Force scales in the cockpit display. A read-out in knots suggests a misleading exactness whereas a Force reading allows for some slack. Force readings make it easier to give instructions to the crew; for example, during the Atlantic crossing, the instructions were to take down the spinnaker at Force 7 so that we wouldn't blow it out.

The following chart will help you understand the forces and sea conditions we encountered during our Night of Sheer Terror during Voyage One:

Beaufort Scale: Comparing Wind Speed and Sea Conditions

Force	Knots	Probable Wave Height (in feet)	Description	Sea Conditions
0	0-1	--	Calm	Sea smooth and mirror like.
1	1-3	1/4	Light Air	Scale-like ripples without foam crests.
2	4-6	1/2	Light Breeze	Small, short wavelets; some crests begin to break; foam of glassy appearance. Occasional white foam crests.
3	7-10	2	Gentle Breeze	Large wavelets; some crests begin to break; foam of glassy appearance. Occasional white foam crests.
4	11-16	4	Moderate Breeze	Small waves, becoming longer; fairly frequent white foam crests.
5	17-21	6	Fresh Breeze	Moderate waves, taking a more pronounced long form, many white foam crests; there may be some spray.
6	22.27	10	Strong Breeze	Large waves begin to form; white foam crests are more extensive everywhere; there may be some spray.
7	28-33	14	Near Gale	Sea heaps up and white foam from breaking waves begins to be blown in =streaks along the direction of the wind; spindrift begins.
8	34-40	18	Gale	Moderately high waves of greater length; edges of crests break into spindrift; foam is blown in well-marked streaks along the direction of the wind.
9	41-47	23	Strong Gale	High waves; dense streaks of foam along the direction of the wind; crests of waves begin to topple, tumble, and roll over; spray may reduce visibility/
10	48-55	29	Storm	Very long waves with overhanging crests. The resulting foam in great patches is blown in dense white streaks along the direction of the wind. On the whole, the surface of the sea is white in appearance. The tumbling of the sea becomes heavy and shock-like. Visibility is
11	56-63	37	Violent	Exceptionally high waves that may obscure small and medium size ships. The sea is completely covered with long white patches of foam lying along the direction of the wind. Everywhere the edges of the wave crests are blown into froth. Visibility reduced.
12	64-71	45	Hurricane	The air is filled with foam and spray. Sea completely white with driving spray; visibility much reduced.

Source: From the Weather Bureau Observing Handbook No. 1, Marine Surface Observations (Wash. D.C. National Weather Service, 1969)

APPENDIX D: POINTS OF SAIL

The points of sail for a monohull are the same for a catamaran.
A. In Irons (into the wind) B. Close Hauled C. Beam Reach D. Broad Reach E. Running

The points of sail are the most important parts of sail theory to remember. The no-go zone (shaded) is about 45° either side of the true wind for a racing hull and sail plan optimized for upwind work. On some cruising yachts, the best course achievable upwind is 50° to 55° to the true wind. On *Pacific Bliss*, we were able to achieve a 45-degree course to the apparent wind. No sailboat can sail directly into the wind; attempting to do so leads to the sails luffing (flapping uncontrollably).

There are 5 main points of sail. In order from the edge of the no-go zone to directly downwind they are:

- close haul (often about 45° to the apparent wind - the least angle that the boat and its rig can manage).

- close reach (between close hauled and a beam reach).

- beam reach (90° to the apparent wind); this was the fastest point of sail for *Pacific Bliss*.

- broad reach (between a beam reach and running).

- running (close to directly downwind), this is the most pleasant point of sail. "May you have fair winds and following seas," is the mariner's blessing, because those conditions allow a boat "to run."

Sail trim relative to the point of sail

On a beam reach sails are mostly let out; on a run sails are all the way out; and close hauled sails are pulled in very tightly. Two main skills of sailing are trimming the sails correctly for the direction and strength of the wind, and maintaining a course relative to the wind that suits the sails once trimmed. With a gentle following wind, the captain might order the sails set wing-on-wing (one sail on each side) or the spinnaker hoisted. The wind pushing the boat from the stern allows the spinnaker to open up, called "ballooning." If the wind is too strong, or the boat suddenly changes course with this light sail up, it can tear; this is called "blowing out the spinnaker."

Reducing and increasing sail

An important safety aspect of sailing is to adjust the amount of sail to suit the wind conditions. As the wind speed increases the crew should progressively reduce the amount of sail. On a boat with only jib (or genoa) and mainsail this is done by furling the jib and by partially lowering the mainsail, a process called "reefing the main."

Reefing means reducing the area of a sail without actually changing it for a smaller sail, such as the storm jib that *Pacific Bliss* had on board. Ideally reefing does not only result in a reduced sail area but also in a lower center of effort from the sails, reducing the heeling and keeping the boat more upright.

We often repeated on board the standard Old Salts' advice: "The first time you even *think* of reducing sail you should go ahead and just do it." As for increasing sail, the English say it best: "When you *think* you are ready to take out a reef, have a cup of tea instead."

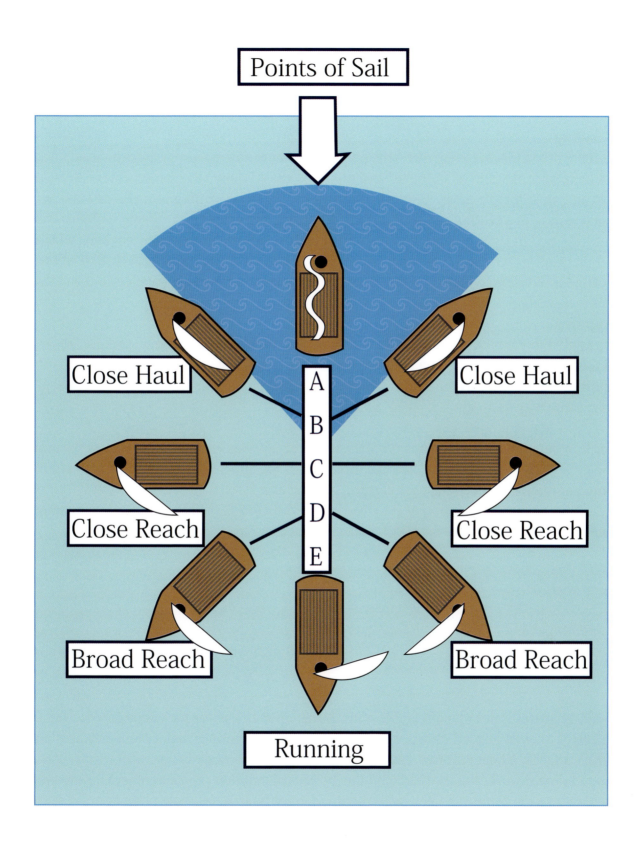

Appendix E: The Physics of Sailing

Sailing is the art of controlling a boat with large (usually fabric) foils called sails. By changing the rigging, rudder, and sometimes the keel or centre board, (or the dagger board in the case of Pacific Bliss) a sailor manages the force of the wind on the sails in order to change the direction and speed of a boat. Mastery of the skill requires experience in varying wind and sea conditions, as well as knowledge concerning sailboats themselves.

Types of Sailing

While there are still some places in Africa and Asia where sail-powered fishing vessels are used, these craft have become rarer as outboard and modified car engines have become available even in the poorest and most remote areas. In most countries people enjoy sailing as a recreational activity. Recreational sailing or yachting can be divided into racing and cruising. Cruising includes extended trips, short trips within sight of land, and daysailing. Most sailors on extended voyages who are not racing call themselves "cruisers." When a cruiser completes an entire circumnavigation of the globe, he or she is called a "circumnavigator," a rare breed of individual with a title coveted in the sailing world.

Energy capture

Sailing is all about capturing energy. Sails are airfoils that work by using an airflow set up by the wind and the motion of the boat. The combination of the two is the apparent wind, which is the relative velocity of the wind relative to the boat's motion. Sails generate lift using the air that flows around them, in the same way as an aircraft wing generates lift.

The air flowing at the sail surface is not the true wind. Sailing into the wind causes the apparent wind to be greater than the true wind and the direction of the apparent wind will be forward of the true wind. Some high-performance boats are capable of traveling faster than the true wind speed on some points of sail; for example, Hydroptère set a world speed record in 2009 by sailing 1.71 times the speed of the wind. Iceboats can typically sail at 5 times the speed of the wind.

The energy that drives a sailboat is harnessed by manipulating the relative movement of wind and water speed: if there is no difference in movement, such as on a calm day or when the wind and water current are moving in the same direction at the same speed, there is no energy to be extracted and the sailboat will not be able to do anything but drift. Where there is a difference in motion, then there is energy to be extracted at the interface. The sailboat does this by placing the sail(s) in the air and the hull(s) in the water.

The sailing vessel is not maneuverable with the sail alone. The torque caused by the sail lift would cause the vessel to twist instead of move forward. In the same manner that a plane requires an elevator with control surfaces, a boat requires a keel and rudder. The sail alone is not sufficient to drive the boat in any desired direction. Sailboats overcome this by having another physical object below the water line. This may take the form of a keel, centerboard, dagger boards, or some other form of underwater foil, or even the hull itself (as in the case of catamarans without centerboard or in a traditional proa). Thus, the physical portion of the boat that is below water can be regarded as functioning as a "second sail." Having two surfaces against the wind and water enables the sailor to travel in almost any direction and to generate an additional source of lift from the water. The flow of water over the underwater hull portions creates a hydrodynamic force. The combination of the aerodynamic force from the sails and the hydrodynamic force from the underwater hull section allows motion in almost any direction except straight into the wind. (Imagine that you are squeezing a wet bar of soap with two hands, causing it to shoot out in a direction perpendicular to both opposing forces.) Depending on the efficiency of the rig, the angle of travel relative to the true wind can be as little as 35° or greater than 80°. This angle is called the "tacking angle."

Tacking is essential when sailing upwind. The sails, when correctly adjusted, will generate aerodynamic lift. When sailing downwind, the sails no longer generate aerodynamic lift and airflow is stalled, with the wind push on the sails giving drag only. As the boat is going downwind, the apparent wind is less than the true wind and this, allied to the fact that the sails are not producing aerodynamic lift, serves to limit the downwind speed.

Effects of wind shear

Wind shear affects sailboats in motion by presenting a different wind speed and direction at different heights along the mast. Wind shear occurs because of friction above a water surface slowing the flow of air. Thus, a difference in true wind creates a different apparent wind at different heights. Sailmakers may introduce sail twist in the design of the sail, where the head of the sail is set at a different angle of attack from the foot of the sail in order to change the lift distribution with height. The effect of wind shear can be factored into the selection of twist in the sail design, but this can be difficult to predict since wind shear may vary widely in different weather conditions.

Appendix F: Bibliography

Bitchin, Bob. *Letters from the Lost Soul: Five-Year Voyage of Discovery and Adventure*. Dobbs Ferry, NY: Sheridan, 2000.

Browne, Christopher and Douglas A. Scott. *Economic Development in Seven Pacific Island Countries.* Washington, D.C.: International Monetary Fund, 1989.

Chesneaux, Jean and Nic Maclellan. *After Moruroa: France in the South Pacific*. Melbourne: Ocean, 1998.

Copeland, Liza. *Just Cruising*. Vancouver: Romany, 1993.

---. *Still Cruising*. Vancouver: Romany, 1995.

Cousineau, Phil. The Art of Pilgrimage: The Seeker's Guide to Making Travel Sacred. San Francisco: Conari, 1998.

Cornell, Jimmy. *World Cruising Routes*. Camden, Maine: International Marine, 1995.

Crawford, Peter. *Nomads of the Wind: A Natural History of Polynesia*. London: BBC, 1993.

Dana, Richard Henry Jr. *Two Years before the Mast and Other Voyages.* New York: Library of America, 2005.

Dugard, Martin. *Farther Than Any Man: The Rise and Fall of Captain James Cook.* New York: Washington Square, 2001.

Dunmore, John. *Who's Who in Pacific Navigation*. Melbourne: Melbourne U P, 1992.

Ebensten, Hanns. *Trespassers on Easter Island.* Key West: The Ketch & Yawl, 2001.

Eustis, Nelson. *The King of Tonga: King Taufa 'ahau Tupou IV.* Adelaide, Aus.: Hyde Park, 1977.

Fiji. 5th ed. Victoria, Aus.: Lonely Planet, 2000.

Fischer, Steven Roger. *A History of the Pacific Islands.* New York: Palgrave, 2002.

Gravelle, Kim. *Fiji's Heritage: A History of Fiji*. Nadi, Fiji: Tiara, 2000.

---. *Romancing the Islands: Journeys in the South Pacific*. Suva, Fiji: Graphics (Pacific), 1997.

Hackett, Joanna. *The Reluctant Mariner.* Chatswood, NZ: New Holland, 2001.

Hansen, Elizabeth assisted by Richard Adams. *Frommer's New Zealand From $50 a Day.* 7th ed. New York: Macmillan Travel, 1998.

Hayden, Sterling. *Wanderer*. Dobbs Ferry, NY: Sheridan, 1963.

Heeren, Fred. *Show Me God: What the Message from Space Is Telling Us about God.* Wheeling, IL: Day Star, 2000.

Helm, A.S. and W.H. Percival. *Sisters in the Sun.* London: The Travel Book Club, 1974.

Heyerdahl, Thor. *Fatu-Hiva: Back to Nature*. Garden City, NY: Doubleday, 1975.

---. *Aku-Aku.* New York: Pocket Books, 1977.

---. *Kon-Tiki.* New York: Washington Square, 1984.

Hinz, Earl R. *Landfalls of Paradise: Cruising Guide to the Pacific Islands.* 4th ed. Honolulu: U of Hawaii P, 1999.

Hiscock, Eric. *Around the World in Wanderer III*. Dobbs Ferry, NY: Sheridan, 1997.

---. *Cruising Adventures, a 3-book series: Wandering Under Sail, Come Aboard, Sou'west in Wanderer IV*. New York: Sheridan House, 1977.

Hixon, Margaret. *Sālote: Queen of Paradise*. Dunedin, NZ: U of Otago P, 2000.

Hough, Richard. *Captain James Cook: A Biography*. New York: Norton, 1997.

Hunt, Terry and Carl Lipo. *Unraveling the Mystery of Easter Island: The Statues That Walked.* New York: Free Press, 2011.

Irwin, Geoffrey. *The Prehistoric Exploration and Colonisation of the Pacific*. Cambridge, Eng.: Cambridge U P, 1992.

Jolly, Margaret and Martha Macintyre. *Family & Gender in the South Pacific: Domestic Contradictions and the*

Colonial Impact. New York: Cambridge U P, 1989.

Jones, Tristan. *The Incredible Voyage: A Personal Odyssey.* 1st paperback ed. New York: Sheridan House, 1996.

Ledyard, Patricia. *'Utulei: My Tongan Home.* Haveluloto Village, Tonga: Vava'u Press, 1993.

Leonard, Beth. *Following Seas: Sailing the Globe, Sounding a Life.* Windsor, CT: Tide-Mark, 1999.

MacClancy, Jeremy. *To Kill a Bird with Two Stones.* Port Vila, Vanuatu: Vanuatu Cultural Centre, 2002.

McLean, Gavin. *Captains's Log: New Zealand's Maritime History.* Auckland: Hodder, 2001.

Mead, Margaret. *Coming of Age in Samoa.* New York: American Museum of Natural History, 1973.

Melville, Herman. *Typee: A Peep at Polynesian Life.* New York: Penguin, 1996.

Miranda, Rosalind. *Best of Multihulls: The Book of Cruising (Volume 2 Cruising Around the World West to East).* Boston: Chiodi, 1991.

Monsarrat, Nicholas. *The Cruel Sea: Classics of War.* Short Hills, NJ: Burford, 2000.

Moore, Denton Rickey. *Gentlemen Never Sail to Weather.* 2nd ed. Bellingham, WA: Prospector, 1993.

Pirie, Marcia. *Travellers on a Trade Wind.* Dobbs Ferry, NY: Sheridan, 1998.

Pocock, Michael. *The Pacific Crossing Guide.* Dobbs Ferry, NY: Sheridan, 1997.

Price, A. Grenfell. *The Explorations of Captain James Cook in the Pacific, as Told by Selections of His Own Journals 1768-1779.* New York: Dover, 1971.

Roth, Hal. *After 50,000 Miles.* London: Stanford Maritime, 1978.

---. *Always a Distant Anchorage.* 1st ed. New York: Norton, 1989.

---. *The Hal Roth Seafaring Trilogy: Three True Stories of Adventure Under Sail.* Camden, ME: International Marine/McGraw, 2006.

Silverberg, Robert. *The Longest Voyage: Circumnavigators in the Age of Discovery.* Athens, OH: Ohio U P, 1972.

Singh, Shubba. *Fiji: A Precarious Coalition.* New Delhi: Har-Anand, 2001.

Slocum, Joshua. *Sailing Alone around the World.* Dobbs Ferry: Sheridan, 1954.

Smith, Percy S. with traditions by Pulekula. *Niue: The Island and Its People.* The Polynesian Society, 1983.

Goodwin, Bill. *Frommer's South Pacific.* 6th ed. New York: MacMillan Travel, 1998.

Stanley, David. *South Pacific Handbook.* 7th ed. Emeryville, CA: Avalon Travel, 2000.

Tahiti & French Polynesia. 5th ed. Victoria, Aus.: Lonely Planet, 2000.

Theroux, Paul. *The Happy Isles of Oceania: Paddling the Pacific.* New York: Putnam's, 1992.

Thomas, Stephen D. *The Last Navigator.* New York: Holt, 1987.

Tonga. Victoria, Aus.: Lonely Planet, 2001.

Thomson, Peter. *Kava in the Blood: A Personal & Political Memoir from the Heart of Fiji.* Auckland: Tandem, 1999.

Thorpe, Nick. *An Improbable Voyage by Reed Boat to Easter Island: 8 Men and a Duck.* New York: Free, 2002.

Vanuatu. 3rd ed. Victoria, Aus.: Lonely Planet, 1999.

Wallis, Mary. *Life in Feejee, or Five Years among the Cannibals, by a Lady.* Suva, Fiji: Fiji Museum, 1986.

Wilson, Derek. *The Circumnavigators, a History.* New York: Carroll, 2003.

Wood, Charles E. *Charlie's Charts of Polynesia.* Surrey, BC: Charlie's Charts, 2000.

Wood, Margo. *A Prairie Chicken Goes to Sea.* Surrey, BC: Charlie's Charts, 2002.